MW01054507

Universities are said to be the 'powerhouses' of modern society. They educate leaders, and advance our basic knowledge of nature and society. Yet historically they have been vulnerable when meeting the challenges of dynamic industrial democracies, let alone modern totalitarian states. Today universities are at the centre of society's attention, and must therefore balance a great number of contradictory demands and pressures. Can this be done within the structure and ethos of an historic institution called a 'university', or are such institutions now *passé* and merely part of a bureaucratically managed higher education 'system'? These essays discuss the ways in which universities have coped with complexity since 1800, while retaining their basic 'idea'. Special attention is accorded to the role of the State and the autonomous professions in defining the mission of universities and their struggle for individuality in the face of mounting pluralistic and bureaucratic pressures.

The European and American university since 1800

The European and American university since 1800

Historical and sociological essays

Edited by

Sheldon Rothblatt and Björn Wittrock

CAMBRIDGE
UNIVERSITY PRESS

Published by the Press Syndicate of the University of Cambridge
The Pitt Building, Trumpington Street, Cambridge CB2 1RP
40 West 20th Street, New York, NY 10011-4211, USA
10 Stamford Road, Oakleigh, Victoria 3166, Australia

First published 1993
Reprinted 1996

A catalogue record for this book is available from the British Library

Library of Congress cataloguing in publication data

ISBN 0 521 43165 4 hardback

The European and American university since 1800: historical and sociological essays – edited by Sheldon Rothblatt and Björn Wittrock.
    p.   cm.
Includes index.
ISBN 0-521-43165-4
1. Universities and colleges – Europe – History – 19th century.
2. Universities and colleges – Europe – History – 20th century.
3. Universities and colleges – United States – History – 19th century.
4. Universities and colleges – United States – History – 20th century.
5. Education, Higher – Social aspects – Europe – History – 19th century.
6. Education, Higher – Social aspects – Europe – History – 20th century.
7. Education, Higher – Social aspects – United States – History – 19th century.
8. Education, Higher – Social aspects – United States – History – 20th century.
9. Higher education and state – Europe – History. 10. Higher education and state – United States – History.
I. Rothblatt, Sheldon. II. Wittrock, Björn.
LA627.E97 1993
378.4 – dc20 92-3170 CIP

ISBN 0 521 43165 4 hardback

Transferred to digital printing 2002

UP

Contents

viii   *Contents*

Part 4   Complexity

Part 5   The ironies of university history

Contributors

MICHAEL BURRAGE is Lecturer in Sociology at the London School of Economics. He has been writing on the history and sociology of professions in France, England, the United States, and Russia, and has contributed to, as well as co-edited (with Rolf Torstendahl), *The Formation of Professions: Knowledge, State, and Strategy* (1990) and *Professions in Theory and History: Rethinking the Study of the Professions* (1990).

BURTON R. CLARK is Allan M. Cartter Professor of Higher Education and Sociology and chairman of the Comparative Higher Education Research Group at the University of California, Los Angeles. He has written, edited, and contributed to books on the sociology of comparative higher education, and is the author of such works as *The Open Door College* (1960), *Academic Power in Italy* (1977), *The Higher Education System* (1983), and *The Academic Life* (1987).

AANT ELZINGA is Professor of the Theory of Science and Research at Gothenburg University and currently President of the European Association for the Study of Science and Technology. He has published articles in the areas of history and philosophy of science, as well as science policy. His books include *Research and Politics in Sweden, the United States, and the Soviet Union* (first published in Swedish 1969) and *On a Research Program in Early Modern Physics* (1972). With Ronny Ambjörnsson, he has published *Tradition and Revolution* (first published in Swedish in 1968), and with Björn Wittrock he has edited *The University Research System* (1985).

ROGER GEIGER is Professor of Higher Education at Pennsylvania State University. His special interests are university history and academic science policy. His publications include *Private Sectors in Higher Education: Structure, Function, and Change in Eight Countries* (1986). The first volume of a two-volume study of the American research university, *To Advance Knowledge: the Growth of American Research Universities, 1900–1940,* appeared in 1986. The second, *Research and Relevant Knowledge: American Research Universities since World War II* is forthcoming.

SVEN-ERIC LIEDMAN is Professor of the History of Ideas and Science at Gothenburg University, and he publishes widely in Swedish and English. His publications include *The Organic Life in German Debate, 1795–1845* (1966), *The Interplay of Antitheses: The Philosophy of Friedrich Engels and the Sciences of the Nineteenth Century* (2 volumes, 1977, with an abridged German edition in 1986), and 'Institutions and Ideas: Mandarins and Non-Mandarins in the German Academic Intelligentsia' (1986). A recent work (in Swedish) is *To Change the World but Moderately: Sweden in the Nineteenth Century as Reflected in the Life and Work of Boström and Agardh* (1991).

SHELDON ROTHBLATT is Professor of History and Director of the Center for Studies in Higher Education at the University of California, Berkeley. He writes on the history of universities in relation to cities, society, and culture. His publications include the books *The Revolution of the Dons: Cambridge and Society in Victorian England* (1968 and 1981), *Tradition and Change in English Liberal Education: An Essay in History and Culture* (1976), and the articles 'The Idea of the Idea of a University and Its Antithesis' (1989), 'George Eliot as a Type of European Intellectual' (1986), 'London: A Metropolitan University?' (1988), and '"A Long Apocrypha of Inquiries": The Humanities and Humanity' (1990).

ROLF TORSTENDAHL is Professor of History at Uppsala University and a former Director of the Swedish Collegium for Advanced Study in the Social Sciences, Uppsala. He is a specialist in nineteenth- and twentieth-century European history with an emphasis on historiography, political ideas, and the history of professions and higher education. He has published extensively in Swedish and English and, with Michael Burrage, has edited books on the sociology and history of professions. His writings include *The Dispersion of Engineers in a Transitional Society* (1975), and *Bureaucratization in Northwestern Europe, 1885–1985: Domination and Governance* (1991).

MARTIN TROW is Professor of Sociology at the Graduate School of Public Policy and former Director of the Center for Studies in Higher Education, University of California, Berkeley. He was Chair of the nine-campus University of California Academic Senate for 1991–2, representing the faculty on the Board of Regents. He is a member of the National Academy of Education and has written or edited books and articles in the fields of political sociology and higher education. Among them are *Union Democracy* (with Seymour M. Lipset, 1977), *The British Academics* (with Albert H. Halsey, 1971), *Right-Wing Radicalism and Political Intolerance* (1980), and 'Problems in the Transition from Elite to Mass Higher Education' (1973).

BJÖRN WITTROCK is Professor of Political Science at the University of Stockholm and a Director of the Swedish Collegium for Advanced Study in the Social Sciences at Uppsala. His special interests are in political theory and institutions, the history of disciplines, and the role of knowledge in modern society and universities. He has edited and published in *Science as a Commodity* (with Michael Gibbons, 1985), *The University Research System* (with Aant Elzinga, 1985), *Discourses on Society* (with Peter Wagner and Richard Whitley, 1991), and *Social Sciences and Modern States* (with Peter Wagner, Carol Weiss, and Hellmut Wollman, 1991).

Introduction: universities and 'higher education'

Sheldon Rothblatt and Björn Wittrock

The university is the second oldest institution with a continuous history in the Western world, the first being the Roman Catholic Church. That much is generally known. Less generally known – except to those who fuss with it – is that the problem of defining 'university' has long preoccupied politicians, planners, reformers, academics, theologians, philosophers, historians, and litterateurs. They have often found the task impossible. So much has this been the case, especially since the eighteenth century, that universities are now subsumed under a broader if less romantic category called 'higher education'. It is less romantic because 'higher education' implies levels of bureaucratic and technocratic organisation and co-ordination that the word 'university' never does.

So this book is also about the tension between universities and 'higher education', between a special sort of cultural inheritance with idealistic, 'spiritual', and 'high-minded' aspirations derived from important philosophical and theological traditions, and a different but no less important set of beliefs which have constantly pushed universities towards a broader and more open set of social or service obligations. Universities have both resisted and accepted, often simultaneously, the broader role. In the process they have redefined their mission and purpose or returned to older conceptions of their 'essence'. The result is a history filled with irony and ambiguity, of a struggle between simplicity and complexity, of outrage and accommodation, of ideals lost and regained; and to understand that history, we are required to narrate how universities have dealt with specific kinds or categories of education – liberal education, the professions, science, technology, research, vocationalism.

The topic of universities and higher education involves every aspect of human activity. It is the study of civilisation itself and requires a multi-disciplinary approach. The contributors represent the academic disciplines of history, the history of science, sociology, and political science. Readers will recognise approaches and conceptions which derive from a wide range of humanistic and social scientific inquiries. They will similarly note a merging of analytical methods from the history of thought, the sociology of science and knowledge, and the social and political study of institutions as these are pursued in their several variations in Britain, the United States, and Continental countries.

Probably it is misleading to invoke the magical (and trendy) academic phrase 'multi-disciplinary'. The best scholarship and writing have always spanned the boundaries of disciplines. Thucydides was a tragedian as well as an historian. The *summas* of the medieval philosophers and theologians comprehended all known forms of reasoning. Politics and law have often been studied together, or in conjunction with economics, history, and especially philosophy. Biographers travel freely into academic territories with or without visas. Literary criticism today is permeated by conceptions deriving from psychology, philosophy, linguistics, and anthropology. Who can determine where sociology stops and anthropology begins?

The Battle of the Books, whether as satirised by Aristophanes, engaged in by the medieval schools of Paris and Orleans, or reduced to absurdity by the savage wit of Jonathan Swift (or present-day attacks on the 'canon'), always leaves the impression that devotion to one's academic interests and riding one's intellectual hobby-horse invariably lead to exclusion and intolerance. Such is only partly the case. Academic boundaries do indeed exist. They are erected for a purpose, but that purpose is not always the same. If boundaries exist to exclude, they also exist to define, concentrate, and 'discipline' the intelligence. Encyclopedism may be a marvelous aim, but it is unattainable by most minds and increasingly unattainable in our own day. If boundaries represent intellectual intolerance, they also help establish the methods for knowing and understanding, and as such become 'professional' and 'legitimate'. Rolf Torstendahl explains how this happened in the case of European engineers.

Sometimes boundaries exist for reasons that are neither intellectual nor professional. They are convenient structural arrangements or a form of bureaucratic rationalisation, permitting accountability and visibility in large-scale structures. The general subject is of obvious interest to the contributors to this volume. With different examples and categories of explanation, they discuss how academic boundaries are created, how they are sanctioned by tradition, reinforced institutionally, serve specific uses, or become a 'problem' in the sociology of knowledge. But boundaries also bend or dissolve, or, paradoxically, create an urge in the disciplined mind to explore other territories and become acquainted with other tribes. Thus, present-day specialists are cognitively, and through the process of 'complexity' explained by Burton Clark, invited to invade foreign lands.[1]

[1] Tony Becher discusses the tendency for sub-fields and sub-disciplines to transcend single institution barriers and even national boundaries, thus diffusing institutional and collegial

As an academic field of study, 'higher education' encompasses battalions of topics and problems for analysis. Elite formation; the professions both liberal and new; the State; labour markets; science policy and research; the organisation, direction and control of schools, institutes, colleges and universities; the academic profession; culture high and low; definitions of creativity and competence; the machinery of selection and the measurement and reward of merit; and the study of occupations: increasingly, these are an indissoluble part of 'higher education'. As a form of inquiry, higher education naturally includes all theories, hypotheses and conceptions, methods of arranging data and sifting through evidence that provide the researcher with distinctions, conclusions, patternings, and meanings. In sum, the study of higher education is no less than the study of human activity itself, as it is ordered and provides for socialisation, culture, skills, competencies, and creativity at those shifting levels of educational demarcation revealed by history.

Yet if good scholarship has always been distinguished by flexibility and openness, the special circumstances of our own age provide particularly impressive opportunities for the cross-fertilisation of academic specialties, arguably greater than in the days of the scholar gypsies of medieval and humanistic learning or when the Western world was tied together by Latin. (The acidic depiction of a peripatetic professoriate in David Lodge's comic novel of the 1980s, *Small World*, has made the reasons embarrassingly familiar.) The size of the international community of scholars, the close ties in some countries between government and the universities, the conjunction of interests of think-tanks, philanthropic societies, civil servants, knowledge-based industries, institutions like the World Bank in Washington and the higher education community, combined with the revolution in communications and transportation, have greatly enlarged the possibilities for frequent collaboration and interchange. Many traditions of thought are today readily accessible – even if not, given the volume of ideas and human limitations, so readily assimilable!

Just how fruitful international collaboration can be is indicated by the broad and intricate definition of 'higher education' employed in this volume. 'Higher education' (in the English language) is very likely a neologism of the last century. It was, and remains, imprecise. Nations do not define 'higher' in the same way, just as they do not define 'lower' education in the same way. Academic work deemed appropriate for a school in one country is inappropriate in another, and courses of study pursued at college or university in one nation are located in an 'upper

loyalties, in *Academic Tribes and Territories: Intellectual Enquiry and the Cultures of Disciplines* (Milton Keynes, 1989).

secondary' or 'post-compulsory sector' in another. These are not merely simple contrasts. They indicate the existence of whole categories of potentially fruitful analysis, ranging from the content of academic subjects and their level, the age of students and conceptions of maturity and suitable conduct, and the relation of advanced to elementary work within specific systems of organisation.

But in fact the dividing line between various levels or types of educational structures was not truly fixed – that is to say, standardised or bureau-cratised – in many countries until late in the last century, or early in this one. That is yet another reason why the definition of a 'university' is so vexed. Admissions policies to universities were often informal or irregular. A frequent complaint of Etonians or Wykehamists at Oxford and Cambridge in the early decades of the nineteenth century was that their undergraduate studies resembled those undertaken at boarding school (or were not nearly so demanding). Later in the century the new English civic universities often functioned as feeder schools for Oxford and Cambridge, much as the University of London and the Scottish universities had in earlier decades. 'Liberal education', the broadest definition of education that the western world possesses, embracing both 'general' as well as 'moral' education, took place in schools and academies as well as in colleges and universities. Indeed, it also took place outside those institutions. Michael Burrage, in his discussion of professions, makes the startling point that in the sense of character shaping or moral education, many forms of practitioner-based education have been more 'liberal' historically than school or university-based experiences. Technical edu-cation as well as professional education, depending upon time and country, was based on apprenticeship as well as on formal teaching. It could and did take place in a great variety of settings, differing radically in aims, methods, and support. Torstendahl makes these points in a discussion that is wide-ranging in chronology, method, and topic. As the essays indicate, the numerous forms of education have often been rivals for public or market attention, resources, and prestige, presenting societies with 'problems' appearing to require resolution. But as to 'who' exactly resolved (or should resolve) those problems – States, civil services, local authorities, professions, privileged elites, the general public, the invisible hand of the market – that is, directly or implicitly, the subject of nearly every essay in the book.

As used today, 'higher education' implies official or formally recognised partitions, systems, and financial controls, setting certain institutions apart from others. The phrase also suggests bureaucratic direction, partial, limited, or permissive, and conscious national attention to institutional differences. In most of the countries discussed in this volume, 'higher education' has in recent decades been elevated to the level of a ministerial or Cabinet post, although in quite a few instances ministerial coordination of higher education or policy-making remains quite loose or ambiguous. In Germany, the *länder* take more vigorous responsibility than does the capital. In the United States, 'higher education' as such is virtually unrepresented in Washington's massive civil service, the Department of Education being principally if not exclusively concerned with schooling. Several essays, notably those of Roger Geiger, Burton Clark, and Martin Trow, discuss the consequences for policy and practice of a higher education sector driven from 'below', that is to say, responsive (but not *absolutely* responsive) in a variety of ways to forces representing 'public opinion', market demand, and consumer or price discipline.

As we write, the question of markets in higher education is receiving more global attention than ever before, and the American 'model' or more properly 'models' of higher education are consequently of special international interest. Once the models were English or Scottish, in the last century more conspicuously German, and here and there, as Torstendahl explains, French. The disenchantment with State planning, 'command economies', and large-scale bureaucracy evident from policy discussions of the 1980s and 1990s, the unification of the Germanies, and the balkanising of former Soviet regimes have predictably led to a search for new and different ways of structuring and financing higher education to achieve the three goals of economic development, social mobility, and 'quality'.

The tendency in today's Europe is for observers and commentators to see the State as the pinnacle of institutional organisation, a body beyond which almost no appeal is possible. In the United States this view is also expressed or assumed, but American history reveals yet another and diametrical conception of the State, one that makes government sub-servient to and responsive to 'society' or public opinion. In this conception the State leads less and follows more.

Once the rhetoric of public argument is set aside, we can see that market behaviour and State or government activity are not always so easily contrasted. The boundaries between the two have not been fixed historically, just as the boundaries between 'private' and 'public' behaviour have not been rigid and firm. These dividing lines have fluctuated. Furthermore, the State is itself a market, operating within a very large and complicated framework of moral and political pressures and arrangements. The same is certainly true of those apparently unregulated 'markets' appearing in classical economics. In general, therefore, it would be an error to view State action as always antithetical to market forces. In 'Liberal Britain' of the nineteenth century, or present-day America, or in any nation for that matter, governments choose the roles they will play, those roles also affected by national patterns of decision-making. Governments can decide whether to strengthen consumer demand, whether to constrain the market in particular ways, or whether to create partnerships between private and public sectors. All these policies are in fact presently in existence, and, indeed, have long been in existence, although not everywhere at the same time nor used in the same way nor likely to produce the same result. A proper recognition of these facts should lead policy-makers and planners away from simple recommendations and panaceas.

Historically, the formation of a higher education public policy has been the result of the interaction between markets, institutions, professional associations, local and national governments, and what ancient historians recognised as chance, fortune or fate, what we today less metaphysically and more technically call 'contingencies'. It is also the result of institutional rivalries. In any case, the essays show how many different and unique responses a set of higher education institutions can make to either government or the market, and that no simplification of the process of inter-institutional interaction is either possible or useful. No two national States are ever wholly alike, although from time to time they may adopt policies or display features that appear similar. Likewise, no two national markets are ever alike. Indeed, each nation contains many markets, and these operate under many degrees of restriction, constraint, competition, or flexibility.

Comparison is the only satisfactory means of determining the relative weight of State policies or of markets, of the degree of 'top-down' or 'bottom-up' innovation, the action of 'autonomous' professions, or combinations of such initiatives, as is so often the case. Comparison is undoubtedly of prime concern to the authors and editors. Indeed, comparison and the virtues of comparison are everywhere evident in the essays. They are evident, for example, in the pairings which discuss two quite distinct if somewhat overlapping traditions of liberal education, those taking hold in countries influenced by Italian humanist values and in those adapting German models of general education. Similarly, other pairings offer comparisons of the history and support for research in very different countries such as Sweden and the United States, or the development at both institutional and ideological levels of professional education in England, the United States, France, Sweden, Germany, and Switzerland.

The Comparative Method (as it was once called and celebrated in a bygone era, especially by philologists, proto-anthropologists, and legal scholars) is certainly not new, nor could we claim for it the virtues and the advantages of our nineteenth-century academic forebears, who were certain they had discovered (as 'laws' of Nature are discovered) a *Method*, a unique intellectual tool laying bare the evolution of language and society. Today there are many means of comparison. They are all in evidence in these essays. They are used, as Trow notes in his contribution, to provide a means for determining just what different institutional arrangements – or the absence of features present in other systems – imply in different national contexts. Asking 'why' a particular development did not occur in one country may be 'whiggish' since the question implies it should have (the danger is pointed out in several essays); but merely posing the question does focus attention on comparison, and this in turn leads us toward new questions, new puzzles, new sequences, and perhaps new data.

As is sometimes observed, comparison brings out contrasts as well as similarities, but it brings them out in relation to a problem, an event, a development, a change of direction, a stopping point for reflection. Very likely, at least in relation to higher education, the tendency at present is to emphasise similarities or at least convergence. The formation of the European Community and the startling changes occurring in Central and Eastern Europe provide an incentive and reason to do so, but changes in the world economy also appear to promote emulation or convergence. International interdependence, linked economies, 'global villages', satellite communications, multi-national corporations, and the disappearance of wholly 'national' manufactured products encourage thinking along lines of unity and similarity. Comparative analysis provides us with rather a finer analytical means for discerning whether recent changes are truly convergent, merely superficial, or simply incomplete combustion. Comparison provides an outside referent for assessment, an external way of defining the volume, the functioning, the purpose, and the success of particular narrative elements in the formation and growth of a nation's institutions. While several of the contributors to this volume are not shy, indirectly suggesting some of the policy consequences implied by their conclusions, our overall task is certainly not to propose but to illuminate and understand the complex processes by which higher education institutions have been created.

Comparative analysis brings out what may be called the second general unifying theme of this volume, already named in passing, that is, 'complexity'. Clark observes that complexity is integral to modern societies and their economies. In our own day, he says, it is leading to the *de facto* breakup of large national higher education structures into a series of 'small worlds' linked by disciplines, the disciplines themselves connected to one another through the process of knowledge expansion and knowledge enhancement.

This is one important view of how specialist inquiry produces a coherent and interdependent cognitive universe. There are others. But our purpose here is not to dogmatise about specialism and universalism but to stress the value of an analytical approach to the study of universities that sees complexity as a fundamental part of the evolution and differentiation of educational institutions. In other words, we are not using the word 'evolution' to depict the unfolding of an all-encompassing rationality in history, nor by referring to 'differentiation' do we mean a straightforward functionalism, as if universities automatically adapt to changing circumstances. It is of course true that modern historians are not exactly united on the question of whether history's 'lessons' are best conveyed through what John Burrow once called the 'cross-section' approach or through a more overarching, more generalized method featuring purposeful accommodation. For the latter, a history without cycles and repetitions has always appeared to be amoral, relativistic, and useless. The historicist[2] assumption that the past is unique therefore disturbs scholars who fear that relativism must inevitably result in a descent into nihilism and anarchy. But a history that acknowledges the special character of past experience can still be 'philosophy teaching by example' as that scamp, Henry St John, Viscount Bolingbroke once maintained, attributing the notion to Dionysius of Halicarnassus. Complexity simply forces us to think more clearly about the meaning and uses of our inheritances.

By and large, therefore, the contributors to this volume agree with Trow that the history of higher education is in large measure a record of 'unique traditions', of inverse and unexplained relations and correlations. As such, it is difficult to reduce that history to relatively simple analytic categories.[3] To be sure, a complex world is in some respects semi-anarchic. That needs to be acknowledged in deference to the anti-historicists. It is untidy. It consists of many actors and of competition for control or influence. But it is the way much history works.

No better instance of this can be cited than Aant Elzinga's detailed study of the unexpected changes in the structure and management of Swedish higher education since 1945. Some of these changes, it is true, were part of the on-going statist and centralising tendencies situated in the third 'great transformation' of higher education described by Wittrock. Sweden's experience very nearly encapsulates the alterations of thought and policy evident in post-war Europe. But the intensity of the changes, and their comprehensiveness, are special. From 1945 to the present, no country in Europe has undergone so many sudden changes in the values and structure

[2] Using the word in its relative or non-Popperian definition.
[3] E.g., 'reproduction', the notion that an understanding of the relationship between institutions and society rests primarily on how institutions 'reproduce' the leading features of society. The view here adopted is much broader and wider ranging.

of its higher education system as has Sweden. Perhaps that is why Swedish scholars have been so concerned with thinking about the 'true' or 'proper' mission of a university. The heralded, socially and politically radical Swedish reorganisation of 1968 known far and wide as 'U68' from the acronym of the government commission preparing the reform is itself now undergoing drastic modification. The policy began, says the famous psychologist Torsten Husén, as an effort of simplification in a world that was by contrast proceeding towards complexity.[4] Elzinga's account is an arresting story of compressed history. Developments which in countries such as the United States took the better part of a century to accomplish have been hurried along by both market forces and State interest. The resulting hurly-burly of events, programmes, and ideologies is bewildering precisely because it is rapid, uncertain, and only intermittently pragmatic.

In a world of complexity, boundaries are constructed only to be torn down. Invisible barriers arise and disappear, as do formal barriers. In countries where a definition of a university has been officially and legally 'protected', as in the 'binary' systems separating 'universities' from 'polytechnics' in Australia or Britain, massive changes under way are removing the distinctions. But in Germany, Switzerland, Austria, and Sweden high quality 'technical universities' have long been in existence, and the question of what constitutes a 'university' or 'higher education' assumes a different form. In the giddy circumstances of the present, historical definitions of a 'university' become meaningless or helpless as the world rushes to meet the extraordinary demand for technological, professional, and research competencies by providing educational alternatives that create highly interdependent educational sectors and partnerships. Systems and institutions emulate one another, or search for their own special niche in highly diversified markets, national but also regional and international. Adult, continuing education divisions, and 'open universities' embark on schemes for mass and universal education. Single-purpose institutions acquire multiple functions and experience the formidable, indeed insoluble difficulties of reconciling opposite missions and values. Research universities form liaisons and alliances with polytechnics and industry according to national conceptions of conflict of interest. They undertake contract work, including contracts for short-cycle courses.

Buried in this dizzying activity, no longer easy to discern or explain, are hallowed or at least hoary cultural ideas like *Bildung, Bildning, Wissenschaft*, 'humanism', and 'liberal education' – ideas, however, that as our authors explain, were filled with ambiguity from the outset and never possessed the clarity of direction or purpose that their present-day

---

[4] A remark arising in conversation with the editors.

advocates claim for them. Gone – one is tempted to say forever – is that secure belief in a single, animating, essentialist 'idea' of a University as represented in different ways by the idealist philosophical traditions of Romantic England and Germany, although its enchantments undoubtedly remain,[5] as Wittrock poignantly but forcefully recalls in his highly-conceptualised discussion of the three great transformations in the history of the university.

The pace of recent change, as well as the remarkable expansion of what in Europe has been regarded as NUS or the 'non-university sector'[6] is both exhilarating and worrisome. It is exhilarating in opening up greater opportunities for social and occupational mobility, in questioning received wisdom, and in challenging long-standing systemic rigidities and bottle-necks. Ideological preconceptions encounter the vigour of competition and human ingenuity. Recent changes also appear to be meeting democratic and egalitarian concerns, although complexity warns us that such 'simple' consequences are not likely to emerge.

It is, however, worrisome – depending upon one's point of view – because established and proven values are threatened, policy changes (as in U68) are hurried through in a rush of enthusiasm, or transitions from one policy to another are given short shrift (how, in fact – the topic sometimes arises when American models are discussed – can a 'top-down' system suddenly become 'bottom-up' in the absence of such experience?). Also, words change their meanings. 'Elite', for example, which once had a neutral meaning, has now become synonymous with economic and social privilege. Ideological attacks on 'elitism', therefore, leave in doubt how the high talent essential to the success of modern societies is to be recruited and trained. Universities are restructured or browbeaten so that they will be more 'accountable' or socially 'responsive', and politicians rush to associate themselves with the latest plans and schemes. At the same time, however, they fully expect that traditional norms of scholarly and educational excellence will be unaffected. This is surely unrealistic.

In the following essays we believe that readers will find many examples of the unexpected. It is almost an axiom of some kinds of historical work that the inquirer should be continually surprised, that the exit of a theme may be quite opposite from its entrance, that the expected patterning takes a different form, or that, through comparison, a familiar generalisation acquires an unusual meaning. We hope that our readers will be surprised by the many faces of *Bildung*, as discussed by Torstendahl and Wittrock

---

[5] See Sheldon Rothblatt, 'The Idea of the Idea of a University and its Antithesis', in *Conversazione* (La Trobe University, Bundoora, Australia, 1989).

[6] See the recent report by the Organisation for Economic Co-operation and Development, *Alternatives to Universities* (Paris, 1991), 20.

and Sven-Eric Liedman, who also traces its influence on the more folkish conception of *Bildning*. Both are connected to, if one more loosely than the other, to what has long been denominated the 'Humboldtian tradition', featuring the disinterested pursuit of knowledge as a value in itself with the university as the appropriate setting. In time the Humboldtian view became the 'idea' of a university as a place for advanced learning, science, and research; and Max Weber, in a famous essay on the German university tradition, restated the idea as a higher 'calling'. But the idea as it moves through history is not always Humboldt's.

The Humboldtian conception of *Bildung* is related to but not exactly identical with a second conception of *Bildung* as spiritual self-development, in which form it appears to be a branch of nineteenth-century individualism. The contrast is yet greater, however, when *Bildung* is compared to Anglo-American conceptions of 'liberal education', with their humanistic rather than pietistic origins and rootedness in an 'Atlantic' tradition of public leadership.[7] The essay by Sheldon Rothblatt discusses the many variations existing on this theme. In this form, liberal education is character formation. The educational focus is less on learning than on behaviour, less on maturity than on youth, leading to a corresponding emphasis on teachers as being *in loco parentis*. The institutional implications – and these also imply certain financial arrangements – are significant. As conceived by Humboldt, *Bildung* also incorporated a public dimension, if perhaps (given the autocratic nature of the Prussian State), a less civic one than in the English-speaking world.[8] That was, in fact, the view of some nineteenth-century British observers. However that may be, Liedman makes the point that the political realities of nineteenth-century Germany produced a distinction within *Bildung* between the inner life, which was free, and the outer one requiring social and political conformity. But the free inner life of the person who was *gebildet* or *bildad* also helped produce the remarkable aesthetic and

[7] The most influential work on the subject of the Atlantic tradition is John Pocock, *The Machiavellian Moment, Florentine Political Thought and the Atlantic Republican Tradition* (Princeton, 1975). Pocock's position has been declared incomplete by Isaac Kramnick, *Republicanism and Bourgeois Radicalism, Political Ideology in Late Eighteenth-Century England and America* (Ithaca and London, 1990), and further criticism appears in Ian Shapiro, 'J. G. A. Pocock's Republicanism and Political Theory: A Critique and Reinterpretation', *Critical Review*, 4 (Summer 1990), 433–72. The debate is hardly academic. It is part of current American controversies concerning the dimensions and responsibilities of citizenship and patriotism and is reflected in arguments over what should be taught in schools.

[8] See David Sorkin, 'Wilhelm von Humboldt: The Theory and Practice of Self-Formation (*Bildung*)', *Journal of the History of Ideas*, 44 (January–March 1983), 55–74. For *Bildung* as general education, if not American-style general education, see Sven-Eric Liedman and Lennart Olausson, 'General Education, Culture, and Specialization', *Studies in Higher Education and Research*, 6 (1987).

intellectual culture of nineteenth-century Germany, and made that nation's universities the centre of international attention for many decades.

We can, nevertheless, fully appreciate how an educational philosophy and theory of self-fulfilment could in time lead away from politics and the responsibilities of active citizenship to become a 'Humboldtian tradition' of intellectual freedom embodied in research, especially when research was of direct and practical interest to the State. For an emerging generation of American scholars, and a revitalised English and Scottish university community, each heavily influenced by German scholarship or student years spent in Berlin, Bonn, and Leipzig, the astonishing intellectual creativity of Germany produced great dissatisfaction with existing ideals of undergraduate education with their heavy emphasis on personal style. These seemed to be more akin to what was expected of schoolboys than to what could be absorbed from scholars on the frontier of knowledge. The mid-Victorian English philosopher (of Scottish background), John Stuart Mill, confided to his diary that the English notion of a rounded or well-adjusted social personality was simply an excuse for conformity, less desirable in a civilised society than the Humboldtian ideal of 'human development in its richest diversity'. That is to say, 'Great and strong and varied faculties are more wanted than faculties well proportioned to one another.' (But in his *Logic* and whenever disgruntled with the quality of British leadership, Mill spoke differently.)[9]

Each nation developed its own institutional arrangements for pursuing the Humboldtian conception of advanced learning. Enamoured of the German 'mandarin' professor who also enjoyed civil service standing, admiring his famous research seminars, the brilliance of the faculties of philosophy, and the depth of German scholarship and science, American reformers realised they could not have this mix at home. For them the route to 'modernity' lay through a different part of the woods. For however important research and graduate education are to Americans today, no part of the higher education system stirs up as much emotion as *alma mater*, or commands as much alumni loyalty as the undergraduate college. This, as Roger Geiger illuminatingly explains, meant and means that research must be grafted onto, or seen to be compatible with, the undergraduate experience.

There are unquestionably 'standing antagonisms'[10] between undergraduate and graduate education in American universities. Multiple

---

[9] Quoted in Stefan Collini, *Public Moralists, Political Thought and Intellectual Life in Britain 1850–1930* (Oxford, 1991), 102.

[10] Sheldon Rothblatt, 'Standing Antagonisms': The Relationship of Undergraduate to Graduate Education', in *The Future of State Universities*, ed. Leslie W. Koepplin and David A. Wilson (New Brunswick, New Jersey, 1985), 39–67.

missions are likely to generate competition for resources in any case, but Geiger explains how those antagonisms are rooted in American history and self-understanding. Whether one believes that the emergence of graduate and professional education has been detrimental to under- graduate education or whether it has in fact strengthened the 'college' years, there can be no doubt that the two are insolubly linked today. The linkages in fact cross the boundaries between separate private liberal arts colleges and research universities. What is probably more interesting than current arguments over the possible deleterious effects of the 'graduate school' is its position in the education system. Far from being the principal driving force in higher education in the last century, the graduate school was itself a rebound effort by scholars who encountered a resilient collegiate structure reinforced by market forces in the shape of a modular system of course instruction. Finding themselves unable to specialise to the same degree as their European counterparts, American professors built a separate institutional structure where the higher criticism might find a home.

They were able to do so because little direct interference came from the State or states or bureaucrats. Local initiative was the American way. Hence, the new generation of post-1900 academic leaders and managers were able to shape consumer interest and mediate the heavy demands for higher education generally. This was an active use of the market, most noticeable as well, Burrage says, in the history of American professional schools like law. These did not displace undergraduate education (as in other countries) but instead used the college to raise the requirements for entrance to the bar by making a first degree necessary for admission to legal training. The popularity of American collegiate education, the development of the modular course system, and the high demand for general education provided the critical mass and diversified curriculum which permitted the establishment of a higher layer of graduate instruction. Thus, the continual claim of mixed-function American universities that undergraduate and graduate education have been partners as well as antagonists proves to have some solid support in the facts of American educational history.

In one way or another, all or most of the essays here presented ring changes on the theme of fact and ideal in the history of higher education institutions. It may well be the case that no part of cultural life can flourish without reference to an ideal, insofar as the absence of a measure also signifies the absence of an aspiration. Religion, politics, trade unionism, the arts all possess ideals. In perhaps prosaic form ideals are meant when references to 'classic' training or a 'classic' method are made. But religion apart, and as this introduction has already indicated, no other historiography of institutional development contains a core of research which puts ideals so squarely into institutional history as does writing on universities.

As the following essays so vividly indicate, the 'fact' is that educational ideals are rarely attainable in the form originally advocated by thinkers and leaders. In some cases – Burrage's point again – they have been attainable but where least expected! However, it is also a 'fact' that educational ideals – most notably the 'idea' of a university – Humboldtian, Weberian, Newmanesque – and 'liberal education', *Bildung, Bildning, allgemeine Bildung, allmänbildning* – have existed and continue to do so. They are often contradictory ideals. They represent within themselves more than one moral order. But they also comprise the cultural or the emotional barrier separating the 'university' from 'higher education'. Their existence and survival act as continual reminders of an alternative vision of higher education bold enough to challenge the laws of supply and demand. They still manage to influence our working notions of what civilised women and men are supposed to be.

Besides, as Wittrock argues, they are part of the historical record and present story. If not, they would be dysfunctional, disappearing long ago as yet another set of useless and cumbersome ideas for the scrapheap of history. One is therefore reminded of the English novelist E. M. Forster's aside that if poets are so unimportant, why do governments spend so much time worrying about them? If *Bildung* is of no consequence, why in its many metamorphoses does it still circulate?

But this is yet another part of the complex world described in the ensuing pages.[11]

The essays in this volume are an outgrowth of an international conference which took place on the pleasant 'island' of Rosenön in Dalarö, Sweden, in June 1987. These meetings were held under the enlightened auspices of

[11] In a thoughtful essay, Margareta Bertilsson suggests that the notion of unified and connected knowledge exemplified by *Bildung* is also symbolized by institutional boundaries and borders. The more 'open' (or trans-national, as in the proposed European Community) a university, the less likely will it possess an 'idea'; and without an idea, there can be no conception of universal learning. The further consequences of this are weak undergraduate education and a depleted sense of citizenship or *Bildungsbürgertum*.

If we pursue these ideas in a different direction, we can see how an alternative view of the idea of a university can arise based not on physical but invisible boundaries. As the guild or collegiate values of academic self-government evaporate under present-day conditions, external professional and specialised networks become more important and satisfying. The Humboldtian ideal of the unencumbered pursuit of knowledge reappears but in the form of 'invisible colleges' (to borrow a pre-nineteenth century term). These, of course, do not bear very directly on the problems of general or undergraduate education. See Margareta Bertilsson, 'From University to Comprehensive Higher Education: On the Widening Gap between *Lehre und Leben*', in *Studies of Higher Education and Research*, 1 (1991).

the Research on Higher Education Programme of the Swedish National Board of Universities and Colleges, since renamed the Council for Studies of Higher Education, with funding directly from the Riksdag. The Council – as the Programme before it – stands for scholarship that is unfettered, undogmatic, cooperative, and open-ended and draws its sustenance from a vigorous international marketplace of ideas. Such a liberal attitude in an era of mission-directed research is hardly casual or accidental. It is the result of careful and thoughtful sponsorship. We are therefore deeply indebted to the Council.[12]

The editors and contributors also wish to acknowledge the help of two other sources of cooperative international scholarship, the Swedish Collegium for Advanced Study in the Social Sciences (SCASSS) in Uppsala and the Center for Studies in Higher Education in Berkeley. Most of the contributors have been associated with either or both, and many of the ideas present in this volume can be traced back to discussions started or continued at Uppsala and Berkeley.

Other colleagues present at Dalarö – Harold Perkin, Torsten Husén, Stuart Blume, Ulrich Teichler, Tony Becher, and Simon Schwartzman – will notice their influence in the separate contributions. Lois McClure assisted us with editorial chores and deserves thanks.

---

[12] And to the two directors. See 'Swedish Research on Higher Education in Perspective – A Conversation between Eskil Bjorklund and Thorsten Nybom', in *University and Society, Essays on the Social Role of Research and Higher Education*, ed. Martin A. Trow and Thorsten Nybom (London, 1991), chapter 12.

Part 1

Fact and ideals in liberal education

1   The limbs of osiris: liberal education in the English-speaking world

Sheldon Rothblatt

> In the following pages I do not pretend to enumerate and analyse all the alien elements which thus gathered round the popular deity. All that I shall attempt to do is to peel off these accretions and to exhibit the god, as far as possible, in his primitive simplicity.
> Sir James George Frazer, *The Golden Bough*, 3rd edn (New York, 1935), II, 3.

A 'primitive simplicity'

What may be possible in science, is not easily achieved in history. The 'alien elements' and 'accretions' are as important as the 'primitive simplicity', for it is in the elaboration of cultural forms and institutions that the human experience is captured, and it is within these forms, certainly as much as in the substance which they have been designed to promote, that argument and confusion arise. To the search for a 'primitive simplicity', therefore, the historian is justified in opposing a sophisticated complexity as a truer approximation of the labyrinthine decisions that take us from the deep past to the near present.

Yet such is the power of science and scientific conceptions of knowing, and the seductive power of logic, which joins fragments through language, that the desire to uncover a clear direction from the remarkable layers of historical time is understandable and possibly pardonable. It is certainly reasonable to expect that a Sir James Frazer, under the spell of late Victorian British rationalism, would want to find in the bones and limbs of ancient cults of dying and rising gods a simple identifiable clue that leads to Christian messianism and connects the centuries, one with the others.

In the chapter that follows I will modify the method of Frazer, at least to this degree, that in pursuing the 'primitive simplicity' presumed to lie at the heart of a tradition, I will not peel off all the accretions and alien elements that in time gathered around the conception of a liberal education, but I will also follow his lead by trying to demonstrate the staying power of an idea that was once, like Osiris himself, conceived as whole and integrated, but over centuries was rent and disconnected, each part forming its own cult and attracting its own votaries. If the heart of Osiris lay at Athribis, the backbone at Busiris and the neck at Letopolis, the head was at Memphis, miraculously duplicated at Abydos.[1] For liberal education, we can say that portions of it remained in ancient Greece, other limbs were to be found in the Italy of the Renaissance, still others in the nations influenced by German conceptions of self-development, and yet others in the English-speaking communities of the world.

As Isis went in search of these fragments, so from time to time have scholars and educators. The most remarkable efforts have been made historically to recover and unite the scattered limbs. But each time this is attempted, it is done so within a new historical context, in reference to a different set of institutions, and with regard to different uses.

The subject of the following interpretation is the problematical character of liberal education as it descended from Hellenic antiquity to become a central feature of the higher education curriculum of English-speaking nations, especially Britain and the United States. In many respects the subject is intimidating. The history of liberal education from its origins is not more difficult to summarise than any other historical theme, such as the history of religious systems, or legal structures or agricultural economies, marriage and the family or the history of diet. But it certainly presents us with a similar range of heuristic and empirical, not to mention interpretive, difficulties. The temporal one by itself is particularly daunting. What is referred to as 'liberal education' or the 'tradition of liberal education' or the 'legacy' of liberal education first took shape in very ancient times in societies and cultures quite different from those of industrial nation-states. The social and occupational structures were scarcely similar, in certain respects only superficially similar. Mass education in any form was unknown. Most of the professional occupations of today did not exist. Governing systems were not like ours. Access and opportunity were not the subjects of widespread public debate, were not under review by bureaucratic policy makers, and liberal education itself was not necessarily 'higher education'. (I have not yet pinned down the origins of the phrase 'higher education' in the English language, but I think it is safe to conjecture that it appears towards the end of the nineteenth century when national systems of education are differentiated into segments.) It is true that 'liberal education' is not necessarily higher education even today, but that depends upon whether we are speaking about the United States, where it is firmly emplaced in the post-secondary education structure, or Europe, where a version of it can be found lower down.

---

[1] Sir James George Frazer, *The Golden Bough*, 3rd edition (New York, 1935), II, 11.

With so much that is profoundly different between past and present, between countries and between cultures, how is it that we so often refer to a common heritage or tradition of liberal education in the Western world? How is it that we can even speak about the 'evolution' of liberal education? However we choose to use that biological and perhaps even Darwinian metaphor, it is certain that educational systems cannot evolve as species evolve. They can mutate, that is, be transformed into some new and unexpected form, but they cannot move from a lower order of functioning and differentiation to a higher one. They cannot, to transfer to a Hegelian metaphor, realise or clarify themselves in time. They do not – I now employ the broader language of philosophical idealism – possess an essence or fundamental animating idea. Yet we have a vast extant literature that does in fact discuss education and especially liberal education as if they have a continuous reality miraculously defying the permutations and revolutions of historical change. The belief in an inner definable reality that can be isolated and employed for the benefit of society generally or for specific groups is a 'problem' in the sociology of knowledge. I do not at this moment wish to discuss it here;[2] but I do want to say rather fleetingly that although liberal education today cannot be what it was in antiquity, there has descended through the *longue durée* a tradition of discussing liberal education as if it were an autonomous and independent set of ideas. Countless generations of writers and commentators, some who might bear the lofty designation 'intellectuals', others, more prosaically, the mental labourers of society – educators, bureaucrats, scholars – have passed on to one another a habit of thinking about the importance and value of liberal education. Insofar as the bearers of this habit have an institutional place in our societies, or have access to publications, they have over the centuries influenced public debate in whatever form it has taken.

Contending powers

I would like to consider a number of leading and interconnected concepts or beliefs that are part of that habit of thinking about liberal education to which I have just referred. Since the subject is vast, I must be unusually selective, but I hope not simplistic.

It has long been the practice to place the origins of liberal education in the great civilisations of antiquity. The contributions of ancient Greece and Rome, especially the first, are demonstrably central. Liberal education is in fact part of the classical corpus; and wherever that corpus is alive or

---

[2] But see Sheldon Rothblatt, 'The Idea of the Idea of a University and Its Antithesis', *Conversazione* (La Trobe University, Bundoora, Australia, 1989).

respected, so will ideas about liberal education be warmly received. It is, however, a 'corpus', which means that the ancient civilisations have bequeathed to us a great many ideas, some of them contradictory and a few of them embarrassing. Any subsequent civilisation, let us say medieval culture or Renaissance Italy or Enlightenment Europe or Republican America, is immediately faced with the problem of selectivity, of choosing from the astonishing productions of Greece and Rome those values and practices or habits that appear best suited to later purposes. Nevertheless, we can start with what may be termed the basic or fundamental attribute of a liberally educated person from which most if not exactly all of the subsequent theories take rise. That starting point is the ideal of the wholeness of the individual, and indeed, by more than implication, of the undefiled, the healthy and secure personality.

This ideal has had a long and seductive history. It states that the purpose of liberal education is to form a character or type, all of whose parts are in harmonious agreement, no one part of the character (or the personality) being over-developed at the expense of another. This statement is not self-evident. Like most other definitions of education, it presupposes a great deal and draws us deeply into some of the most fundamental concerns of a particular culture. We are instantly in a strange world of metaphysics or meta-psychology, and we recognise the characteristically Greek notion of a world in balance and good order. When we speak of the whole man, then, we are also speaking about Hellenic cosmology and philosophy and about conceptions of human nature and being in relation to the structure of nature itself and to the organisation of social existence.

What exactly, then, does it mean to be whole? It means that we start with an axiom about the human personality, we posit an ideal or preferable condition, and we then create educational systems to reproduce that ideal. The Greek view of human personality holds that the individual person is divided into mental, emotional, and bodily parts. Unfortunately, each part is at war with the other. Just as in the cosmology of Heraclitus the powers of Love and Strife, or Justice and Injustice contend, each gaining supremacy only in the short run – their universal contest producing flux and instability – so do the several divisions of the self struggle for its mastery. This notion of fundamental contending powers appears everywhere in Hellenic thought, in humoral physiology, for example, where an imbalance in the bodily fluids produces illness. But not only physical health is linked to bodily fluids: psychological health is also involved. As it is possible to have too much blood and too much black bile, so is it possible to be overly cheerful or congenitally angry. These are personality defects in need of correction, and if the physician is stymied, the educator is summoned to the rescue.

Whatever the parts, they are to be integrated. However we designate them, they are to respect one another, otherwise we are illiberally educated. Our body, mind, and emotions will contend for mastery of the self, and the result will be an unstable personality, or a one-sided personality and surely, since the personality is tied directly to the body's physiology, an unhealthy personality.

These ideas can be illustrated by a rather free rendering of the Greek apophthegm that a liberally educated man must learn to play the flute but not too well. The distance between the modern and ancient worlds is captured in this sentiment. In the holistic conception, division in any form prevents the 'natural' or the 'original' self from emerging. So proficiency, playing the flute well, divides the self by drawing attention to the accomplishment. Nowhere is this more dangerous than when proficiency assumes priority in the definition of life chances. But for us, proficiency above all is the object of education. Division is the means by which proficiency is advanced, and both proficiency and the results of division are measurable.

When carried to its logical conclusion, measurement becomes the absolute antithesis of the view that human nature is indivisible and unmeasurable. It is consequently decried as denaturing, a profanation of the essential self. For the Greek, dire consequences follow from playing the flute too well. The self inevitably becomes fascinated by the skill, which is then regarded as an end in itself, something to be mastered and indeed, as I indicated, measured. 'Any particular technique tends by its own inner logic to develop exclusively along its own line', writes Henri Marrou in his indispensable study of classical education, 'in and for itself, and thus it ends by enslaving the man whom it should serve'.[3] Safeguarding the personality from this perennial temptation requires eternal vigilance. Once we admit to the pleasure of being proficient, or still worse, submit to measuring proficiency, we will next wish to do so competitively, and we are back in a world where conflict and ambition produce instability and disharmony.

The educational institutions of today reflect the reality of the modern world through division in the organisation of disciplines, the arrangements for teaching, the facts of publication, and the basis for professional reputations. In other words, in modern culture we have accepted the belief in, and the necessity for, a fundamental compartmentalisation of mental labour. And far from considering these arrangements as harmful to the human spirit, or a violation of human nature, the position is maintained

---

[3] Henri Marrou, *A History of Education in Antiquity* (Madison, 1982), 225. See also Charles Norris Cochrane, *Christianity and Classical Culture* (New York, 1957).

that it is only in discordance, it is only when all notions of a natural, whole self are discarded, only when the partitioning from the world is achieved, that mental health is assured. Here, for example, are the words of the contemporary American novelist, Philip Roth;

[T]here are those whose sanity flows from the conscious separation of [self-consciousness and natural being]. If there even is a natural being, an irreducible self, it is rather small ... and may even be the root of all impersonation – the natural being may be the skill itself, the innate capacity to impersonate. I'm talking about recognizing that one is acutely a performer, rather than swallowing whole the guise of naturalness and pretending that it isn't a performance but you.[4]

This hardly disposes of the issues, as Roth himself understands, introducing his refutation with the correct generalisation that 'The whole Western idea of mental health runs in precisely the opposite direction'.[5] The 'problem' for the Greeks has remained the problem for many modern thinkers and writers, theorists, and indeed social workers, the problem of human nature forever rebelling against itself, as Thucydides says in his history of the Peloponnesian War. It is not fanciful to notice in the ancient philosophies, several ideas or attitudes also to be found in the writings of Sigmund Freud, for he too has constructed a psychology partly on the basis of contending inner constituencies. But in Freud, as in ancient thought, contending inner constituencies are manifestations of outer rivalries. The larger struggle, of which the individual is a representation, is one of barbarism in perpetual conflict with civilisation. Barbarism is the equivalent of the personality over – developed in one direction. Civilisation is the opposite, the personality under control, mastered and quiescent.

These remarks can now be re-stated in another way. Not only is a state of internal equilibrium or a balance between psychology and physiology the ideal expression of human nature, there must also exist a happy correspondence between the individual and society, a harmonisation of interest, for otherwise both entities are in disarray.

On the town

Enough has now been said to show how a great many different educational ideas entangled in the complexities of the Hellenic ideal of a liberal education originate in a profound fear that the integrity of the human personality is constantly threatened by very great forces of division. These are inherent in the construction of the self and in the very organisation of

---

[4] Philip Roth, *The Counterlife* (New York, 1988), 365–6.   [5] *Ibid.*, 365.

society and the cosmos. From here we can easily understand some of the appeal and the power of later theories of learning, such as the phrenological notions of the nineteenth century which also have an ancient origin. The theory that various mental functions are located in distinct compartments of the brain is in some sense a descendant of the theory of bodily humours, for the over-development of one part of the brain also threatens to introduce a mental imbalance and must be corrected by the application of an appropriate pedagogy. The appeal of the ideal of the breadth of learning, also originates in the ideal of wholeness, for to learn one thing without learning another is to invite imbalance. 'When certain mental endowments receive a much higher culture than others, there is a distortion in the intellectual culture' – thus the opinion of a self-described 'Member' of Yale University in 1842.[6]

From breadth of learning we elide to the problem that has caused advocates of liberal education their greatest difficulties and which has endlessly confused the historiography of the subject, namely the question of the utility of liberal education, where utility is commonly regarded as a vocation or occupation requiring precisely that element of skill concentration that the liberally educated person has been advised to avoid.

Recently, however, one historian has cautioned us to avoid concluding that the conflict between utility and inutility is the cardinal historical distinction between what the fourth-century Greeks called *eleutherios* or liberal education and *banausos* or mechanical, technical, 'vulgar' education. He quite soundly notes that through the ages many writers have found – that is to say, have assumed – that liberal forms of education were thoroughly useful. However, what made a subject 'useful' was not whether it was united to a specific career or occupation, more or less socially acceptable or dignified, but whether or not the career in question and the education for it either elevated or degraded the mind. Did education focus the personality on narrow pursuits, generally material in nature, or did it encourage 'free' speculation, breadth, and disinterest?[7]

I have arrived at similar conclusions: historically, curriculum and occupation have been less important in defining traditions of liberal education than the spirit in which a given subject was pursued.[8] Yet the very fact that debate has so often centred on practicality, or taken the form of

[6] Mary Lovett Smallwood, *An Historical Study of Examinations and Grading Systems in Early American Universities* (Cambridge, MA, 1935), 88.
[7] Bruce A. Kimball, 'Liberal versus Useful Education: Reconsidering the Contrast and Its Lineage', *Teachers College Record*, 87 (Summer, 1986), 575–87.
[8] Rothblatt, '"Standing Antagonisms": The Relationship of Undergraduate to Graduate Education', in *The Future of State Universities*, ed. Leslie W. Koepplin and David A. Wilson (New Brunswick, 1985), 63. The difficulty was certainly noted in the nineteenth century:

a battle of the books, or rests on semantic paradoxes and a confusion of terms is also evidence for a deep-seated historical ambiguity and malaise. These arise, it should be added, not so much from the intrinsic meaning of words like *eleutherios*, *liberalis*, or liberal, but from the need to make educational ideas work in specific historical contexts.

Here again we encounter the conflict between fact and idea. In social matters, ideas are necessary, but they are rarely sufficient. If bridge-building is needed, and a liberally-educated person cannot build a bridge, then in that context a liberal education is worthless or limited; but if a broad knowledge of human affairs is required as an aid to good governance, then in that context a splendid civil engineer may be helpless. Yet if over many centuries the practice has arisen of associating education with the leisure to reflect, to devote one's energies to civic life, to attend the prince at court, or to spend one's mornings in the library of a great manor house, one's afternoons in the fields chatting up the tenants, then the record is likely to show that such an education will be labelled 'liberal', that is to say, the education suitable for 'free' men, for the unencumbered personality. By comparison (and it is 'logical' or 'reasonable' or 'natural' for the mind to compare), any other form of education is likely to be dismissed as 'servile'. Historical comparisons do not stop even here. To make the distinctions between forms of education yet finer and more complicated, it is possible to contrast what surely in our time would be considered a grouping of subjects in a liberal education curriculum but in London in 1826 was divided into liberal and 'ornamental accomplish-ment', the latter comprising such sciences as geology, mineralogy, botany and zoology, and such arts as modern languages and oriental literature.[9]

Finally, to complete this introduction, I would like to re-emphasise that from the perspective I have developed, the ideal of being whole cannot be accommodated anywhere except in the larger world itself. To realise or express its fullest human capacity, the personality must exist in the largest and freest possible social space. A liberal education is therefore preparation

Almost every subject has some value, both in itself and as a mental discipline. Some voices are still lifted in defence of a classical education, which, if in its origin an accident, is nevertheless, it is urged, invaluable in disciplining the mind and forming a cultured taste, while it furnishes the key to European history and literature and thought. Study science is the cry of another party: the hopes of mankind lie in the increase of that knowledge of nature which alone is power. And a third voice is heard – the voice of poverty, suggesting that it will be best to study whatever subject is most marketable, – for life has become more complex and the struggle is harder, and the strugglers more numerous: it is more difficult to ascertain what society wants, and the penalties of mis-take have not been diminished (Walter Hobhouse, *The Theory and Practice of Ancient Education* (1885; New York, 1910), 54).

[9] H. Hale Bellot, *University College London 1826–1926* (London, 1929), 53.

for life in society. But how that life is lived is central to the problem. Not every activity or career or occupation can be connected to 'liberal' education. For the Greeks, both Attic and Spartan, the proper sphere of a liberally educated person was public service. The best disposition of one's talents was in relation to the political or military realm where decisions essential to the well-being and preservation of the ancient city-states were taken. Isolation from the world, withdrawal from it or political ostracism, was virtually the worst fate that could befall the citizen of the ancient polis. Not only did voluntary or forcible departure lose him friends, fortune, and influence: it also removed him from that environment, cut him off from the sources of knowledge and information, and deprived him of that wider view of social affairs which nourished and guaranteed his wholeness. Once out of society, the descent into fantasy was rapid. Wherever ancient ideals of living in the world remained powerful, as in eighteenth-century England, historians will notice the staying power of the belief that only in the world, or on the town, was a fully rounded personality likely.[10]

In common with some recent authorities,[11] I am suggesting that the view of human nature and potential here elaborated, albeit in a special way, remained the dominant and most influential theory of the purpose and meaning of liberal education in the English-speaking world until virtually the present. But a second also makes an early appearance. It is sometimes known as the platonic-pythagorean or 'philosophical' theory. This theory stresses intellectual more than civic dimensions. It holds that the temptations, compromises, and disappointments of the world do not nourish and sustain but instead overwhelm the personality. Isolation does

[10] See, for example, Samuel Johnson's eighteenth-century romance about the consequences of social and intellectual isolation, *The History of Rasselas, Prince of Abyssinia*.

[11] An interesting work appearing since this chapter was first composed, Robert E. Proctor, *Education's Great Amnesia, Reconsidering the Humanities from Petrarch to Freud* (Indiana, 1988), singles out the holistic conception of education as the essence of the *studie humanitatis*, that is, liberal arts teaching. See especially pp. 21, 109, 113, 128. Following Jacob Burckhardt (and others), Proctor places the origins of the modern self in the Italian Renaissance and relates the modern curriculum to the desire to explicate that self. From this perspective, disciplines are valued insofar as they can be personalised. The logical end result of an intense, internalised pursuit of self-understanding is, Porter observes, the belief in an unconscious self. As education is the process by which the self is formed, a belief in the unconscious actually undermines the very possibility of liberal education as holism. Undeterred by this conclusion, Proctor appends his own recommendations for an undergraduate curriculum to his valuable study, describing it as an attempt to restore the Renaissance conception of 'good' behaviour and basing it more on self-understanding than on values implicit in institutional aims and forms.

The historical version of liberal education elaborated in my own essay is not so normative. It places less emphasis on curriculum and more on a learning environment and on the necessary tension between 'liberal' and 'servile', life and the counterlife. Why? because historically liberal education is filled with contradiction and ambiguity.

not imperil the personality but preserves it and allows the self perfect freedom to pursue thought at its highest, purest, and most disinterested. Alone or surrounded by a knot of like minded companions 'we few, we happy few' – the philosopher reflects upon the nature of things and allows his attention to be drawn towards the contemplation of eternity. Losing himself in the pursuit of pure and abstract studies, such as mathematics, he resists every temptation to placate others or to place his knowledge at the immediate service of society.

Each of the different conceptions of liberal education produces a different career track. To live in the world means a career in the world, and the careers that successfully embody the attributes of a liberal education are leadership positions, usually political or military. To live out of the world suggests an utterly different career, if 'career' is even the right word. In fact, no career is truly possible under these conditions. So the philosophers face the continual historical prospect of unemployment, unless they are independently wealthy, supported by benign patronage, or compromise with society by hiring themselves out as teachers and instructors.

These opposing conceptions of the purpose of liberal education nevertheless reinforce one another at certain points. It therefore can be said that the attributes of a liberal education are:

1. liberation from the self or parts of the self, mentally and emotionally, or from society or the prejudices and limitations of society;
2. breadth of outlook, a capacity to see connections and hence an ability to make fundamental decisions and judgements;
3. independence of mind, born of a breadth of outlook and freedom from prejudice and pre-conception;
4. an understanding of human nature, the motives and springs of action in human conduct, and by extension, institutions and basic human structures.

Possibly the most vexing historical problem – it is certainly true of American educational systems today – is translating a complicated set of interlocked conceptions and assumptions about human nature into actual educational systems. How does a society guarantee that the personality will be liberated from itself or remain free from general prejudice? How does it encourage independence of mind or promote an understanding of human nature and the functioning of institutions? How does it create whole people who are, precisely because they are free of the burden of themselves, comfortable in the world? And how does a society mediate the conflicts between two opposing ideals that have come down through the centuries packaged so very similarly, but the one insisting on a wholeness that is gained in and through the world and the other apart and in contempt of it?

How 'liberal'?

The historical task of liberal education is to attach itself to some solid function, otherwise it will be useless. The curriculum, it appears, follows the function. Yet given the nature of the historical transmission of ideas and institutions, their slow transformation and adaptation, even sometimes in periods of revolutionary change, it more often happens that the curriculum precedes the function and is only loosely attached to it. This does not necessarily render the curriculum dysfunctional, because it may happen that the historian is looking for connections in the wrong places, but it does mean that we can expect the fit between liberal education and society to be uncertain. When this happens, as in the Hellenistic period (according to Marrou), the philosophical tradition of liberal education tended to be more appealing that the rhetorical one. '[C]lassical humanism turned inwards in search of an immanent perfection and became absorbed in an egoistic aesthetic contemplation.'[12]

But historically there has in fact existed another means for ensuring that the Greek ideal of the whole person remained alive: that was to connect it more closely to the social than to the occupational structure. This solved the problem of the utility of liberal education by freeing its recipient from the need to make a living. Hence we find that from the earliest times it is mainly wealthy families that furnish sons with a liberal education. Consequently over the centuries there exists an explicit connection between high social standing and liberal education. As a form of insurance it becomes possible to graft a more utilitarian form of education onto a liberal arts exposure once the pupil reaches mid-adolescence – for example, the law, but a frugal parent will not wish to stretch the family purse any further than circumstances require.

Liberal education historically is associated with privileged elites, especially elites in government, at princely courts, in the great State churches, in universities, expensive schools, and the leading professions. It is associated with leisured classes and groups aspiring to high social position. Perhaps this generalisation is glib. Every Western society since antiquity has a different social configuration, a different set of hierarchies, and a different code of rules. The kind of liberal education adopted for each elite group, the emphases within the tradition of the liberal arts, the texts selected for study and the institutional delivery systems are sufficiently

---

[12] Marrou, *Education in Antiquity*, 226.

dissimilar to warrant comment and qualification. However, the generalisation is broadly accurate if unexceptional. The higher type of character which it was the singular responsibility of liberal education to produce, a character who can, as Marrou says, transcend himself and society (if such a character can ever be said to truly exist), is the result of relatively long years of schooling and unemployment and must be therefore subsidised. If prosperous parents and guardians are lacking, then a network of support in the form of scholarships, patronage, and sponsorship must be created, along with subsidies for room, board, and transportation.

These social facts account for the liberal arts curriculum, that is, account for the heavy emphasis on texts and authors whose utility is not self-evident, and leaves the reviewer with the strong impression that general education is indeed a central concern of liberal education. It is possible, in reviewing the long lists of authors, to produce an impressive catalogue of instructional materials in ancient Greece, the Hellenistic, and Roman Republic periods, the Empires of Rome, East and West, the middle ages, the Renaissance and so on, to name only those segments of the past where a classical curriculum was featured. In one way or another every major subject known to those times was touched upon: drama, history, the grammatical arts, geography, religion, the mathematical sciences, physics and poetry in all their varied forms. Foreign languages entered the liberal arts curriculum when Rome took over the tradition of Hellenistic learning and made Greek compulsory. When vernacular languages appeared, Latin became essential, and in time a canon was established.

As I write, the subject of an educational canon is being hotly debated in the United States. Several observations about it are therefore in order: 1) instruction in it is not thorough but selective – there is, after all, insufficient time to teach everything as one civilisation builds upon another; 2) an organising principle is required, and the favoured one is rhetoric, oratory, or declamation, the tradition of the sophists, of the rhetors, of Isocrates, that is, of educators who promoted the belief that the purpose of liberal education was public service; 3) the canon is for the most part schoolboyish. In other words, while it may well be true, as has been said, that the aim of liberal education is to free the adult in the child, that antiquity has no text like *Émile* which instructs teachers in the special needs and requirements of children and adolescents,[13] in practice, paradoxically, the teaching of the liberal arts tended to be astonishingly illiberal. It was characterised by the inculcation of skills and proficiencies, especially language skills, spoken and written. Liberal education was drill, rote,

---

[13] *Ibid.*, 218.

emulation, memorisation, repetition, and (since those so educated were boys or youths) the rod.[14]

From the beginning, therefore, liberal education was beset by philosophical and practical difficulties. The correlation between the intentions behind a given curriculum, the actual content of the curriculum, and its alleged consequences were most often hopelessly confused or contradictory. The claims made for one were at variance with the defences constructed for another. A liberal education was *supposed* to do this, the content was said to do that, the results were *meant* to be such. Yet all three were not and could not be synchronised.[15]

A canon is sanctioned by tradition and use. It derives legitimacy from association. It is essentially conservative, but it never stands absolutely still. As time passes, it acquires additional refinements as well as accretions, much like the knowledge paradigms discussed by Thomas Kuhn in the *Structure of Scientific Revolutions*. (2nd edn, 1970). Inevitably the unwieldy mass of information and justifications that it must promote place considerable strain on its coherence and plausibility. The canon comes under periodic review and discussion, yielding to differences of view such as we experience in a reading of treatises like Baldesar Castiglione's sixteenth-century *The Book of the Courtier*. However, the canon remains more or less intact, by which I mean more or less acceptable, because its stated objectives are legitimate and because the correlation between means and ends is still widely respected. It is respected because the conservative impulse yields positive advantages. A mastery of the traditional forms promotes self-confidence, and to this extent even a schoolboy proficiency is particularly useful for a social and political elite.

Interruption or intermission?

The transmission of the liberal education heritage from classical antiquity to and through the 'middle ages' is almost impossible to summarise, even if by that designation we mean a Europe wholly united in purpose and institutions. Nevertheless, a few properly qualified generalisations regarding the fate of liberal education may be in order.

The conception of the whole person, of mind and body in pleasing balance, does not appear to have been as central to medieval as to classical culture. A Carolingian scholar such as Alcuin, by drawing on the rhetorical

---

[14] Plato's jaundiced view of rhetoric as practiced by the sophists is familiar. Since he believed that in their hands rhetoric had degenerated into style not sense, he forbade its teaching in the Platonic republic. Kenneth J. Freeman, *Schools of Hellas* (New York, 1969), 562, 174–6.

[15] Andrew Ahlgren and Carol M. Boyer, 'Visceral Priorities, Roots of Confusion in Liberal Education', *Journal of Higher Education*, 52 (1981), 173–80.

traditions, could still demonstrate the importance of being a good citizen and leader of society,[16] but other quasi-vocational objectives were equally valid: hermitic withdrawal, for example, or, once universities were established in the high middle ages, preparation for careers in law, and medicine, and the Church. The ideal of public life, for which self-integration was absolutely necessary, did not customarily drive the curriculum. Of course political concerns certainly appear in the writings of medieval theorists. Quentin Skinner has shown how much early Renaissance political thought is in fact indebted to the scholastics,[17] and direct connections between the liberal arts curriculum and public occupations were widespread, as in the case of the legal profession. Rhetoric was useful to the lawyer, for oratory, logic, and argument were obviously instrumental; both Cicero and Quintilian had given their blessings to the union.[18] But this only means that the bend and direction of a given discipline can be determined by the uses to which it will be put. Whether we call the study of law a liberal subject or something else – a professional subject, for example, or compromise by naming it a 'liberal profession' – is more a matter of the profession's historic associations with portions of the liberal arts than with its alleged intrinsic properties.

In the middle ages the liberal arts curriculum was divided into mathematical studies, the quadrivium, and language studies, the trivium (the Romans had known as many as nine liberal arts, adding architecture and medicine), and for centuries the schoolmen debated which methods were appropriate to each of the seven studies thus partitioned. They debated whether grammar was the pathway to metaphysical truth, whether (after the revival of Aristotelian learning) the New Logic was superior to the Old, whether the liberal arts were of independent use or subservient to an understanding of Scripture, or whether pagan learning had any place at all in Christian civilisation. (Apparently so, or to use the words of Ermenric of Ellwangen in the ninth century: 'Since even as dung spread upon the field enriches it to good harvest, so the filthy writings of the pagan poets are a mighty aid to divine eloquence.'[19] Knowledge through Revelation contested with knowledge through empirical or at least logical systems of explanation.

Bruce Kimball argues that the Aristotelian revolution in medieval thought, principally associated with Aquinas, 'made logic the heart and soul of the *artes liberales*, which were stripped of direct connection to ethics

---

[16] Bruce A. Kimball, *Orators and Philosophers, A History of the Idea of Liberal Education* (New York, 1986), 53.
[17] Albert Rabil, Jr., 'The Significance of "Civic Humanism" in the Interpretation of the Italian Renaissance', in Albert Rabil, Jr. (ed.), *Renaissance Humanism, Foundations, Forms, and Legacy*, (Philadelphia, 1988), I, 164–6.   [18] Kimball, *Orators*, 70.
[19] *Ibid.*, 45.

and oriented purely to intellectual formation'. Rhetoric, he observes, practically dropped from sight, as the platonic/pythagorean speculative tradition nearly replaced it.[20] If so, we can see how these long centuries took the history of liberal education further and further away from the most fundamental concerns of classical civilisation. It would be imprudent, not to mention arrogant, for an historian of the modern period to assert that in the middle ages liberal education nearly ceased to exist. How else explain the constant preoccupation with the Roman repertory of terms and phrases so essential to the understanding of the ideas of a liberal education? Yet this preoccupation seems so distant from the most vital concerns of ancient culture. In spirit and purpose, in metaphysical orientation towards the cosmos, in its social meanings, it would be difficult to locate within medieval uses of the liberal arts a concern for the gentlemen who had to learn to play the flute, if not too well.

Playing the flute

The recent work of Anthony Grafton and Lisa Jardine is notable for attempting to recover the atmosphere of humanistic and liberal arts teaching in the Italian classroom. Their description of the famous educator, Guarino Guarini of Verona, returns us to the central concerns of the liberal education tradition. These authors lay out the dimensions of a liberal education in its quattrocento form and explain the connections between a highly standardised curriculum, a servile set of pedagogical methods, and the goal of promoting self-confidence. The 'greatest teacher in a century of great teachers', Guarino subjected his pupils to a detailed and severely-disciplined regimen of 'pure' Latin (i.e., the Latin of Cicero and Virgil) and its correct pronunciation, the indispensable beginnings to a programme of studies that included history, geography, and mythology. Guarino's own manual, the *Regulae*, laid out the methods of instruction to be used, the parts of Latin speech, mnemonic devices to assist the lazy memory, all of which were derived from learned grammarians of the medieval and ancient periods. Objectives of liberal education promoted in our own time, such as the ability to think freshly upon a given topic and to develop independent ideas, were not only ignored: they were actively discouraged. Nor was the knowledge imparted systematically interrelated. Familiarity with a canon, facility in its use according to the conventional standards of the day – these were given primacy in a highly-stylised curriculum.[21]

[20] *Ibid.*, 66, 73.
[21] Lisa Jardine and Anthony T. Grafton, 'Humanism and the School of Guarino: A Problem of Evaluation', *Past and Present*, 96 (August 1982), 61–73, and *From Humanism to the Humanities: Education and the Liberal Arts in Fifteenth- and Sixteenth-Century Europe* (Cambridge, MA, 1986). Bruce Kimball's stylish critique of Grafton and Jardine,

Such a curriculum, or rather, the methods employed in meeting the requirements of the curriculum, belie the ancient injunction to avoid servility at all costs. The personality must never become subordinated to the skill. But what if the skill is employed in public service, broadly that is, rather than narrowly in the pursuit of a vocation? That, we have seen, defined the great tradition. For such educators as Guarino, the world of practical affairs was the pre-eminent justification of a minutely crafted curriculum in the arts of language. Potential men of affairs drawn from the families of the rich and powerful, or simply those intended for service in the courts of princes, or in law, administration, and even teaching, must be proficient in the arts of diplomacy, conversation, and persuasion, in the formulation and defence of policy, in written and oral communication skills as we might say, and such proficiency promoted and sustained the self-confidence of a governing and administrative elite. For those not high born but destined to mingle with the privileged, there were careers like Guarino's, for which anything less than perfection in language studies was potentially fatal.

The ambiguities surrounding proficiency in relation to the ideal of the whole man do not disappear, however, and remain a permanent part of discussion about the ends and purposes of liberal education. The dialogue between the Count of Urbino and Caesare Gonzaga in Castiglione is one illustration of the problems a reverence for a canon can produce. The parties are discussing affectation, that is, exchanging views on the best means of presenting the self to the world at large. Gonzaga takes the position, by now wholly familiar to us, that the liberally educated man must not labour or belabour whatever he does. Understatement and nonchalance should be his style.[22] The position adopted is precisely rooted in the reverse social psychology and ambiguities of public cultures. The greater the effort made to impress, the more sceptical is the likely reception. Conversely, the more effortless the exhibition, the greater its impact. But an equally deceitful but absolutely necessary reason for the Renaissance courtier to dissemble his real talent is the fear and jealousy it will arouse in proud but insecure rulers.

The Count responds along the same lines but in reverse. Even too much nonchalance is suspect. Moderation in all things is preferred.[23] The whole

raising valuable methodological and historiographical points, appears in *History of Education Quarterly*, 28 (Summer, 1988), 243–56.

[22] *Nonchalance* is the Anglo-French rendering of Castiglione's *sprezzatura*, cognate to the German *spritz*, which is a better onomatopoeic clue to the violence of feeling underlying use of the word. I am indebted to Randolph Starn for sharing his knowledge of things Italian.

[23] Baldesar Castiglione, *The Book of the Courtier* (Completed 1518) (Hardmondsworth, 1978), 67–70.

or complete man avoids excess in any form (and, whispers the attendant but invisible cynic, thereby saves his neck).

The ideal of the whole man, to repeat, aspired to the over-arching if rather lofty requirement of self-mastery. It developed from a fear that individuals would readily submit to the self-tyranny of a particular passion, disposition, or impulse, or become enslaved to a particular activity not befitting a free man with civic responsibilities. The ideal was extremely difficult to achieve in practice, for there was no line that could be drawn by the schoolmaster that fulfilled the delicate requirement that a gentleman ought to play the flute but not too well. Since the gentleman had to be self-confident, a high level of proficiency was necessary.

Furthermore, even in the highly stylised classical curriculum of the courtier or servant of the State, certain proficiencies were absolutely indispensable. Military prowess may be immediately identified, and military prowess also meant training in horsemanship, gymnastics, and the martial arts. The most popular and widely influential educational tract of the Italian Renaissance, *De ingenius moribus* written in 1403 by Pier Paolo Vergerio the Elder, places the martial arts into the humanist curriculum as indispensable to the survival of the city-state.[24] Castiglione, in speaking of the place of drawing in the curriculum of the courtier, has one of his characters mention its utility in connection with military skills such as map-making or the depiction of military targets.[25] The study of martial music could be similarly justified. In other words, occupation, no matter how amateurish, and social standing have a critical bearing on the education of a public man. Knowledge, as we might put it, is applied.

Grafton and Jardine underscore this point in a special way in their application of reader-response theory to the education of practical men of affairs in early modern England. They discuss the 'book-wheel', a device permitting the nearly simultaneous but selective reading of texts. The reader concentrates on specific passages or examples which serve as a guide to action and decision-making. 'Renaissance readers (and annotators) persistently envisage action as the outcome of reading ... reading as trigger for action.'[26] Action was military, political, or careerist (e.g., as a courtier).[27] In other words, reading was purposeful, goal-oriented, and less

---

[24] Benjamin G. Kohl, 'Humanism and Education', in Rabil (ed.), *Renaissance Humanism*, III, 12–13.   [25] Castiglione, *Courtier*, 97.

[26] Jardine and Grafton, '"Studied for Action": How Gabriel Harvey Read His Livy', in *Past and Present*, 129 (November 1990), 40.

[27] *Ibid.*, 52. The centrality of civic humanism to the Renaissance liberal arts curriculum is currently hotly disputed. Scholars divide on whether the primary emphasis was on preparation for public or active life, training for critical, textual, or scholarly work, or whether schoolmasters were interested in the production of imaginative literature. The exact content and derivation of ideas of *civile vivere* are also disputed. Is civic humanism only relevant to popular or elite but not hereditary governments; does it view wealth

private or personal than we of another, more individualistic era prefer to
believe.

Perfection lost

Before embarking on new topics, a few lines on the place of Christianity in
the history of liberal education are required. These of necessity must be
brief. The ideal of a liberal education, commencing as it did in pagan
antiquity and intended as a preparation for civic or public affairs, was not
conspicuously religious in orientation. The sophistical tradition of
dialectic, argument, rhetoric and declamation was not distinguished for
piety and reverence, as we have noticed in the case of the Italian courtier.
In fact, there was an implicit if not comfortable understanding that
participation in the realm of public affairs might require behaviour that
was, to say the least, disingenuous. Pagan philosophies such as Epicureanism, Stoicism, and Neo-stoicism were designed to cope with practical
dilemmas by spurning common rewards like power or wealth, by
withdrawal as an extreme measure, or by contemplation of the eternal and
unchanging above. Christianity, in coming to terms with the same problem,
introduced a vital distinction which affected the liberal education inheritance and its uses. Christianity challenged the belief that liberal
education was truly capable of producing a whole person, whose wholeness
was 'natural', i.e., conformed to the order of the cosmos itself. There was
an unbridgeable gap between the secular and divine worlds, between the
gifts of a liberal education and the blessings of a redemptive Heaven. There
was a clear and unreconcilable distinction between serving Caesar and
serving God.

I have referred to the liberal education ideal as essentially pagan or
secular, by which I mean that it celebrated the primacy of mind and body.
But in another sense, as explained by William Bouwsma,[28] it was,

acquisition as positive or negative; did the humanists themselves believe in the efficacy of
human agency or submit to the view that human affairs are subject to the caprice of
fortune? Can it even be the case that humanism was fundamentally apolitical? This last
view does not appear to enjoy wide support.

It has been estimated that some 1,412 Italian scholars, critics, lawyers, editors, or writers
living in the two centuries between 1300 and 1527 deserve the label 'humanist'. The size
of this cohort makes generalisation awkward; yet whether or not civic humanism
incorporates views and traditions of full or partial withdrawal from the world (e.g., neo-
stoicism or Franciscanism), scholarly opinion appears inclined to support the notion of the
importance of an active and industrious life, probably political if not exclusively such, as
central to the ideal. Over 30 per cent of the humanists in the above survey were wholly,
partly, or occasionally employed in teaching of some kind. See Kohl, 'Humanism and
Education', 18–19.
28 William J. Bouwsma, 'Models of the Educated Man', *The American Scholar*, 44 (Spring
1975), 204–5.

paradoxically, the Christian view of education that was secular and the ancient one that was religious. The balanced person reflected the balance obtaining in the natural and cosmic order, represented that ideal and order, and was brought into correspondence with it. The cosmos itself was divine. Balance, therefore, was a divine state (or, as sometimes called, 'perfection').

This was not the Christian view, which, insofar as it influenced subsequent theories and practices of liberal education, had both a positive and a negative effect upon them. The positive effect was to encourage the self-control that lay at the heart of liberal education. (The step from this happy assumption to corporal punishment follows almost automatically. In order to restrain the innate and continuing sinfulness of children, discipline is essential.) This led educators to consider the importance of the environment in education. The negative effect was to inhibit the seductions and social imperialism inherent in the theory of the whole person and to render it subject to challenges from other educational quarters.

Of markets, individuals, and new knowledge

By the end of the Italian Renaissance, the main lines of the liberal education canon were set. The basic ideals, purposes, and meanings that determined the parameters of future debate were essentially in place, but also the internal contradictions to which the tradition was prone, as well as the tensions arising from changing social contexts. It would be quite impossible in this presentation to carry the story of the liberal arts forward into the present century, making allowances for all the permutations and consequences and for national variations on the theme in detailed fashion. Therefore, in the remainder of this chapter I would like to follow the modern history of liberal education by considering it in relation to a series of major developments or challenges of importance to the contemporary world. These are the rise and spread of liberal individualism, the question of new knowledge, and the problem of mass education and the open market. All of these variables have independent origins, but they become interrelated in time.

Kimball speaks of the liberal-free ideal in modern culture, the rational, critical intellectual shift associated with the Scientific Revolution and its diffusion through the Enlightenment.[29] Other authors have spoken about the rise of possessive individualism, elaborating for us the dissemination of a conception of human action grounded in egoism and the association of ideas, which in time produced a psychology of individual differences. Still

[29] Kimball, *Orators*, 119ff.

others, in countless books and articles, have discussed the Romantic movement as a form of cultural rebellion wherein existing literary models and inherited standards of taste were overthrown, or at least severely questioned, in the name of personal freedom and the unrestricted, the creative intelligence. The 'long eighteenth century' contained all these changes, but in every case a counter-thrust occurred, such as in theories of the collective or general will, the revival of socialist and communitarian ideals, and the return of an epistemology derived from platonic idealism. The tensions between opposing trends, ideas, and positions draw the historian's attention away from outcomes to processes as providing a truer picture of the course of historical change. Yet in the interests of economy I will have to place more emphasis on outcomes, returning to some of the larger methodological questions at the end of my discussion.

We must make some effort to distance ourselves from the difficulties caused by the semantic confusion of 'liberalism' with 'liberal education'. The rhetorical tradition of liberal education was not individualistic. Classical culture, especially and particularly Hellenistic culture, did not assume that all people were exactly the same in everyday life. It did however believe in the existence of a common human nature, or as Robert Proctor says, the ancient world knew individuality but not personality.[30] It was this bedrock belief, in fact, as many scholars have noticed, that made classical epistemology and hence education possible. Young people could be socialised through a firm instructional regimen consisting of explicit rules or examples for proper behaviour. Classical literature is filled with exemplary accounts of virtuous and vicious conduct, and classical biographies and histories offer a gallery of possible moral types. Not to simplify overmuch, it can be said that the liberal individualistic notion of struggle and experience as essential to the shaping of the personality is not classical. There it is sufficient to borrow and copy without personality undergoing similar ordeals or temptations. Individualism has Biblical affinities and thus belongs to religious traditions of the West; but it does not form a significant part of the history of liberal education until we reach the more recent centuries.

The vast and influential corpus of Hellenistic philosophy, especially Stoicism, may be offered as a refutation of the foregoing generalisation, as may Hellenistic sculpture. In both instances there existed a recognition of individual differences and consequently of the necessity to take individual diversity into account when planning the education of young persons.[31] In Epicureanism we even find notions that strike us as contemporary, such as

---

[30] Proctor, *Amnesia*, 109.
[31] Anthony A. Long, *Hellenistic Philosophy, Stoics, Epicureans, Sceptics* (New York, 1974), 3–13, 108–12, 124, 146–7, 177–8, 183–4, 187–8, 199–209.

the value of private life and education as a form of consumption to enhance that life.[32] In Stoicism, especially in the first-century Roman, Musonius Rufus, the teacher of Epictetus, there was also a recognition of the importance of educating women,[33] who in the preceding centuries, because of their exclusion from public life, were not deemed suitable recipients of liberal education. Yet the world-view against which the Stoic view of individual differences is placed is profoundly different from that of post-seventeenth-century liberal individualism. The Stoics presupposed the supremacy of nature and the necessity of shaping character in conformity with it, requiring, if necessary, submission to the order of events. The purpose of education was to prepare individuals to comprehend that order and so bring personality into harmony with it. The result was called wisdom or virtue,[34] and in these fundamental respects Stoicism is therefore in agreement with the other ancient philosophies that posited the necessity of some essential correspondence between the inner man and the outer world.

[32] The Epicurean symbol of private life was the walled or 'secret' garden, and it is instructive to see how the Stoics later challenged and changed the meaning of the Epicurean garden to bring it more in line with the dominant public traditions of Greek philosophy. The changes included an attack on the pleasure grounds of the rich and praise for the simple garden as a place of education, intellectual exchange, and reflection and as a model of disciplined living. The Roman Stoic view of the purposes of the garden was passed on to the neo-stoics of the Early Modern Period. Mark Morford, 'The Stoic Garden', *Journal of Garden History*, 7 (April–June 1987), 157–9.

In a broader sense, the success of this strategy may be noticed in one of the most fascinating of all reversals in the history of liberal education, the change of venue for the whole person from polis to garden. When the polis became the modern city or metropolis, it also became the source and reason for the fragmentation of the personality, encouraging (according to George Simmel) idiosyncrasy and the division of labour. The garden, as the freer and more leisured environment, permitted the unfettered, disinterested pursuit of understanding. The conflict between city and garden, town and country, has produced a stimulating set of writings. For a discussion of nineteenth-century England, see Raymond Williams, *The Garden and the City* (London, 1973). For the argument on behalf of the city as 'polis', as the ideal place for achieving a full and rounded life, see the very different works of Richard Bennett, *The Fall of Public Man* (Cambridge, 1974), and Donald J. Olsen, *The City as a Work of Art, London, Paris, Vienna* (New Haven, 1986). George Simmel, *On Individuality and Social Forms* (Chicago, 1971), 325–337, remarks on the implications of city life for personality development. Educationally, the conflict between the two loci of city and garden is repeated in the struggle between two types of higher education institutions, the urban or city university and the collegiate university and 'campus' (used in eighteenth-century America to designate the greensward around the new Nassau Hall at Princeton University). See the introduction and essays in *The University and the City, from Medieval Origins to the Present* (New York and Oxford, 1988), ed. Thomas Bender, and the review of Bender *et al* by Jeremy Catto, *Times Literary Supplement* (May 26–June 1, 1989), 584–5.

[33] Martha Nussbaum, review of Allan Bloom, *The Closing of the American Mind: How Higher Education has Failed Democracy and Impoverished the Souls of Today's Students* (New York, 1987), in *New York Review of Books* (November 5, 1987).

[34] Long, *Hellenistic Philosophy*.

Neither the final triumph of nature nor the necessity to bring the individual through education into conformity with such a conception of universal order is characteristic of liberal individualism in its more developed, nineteenth-century forms.[35] Liberal individualism does not aim at wisdom or virtue so much as individual success and achievement in competition with, and, depending upon the circumstances, at the expense of others. Nor does liberal individualism stress the primary objective of living in accord with a nature conceived as perfect. Perfection is instead regarded as regularity, which provides the basis for calculation and self-interest.

Liberal individualism is in conflict with the character-forming legacy of liberal education for the simple reason that it is suspicious of any form of education that does not allow free play to the personality. Ibsen's Buttonmolder offered to release Peer Gynt from his exaggerated sense of self by melting him down, a horrific prospect from a Romantic point of view. Major aspects of the more recent history of liberal education resemble a contest between liberal education and liberal individualism, especially in present-day America. The quarrel between advocates of a wholly unrestricted curriculum and proponents of a core curriculum or core curricula is an extreme example of the contest, as is the demand by students to be judged exclusively on the basis of their personal qualities without reference to either absolute or competitive standards of measurement.

Polemically, the correlation between liberal education and free expression and individuality is proclaimed repeatedly with the kind of self-assurance that assumes that the end of liberal instruction has always been the liberation of the personality from all restraints and conditions, enabling the untrammelled Gyntian self to pursue its own true nature. The object is to unbind Prometheus. Is this a total perversion of the great tradition or a misreading of the ideal of the whole man?

The answer may well turn upon how one interprets an ancient and diffuse corpus of writings, but it can also be maintained that the equation of liberalism and liberal education is an example of the familiar practice of selective borrowing from history. The equation takes its legitimacy in part from the platonic/pythagorean or 'philosophic' version of liberal education that postulates an unresolvable conflict between the individual and

---

[35] However, eighteenth-century association psychology resembles Stoicism in one particular, the over-riding influence of external environment in creating mental attitudes. But philosophically this was successfully challenged by the revival of idealistic philosophy, especially in Kant's version. Furthermore, even in eighteenth-century association psychology the outside world is not equated with a cosmic order but approximates what we call 'society'. Intellectually, it is easier to change society than to change nature, and associationists consequently tended to be social and legal reformers.

society and advocates withdrawal as a final measure. However, the philosophical ideal is not so much individualistic in leaning as spiritual and contemplative. It is an ideal of how to pursue knowledge and gain wisdom. Its closest modern variant is not American individualism but nineteenth-century German idealism, especially in the concept of *Bildung* (the Swedish *Bildning*) or spiritual and aesthetic self-development. As Sven-Eric Liedman remarks in the subsequent chapter, in the northern European conception of *Bildung* only the inner life is genuinely free. The outer must conform. *Bildung* is to be found exquisitely articulated in novels like Thomas Mann's *The Magic Mountain*, where the body is allowed to waste away while mind and spirit develop in the rarefied surroundings of an alpine sanitarium. It appears in Hermann Hesse's remarkable *The Glass Bead Game*, where an obscure, subtle, and excruciatingly difficult and perfectly impractical intellectual exercise symbolises the purest reachings of the spirit in a fratricidal universe. It infuses Jacob Burkhardt's 1860s recreation of Renaissance Italian civilisation, wherein is avowed the primacy in life of self-fashioning according to an ideal of human perfection. It is not an English ideal, for the English intelligentsia was not detached from the world of decision-making and opinion-forming. Indeed, the opposite was closer to reality, although in the case of one Victorian writer the ideal comes within an ace of acceptance.[36]

Traces of the German conception of *Bildung* are to be found in American writers, particularly those who reacted strenuously to the powerful and at times very crude materialism of American culture and its periodic outbreaks of know-nothingism and populism. There is a genre of American writing on anti-intellectualism in United States history, but there is also a body of writing on anti-intellectualism in Britain, and it is perhaps not to our purpose to delve into these at the moment. Suffice it to say that the Anglo-American political constitutions require an active citizenry; and while there are differences between the two countries on how that citizenry is to be educated, and differences of opinion within the countries themselves, traditions of representative government have inhibited if they cannot altogether prevent the penetration into the liberal education curriculum of idealist conceptions like *Bildung*.

Of minds and canons

No one part of the liberal education inheritance has been more vexing or produces more difficulties than the canon itself. A curriculum needs more than the reiteration of lofty ideals. It must be a workable set of procedures.

---

[36] I refer to Matthew Arnold and credit discussions with Fritz Ringer for enabling me to see the limits of Arnold's Germanising.

It requires considerable organisation of effort and systematic instruction supported by complex financial structures. Courses must be arranged and course objectives of a narrow sort laid out as working guides. In short, all of the paraphernalia of academic culture that goes with teaching ultimately detracts from the sublime aspirations with which the liberal arts teacher selects texts and teaching materials.

I have already described the inherited liberal arts canon as essentially mimetic in method, highly stylised and based on classical languages but also (except for the medieval period), on the best stylistic examples of literary production. Facility in written and oral expression was the necessary intermediate aim of a curriculum prepared for an elite destined for public life. We have seen that other subjects – the courtly and martial arts, for example – were considered liberal because, by circular reasoning, they were essential parts of a gentleman's education, and a gentleman by definition was liberally educated. In this connection, two questions need to be asked:

1. Can the canon be indefinitely altered and still be liberal?
2. Is liberal education applicable to those who are not gentlemen and cannot be expected to be gentlemen?

From past evidence, the answer to the first is yes, but only insofar as the recipient is a gentleman or capable of being transformed into one. On the same grounds, the answer to the second is no. Yet the history of liberal education in the modern period is precisely the history of a canon that is being continually augmented by new subjects and fed into the curriculum of new kinds of recipients: 'provincial' people like eighteenth-century Scots, Scots-Irish, and Americans; 'marginal' groups like English Dissenters of the same period; 'meritocracies' in the nineteenth century. The paradoxes and difficulties require examples.

The liberal arts canon in Enlightenment Scotland was transformed in several ways. The classical languages core remained, but modern languages and modern social science were added to the educational enterprise. An even bigger change was the substitution of moral philosophy in at least two forms as the integrating medium, replacing rhetoric. Eighteenth-century Presbyterian Scotland also influenced English Dissent. The non-Anglican Protestant sects created academies that incorporated the Scottish mixture, adding some of the concerns and some of the methods of modern experimental science, especially chemistry. All of this was designated 'liberal'.

The new mix was imported into America's eight colonial colleges and remained their staple, especially and particularly because it was easily harmonised with the relaxed forms of most American Protestant denominations, at least until the middle of the nineteenth century.[37] In the American setting the mix soon became 'traditional' and formed a new canon. Despite its broadened base, the canon was still 'canonical'. It therefore had to be defended, most notably against attempts to reduce and then eliminate the classical languages component and make the curriculum wholly modern. The modernists were accused of the two sins of making liberal education 'relevant' or 'practical' and of subjugating it to the market, thus turning a 'liberal' tradition into a 'servile' one.

How, historically, is it possible to legitimise departures from a canon if it is still believed necessary to retain the notion of a canon? This remains a fundamental question in the sociology of knowledge. In the eighteenth century one way was to assert that all the new subjects quite satisfactorily fulfilled the purposes of the old, and so it could and was suggested that chemistry was no more than polite learning, very useful in making conversation. Another way, more typical of our own day, was to maintain that the curriculum was *general education*. The introduction of new subjects was merely a necessary step in updating the canon, which had always aimed at comprehension. After all, no subjects had been actually displaced. The classical corpus was intact, *a fortiori* enhanced, since from the nineteenth-century onwards the Greek language and Greek culture, historically in second place to Latin, was accorded higher status. The substitution of moral philosophy for rhetoric did not make the curriculum any more or less useful than it once had been. Whosoever received an updated version of liberal education was not obtaining a professional or vocational education. Liberally educated people were still gentlemen, if not aristocratic gentlemen, and many of them, particularly in Scotland and America, would enter gentlemanly occupations, such as those in the Protestant churches, from which much in the way of leadership in public affairs was expected.

It could be further explained that updating the canon was exactly what had happened in antiquity when the Romans took over Hellenistic learning, added their own language and literature to the canon, and, incidentally, systematised the educational system into the seven liberal arts which had such an influence on medieval cathedral schools and universities.

However, a change was already underway in Scotland and America that was to alter the meaning of the ancient inheritance quite dramatically. Under the influence of the new psychology of the eighteenth century, and the phrenological psychology of the nineteenth century, a shift was

[37] The Scottish philosophical school of Common Sense, imported into the United States, provided a reasonably successful means of integrating the curriculum. It should be pointed out that neither the Scottish nor American versions of the Enlightenment were anti-clerical.

occurring that was pushing liberal education away from a holistic theory of character formation to an intellectual one. Mind counted more than the body and the emotions, at least insofar as the curriculum itself was a factor in education; and although it was important to achieve a balance of skills and proficiencies, to warm or excite the imagination where deficiencies were noticed, or sharpen the intelligence when it became dull, or stimulate memory, or strengthen the will and so on, wholeness was now considered in the light of the mental powers or cerebral functions.

The Scientific Revolution had altered the human-cosmos relationship. The Romantic Rebellion was altering the human-societal relationship. Even in England, where an extraordinarily influential aristocratic culture remained until long into the nineteenth century, signs of a departure were in evidence. While the sentiment that a gentleman should learn to play the flute but not too well could still be encountered wherever wealthy and relaxed young men gathered to play, and whereas classical languages, translations, literary composition still dominated the curriculum of elite schools and universities, competitive examinations had entered along with the methods of objective evaluation. One means of making evaluation genuinely objective was to narrow the curriculum down to a point where arithmetical marks could be assigned. Thus gradually, first in a small but significant way at Cambridge in the eighteenth century, second at Oxford in the early nineteenth century, the English single-subject honours degree took hold in universities. By the middle years of Victoria's reign the practice spread to Scotland, although in broader form as suited its own traditions. In the twentieth century the Oxbridge honours degree has become more or less the norm until the experiment at Keele following World Way II suggested new possibilities and combinations,[38] which, in the 1980s, increasingly took the form of American-style modular or unit-credit course systems.

'Integrity' by other means

George Malcolm Young, a distinguished civil servant, 'classic' and historian, exemplifying the Oxford theory of a liberally-educated man and (naturally) eccentric, has remarked on the longevity of the gentlemanly ideal in England.[39] This would not be quite so apparent from what I have

---

[38] There is an exception to every historical rule. Literae Humaniores ('Greats') at Oxford was interdisciplinary from its creation in 1800, albeit confined to classical subjects.

[39] An amusing portrait of Young appears in the reminiscences of the English publisher, Rupert Hart-Davis (ed.), *The George Lyttelton-Rupert Hard-Davis Letters* (London, *c.* 1978), I, 132–4.
    I am indebted to David Spring for this reference.

just been saying about liberal education in English universities, but I think that Young is essentially correct. There is more than one way to realise an ideal, and the nineteenth-century English way was to implant responsibility for a liberal education in residential institutions such as colleges and public schools. There are frequent discussions in nineteenth-century educational circles, and among the political and intellectual elite, concerning the differences between universities and residential colleges and debates over how to redesign or adapt the liberal education canon to make it suitable for a meritocratic society within an increasingly democratic polity. But it was widely agreed that the most effective form of liberal education was character shaping. If the curriculum could not carry that burden, it was necessary to expand the provision for 'total' institutions.[40] In total institutions, young people live together, share a common life, and are socialised into an elite stratum. The total institution is also the home of an extensive array of extra-curricular activities: games, student journalism, poetry readings, plays, balls and so on.

It is interesting to see that the emergence of new ideas about schoolmastering in the Renaissance was from the start in some respects associated with the residential conception. In the *contubernium* pupils boarded in the schoolmaster's house. Actually, the pedagogical or educational advantages of students and teachers in residence together appear to have been appreciated early. Residential colleges for poor scholars, students living away from home, or reading a particular subject like law or medicine, emerged at Italian universities in the late fourteenth century. At one time there may have been as many as twenty-seven such colleges, houses or residences in Padua. They tended to be small, in the range of six to twelve boarders.[41] Many later examples of living and learning can be cited, as in the case of the Historicum at Uppsala University, the History Institute today which began life as a fine eighteenth-century professor's house where students boarded.

Living and learning are closely associated in the liberal education tradition. For the nineteenth century I would even suggest that there is a dialectical relationship between the spread of an intellectual ideal of liberal education and the revival of the college as a model institution. The English practice of clustering student rooms around staircases rather than corridors is an architectural refinement of the collegiate idea well worth further

---

[40] The term 'total institutions' was created by the late Erving Goffman and has been applied to the English public schools by Ian Weinberg, *The English Public Schools, the Sociology of Elite Education* (New York, 1967).

[41] Kohl, 'Humanism and Education', 14–15. Pearl Kibre, *Scholarly Privileges in the Middle Ages, the Rights, Privileges and Immunities of Scholars and Universities at Bologna, Padua, Paris, and Oxford* (Cambridge, MA, 1962), 66–8, 67n, 68n.

thought, but in any case the ideal of the whole person is kept alive by the idea of the college. It is the college, said John Henry, Cardinal Newman, in his famous discourses on a university, that lends 'integrity' to a university, the word being his adaptation of an Aristotelian concept to denote completeness or substantiality.[42]

From canon to sampler

American changes are both similar and different from those occurring in Britain. They are similar because the curriculum also falls under the spell of the theory of mental powers, leaving liberal education to the fellowship of the college, especially the liberal arts college. As in England, a transformation in the quality and character of student life is noticeable from the 1790s onwards.[43] The changes are different because the social and cultural characteristics of American life are different. The nation is ideologically egalitarian, and it has populist waves, especially after the coming of Jacksonian democracy in the first half of the nineteenth century. It is more conspicuously individualistic and plural, and it is a frontier society, expansionist and consequently pragmatic and opportunistic. Each of these points is an essay in itself. For the moment I must content myself with saying that these features of American history are translated into a series of new higher education structures that challenge the hegemony of the small liberal arts colleges of colonial origin and their southern and mid-western clones. The challenge appears in the form of specialised institutions or mixed-purpose universities supported by states. (These, as the chapters following note, appeared in Europe at roughly the same time.) Agricultural and engineering colleges are founded in the early nineteenth-century, the most famous of the latter being the national military academy at West Point established in 1802, followed by proprietary medical schools.

Most of these are typified by market response. The older colonial foundations like Harvard, Yale, and Dartmouth eventually responded to the competition by offering a similar number of professionally based studies or applied science courses,[44] although Harvard's medical school actually dates from the end of the previous century. The market for some kind of general or liberal studies without specific vocational reference (except where useful for teaching or the Protestant ministry) certainly continued to exist. Comprehensive or multiple-purpose institutions

[42] John Henry Newman, *Historical Sketches* (London, 1881), III, 182–228.
[43] See the contribution by James McLachlan, 'The Choice of Hercules: American Student Societies in the Early Nineteenth Century', in *The University in Society*, ed. Lawrence Stone (Princeton, 1974), II, 449–94.
[44] Jurgen Herbst, 'American Higher Education in the Age of the College', in *History of Universities*, 7 (1988), 52–4.

whether public or private met the demand through core colleges of liberal arts or letters and science. The newer land-grant colleges and universities of the Civil War era followed suit.

The founders and proponents of new and cheap, easy-access institutions assumed with characteristic nineteenth-century American confidence that educational institutions could adopt multiple missions without contradiction. They also assumed that resources could be found to support all missions. Expanding markets gave substance to optimism. The impetus behind the great changes of the 1860s was to broaden access and opportunity and to open public-sector institutions to all forms of educational demand, to serve as many constituencies as possible. Yet the reality was always that the liberal arts had to be marketed, governors of states cosseted, legislatures lobbied, and elected officials persuaded. The ideals of a liberal education needed to be constantly trumpeted, while colleges and universities claimed allegiance to every educational ideal, past or present, simultaneously and unabashedly, as well as to the uniquely democratic principles celebrated at the Revolution and redefined in the political changes of the 1820s onwards.

Diverse in curriculum and intake, the new American institutions could not and did not exemplify the principle of the unity of knowledge as found in the whole person of balance and moderation. Their missions derived from many sources and traditions. They were heirs of the Enlightenment principle of useful knowledge, as incorporated in popular education movements such as one finds in the early nineteenth century in both England and America. They were (and remain) mass education institutions, with low teaching costs (by elite standards) and for the most part (with exceptions) extremely sensitive to public opinion. They have few or none of the institutional traits that long characterised elite liberal education: low faculty-student ratios; an intimate, collegiate, character-shaping environment under the control of faculty; a socially, if not always academically, select student body; an atmosphere of privilege, and occasionally an air of *noblesse oblige*. They are secular or lay and know only one religion, America's civil religion of 'progress'.[45]

In both Britain and America, as in Europe generally, the question of the generation of new knowledge and its effect on the liberal arts canon had to be faced. We have noticed the Scottish and English responses, with the Scottish institutions of the nineteenth century coming increasingly under the influence of the English honours degree, which for the most part meant a movement towards specialism without wholly embracing it. However, academic specialism is, like the theory of the whole man, a constant in the

---

[45] For which see Henry F. May, *The Divided Heart: Essays on Protestantism and the Enlightenment in America* (New York, 1991).

history of education not a nineteenth-century innovation. Historically, especially since the Scientific Revolution, specialised scholars and scientists had always sought regular positions in established teaching institutions, although they were not always successful in gaining entry. From the standpoint of the ancient theory of completeness, specialism was un-fortunate, but the very fact that continual warnings were issued against it indicates both its prevalence and in some respects (as Alfred North Whitehead was to say in one of his essays) its naturalness. It is 'natural' to have an interest, only 'natural' to wish to excel at some task or invite attention for some specific achievement. In the counterlife – we recall the words of Roth – the only defining point of personality may indeed be the skill itself.

But the historical question is not specialism *per se*. It is the institution-alisation of specialism as the basis of academic appointments. It is support for those appointments under the headings of reduced hours of teaching or full-time research posts and research subsidies in the form of libraries, laboratories, postgraduates assistants, travel, and publication. Specialist study in the later nineteenth century consequently differed from earlier versions in being a permanent and dominant part of the undergraduate curriculum.

In relation to the tradition of thought and practice we are following, nineteenth-century specialism shattered the idea of the unity of knowledge and in America, as in other countries, was responsible for the creation of wholly new internal teaching structures and programmes: departments, departmental majors, the elective, and the course-unit systems (or modular system in Britain), which, although available in many forms, is most often found as the single or autonomous lecture or seminar course, only tangentially related (outside the 'building-block' sequences of the sciences and foreign languages) in subject matter or approach to other courses. Interestingly enough, the move to modules and student options was not an evolutionary process. It was a radical step, a sharp initial break with past practice, appearing first at the University of Virginia in the 1820s, but known better in its post-mid-century Harvard form. So revolutionary was the change that the elective system needed to be modified later, for it assumed a degree of preparedness and maturity totally at variance with the actual academic achievement levels of undergraduates.

Electives are associated with American consumerism but also with a democratic ideology and only later with specialism. The course-unit system was the means by which new demands could be incorporated into the existing curriculum and new groups given access without displacing the old. Diversity therefore replaced unity. Refinements, adaptations, and even retreats have marked the history of modularity in the United States, but the union of teacher and examiner in a single person teaching an autonomous course remains the backbone of all American college and university instruction, whether in undergraduate or graduate programmes. Ever since the last decade of the nineteenth century, American higher education has resembled a seventeenth-century corpuscular universe of particles of varying shape, weight, and colour bombarding one another within academic space.

This is hardly the entire historical tale. There have been and remain critical attempts to tame the anarchy of the American curriculum and to push it back towards some notion of a unified and connected programme of studies. In the last three decades of the nineteenth century, the implications of the course-unit system caused considerable alarm. Few institutions shifted from the old moral philosophy curriculum to the autonomous course system as quickly as did Harvard, which eventually pulled back. Most of them adopted an array of alternatives which have not in principle changed all that much. The choices were compulsory first- or second-year courses, quasi-specialised or what were termed 'parallel courses', majors and minors. Embedded in the undergraduate curriculum was a conception of liberal education scarcely recognisable even as an ideal. Modules were combined and re-combined to produce a general or broad curriculum; but since the modules were independently devised and taught, no single conception of breadth was possible. As the list of modular possibilities increased as a consequence of the knowledge revolution, breadth was largely determined by consumer, that is, student choice. But the choices produced a very odd conception of general education and a very confusing definition of breadth. Relatively specialised modules could be chosen in satisfaction of breadth requirements and relatively broad courses could be used to satisfy major specialised subject requirements. As an extreme measure to protect a canon rapidly disappearing in the nineteenth century, new subjects were housed in separate schools or degree programmes, but this was not a universal practice.

What emerged in twentieth-century America was not a liberal education canon but a liberal education sampler. The system remains popular with students and, it may be ventured, with most teachers who value the classroom independence which modularity provides as a form of *Lehrfreiheit*, a palladium of academic freedom. The chorus of disapproval, the numerous conferences on the teaching and meaning of the liberal arts and humanities, the debates over the canon, the books and articles deploring the incoherence of the undergraduate curriculum, suggest the opposite. But both conclusions are accurate. Doubtless there is satisfaction; but doubtless also there is sufficient dissatisfaction to produce a reform industry both within and outside universities. The external sources lie in the media, in various 'professional' academic associations, especially those formed to protect the undergraduate curriculum against the graduate and professional schools, and in philanthropic associations which have long played an important part in supporting the American college idea.

In truth the American undergraduate curriculum has almost never been without critics, and it has been experimented with continually since the evanescence of the 'old time college' in the second half of the last century. Historically, two main lines of reform can be distinguished. The first is really no more than a continuation of the reaction against the independent course and the free elective system. New names are often given to very old ideas, so today reformers talk about instituting core curricula, or capstone senior courses, or 'writing across the curriculum', or interdisciplinary majors. But even in these proposals, options are as prevalent as outright requirements, and the requirements themselves often contain choices.

A second line of reform is more ambitious, but being more expensive, or more elite in character, its effects are limited. It consists of efforts to establish liberal arts programmes in colleges within state universities or in wholly separate institutions. The famous 1940s and 1950s Robert Maynard Hutchins collegiate programme at the University of Chicago falls into this category, as do the Contemporary Civilisation course at Columbia (1919) or the 'great books' course of study at the two St John's colleges, Annapolis and Santa Fe. These latter are perforce private institutions. Public institutions must function with external pressures for multiple programmes and the need to satisfy numerous constituencies.

'Great books' is an attempt to keep alive the idea of a canon. The origin of an effort to compile a list of the best and most important authors lies in the survival of classical literature and in the transformation of the words 'classic' and 'classical' in the late seventeenth or eighteenth century to mean the best and the timeless. The Battle of the Books, the quarrel between Ancients and Moderns which took place during the Enlightenment, has left a permanent legacy of compiling lists of authors or names which are taken to represent the essence of Western culture, or its most sublime aspirations, or, more functionally, merely those ideas and beliefs that all well-educated people should know. Courses built on great books are often satirised as teaching texts from 'Plato to Nato' or from 'Beowulf to Virginia Woolf'. The lists of great books never remain wholly the same, and some efforts at upgrading lend themselves to parody as a form of trivial pursuit.[46]

---

[46] Eric Donald Hirsch, Jr., *Cultural Literacy, What Every American Needs to Know* (New York, 1988) has been so treated by sceptical reviewers for its unstylish writing and quiz show format – the paperback edition cover boasts of '5,000 essential names, phrases, dates, and concepts'.

The restlessness of American life, but also its ideology of education in the service of society make 'reform' an imperative. Higher education must be seen to be responsive and changing. But 'reform' is an ambiguous word. It implies a world divided into two sets of people: reformers who are 'progressive' and anti-reformers who are 'reactionary'. But in *fin de siècle* America the demands for change in the curriculum are so contradictory as to render many interested bystanders virtually speechless. The curious fact is that the broad polarities remain nearly as they were a century ago when the modular system attained its predominance. Since then, cries for unity and integrity in the American curriculum have competed with demands for additional diversification of subjects and disciplines. A national educational schizophrenia occurred which is as pronounced today as earlier. For every national or local report advocating a core curriculum, there is one calling for new interdisciplinary majors, such as women's or ethnic studies. There are proponents of compulsory cores and advocates of optional ones. For every appeal for a programme of studies common to every student, there is an eloquent plea for the importance of individuality and creativity. For every request that civic responsibility be made the object of the curriculum, there is the counter-suggestion that the needs of individual groups be met first. For every call to patriotism, there is one for general recognition of the right to dissent and to be allowed openly and even aggressively to declare that right. Teaching resources are contested for by departments and intercollegiate programmes, and in this welter of competing demands is captured the historical dilemmas of a theory of general education that is recognisable but only vaguely.

Taken in the aggregate, or even singly, it is nearly impossible for one historian to find in these extraordinarily time-consuming efforts to keep an old inheritance alive more than a suggestion of its former purpose and traits. Even the exact sources of inspiration for American experiments are hard to pinpoint. Liberal individualism, for example, falls outside the historical liberal education canon, yet many American educational reforms of the present century owe their beginnings to it. The justification of liberal education as the unhampered pursuit of knowledge, especially original knowledge, perhaps with no applied dimension but solely for its own sake or as a form of truth, is, as observed, related to the platonic/pythagorean strain in the tradition. Still, it owes just as much and possibly more to the research ethic which was penetrating higher education systems throughout Western society in the second half of the nineteenth century.

But the idea that living in the world 'successfully' requires recognition of and familiarity with a very great range of information and knowledge and presupposes some facility in their employment is certainly not trivial. Still, the practical problem remains how to pack learning into a canonical curriculum competed for by so many interests.

Research as liberal education

The research ethic is antithetical to most of the essential aims of American versions of liberal education. The language of its internal discourse is different. It is intellectual. It repudiates the notion of a canon and replaces it with the celebration of discovery. It is sceptical of received opinions and traditions. It is specialist in outlook, in that discovery is more possible in a concentrated than in a broad focus. It is particularistic and deliberately focused. Liberal education was born, I said, in a fear that individuals would live only partial lives. The research ethic says that it is 'natural' to do so. It is healthy to have an interest in life that can be continually developed. Researchers do not commonly speak about the need for inner harmony or about reconciliation of the self and society. The skill itself is the connection, proficiency rather than personality. Nor is the research ethic necessarily concerned with civic traditions of responsibility, unless 'civic responsibility' is a research interest.

Yet one significant qualification must surely be heard, particularly in connection with the accusation that the specialism associated with research is in most respects hostile to the theory of the well-rounded person, promoting and sustaining a narrow sort of person who knows only the one thing. Mark Pattison was the Rector of Lincoln College, Oxford University in the middle decades of the nineteenth century, a remarkable if eccentric figure who appears prominently in Victorian novels. No one of his era was more sophisticated or original in comprehending the social or intellectual assumptions behind the several forms of learning. In 1870 he testified before a royal commission appointed to inquire into the state of scientific and technical education in the United Kingdom, and he put the case for the educational importance of specialised learning in compelling terms:

the system of general information, knowing a little of the surface of half a dozen things, has its value, but...on the whole, the result of such an education is an inferior result to the result of a deep and thorough investigation of some one great branch of knowledge...I think that true thoroughness in a scientific man, and true thoroughness in a philosophical [i.e., a literary] man would not tend to isolate him from other branches...If you have got past a certain stratum in investigation, your sympathies begin to widen, and the more you know of your subject, the more that you begin to see that it has its ramifications into every other subject.[47]

These responses are especially interesting because they were answers to questions put by a member of the commission who was himself a great

---

[47] Royal Commission on Scientific Instruction and the Advancement of Science, Parliamentary Papers 1872, XXV, Supplement to First Report, with Minutes of Each, no. 3853 and no. 3855 (November 15, 1870).

Victorian intellectual and scientist, Thomas Huxley. In his questioning, probably deliberately designed to elicit an expected response, Huxley queried whether specialisation was not, in fact, 'a very great evil' that could be corrected 'to some considerable extent' if persons of 'the higher culture...were obliged...to pass through some common discipline'. Pattison gave an 'advanced' answer. He thoroughly understood the schoolboyish characteristics of Oxford's collegiate education, its pedantry, tedium, and lack of intellectual bite. He also knew about Oxford's tendency to rely on the new and trendy phrase the 'higher culture' to deflect attention from the pedestrian pedagogy of much that passed for teaching in the classroom. For him, who so clearly understood the character of modern intellectual thought, research specialism was not the enemy of breadth, but a different way of achieving it in an age when the knowledge base was expanding. In Pattison's view, the canon could no longer rally the support of a majority of educators. And although he does no say so, there is implicit in his position a recognition of the question of self-esteem and self-confidence that had always been one of the principal assumptions of elite education.

In the modern world, the world of the division of labour, it is not the harmonious development of character that provides a sense of self-satisfaction. It is the pride that attends the successful pursuit of a special interest, the assumption being that special interests are as natural to a (liberal) culture in which each person is unique as broad interests are natural to a culture in which each person shares a nature common to all. Some proponents of general (and they would also call it 'liberal') education simply ask that the research ethic be accepted as the basis of modern education and extended to undergraduates. The antithesis between liberal learning and research is false, they argue, and undergraduates (as well as outside critics of the academy) who are exposed to the assumptions, procedures, and values of original inquiry early in their university careers are soon caught up in the excitement of discovery and the testing of hypotheses against empirically-derived evidence. This argument sometimes passes under the banner of 'collaborative learning'. It underscores the importance of the authority of knowledge rather than the authority of the teacher. It also releases the scholar or scientist from the historical obligation of appearing before the student as a model of the whole person. 'Truth' is more important than personality, and research leads to truth. We are today more inclined to substitute 'accuracy' for 'truth' as a more comfortable if mitigated word.

Research is also the creation of new knowledge and new ideas and is therefore the pursuit of methods for conducting research. Any new field of inquiry is immediately concerned with the development of explanatory theories and hypotheses, paradigms and frameworks, logical systems of explanation and conceptions that guide and monitor empirical investigation. In this regard the research ethic has had another influence on the liberal arts curriculum, rather 'medieval' in character. It has pushed the general education component towards a concern for method and methodologies as the integrating medium. Since there is far more new knowledge than can be mastered, undergraduates must learn to ask questions rather then to expect answers. Consequently we find that the present-day American liberal arts curriculum is loosely designed to impart an understanding of the methods of four (and occasionally five) major divisions of knowledge. In some institutions compulsory courses are given in the form of special introductory courses to the social sciences, the humanities, the biological, and physical sciences. In others it is more hoped than believed that a similar understanding can be imparted through the regular curriculum. In yet others new areas of knowledge – not necessarily 'basic' knowledge – have been added, such as the environmental sciences. The search for an integrating subject or approach continues. Most often it is through courses in Western or world civilisation, very often as a form of the history of ideas.

History has in fact replaced rhetoric and philosophy as the integrating subject. History was the approach essentially selected in the famous Harvard Report issued after the Second World War. The case method approach adopted in professional schools like law and business has also been suggested as appropriate for liberal education. It combines theory and application and is interdisciplinary in method. Therefore, it appears to restore the ideal of the unity of knowledge but with a broadly functional purpose. Since the modern intelligence, it is argued, is above all a problem-solving intelligence, techniques for problem-solving comprise the highest form of liberal education.[48]

The hidden or co-curriculum

I want now to turn to the non-intellectual side of the liberal education story and mention an interesting development, essentially recent, which shows

[48] On the case method, see Daniel Bell, *The Reforming of General Education, The Columbia College Experience in its National Setting* (New York, 1966). For an original critique of the intellectualist position in liberal education from the standpoint of theories of personality development, showing how modern learning strategies favour the curriculum over students and isolate them from one another, see Joseph Katz and Nevitt Sanford, 'The Curriculum in the Perspective of the Theory of Personality Development', in *The American College, a Psychological and Social Interpretation of the Higher Learning*, ed. Nevitt Sanford (New York, 1962), 418–44. Insofar as the learning strategies discussed by the authors contribute to the separations that alienate the personality from itself and from society, they are in historical language 'illiberal' or 'servile'.

the survival of the conception of the whole person in a different light. It represents an effort to reproduce balanced men and women within the bewildering context of a mass education system which includes large and small institutions, colleges and universities; private and public sectors; low and high cost, elite and universal access programmes; urban, small-town, and semi-rural facilities; and non-residential, full-time, and part-time students, the typical 18–21-year-old undergraduate but also graduate and 'mature' students. I refer to the interest in combining the numerous campus services, its advisory and student assistance components (housing, financial aid, health, and counselling centres, remedial education, pre-professional advising, placement services, intern programmes), which have grown to substantial proportions into a 'co-curriculum' or union of academic and non-academic functions to create a total learning environment.

Such a notable effort is faithful to the spirit of liberal education; but impressive as is the undertaking, it is not free of special difficulties. The logistical problems alone are insurmountable, but ethical and certainly legal questions also arise. Do the efforts to create a co-curriculum represent a return to some form of *in loco parentis* only to be resisted by contemporary students who have grown up in an atmosphere of permissive conduct? Can such efforts be interpreted as increasing institutional responsibility for the moral welfare of students and therefore, in the litigious environment of America, lead inevitably to a large number of expensive law suits if something is presumed to have gone wrong? There is also the question of the diversion of resources into these areas and the expansion of staff and programmes that dilute more purely academic programmes. Students have an obvious vested interest in services designed to maintain their physical and mental well-being. Once established, such services are difficult to trim back. Since the quality of American public sector mass academic education is a perennial issue, even apart from any consideration of liberal education, the resource question is truly paramount.[49]

---

[49] Nothing touched by human hands is safe from perversion. The German National Socialists were also fascinated by the co-curriculum, especially in its Oxbridge dimensions, seeing in the English universities a successful example of their own efforts to use education to promote military prowess and team spirit, a more down-to-earth, to put it gently, means of socialisation than *Bildung*. On this subject I am indebted to Geoffrey Giles for sending me a copy of his paper, 'Oxbridge in Jackboots? The Attraction of Oxford and Cambridge University Reformers in National Socialist Germany' (1987).

School, university, and liberal education

The responsibility for perpetuating traditions of liberal education has in America fallen to the post-compulsory sector. Liberal education has most often been interpreted as general education of some kind, with general education in fierce competition for credit hours with electives and major requirements. Except for some notable experiments, there has been no integrating discipline or unified aim capable of gathering the great variety of modern disciplines and courses into a fundamental conception of a common liberal arts education. Attempts to round out the undergraduate personality by attending to the non-intellectual dimensions of the human personality must always be undertaken in consideration of the mass market and with respect to the popular American belief that education is an item of consumption whose value fluctuates according to supply and demand cycles. Perhaps it is accurate to say that under these conditions liberal education in America can only flourish wherever an institution has successfully resisted market forces. The Chicago college of 1942 appears almost deliberately designed to inhibit student consumer influence,[50] although even in such circumstances the definition of liberal education has been permanently affected by modern history.

Against the special developments in the United States we can set certain differences in British and Continental practice. First, it can be said that responsibility for liberal education on the Continent has more often been assigned to schools than to the tertiary sector. This is in fact a more faithful reflection of the distant past than is American practice. From Hellenic times onwards the period of liberal education extended to about 14–16 years of age and then ceased, except where, as in the case of eighteenth-century Oxford and Cambridge, additional years of liberal education were thought to be mildly useful for a landed aristocracy. This explains why corporal punishment and a concern for 'discipline', rote learning, and moral education have been such conspicuous features of the institutional history of liberal education. Younger minds, it was thought, did not require liberating. Quite the opposite. In Scotland and America, until the rise in the age of entry about the middle of the nineteenth century, secondary school and university were virtually indistinguishable, which is why the early Republic's liberal arts colleges like Yale reacted strongly to the growth of what today we might call 'mere' high schools but were viewed then as serious competition for students. A certain confusion of identity and function remained long after. A German visitor who taught at

---

[50] Joseph J. Schwab, *Science, Curriculum, and Liberal Education, Selected Essays*, ed. Ian Westbury and Neil J. Wilkof (Chicago and London, 1978), 4–5.

New England's Amherst College later in the nineteenth century remarked that, 'I confess I am unable to divine what is to be ultimately the position of the Colleges which cannot become Universities and which will not be Gymnasia. I cannot see what reason they will have to exist.'[51] Only the creation of another tier of tertiary education dissolved the confusion between school and college. The arrival of the American graduate school at the end of the century mitigated some of the influence of school over college, but the result was today's situation where the 'college years' are squeezed between two other segments of education. The undergraduate curriculum is competed for by both school and graduate school. Overlap with the former continues, while the graduate school presses down upon the undergraduate curriculum and forces the departmental major towards pre-professional work.

At the beginning of the graduate school development a few reformers influenced by European, especially German conceptions of the higher learning, abandoned the comprehensive model of a university and developed separatist conceptions of a university as a place of advanced knowledge and professional education. The Johns Hopkins University of Baltimore was the most notable example of this movement, which, in fact, was destined to have only a limited effect. The comprehensive university remained the main source of mass education, acquiring new layers of responsibility with each new shift in educational thinking.

The one shift that did not occur in the United States was the establishment and spread of an elite upper secondary sector supported at public expense. Schooling of this kind emerged locally in the twentieth century in metropolitan areas like New York City, but the common school was really the national norm. Nothing marks the difference between American and European education more than the absence of a significant select post-compulsory secondary education sector preparing students for university-level work. Given mass market pressures, American faith in individual worth and a preference for the second and third chance, as well as the need to assimilate very large groups of immigrants, schooling and higher education continue to overlap. The result is a situation in which the standards of student performance in certain private schools exceed those in certain colleges and state universities, at least in the first two years of the higher education curriculum.

In the absence of a strong preparatory relationship between the secondary and tertiary sectors, it is hardly surprising that the words 'school' and 'college' (and 'university') are used interchangeably in America (as the first two were once in Scotland), or that 'general

---

[51] Kimball, *Orators*, 164.

education' and 'liberal education' are virtually synonymous. It is also not surprising that under conditions of mass higher education it is the general education component of liberal education that is actually most at issue whenever the curriculum is discussed. 'Liberal education' carries too much historical freight to be easily unloaded in the present day. But 'general education' is possible precisely because it suggests and promises less.

General education is, historically, the mission of schools or their functional equivalents, for example, tutorial systems; but the American common school has proven to be an unreliable feeder institution, undependable as a source of undergraduates whose skills, proficiencies, and basic knowledge are developed to the point where a capacity to specialise is safely assumed. Universities have therefore acquired responsibility for general education by default. Overlap is the result, as are repetitive courses in mathematics and languages, a heavy emphasis on learning to write, and remedial work, either as a substitute for regular courses or as supplementary instruction. As we might expect from a course-unit system, students in remedial courses prefer to be given credit for them, while many faculties resist such assaults on their vision of the higher learning.

The separation between secondary and tertiary education is, as Burton Clark has carefully observed, illustrated by the tendency of high school teachers to identify in status and professional interests with colleagues in the lower schools rather than with professors at the universities.[52] The status of the two-year community college teacher continues to be ambiguous in some respects.

In the post-compulsory sectors of European schools, the opposite has been historically true. In nineteenth-century Britain or France or Sweden (as Aant Elzinga's contribution to this volume notes), schoolmasters in university-preparatory sectors identified with the professors above them – indeed, one held the title 'professor' while teaching in the *lycée*. Something of this spirit remains in elite private schools in America today, where headmasters will take graduating seniors on a Cook's tour of colleges and universities to acquaint them with options and perhaps provide them with the advantages of interviews with admissions officers. But in the public sector the orientation of the schools is largely to the surrounding communities, which on the whole tend to put academic achievement second to broad social aims, and the result is a standing conflict between secondary and tertiary education. The schools wish to be free to determine their own programme of studies in relation to the pressures brought by parents and local school boards, and the universities wish to be free to

[52] See Burton Clark (ed.), *The School and the University, an International Perspective* (Berkeley, Los Angeles, and London, 1985).

pursue modern notions of higher education without having to teach the elementary skills that divert resources to areas of instruction considered the historic responsibility of schools. Counter-factual history does not enjoy widespread approval, but perhaps I may take some license with historical method and suggest that if left to their own devices, the higher education sector in America and possibly elsewhere would not be as concerned with liberal education and liberal education ideals if the preparatory segment were more proficient. Given the pressures exerted by nation-states on higher education (see the concluding chapter by Björn Wittrock), specialism, professionalism, and research, basic and applied, would dominate the curriculum to a far greater extent than at present.

Liberal education as 'corrective'

Throughout this chapter I have been discussing ancient ideals and values as they have reappeared under modern conditions, showing how under present circumstances the past inheritance has been modified or simply reversed. I want to conclude with yet another example of the importance of analysing institutions and cultural legacies in their historical contexts.

We have noticed that a minor strain in the history of liberal education can be attributed to the influence of the platonic/pythagorean school which maintained that the fullest realisation of the personality took place in isolation from the world. Self and society were presumed in conflict, since society was not interested in the pursuit of truth, preferring men of action to philosophers. The fate of this conception of liberal education has been partially tied to the fate of platonic influences generally. The great revival of platonic study *per se* (as opposed to specific neo-platonic influences, such as first-century Jewish philosophy, Renaissance astronomy, or Georgian architecture) is in the nineteenth century when platonic scholarship was made into a field of specialised academic study. As scholars began to study the corpus of Plato's writings, idealist philosophy was revived once again, achieved a certain currency, and entered Western intellectual culture generally. The prestige of German philosophy in the form of *Bildung* was particularly important and begins to appear in discussions of British and American liberal education around the middle of the nineteenth century. By no means does it displace the civic emphasis of the dominant Anglo-American theory of liberal education. In America particularly, where the republican idea of political participation remained strong, liberal education was still regarded as a broad preparation for living in society. *Bildung*, best known in the English-speaking world in the form of personal or spiritual development, had limited influence in a mass education system. It did, however, affect individual thinkers, and in some cases reinforced an inclination to stand aloof from the vulgarities of contemporary culture.

In an opposite way, it also led to a new view of the role of liberal education, especially in the developing mass higher education system of the United States. Idealism provided the sense of a standard or superior model of higher education which could then be used to assess the validity of mass culture, democratic but also populist and consumer-led, in a nation heavily dependent upon immigration from non-English-speaking parts of Europe. The function of universities and colleges was to educate young men and women to recognize the serious deficiencies in American culture and to use liberal education to 'correct' them.

In America expansion and diversification of the higher education sector and market forces had greatly attenuated the ideal of liberal education as character formation, but liberal education as a series of 'correctives' gained a certain appeal. In England, given the surviving strength of elite collegiate education, the response was to place trust in the capacity of colleges and universities to socialise a meritocracy to its responsibilities as leaders of society or, as a last resort, to stand up to public opinion.[53]

Thus in both nations we find a vast body of twentieth-century writings on liberal education which claims for liberal arts, or for 'the humanities' with which the liberal arts are nearly always synonymous, such diverse and contradictory responsibilities as combating demagoguery or communism, opposing the spread of modern relativism and utilitarianism, amoralism, secularism, and bohemianism, counter-attacking the pernicious influence of technology and applied science or promoting the high aristocratic 'culture' associated with Oxbridge colleges. In the United States there exists a liberal education corpus advancing the special claims of American visions of democracy and religious morality and even, in one instance, advocating the spread of cost effective forms of higher education! Wars and periods of heavy immigration have produced cries for a form of liberal education which will bind the nation together again by giving it common values or a common 'culture'.[54]

The corrective notion also requires a concentration of resources that mixed-function institutions cannot achieve, as well as a much more expensive labour-intensive teaching effort only possible in a small number

[53] Rothblatt, *The Revolution of the Dons, Cambridge and Society in Victorian England* (1968; Cambridge, 1981).
[54] Ernest L. Boyer and Arthur Levine, *A Quest for Common Learning, the Aims of General Education* (Carnegie Foundation for the Advancement of Teaching, Washington, D.C., n.d.), particularly Appendix A. Ian Carter, *Ancient Cultures of Conceit, British University Fiction in the Post-war Years* (London, 1990), examines hundreds of British academic novels which more or less assume that a liberal education can be obtained in an Oxford and Cambridge college and nowhere else.

of elite centres. To be genuinely effective as educational ends, 'correctives' would also have to be systematically linked together in a highly-focused undergraduate curriculum, organised from a centre and reflecting the opinions and experiences of faculty united in their social and political beliefs. It would need to be based on a universe of assumptions and references shared by teachers and students. In the contemporary American experience, and perhaps too in the European, generation gaps and changes in popular culture produce a knowledge gulf between young and old. Most of the allusions and references taken for granted in the past (at least in elite institutions) have either disappeared or are moribund.

Yet formidable obstacles notwithstanding, there remains in America strong sentiment in favour of something that may be called liberal or general education, and among the reasons for it must surely be the special quality of American ethnic and religious pluralism. A nation composed of immigrants from the start and still very much a nation of immigrants places upon schools, colleges, and universities the responsibility for creating an 'American'. Similar efforts are comparatively unnecessary in societies with more homogeneous populations, or, as in The Netherlands or Switzerland, societies where religious and language separatism is both more acceptable and officially recognised by the State. We can perhaps hypothesise that as other European countries begin to display some of the ethnic diversity of the United States as well as its assimilationist objectives, a concern for liberal and general education may well appear in more pronounced form. Indeed, there are signs that this may now be happening in the United Kingdom or in Eastern Europe or reviving, according to the analysis of Liedman in a following chapter, in Sweden with its very special traditions of *Bildning* and *allmänbildning*.

Everything I have said about the corpuscular universe of the American curriculum indicates the will-o'-the-wisp nature of present-day liberal education; but I did also wish to point out just how the platonic/pythagorean tradition of liberal education has managed to reappear as a tradition of protest from on high.

Looking backwards

So much has been written in praise of the (contradictory) principles and practices of liberal education that it is necessary to use historical perspective to identify certain possibly unpleasant facts. Historically, liberal education in practice has reinforced existing status distinctions and has encouraged social snobbery. (The English case is generally familiar, but Wittrock has noted similar tendencies in other countries.) Insofar as liberal education became associated with aristocracies and leisured classes generally, it encouraged superficiality of learning. It emphasised the ornamental arts and the importance of physical appearance, body movement, manners, and style. Since it was mainly intended for adolescents, it assumed the form of finishing school education. The emphasis on youth means less in modern societies where universities and colleges educate mixed-aged students and where so much higher education is part-time, 'open', or continuing (adult) education. Mature students have their own lives and do not care to be shaped or formed by teachers often no older than they.

Historically, liberal education was heavily literary, oriented towards the book or text and often *retardataire*, looking back towards precedents and past models, towards authorities such as 'great books'. The history of liberal education is partly *mythistoire*. It has left us in great confusion about the differences between liberal and servile education and by what exactly is meant by such rhapsodic phrases as the pursuit of knowledge in and for itself.

Breadth and where to find it

Liberal education is a set of ideals whose implementation has proved difficult. Major contradictions appeared early in the corpus and have given rise to different historical forms in different centuries. I have taken the position that ideas about liberal education have not 'evolved', that is, developed over time from one form to another with some identifiable thread of continuity between them, but have interacted with other historical variables to produce quite different and even unrelated species. I have suggested that in some instances liberal arts ideals were turned upside down and asked to serve ends for which they were never designed. I have stressed the discontinuities in the tradition of liberal education and the rather free-for-all attitude that generations of writers and educators have taken towards the canon, redefining it cavalierly as suited their objectives, which today includes gender and ethnic interests.

But I have also suggested the existence of continuities, sometimes of thought and at other times of feeling, that have retained a considerable amount of historical appeal even as they have proved elusive. The continuities are rooted in ambiguities in the corpus of liberal education ideals and in the religious, ethnic, or class diversity of society and its occupational structure. Some of the ambiguities are metaphysical, as in the conception of the whole person. Others are philosophical, as in the notion of the unencumbered intelligence in pursuit of truth perceived as a thing-in-itself. Some or many of them are social, as in the various leadership conceptions of the purposes of liberal education that have defined the tradition's mainstream. And some of them may be termed social-psychological, in that the purpose of the liberal education experience was to produce self-confident personalities. This extremely critical part of the inheritance is almost always ignored in current discussions of liberal education and has clearly not survived as well as some of the others. There is a reason. Meritocratic systems of evaluation such as competitive examinations are not so much confidence-building as anxiety-producing. They cannot be eliminated, however, without altering the means by which both democratic and occupational objectives are attained.

Historically considered, liberal education was education for the very few, usually from wealthy families willing to pay for the service. It was 'face-to-face' education by tutors, who could adjust the pace of instruction to their expensive charges and closely monitor their progress, or it was education in total institutions where the conditions of selection and privilege obtained. It was education for adolescents, not for young adults, and in the education of adolescents the rod had occasionally to be employed, a practice that may strike the impartial observer as rather at variance with many of the lofty notions associated with liberal education's history of self-praise. And, not to belabour the point unnecessarily, liberal education – except for the platonic strain within it – was practical. The curriculum was not and could not have been impractical, and it was continually modified to render it more practical as needed.

Practicality, however, was related to the requirements of an elite. The notion of the utility of liberal education has caused more difficulty than perhaps any other part of the inheritance precisely because definitions of utility are subject to historical change. The decline and disappearance of an aristocratic class did not immediately produce the decline and disappearance of aristocratic notions of how liberal education was to be used, and objectives long associated with privileged social hierarchies continued to exist in societies where cheap mass education was replacing expensive elite education. This, in combination with *Bildung* and with the tradition of intellectual protest briefly mentioned, produced a situation in which the impracticality of liberal education or its utter devotion to the search for truth were and are often proclaimed to be the most enduring part of the canon.

But fairness to the devotees of the tradition is necessary. Practicality is best understood mainly as non-vocational education, except for military training – a large exception one might say. Liberal education in this regard is correctly defined as a broad understanding of human nature, society, and institutions, accompanied by a critical capacity to make choices and distinctions and to exercise, where necessary, a responsible independence of mind. In the dominant liberal arts tradition, this would also require the exercise of such attributes in a generally public dimension, as, under Western conditions, a participant in a democratic polity where decision-making is widely shared. The desire to turn liberal education into an article of private consumption, which individualistic and relatively wealthy societies permit, thwarts this larger purpose but is itself able to draw on historical sources of support and justification.

It is, I must say rather boldly, easy enough to re-state what liberal education is supposed to do, much harder to stipulate how liberal education ideals are to be incorporated into a curriculum in a mass higher education system where competing forms of education exist, will continue to exist, and by the very structure and nature of present-day societies finally must exist. The question that cannot be answered, that could not always be answered historically without confusion and contradiction, is how to select subjects, methods, and a point of view from the staggering accumulation of educational ideas and information in order to fit the possible means of a liberal education to its presumed ends. No Benthamic calculus exists with which to measure precisely the liberal education quotient in mathematics, history, business, epigraphy, photography, dance, fencing, chemistry, sociology, or the study of Chinese languages.

There is no subject that cannot be taught illiberally, no subject that cannot be taught liberally. The philosophical and sociological as well as psychological implications of virtually any subject can be drawn out and developed to a point where they meet the broad requirements of a liberal education; but this point is not popular, which is why the history of liberal education has been a perpetual Battle of the Books, with one medieval school of logic and dialectic pitted against another, with the classical languages in conflict with experimental science, with one modern subject or another clamouring for entrance to the canon while defenders are anxious to close the door.

No one can satisfactorily and rigorously specify the amount of breadth required to produce a broadly educated person. Indeed, how broad is broad? Surely it is possible to argue along lines suggested by Liedman that a 'single' discipline with a long internal history of debate, differentiation, and reference provides as fine a general education as a *macédoine* or sampler of subjects expressed, for example, in the form of the typical American set of distribution requirements. Interdisciplinary courses may not be any more interdisciplinary than other kinds of courses; and if they are not made compulsory, they simply add yet another layer of choice to a college curriculum already overwhelmed (in America) with modular options. But even where compulsory, it is not certain that interdisciplinary or even core courses allow for that extra and higher academic step any better than traditional subjects, that step wherein the mind is encouraged to make connections and associations between ideas not readily apparent. It is not certain that cores have this step in mind, or indeed, the wholeness so embedded in liberal education's historical odyssey.

In fact, the modern experience should warn us of the limits of the curriculum in creating the whole person. Wholeness, it would appear, is not merely a question of the curriculum. It is a question of total experience, of the influences that come from families and communities, from teachers who have the time for close and attentive instruction, from peer and affinity groups, from all of the other institutions and activities of greatly plural societies. So it has been historically; and the particular, it can be said the peculiar, emphasis on liberal education in the twentieth century is in large measure caused by the confusion existing in all those other social institutions assumed to provide stability and reassurance to young people passing through the several stages of growth to maturity. The 'burden' – one might say the 'obligation' – of providing the generations with a broad understanding of what in the eighteenth century was called 'men and manners' has been pushed up the educational ladder. The years once spent in preparing for a profession, or earning a living, are now to be spent acquiring a general education. Those undergraduates in the United States who proceed directly from high school to professional training, e.g., engineers, some architecture and business administration students, are often derided as illiberal and narrow, and their crowded academic schedules are scrutinised for openings that might admit some of the light emanating from the distant centuries of liberal learning.

It is relatively easy to train an engineer and relatively simple to produce an accountant. The technical competencies required for success in these occupations are familiar enough, and it is always possible to upgrade skills when changes in professional practice occur. But it is almost impossible to determine which of the many subjects to which higher education gives place and prominence are absolutely essential for living in the world. Facility in reading, writing and speaking almost certainly: should there also be instruction in how to make friends and influence people, in how to repair electrical wiring, in how to start a consulting firm, or operate a governmental lobby group? Is an introduction to understanding the natural and urban environment a *desideratum*? Should undergraduates take a compulsory course in world civilisation, in ethnic studies? Is art appreciation absolutely essential? Particle physics and bio-engineering? Morality: a topic of recurrent interest in a tradition which began with an ethological, that is, characterological theory of conduct. But which code of morality? Hammurabi's, something faintly called Judaeo-Christian, liberal individualism, utilitarianism, idealism, authoritarianism? And is exposure to a specified set of morals a guarantee of their efficacy? The historical answer to that question is not hopeful. One has only to read Friedrich Meinecke on *The German Catastrophe* to notice how the most sublime theories of liberal education are horribly perverted in practice. But supposing the answer to most of the questions was 'yes': we would still have to apportion a certain number of hours to each subject and decide whether there was any practical correlation between those hours and the quantity of knowledge that resulted.

The final difficulty is really insurmountable. In a mass society it is not possible to devise a test or even design a social survey that will tell us whether we have firmly implanted in the minds and characters of educated people something recognisable as a liberal education, especially since the historical test was not a grasp of information or even knowing but how the life was actually lived in the world.

'Splitting up is the historical way of mankind.'

Liberal education, its ideas and assumptions about human nature, its institutionalised forms, is a mixture of hopes and rationalisations. It is irretrievably connected to the severest dichotomies of Western civilisation. On the one side, liberal education holds out the possibility of a union of all parts and a harmonisation with the natural order. On the other, it declares the autonomy of the self and the necessity for its fullest free-flowering. In between – again in correspondence with the great range of mixtures produced by its host culture – liberal education shifts its aims continually, sometimes connecting individuals with nature, sometimes with socio-political artifacts like the polis or the nation-state, or just the city alone, sometimes mitigating philosophical egoism with an ethic of social responsibility. Still at other times the harmonisation with nature or society so long a part of the aspiration of liberal educators is overthrown in favour of the educational aim of inculcating in the student a rigorous critical discrimination. Thereupon liberal education does not so much take its source of understanding passively from the world but is itself the active source of the world's self-understanding.

There is a sense in which educational history is the story of the continual partitioning of the human personality. From this perspective, the history of liberal education is the history of attempts to reunite the segments and join the scattered limbs of a long-suffering deity, restoring him to health and activity. The history of liberal education does not evolve or descend: it dissolves. It is the narrative of a series of departures from a conception of wholeness or integration which appears to be a 'natural' way of viewing the human condition, beginning with the balance presumed essential to mental and bodily health and extending to the necessary and palpable interdependence of people. In everyday language such interdependencies seem 'reasonable'. Appeals to an ideal of roundedness rarely fall on deaf ears. But the deeper assumptions upon which ancient ideas of liberal education rest are actually incomprehensible from the standpoint of present-day conceptions of personality. They are not compatible with the idea of an autonomous self in competition with other selves for status, income, position, and influence, or with our belief in the importance of skills, proficiencies, and specialities.

A momentary suspension of the assumptions behind the development of liberal individualism reveals a different set of preoccupations. Whether defined as Renaissance universalism, the acquisitive instinct, constitutional rights, and negative freedoms, personal creativity or spiritual self-realisation, liberal individualism is not the inheritor of ancient ideals of liberal education. It is the end result only of the breakup of those ideals, the history of continuing disjunctions, of dichotomies and separations, all of which have the profoundest implications for the kind of cultures that have developed in the West, quite possibly anywhere.

In religious thought, the union of the divine and the human is a fundamental aspiration, and the hybrid man-gods of ancient polytheism may represent a logical if implausible compromise, as, in yet another way, does the ancient Egyptian denial of mortality. In Hebraic theology, where the human and the divine are forever parted (except in certain mystical, cabbalistic traditions where even gender is confused), wholeness nevertheless remains an ideal. In practical terms it consists in living according to the divine standard and of following the 613 heavenly commandments essential to the righteous life. In politics, the long tradition of defining essential human attributes in relation to the demands of living in city-state communities made wholeness dependent upon the active or public life. Separation from the city, from public life itself, led to alienation and idiocy, two Greek words that continue to convey strong and even violent meanings. The underlying assumption was always and everywhere the same: social life is the natural condition of men and women. Anything less is unnatural or denaturing, contrary to the facts of our very existence. It is therefore necessary at all times to forestall separation from the larger communities and institutions that contribute to and guarantee the compatibility of our inner and outer lives. Matthew Arnold consistently clings to this view when he advocates the necessity for a holistic culture and when he (as well as other nineteenth-century Victorians) talks about the superiority of a national or Broad Church when contrasted to the particularistic tendencies of religious denominations.

The enemy of liberal education is therefore the many dividing forces of history: that which divides the earthly from the spiritual; the person from the community, the city-state, the nation-state; the mind from the body, and reason from the passions; the mind from itself, as represented, for example, in the many forms of faculty psychology that have existed, such as the phrenology of the last century, which separate the mind into numerous autonomous compartments. The enemy too is, paradoxically, the repudiation of liberal education's oldest axiom, the belief in a universal human nature. This is a paradox because some of the most devoted and passionate advocates of twentieth-century American liberal education have tried to eliminate the theory of a pre-existing human nature precisely because it is an educational bottleneck. For them the end of a liberal education is not the liberation of an internal self which is our 'humanity' or 'essence' but something else more external or the result of human effort – let us say 'culture', or in any case, that which can become an end in itself and can be contemplated by the mind.[55]

In the history of educational institutions it is possible to plot the steady parting of socialising elements as when, in the first half of the nineteenth century, American colleges and universities began to distinguish between mental ability and personal behaviour, assessing each separately where the practice had been to lump them together.[56] Many movements and ideologies have arisen purporting to return the fractured personality to its ideal state of balance, some of them bizarre, destructive, and extreme – totalitarianism and religious cults, for examples – other belonging more clearly to the traditions comprising liberal education, such as civic humanism or the notion of a 'core' curriculum, or ideas about the integration of work and leisure.

In the foregoing discussion much perforce has been left out.[57] Much

---

[55] Schwab, *Science, Curriculum, and Liberal Education*, 11.
[56] Smallwood, *Examinations*, 70.
[57] The topic of women and liberal education has been alluded to in passing and can be elaborated in several dimensions. The ancient theory of personality development through self-restraint, for example, became connected to the Enlightenment civilising ethic as described by writers such as Norbert Elias. Civilised behaviour was characterised by self-control, politesse, and humanity – it was in a sense 'feminine'. Aggressive, self-interested, or war-like behaviour was by contrast 'masculine' or 'manly'. These 'gender' words or their equivalent could be applied to either men or women.

However, in the new American women's colleges of the nineteenth century there was a tendency to equate the curriculum with gender. 'Soft' subjects were language, literature, and the fine arts or dance; 'hard' subjects were the physical sciences and engineering. Women were often thought of as the 'carriers' of civilisation. They were the civilising forces in society and needed to be prepared for that role. See Rothblatt, 'The Carriers of Civilization', *Higher Education Policy*, 3 (March 1990), 9–12.

Yet caution is advisable in these speculations. American Roman Catholic women's colleges like St Mary's of Notre Dame, South Bend, Indiana, founded in 1844, had a very substantial science laboratory programme in the 1890s. For England, the investigations of Robert Fox and Anna Guagnini indicate that undergraduate women at Oxford and Cambridge in the thirty years before the First World War were willing to read for the

needs to be further qualified, especially with respect to the different countries of the Western world, but perhaps the general argument will prove sobering or at least provide some stiffening in the discourse. For our present discussions usually take place in an historical vacuum and are far too often reduced to platitude, special pleading, and misconceptions as to the place and character of those traditions of education confusingly called 'liberal'.

Today, whenever liberal education is discussed, the question of the curriculum is uppermost. Nearly all of the well-publicised American reports and books on the liberal curriculum of recent years – Allan Bloom, the report of the American Association of Colleges, the report of the former Secretary of Education, William Bennett – concentrate on the range of subjects appropriate to liberal or general education, with attention in some cases paid to their cognitive dimensions and the analytic or synthetic reasoning skills they are said to advance.[58]

However, the recent report by the Carnegie Foundation for the Advancement of Teaching which mentions the 'co-curriculum' alerts us to a different strain of reasoning.[59] Historically, the curriculum has been only one factor in the creation of liberal education. Wholeness, or the unity of personality, required attention to all aspects of living. This was possible because liberal education was education for an elite, and the cost of educating future leaders could be borne by wealthy parents, guardians, and patrons. Cost alone is one strong reason why a liberal education cast in a more traditional mould is difficult to achieve under conditions of mass access, market discipline, and plural cultures. Another is the fact that the socialisation objectives of liberal education were customarily located in the years of schooling not university, when young people were of a more pliable age and subject to a great variety of restraints. In America even more than in Britain, the period of liberal education has been progressively pushed into higher education, where young persons are older and in the process of detaching themselves from home and family. And in institutions

mathematics, biological, and physical sciences honours degree. Paradoxically, if Oxford women avoided any subject at all it was a 'traditional one like "Greats" or *Literae Humaniores*, possibly because their prior schooling was weak in classical languages'. See Fox and Guagnini, 'Classical Values and Useful Knowledge: The Problem of Access to Technical Careers in Modern Europe', *Daedalus*, 116 (Fall 1987), 160–3. And with respect to the use of gender words, Stefan Collini, *Public Moralists, Political Thought and Intellectual Life in Britain 1850–1930* (Cambridge, 1991), 186, has shown how 'manly' or 'masculine' could be used in quite different senses from what is now commonly assumed.

[58] Allan Bloom, *The Closing of the American Mind: How Higher Education Has Failed Democracy and Impoverished the Souls of Today's Students* (New York, 1987); *A New Vitality in General Education* (Association of American Colleges, 1988); William Bennett, *To Reclaim a Legacy* (November, 1984).

[59] Ernest, L. Boyer, *College, The Undergraduate Experience in America* (New York, 1987).

of higher education, the ideals of liberal education come into conflict with yet other educational ideals, arising from yet other historical circumstances: professionalism, research, specialisation, the 'higher culture of the mind', *Bildung*, and liberal individualism. These have inevitably transformed the intellectual character of liberal education which, when combined with the greater age and social experience of the student (to include the adult or 'mature' student of America, Britain, Denmark, and Sweden), becomes a very different kind of education from what was known earlier. The conflicts between educational missions are not likely to diminish, and they will continue to produce differences of aims, competing demands on university teachers and their timetables, and disagreements over resources.

Ideals and idols

In a book on the history of liberal education in England published in 1976,[60] I adopted the melancholy position that the ideals of liberal education in their historically dominant form cannot be realised under present circumstances. I still believe that liberal education is almost incapable of accomplishing the rather etherial objectives assigned to it; but having said as much, I want now to end with a reflection far more sensitive to the place and importance of ideals in the organisation of cultural life.

An ideal resembles an experiment. It may or may not work in practice, but its value is in the trying and reaching. Its function is to explore alternatives and to exercise a creative reach in order to prevent human life from being overrun by the humdrum and banal. An ideal sets an example or standard and puts us on the road to a vision of perfection. But a perfectly realised ideal would surely be dangerous. Once imposed, or universally accepted, it would lose its power to lift the imagination or ennoble conduct, becoming instead yet another new orthodoxy. As with the humanist school curriculum of the Italian fifteenth century, or any highly institutionalised curriculum, it is likely soon to be stilted and flat, a matter of routine, but routine that is dogmatically, even tyranically defended. There also remains the possibility that the new ideal may well prove wrong in practice, incomplete or misconceived, or simply at variance with other equally valid but hitherto overlooked ideals. Consequently, there is some value in thinking that an ideal should always retain its original singularity as an ideal, remain a vision, even a torment of Tantalus, never wholly within reach, but an inspiration and aspiration, a

---

[60] Rothblatt, *Tradition and Change in English Liberal Education, an Essay in History and Culture* (London, 1976).

reminder of what might exist were we divine and not human. The readiness, the reaching, is all, but the distinction is crucial.

As we have noticed, many ideals have comprised the history of liberal education, several of them remarkably contradictory, either in theory or in historical context. Wholeness has not been the only ideal associated with liberal education historically. Withdrawal and the 'counterlife' have been others. The partitioning of the human personality has had its own advocates and historical attractions, if only because it provides relief from the relentless necessity to fulfil a centuries-old dream of oneness, of union with the cosmos, nature and society. In the mental life, the division of knowledge is the only path – to recall the words spoken in 1870 by the Rector of Lincoln College, Oxford – that leads to the creation of 'all real culture'. 'Knowing a little of the surface of half a dozen things' was 'inferior'. Partitioning means the freedom to follow an interest, a specialty, but also a whim or 'hobby' – an eighteenth-century English neologism to describe the pastimes occurring under conditions of leisure. It means the right to be an antiquarian, or to impersonate, as Roth declares in his novels, the right to embrace the artificial in preference to the natural. In short, as an ideal, the dividing of the self and its separation from a larger controlling sphere of activity also means the liberty to indulge the pleasures of human curiosity. In the process, one self is distinguished from another.

Yet the counterlife too holds its own dangers. It may disregard the boundaries upon which it depends and encroach upon the lives and specialties of others.[61] It may lose its sense of limits and re-make the world in its own image. Enter once again the story of the fluteplayer and the flute, the skill or act taking precedence over the person. The counterlife provides no guarantee of responsibility, no sure and certain moral authority outside the individual; and so it has been continually in conflict with what I regard as the principal telos of liberal education.

The ideal of the whole and harmoniously composed individual is a tradition pedagogically associated with ancient Greek thought and culture, but in some respects it is wider and includes the non-pagan cultures that have had such a profound influence on Western values. It goes back to the Covenant, the alliance, the union of a people about to be made holy by accepting the transparent Spirit of the Divine. Our world below and the world above were to be one, and the great leader Moses requested this consummation by combining within himself the roles of judge and priest. 'Moses wished for an entire, undivided human life, as the right answer to the Divine revaluation.' But upon his death the roles divided. Prophet, priest, judge, political leader – it was no longer possible to combine them

---

[61] See the discussion by John P. Sisk, 'The Bias against Specialization', *This World, a Journal of Religion and Public Life*, 26 (Summer 1989), 101.

into one. The existential philosopher Martin Buber continues his discussion in this answer: '[S]plitting up is the historical way of mankind, and the unsplit person cannot do anything more than raise man to a higher level on which he may thereafter follow his course, as long as he is bound by the law of his history'.[62]

'Splitting up is the historical way of mankind', and to this many responses have been given, although, as Buber concludes, they can never be arbitrary, being bound by history, that is, circumstances. One primary response in Western society has been through liberal education. Had there been no such body of thought as liberal education, it would have been necessary to invent one. We might well ask ourselves what our traditions of Western education would be without a view of human potential that holds we are greater than the sum of our proficiencies. How relatively easy it has been for educational systems to divide those proficiencies from personality, and to measure them, often mechanically or coldly, the excitement of measurement becoming in time its own justification.

It is, furthermore, certainly desirable to teach young people how to think about the issues of living in society as distinguished from issues that are more properly abstract or technical. Living in the world is the critical point. We might well wonder what our traditions of Western education would be without an educational ideal stressing the importance of civic participation, wherein we are instructed to think of ourselves as part of a larger community of shared public responsibilities and values. It is important to have an ideal which does not continually direct the mind into itself.

Finally, it is necessary to say that it is important to have an ideal where many of the assumptions of the counterlife are challenged and the seductions of exclusion and limited loyalties are questioned. The counterlife provides identity, but we should also recall those other theories which tell us that identify is often purchased at the price of anger.

Liberal education historically was not, in my view, either as privatistic or as antagonistic as it became in the last two centuries but was meant to provide recipients with a solid sense of confidence in their ability to understand and live within the world in a condition of mutual respect. It is true that this solid sense of confidence was supported by wealth and birth, but liberal education played a part, if by no means the whole part.

Ironically, the search for a means of instilling self-confidence was also a reaction to the realisation – I have called it a 'fear' – that in human nature lay a destructive impulse, another self, needing to be calmed, controlled, and re-directed through education into purposeful activity, in a word,

---

[62] Martin Buber, *Moses, the Revelation and the Covenant* (New York, 1958), 199.

needing to be 'civilised'. Sigmund Freud addressed the problem psychoanalytically in the theory of sublimation. But the postulate of two selves is not a peculiarly 'modern disease'.[63] It is a constant. It appears and reappears in theology, in literature, and in the psychological theory of schizophrenia. It goes under many names that refer to the doubling and disintegration of the personality – the 'other self' of Renaissance writers, the stolen mirror image of Romantic writers, the *doppelgänger*, the best and ordinary selves of Matthew Arnold, the secret sharer of Joseph Conrad, the *dybbuk* of Jewish folklore.

Ideals can only be successfully held in conscious relation to realities, 'for, alas, the Ideal always has to grow in the Real, and to seek out its bed and board there, often in a very sorry way'.[64] Nevertheless, I submit that as an historical ideal civilising oneself through liberal education is not at all bad. The fight against a narrow and limited view of human nature was on balance a noble undertaking, and the effort to unearth the buried parts of Osiris was well worth the trouble.

[63] Matthew Arnold's phrase. See also Margaret Scanlan, *Traces of Another Time, History and Politics in Postwar British Fiction* (Princeton, 1990), 101–2.
[64] Thomas Carlyle, *Past and Present* (London and New York, 1947), 55.

2   In search of Isis: general education in Germany and Sweden

Sven-Eric Liedman

> In her aspect as the wife of Osiris she is the chief actor, but only after his death: she finds his corpse at Byblos, she finds the fragments of the dismembered body scattered throughout Egypt, she is the chief mourner at the funeral, she unites the fragments of the body and, by her divine power, brings Osiris to life again.
>
> Encyclopaedia Brittanica

In this chapter, I intend to call attention to the German concept of *Bildung* as well as to its generally less well-known Swedish counterpart of *Bildning*. These words have much to tell us about both German and Swedish intellectual traditions. *Bildung* and *Bildning* start their careers at the end of the eighteenth century, and even today they are quite central to actual discussions about school and society. Of course, their meanings have shifted over the centuries, and these changes were closely linked to the social, political, and institutional circumstances in both countries.

The German Ideology of *Bildung*

Culture and enlightenment

In 1784 in the *Berliner Monatsschrift* there appeared some articles concerning the meaning of the word 'enlightenment', its supposed 'real' meaning. Immanuel Kant's little masterpiece, *An Answer to the Question of Enlightenment (Beantwortung der Frage: Was ist Aufklärung?)*[1] is still widely read and commented upon. The great German-Jewish philosopher, Moses Mendelssohn, contributed to the discussion with a succinct and lucid article called, *On the Subject of the Meaning of Enlightenment (Über die Frage: was heisst Aufklären?)*.[2] Mendelssohn started his essay with the remark that the words *Aufklärung*, *Kultur*, and *Bildung* were newcomers to

---

[1] Immanuel Kant, 'An Answer to the Question of Enlightenment', *Werksausgabe*, XI (Frankfurt, 1977), 553–61.
[2] Moses Mendelssohn, 'On the Subject of the Meaning of Enlightenment', *Gesammelte Schriften*, Jubiläumsausgabe, VI (Stuttgart, 1981), 115ff.

the German language. Ordinary people hardly understood them. Mendelssohn tended to define them in a clear-cut way, declaring that *Bildung* was the more comprehensive concept, standing for the human maturity of a people possessing *Kultur* and *Aufklärung*. *Kultur* or culture was a more restricted term, but only relatively so. It described practical matters, such as standards in handicrafts and arts, but also general character traits, such as industry and assiduity, cleverness and good manners. Enlightenment, on the other hand, was a term that referred to more abstract qualities. For example, a people that was enlightened would possess rational knowledge and have insight into human life and the human mission (*Bestimmung*). The vehicles of enlightenment were science and philosophy, whereas social intercourse, poetry and eloquence or rhetoric (*Beredsamkeit*) advanced culture.

When he applied these ideas to nations, Mendelssohn found that the French had culture and the English enlightenment, while the Chinese, who also had culture, were weak on enlightenment. By contrast with all others, the ancient Greeks possessed both enlightenment and culture and hence alone possessed true *Bildung*.

Mendelssohn's argument was easier to grasp in his own day than in our own because several of his key distinctions and presuppositions were more acceptable to his contemporaries. He made a sharp distinction between man *qua* man and man as a member of society or a certain society. For example, a German peasant and an English professor shared a common human essence (*Wesen*); and insofar as this was the case, both shared common needs. Both, to pursue the example, could be said to be in need of enlightenment (Americans understood this argument in the context of philosophical and constitutional assumptions about the equality of people). Nevertheless, while all people share an essence, they also exhibit cultural differences. The residents of different countries have cultures different from one another, and even within a single country there are cultural distinctions of social ranks and standing. Mendelssohn went on to say that in his essence man *qua* man did not need culture: only enlightenment. However, man as a member of civil society, man *qua* citizen, certainly needed culture in order to participate in the affairs of society, and the kind and quantity of culture essential to the normal everyday functioning of society was determined by rank and position. Enlightenment, on the contrary, was not a 'given'. It was not a concomitant of a person's social standing but independent of it.

Now, according to Mendelssohn there was a latent conflict between culture and enlightenment. Enlightenment was limitless, whereas culture had the task of defining and making clear social limitations and barriers. Both were needed, however, and a State was unfortunate (*unglücklich*) if it could not harmonise the prerequisites of enlightenment with those of culture.

The emergence of Bildung

The circumstances in which Mendelssohn's and Kant's articles on enlightenment and *Bildung* had their origin have much to say about the milieu in which the German word *Bildung* – a word without a direct equivalent in English or French but borrowed into Swedish as *Bildning* and into Russian as *Obrazovannost* – received its modern, very broad, unstable, but still identifiable meanings. We can trace the origins of the German *Bildung* and its borrowed forms back to the debate on freedom of public speech that emerged in the German *Aufklärung*.

The debate started with a lecture by another representative of the German Enlightenment, J. K. W. Mohsen, given before a Berlin discussion club called the Berliner Mittwochgesellschaft (The Wednesday Society of Berlin). The society, as well as the *Berliner Monatsschrift*, the journal in which Kant and Mendelssohn published their articles, represented the belated emergence in Germany of a real civil 'public sphere', about which Jürgen Habermas has published a famous book.[3] The journal and the Berliner Mittwochgesellschaft were significant arenas of discussion because they were regarded as being outside the domain of the State and hence less restricted in their range of reference than other institutions, for example, the German universities.

The point under consideration was no less than the issue of freedom of speech itself. Mendelssohn, Mohsen, and even more explicitly, Kant, defended the importance of such freedom. According to Kant, a sharp distinction was to be made between the private and public spheres. In the first, for example, a university professor instructing his students was obliged to follow the university statutes and regulations instituted by the State. But in the second sphere, represented by journals, books, and lectures, all views were in principle openly accessible, and all people could instruct themselves according to their own convictions. This distinction between 'private' and 'public' may seem strange, but it is rooted in the special circumstances of Kant's time. Kant explained that university instruction, for example, was private because it was directed only to a few who have a special career with special duties before them, whereas a public dialogue was by its very nature an open exchange in which people could participate freely. In order to assure political order and security, it was

---

[3] Jürgen Habermas, *Strukturwandel der bürgerlichen Öffentlichkeit. Untersuchungen zu einer Kategorie der bürgerlichen Gesellschaft*, 9th edn (Darmstadt, 1978).

probably necessary to restrict the freedom of speech of State employees discharging their official duties, but progress and intellectual development – which Kant certainly advocated – were different matters and depended upon freedom of opinion and belief.

In his *Aufklärung* article, Kant did not hint at the possibility that any part of the university would have a special claim to extra freedom. It was only in his later booklet, *The Conflict between the Faculties* (*Der Streit der Fakultäten*), that he argued that the philosophical faculty – the faculty of humanities and science – could enjoy a less restricted activity than other university faculties. While theologians were bound to the Holy Bible, lawyers to the law in force, and doctors to the official regulations concerning health, philosophers were only limited by reason itself. In this respect, Kant maintained, the philosophical faculty was surely superior to the others, not inferior as he said was the customary view, wherein liberal education usually took a back seat to professional education.[4]

Neither in his *Streit* pamphlet nor in the *Aufklärung* article did Kant use the word *Bildung* in order to characterise the independence of the public in a free public sphere or put a label on the mission of a philosophical faculty. But, in another booklet, *On Teaching* (*Über Pädagogik*),[5] he very briefly developed his own idea of this new word, use of which was spreading, declaring that *Bildung* encompasses both discipline (*Zucht*) and education (*Unterweisung*). Here, evidently, *Bildung* was much more precisely related to ideas of the formation of individual character than it was in Mendelssohn's article some twenty years before. Kant intended to make a contribution to the intense debate on education going on around 1800. The word *Bildung* was already so common that it was impossible to avoid its use in dealing with the problems of pedagogy.

Kant, like Mendelssohn, used the word *Bildung* broadly to mean not only the intellectual but also the moral and emotional development of individuals. Their younger contemporary, Johann Gottfried Herder, philosopher, historian, and preacher, employed the word in a much wider sense and was very likely the first to use *Bildung* to denote the education of man and mankind generally. He did so, as early as the 1760s, and in his famous *Account of My Travels in 1769* (*Journal meiner Reise im Jahr 1769*) he sketched out a philosophy of *Bildung* which turned out to be seminal for not only his own future but for all German post-Kantian idealist thought. He employed *Bildung* in a universal but also in a dynamical sense, speaking about an 'Universalgeschichte der Bildung der Welt'.[6] Here the meaning is

---

[4] Kant, 'The Conflict between the Faculties', in *Werksausgabe*, XI, 267ff.
[5] Kant, 'Über Pädagogick', (1803) in *Werksausgabe*, XII, 696–707.
[6] Johann Gottfried Herder, 'A Universal History of *Bildung*', in *Herders Werke*, ed. Ernst Naumann (Berlin, 1908), III, 32.

equivalent to a description of change and development in all aspects and respects – geological, biological, historical, individual. According to Herder's all-embracing conception, every form of development is related to another. The laws of change are comprehensive, uniform, and universal. They operate on all levels of reality simultaneously, and all reality is in fact always in a state of flux.

In his *Journal*, Herder outlined a broad programme for individual *Bildung*. Like Kant, he was very impressed by Rousseau's *Emile*. In contrast to Kant, however, who also learned from Rousseau and agreed with him that all men fundamentally have the same ethical capacity and insight, at the same time rejecting Rousseau's love for original, 'primitive' man, Herder sought for precisely the original, the unchanging constitution of human nature. Rousseau had said that this nature was to be found in the child, and the teacher's task was to preserve it, or, more correctly, to extract all its slumbering qualities in the process of learning. But this process of teaching always presupposed the active participation of the pupil. Knowledge and insight were not external qualities which could be later attached or acquired. They existed internally in the pupil and had to be encouraged or developed. Like Rousseau, Herder criticised the traditional forms of education such as the teaching of ancient languages for their coerciveness and neglect of the child's inner capacities, including natural innocence. As with many of the later romanticists, Herder's attitude to Latin as a main school subject was very negative, and he advocated the study of living languages, as well as other kinds of knowledge close to the pupil's own immediate experience.

These pedagogical ideas were new in the late eighteenth and early nineteenth centuries. The Swiss reformer Pestalozzi was their most remarkable and foremost advocate. He too, in fact, was one of the prominent philosophers of *Bildung*, even going so far as to maintain that *Bildung* was suitable for the lower classes in society.[7] It is important to keep this radically democratic or at least egalitarian view of *Bildung* in mind, as its part in later German and still more in Swedish development is absolutely central.

Two directions for Bildung

These early examples of how the word *Bildung* could be used in the late eighteenth century might seem more bewildering than clarifying. Most of all, they seem to demonstrate the enormous breadth of the word and its

---

[7] Johann Heinrich Pestalozzi, 'Die niedere Menschheit', in *Abendstunde eines Einsiedlers* (1780), republished in *Sämmtliche Werke*, ed. Artur Buchenau *et al.* (1927), I, 267.

uses, although the central or crucial characteristics of the philosophy of *Bildung* have been touched upon. But before elaborating these further, we must add some remarks on the etymological origin of the word itself.

Bildung is constructed out of *Bild*, which here has to be translated as 'image' rather than 'picture'.[8] The origins of *Bildung* must therefore be searched for in mysticism, where the idea that man has to be an image of God (*imago dei*) is fundamental. However, in the eighteenth century these ideas were secularised. For example, they were used in Germany to clarify the meaning of the aesthetic ideas of the seventeenth-century Englishman, Lord Shaftesbury, whose idealist thinking heavily influenced German intellectual life, penetrating many fields of learning. Even in biology, *Bildung* became a common word. The German biologist, J. F. Blumenbach of the University of Göttingen, called the supposed vital force in all living creatures their *Bildungstrieb* or life principle.

In order to understand the success of the new word, it is necessary to realise that it seemed to be in accord with traditional German ideas about macro- and micro-cosmos, the individual person reflecting or being an 'image' of the historical development of mankind. Traditional ideas seem to have been especially important for Herder. A *gebildeter* man, that is to say, a man who possesses *Bildung*, is thus an image of mankind in its true reality. However, the strong stress on historical process in Herder's thinking represents something radically new. A willingness or tendency to see everything as changing and developing was indeed a constitutive feature of the new meaning of the word *Bildung*. In the changing historicistic environment of the time, a dynamic connotation was virtually a prerequisite for the word's widespread acceptance in both academic and social discourse.

Thus *Bildung* came to signify either a process or the result of a process – it might be a process in nature or history or in an individual's life, but development of some kind is always essential to the word's use. In this chapter, the educational meaning of *Bildung* will be particularly emphasised; but that is fully in keeping with the historical origins, development, and actual employment of the concept. It is the use of the idea in the broad context of education – and not in, say, the life sciences – which has survived the more than 200 years separating us from its modern beginnings.

It has been shown[9] that the word *Bildung* replaced such words as 'education' and 'information', both of course of Latin origin and in their familiar meanings not radically different from the English understanding

---

[8] In fact, *Bildung* has affinities with 'imagination'. *Einbildung*, the German counterpart of the English word, is central to its early philosophical formulation.

[9] Ilse Schaarschmidt, *Der Bedeutungswandel der Worte 'bilden' und 'Bildung' in der Literatur-Epoche von Gottsched bis Herder* (Koenigsberg, 1931), 46.

of 'education'. The English 'education' and the German *Bildung* also possess similarities. There is certainly overlap in meaning, since 'education' also carries a dynamic implication. It too can refer to a process; but it is also a word with static connotations and can be used to describe an existing state or condition, a process that is in fact ended or complete, as in the phrase an 'educated person' or someone whose 'education' has been professional, technical, or liberal. Perhaps the difference is only one of emphasis, but it is useful to remember that *Bildung* is always forceful. It nearly always means or meant a process (or the result of a process) and implies, as 'education' invariably does not, the tacit cooperation of the pupil or student in the learning experience. The subjective side of acquiring knowledge is stressed. The role of the teacher is never to impose knowledge on the pupil, but rather to elicit talents and predispositions which every human being possesses. Therefore, the process of learning in this context means self-fulfillment, as the boy or girl (or adult student) who gets *gebildet* learns to actualise something which he or she already potentially has.

This idea that all genuine education is self-education is the hard core of the well-known pedagogical projects of Rousseau, Pestalozzi, and many others. It is strengthened by the totally new, activist theory of knowledge, which Rousseau sketches in his *On Inequality Among Mankind – the Profession of Faith of a Savoyard Vicar* and which Kant achieved in his *Critique of Pure Reason* (*Kritik der reinen Vernunft*). According to this treatise, even pure sense-perception is an active process, man never merely mirroring or passively depicting the external world through his senses – Kant's response to the Enlightenment English associationists and Lockeans, who subordinated ideation to sensation for their own political purposes.

In the revolutionary decades just before and after the turn of the eighteenth century, these conceptions about learning and knowledge had a certain affinity with ideals about the active citizen. This was true of most Rousseauists in the French Revolution, Robespierre being their head, and it was also true of many early German adherents of the revolutionary process. However, the stress on *Bildung* as an inner process could lead to the opposite conclusions, too. The internal world could be seen as the real one, where man was unbound and creative, whereas his life in State and society had to follow fixed rules.

It would be a mistake, however, to presume that *Bildung* was an exclusively subjective affair. Literally, by the process of *Bildung* a man's life was an 'image'. To be *gebildet*, his development had to correspond to a certain ideal, be it his real essence or the ideal of the true artist, the loyal and conscientious civil servant, or the perfect Christian. He had the capacity within himself to reach such objectives. Indeed, it was an obligation for him to do so, but the goal itself was not regarded as automatically achievable. It was seen as an external standard that had to be positively striven for.

The subjective-objective character of the concept of *Bildung* was its strength – but also its weakness. As far as the subjective and objective worlds could be kept together, the correlation was very efficient. Learning was not a personal affair. True self-fulfillment meant correspondence to an objective, external standard. But real knowledge was also man's own knowledge, and the process of learning was active in the sense that it required both hard work and the pupil's whole attention and creativity.

The complexity of the concept, balancing the two worlds of subject and object, was its weakness. It could easily turn out to be either something merely internal or *innerlich* or (which was more common) wholly external, in which case the process of self-realisation essential to *Bildung* stagnated, becoming machine-like, repetitious, a question of a fixed curriculum, or prescribed behaviour and social position. In light of the later eighteenth-century preference for 'organic' over 'mechanical' thinking and images, this prospect for *Bildung* was particularly unfortunate. As a concept, therefore, *Bildung* could go in two directions. In its ideal form, it was educationally radical; but in its second form, both conservative and conventional.

There is also another ambiguity or duality in the concept of *Bildung* which could in fact be noticed from the beginning. To Herder, the pioneer, *Bildung* was opposed to enlightenment, where enlightenment stood for reason. To Mendelssohn, as we have already seen, enlightenment in the eighteenth century meaning was a central part of *Bildung*. In its long history, thereafter, the concept could be used to signify both rationalist and irrationalist ideals.

Bildung *and the German university*

To Moses Mendelssohn, the guarantee of *Bildung* appears to have lain in the public sphere. To Pestalozzi, it was the elementary school, open to poor and rich alike. For many others, the institution that appeared to have the most potential for encouraging the spread of *Bildung* was the university.

In the early nineteenth century, a whole series of important philosophers and scientists followed the example of Kant and wrote booklets, essays, or articles on the real purpose or meaning of universities. Due both to the French Revolution and the ferment preceding it, many basic institutions were being questioned, and higher education was certainly no exception. In Revolutionary France, the old universities were by-passed as centres of innovation and importance and their place taken by a specialised group of

82   Sven-Eric Liedman

institutions called *grandes écoles*. As in the case of religion, when Napoleon broke with the past, he created new forms and institutions as replacements, so in the first instance he established a new kind of highly centralised higher education system, abolishing 'universities' while however retaining their faculties structure.

In Germany, especially in Prussia, university reforms went in another direction. The foundation of the University of Berlin was decisive, and *Bildung* played a role in its conception. Berlin was the first university in the world where research and not only instruction was regarded as a primary duty of its professors.[10] According to the founder of the university, Wilhelm von Humboldt, research and instruction were naturally inseparable. They were also endless processes. Just as a student could never complete his education because intellectual (or spiritual) development was endless, so too was research a never-ending story.

Humboldt was not only a university reformer but also a philologist and a philosopher and by far the most influential of all ideologists of *Bildung* in this period. His influence was due to his rare way of combining theory and practice. During his years as a high-ranking civil servant responsible for education and culture in Prussia, he was able to translate his ideas into actual institutions and regulations. While his thoughts about *Bildung* were not very original, his way of transforming them into concrete institutional arrangements was special.

The Berlin type of university was unique because the research mission added to the official duties of the professor. But it was also unique because, just as Kant once proposed, it made the philosophy faculty central. It was most of all there that the student received *Bildung*, and it was also there that research had its natural home. Remarkable, too, was the crucial role allotted to philosophy itself. The spirit of philosophy was intended to imbue all branches of the university; the universality and unity of the university were to be guaranteed by philosophical research and the

[10] A huge secondary literature exists on the foundation of the University of Berlin and its importance. A classic overview is expressed in Stephen d'Irsay, *Histoire des universitées françaises et étrangères des origines à nos jours* (Paris, 1932), II, where significant comparisons are made. The more recent, largely English-language literature is well summarised in Björn Wittrock, 'Dinosaurs or Dolphins? The Rise and Resurgence of the Research-oriented University', in *The University System*, ed. Björn Wittrock and Aant Elzinga (Stockholm, 1985), 13ff. A good survey of the development of the German University is Charles E. McClelland, *State, Society, and University in Germany, 1700–1914* (Cambridge 1980). A fairly recent, very influential German interpretation of Berlin's history and still more of the university ideology represented there is Helmut Schelsky, *Einsamkeit und Freiheit, Idee and Gestalt der deutschen Universität*, 2nd edn (Düsseldorf, 1971). Schelsky's interpretation of Humboldt's ideas has been fundamentally challenged in Manfred Riedel's succinct article, 'Wilhelm von Homboldts Begründing der "Einheit von Forschung und Lehre" als Leitidee der Universität', *Zeitschrift fur Pädagogik*, 14 (1977), *Beiheft: Historische Pädagogik*, ed. Ulrich Herrmann, 231ff.

philosophical training of students. Moreover, according to Humboldt, the new university should realise the old but seldom fulfilled ideal of academic freedom, and this view appears to have achieved some success. In the course of the nineteenth century, the German university acquired a reputation for *Lehr- und Lernfreiheit*, i.e., for the freedom of the teacher to disseminate those theories deemed true, and the freedom for the student to choose both subjects of study and professor with whom to study. Of course, both liberties had their limitations and flaws in the highly illiberal Prusso-German society; but in comparison to other European and to North American universities of the day, the license, especially in religious matters, was substantial. The student really could choose a favourite teacher.

In order to comprehend Humboldt's contributions to the history of *Bildung*, it is more fruitful to study the documents concerning the institutional framework of the university than to scrutinise his philosophical writings on the topic. During his years in power, Humboldt composed a whole series of proposals, memoranda, and instructions. In many respects, the most down-to-earth is a report concerning the examination of State officials. Here, Humboldt stressed the necessity to assess both the candidate's natural talents and his acquired *Bildung*. The amount of cramming must not, says Humboldt – implying that it has usually been the practice – be decisive for the fate of the examinee. Needless to say, the candidate must have a certain amount of knowledge fitted exactly for his occupation *in spe*. However, this, the 'slavish' part of the examination, does not catch much of Humboldt's attention. It is the general part of the examination which excites and leads him to make some very interesting remarks.

It is definitely not expert, still less encyclopædic knowledge that Humboldt insists upon. Even the future financier may be excellent in his job without a full understanding of statistics, and a good diplomat does not necessarily need to master history. Two kinds of insight are, however, absolutely indispensable. Humboldt labels them the 'really material part' and the 'formal'. Central to the first is that portion of 'practical philosophy' (i.e., ethics and politics) upon which the law in force is founded and which concerns the aim and purpose of mankind and, in accordance therewith, of the State. Humboldt, whose ideas of *Bildung* mainly and in contrast to Herder and Mendelssohn, not to mention Pestalozzi, are limited to the university sphere, declares that 'nothing is as important to a high-ranking civil servant' as the conception that he 'in all respects has of mankind, its dignity and its ideal in its entirety'. Decisive here is both the 'intellectual limpidity' and the 'warmth and sensitivity' with which the civil servant can express his insights. Even respect for the 'lower social classes' is needed, and the examiner should be able to discern if the future civil servant will be a reformer or a conservative. Humboldt openly prefers the former, calling him 'liberal'[11] as contrasted to the 'narrow-minded' (*bornierter*) conservative. Humboldt stresses in a way very typical of the ideology of *Bildung* that the examiner must not follow any fixed questionnaire when evaluating the fundamental general knowledge and attitudes of his examinee. There are, he argues, thousands of ways to determine if the candidate is sufficiently open-minded. The formal portion of the required general knowledge of course is naturally always easier to mark. Here, the student's delivery and discourse are decisive, as is his capacity to follow and summarise an argument.[12]

From this document, we can see what *Bildung* according to Humboldt would be like in actual life. Reality itself, represented by the Prussian State and society in its rapid but far from harmonious development from the first decade of the nineteenth century up to the *Reichsgründung*, the formation of the German Empire in 1871, transformed Humboldt's design for a university and examination system. But while the new arrangements certainly had some remarkable traits in common with the original project, substantial differences existed. In the early nineteenth century the reshaped higher education system was intended to give spiritual strength to a country which had been subdued in a degrading war. In 1871, the new German empire was a dominating political and military power in Europe. Its economic and industrial growth was precipitous, and its universities – especially that of Berlin – and its *Wissenschaft* or output and methods of learning commanded the highest international esteem. In such a society, neither the university nor *Bildung* could possibly play the same role or be the same as before.

The best presentation of the German university at its apogee is still Friedrich Paulsen's far from objective but still marvellous account, *Essence and Historical Development of the German Universities* (1893) and *The German Universities* (*Die deutschen Universitäten*), published in 1902. But here we will follow the line of argument in a more eloquent and less comprehensive presentation, that of Hermann von Helmholtz' 1887 oration, *On the Academic Freedom of German Universities* (*Ueber die Akademische Freiheit der Deutschen Universitäten*). With this speech, Helmholtz, the famous physicist and physiologist, commenced his duties as Rector of the Berlin University.

---

[11] 'Liberal' as used here has the general meaning of open-hearted, generous, unprejudiced, and progressive. Not until some years after 1809 did it become the name of a political ideology.

[12] Wilhelm von Humboldt, 'Gutachten über die Organisation der Ober-Examinations-Kommission', in *Werke in fünf Bänden* (Darmstadt, 1960), IV, 79ff.

Helmholtz the scientist begins with the admission that historically the humanities not the physical sciences have been the centre of gravity of the German university. The physical sciences may therefore be regarded as intruders, pushed along by their accelerated growth in the nineteenth century and challenging the traditional organisational and philosophically curricular framework of the university. But he also maintains that the sciences have been successfully integrated into the university, and he points to his own rectorship as evidence of that fact.

A substantial part of his oration consists of a comparison between German, English, and French universities. In England, Helmholtz says, the students are trained to master their own language in a marvellous way, and the universities take special interest in the physical health and strength of undergraduates. Especially in the last respect, Oxford and Cambridge are far superior to the German universities, where duelling and fencing are the only sporting activities.

The French university, he says, is different again. It is a very rational construction. Helmholtz does not hide the fact that he greatly dislikes it. There, all research is located outside the universities, in special institutes, and university training is substantially vocational. Conventional talent is favoured at the expense of creative talent.

To Helmholtz, it is especially remarkable that the French university professors hold their positions quite independently of the approval of their students. Since attendance at lectures is compulsory, numbers are no proof of the teacher's success. How different in Germany! There, the students have their famous *Lernfreiheit*. When studying a subject, they have always several professors to choose from. In some cases, lectures and classes are compulsory – but this is never due to the demands of the university, but to the requirements of the State examination system. Furthermore, outside the university the student is totally free to behave as he or she desires, the penal code being the only limit on personal freedom.

Evidently, to Helmholtz *Lernfreiheit* formed the absolute prerequisite of *Bildung* which the university must further among its students. Another prerequisite was the *Lehrfreiheit* of the professors, which meant, for example, that in 1877 it was possible to propagate both the crudest materialism and the dogma of infallibility. However, while Helmholtz can state that the freedom to learn and the freedom to teach are essential prerequisites for obtaining *Bildung*, he cannot actually define the content of this compelling yet elusive conception.

Helmholtz is not unaware of the limitations of the university which he represents. It is far from a wealthy institution, and already this fact makes it dependent on the State. But as a typically loyal German professor of his day, he prefers to believe that the patronage of the State is propitious and that the State itself does in fact respect and guarantee university autonomy.[13]

The political context of Bildung

So far, we have only followed the German conception of *Bildung* in some of its German manifestations. Now, we must broaden the perspective. We need, for example, to compare *Bildung* with something called 'liberal education' and its varieties in Britain and the United States. Only comparative history can truly explain or illustrate the singularities of German intellectual development.

It was in the Reformation era that German universities acquired a strongly humanistic character.[14] The ideal was, however, far from that of Renaissance Italy. It was not the universal and harmonious man that was aimed at. According to the dismal Lutheran conception, after the Fall man's nature was destroyed by sin, and only divine grace could save him. The humanities, therefore, acquired a fundamentally different purpose, more immediate and more narrowly focused. Luther's own view of the usefulness of the humanities seems to have been rather down to earth. When talking about education, he exclaims: where are the preachers, jurists, and physicians to come from, if grammar and other rhetorical arts are not taught? Philip Melanchthon, his follower and the 'preceptor Germaniae' was a decided Aristotelian and paved the way for the Lutheran orthodoxy with its stiffness, intolerance, and strong sense of logical order and classification. In this special version of Aristotelianism, Aristotle's secular ethics played a limited role.

The devastating effects of the Thirty Years' War on German society and culture are well known. The negative effects on German language and German cultural self-confidence were far-reaching. It is instructive that the first German intellectual giant in the period after that war, Gottfried Wilhelm Leibniz, wrote in Latin or French and not in German. His pupil Christian Wolff was the first to make the German language peculiarly amenable to philosophy.

Prussia, which soon became the strongest single German state, underwent a rapid change in the eighteenth century. State power was strengthened not only through a very efficient army, but also through massive bureaucratisation requiring civil servants educated at universities. In the school and university reforms which followed, subjects seen as especially marked by their utility were decidedly favoured.

---

[13] Hermann von Helmholtz, *Ueber die akademische Freiheit der deutschen Universitäten. Rede beim Antritt des Rectorats an der Friedrichs-Universität zu Berlin ...* (Berlin, 1977), 5ff.

[14] Bruce A. Kimball, *Orators and Philosophers: A History of the Idea of Liberal Education* (New York, 1986). 90ff.

In a rather peculiar way, this very practical and somewhat ruthless tendency was sometimes counteracted by, sometimes helped by, new religious trends running somewhat counter to the effects of the Reformation. Most of all these were of a Pietist character distinguished by unworldliness, inner-direction (*Innerlichkeit*), and sentimentality. Life tended to be split up into private and public spheres, each with very different ideals: one favouring efficiency, the other meekness; one inclined towards activity, the other towards passivity; one leaning towards rationality, the other towards irrationality.

The Enlightenment came late to Germany and acquired its own direction for both political and religious reasons. It was nearly without exception favourable to religion but also propagated tolerance, openness, and once again *Innerlichkeit*. Politically, it was not very revolutionary (at least not before 1789) but aimed at the greater extension of freedom of speech, as we have already seen in the cases of Kant and Mendelssohn.

Given this rather humbling ancestry, it is not a simple task to explain how a period of remarkable cultural prosperity followed after about 1780. However, this epoch with all its great philosophers, scientists, writers, artists, and composers was the one in which the conception of *Bildung* thrived. As in the culture generally, *Bildung* itself was characterised by a tension between outer and inner, between activity and passivity, all of which could be traced back to an earlier epoch.

In his book *The German Catastrophe* (*Die Deutsche Katastrophe*), written immediately after the collapse of Hitler's 'empire', the noted historian Friedrich Meinecke, who was himself a representative of the old German tradition of *Bildung*, described the long period from 'die Goethezeit' as an ominous decline, reaching its logical culmination in the Nazi Reich. Originally, he says, there was a balance between reason and emotion and between power and intellect. Militarism, industrialism, and the mass movements – socialism and nationalism above all – destroyed a formerly prosperous culture, leaving only ruins in 1945.[15]

Meinecke's conception of history is a highly idealistic one. To him, ideas and ideals reign in the world and determine political, social, and economic circumstances. However, there is much that favours his view of German development. In the case of *Bildung*, the original, brittle balance between subjective and objective moments was lost, the *Bildung* became either something highly *Innerlich* or an attribute easily defined by university degrees, marks, and social rank.

The German university, about which Helmholtz uttered such impressive words, tended to be a free zone where freedom of speech was much more

---

[15] Friedrich Meinecke, *Die Deutsche Katastrophe. Betrachtungen und Erinnerungen* (Leipzig-Wiesbaden, 1946).

recognised than outside and where the search for an even 'higher' or *höhere Bildung* liberated students and teachers from the otherwise stiff demands for exacting and immediately useful work.

As Fritz K. Ringer has shown in his famous study of the 'German Mandarins', university educated people and most of all the professors defended their position and privileges against all changes. Especially after the World War, this defensive struggle was fierce and embittered, and it is remarkable that the allegedly unique *Bildung* accessible only at the universities was used as a weapon by the conservative defenders of the university.[16]

It must not be denied, however, that there were also earnest endeavours to revive the classical concept of *Bildung* in the 1920s. Eduard Spranger published a whole series of books dealing with the original philosophy of *Bildung* and its possible modern applications. Although an outspokenly conservative adherent of the German university system, his conception of *Bildung* cannot be called superficial in any respect.[17]

Originally, as we have shown, *Bildung* was the heart of the faculty of philosophy, and the subject of philosophy was regarded as the one which pre-eminently united all the different branches of learning. Yet in the nineteenth century, the great systems of integrated knowledge descending from the days of Schelling and Hegel divided into specialised studies. Epistemology, ethics, psychology, and the many other disciplines of the faculty of philosophy ceased to provide a unitary perspective. Historical study itself came to be regarded as yet another separate and privileged field of knowledge, although the advance of a historicist viewpoint brought with it a belief that as nothing could be understood except in an historical context, so the history of a discipline was the best method for understanding it. The philosophers themselves were after all historicists, and in actuality history and philosophy merged into one field of *Bildung*.

Classical studies and especially Greek, whose position was once central to the Humboldtian conception of *Bildung*, retained their prestige but turned out to be more and more specialised as separate philosophical or archaeological fields.

Despite fragmentation of the old philosophical faculty, so strong was the inherited belief in the special character of philosophy itself that its defenders continued to maintain the former premise that only through the study of philosophy could one become *gebildet*. Philosophy, they claimed,

---

[16] Fritz K. Ringer, *The Decline of the German Mandarins: The German Academic Community, 1890–1933* (Cambridge, MA, 1969), 87, argues that *Bildung* was the singlemost important tenet of the mandarin tradition.

[17] Eduard Spranger's main work is *Lebensformen. Geisteswissenschaftliche Psychologie und Ethik der Persönlichkeit*, 7th edn (Leipzig, 1930).

featured the basic principles behind all knowledge and provided a fundamental overall perspective. The strength and tenacity of this view is best demonstrated by saying that despite the growth of specialism in the German university, philosophy as a subject managed to retain its unique position in the German examination system.

After the World War, some radical university professors headed by Carl Heinrich Becker, who also served as minister of cultural affairs in the State of Prussia in the 1920s, faced up to the fact of the disintegration of the philosophical ideal of universal knowledge and tried to introduce sociology as the new unifying subject. Their efforts were not really successful in a Germany on the threshold of Nazism. Nor, one might add, could the classical Weberian conception of sociology as a comprehensive and historically-oriented science of society in its cultural, political, and economic evolution compete with the strength of formalised, self-referential systems of discourse in the economics of neo-classical marginalism and a correspondingly influential legal positivism. In fact, in the 1920s German sociology gradually developed in the direction of an equally formal and ahistorical mode of inquiry in the wake of efforts, most notably by von Wiese, to create a 'pure' relational and behavioural sociology.

The difficulties of bridging the widening gap between different specialties at the university were quite the same in Germany as in Britain and the United States. In all countries, specialism and professionalism made the idea of a fundamental stock of knowledge difficult to achieve. The simplest solution to this dilemma was a patchwork quilt of bits of knowledge from all or many different branches of knowledge. Sometimes, this kind of broad education was called *allgemeine Bildung*, the German counterpart of the Anglo-American notion of 'general education'. However, the history of *allgemeine Bildung* is rather more 'honourable', that is to say, represents a more forthright or sustained attempt to broaden a university education for technicians such as engineers than the piecemeal efforts characterising the history of general education in the English-speaking world, particularly America. For example, in the nineteenth century when subjects such as history and philosophy were introduced at the new universities of technology, it was to give future engineers the necessary *allgemeine Bildung*.[18] As in the case of *Bildung*, the humanist content of *allgemeine Bildung* was predominant.

After World War II the old ideas of *Bildung* and *allgemeine Bildung* met still more difficult obstacles when confronted with mass education. Even the outstanding spokesman for the old conceptions, Helmut Schelsky,

[18] Mikael Hård, 'Forskning, skolning, bildning. Carl Linde som teknikens institutionsbyggare' ('Research, Schooling, *Bildning*'), *Daedalus, Sveriges Tekniska museums årsbok*, 55 (1986).

whose *Solitude and Freedom* (*Einsamkeit und Freiheit*, 1910) is still the standard work on the classical German university tradition, seems to have surrendered to the increasing difficulties as indicated by the introduction to the second edition of his work in 1971. However, Schelsky found at least one remedy in interdisciplinary research, and the interdisciplinary University of Bielefeld is his creation just as much as Berlin is Humboldt's.[19]

Swedish *Bildning* in idea and practice

The social context of Bildning

As already mentioned, the German *Bildung* had its immediate counterpart in the Swedish *Bildning*. After only a few years, Herder's way of using *Bildung* to signify an educational process first and foremost was introduced into the Swedish language,[20] and a rich and varied use of the word *Bildning* especially distinguished the earlier decades of the nineteenth century. This period, labelled the Romantic or even the Neo-romantic in Swedish intellectual history, was characterised by heavy German influence. Kant, Schelling, and Hegel were the epigones, Goethe's and Hölderlin's poetry was imitated, German political ideas were introduced, and pedagogical ideas from the German-speaking world heavily influenced the school system at all levels.

German models succeeded a period in which France had been the cultural paragon. French influence, however (as is not surprising), had been strongest at court, capital, and among the nobility. German influence had its stronghold in the small towns of Uppsala and Lund, where the only universities were situated, and their character (as we might expect) was much more bourgeois, perhaps even petty-bourgeois, than aristocratic.

In modern Swedish, there is a fairly clear distinction between the words *Utbildning* (the German *Ausbildung*) and *Bildning*, the first denoting vocational training or at least a learning process aimed at a clearly-defined actual or practical goal. In short, one became *utbildad* in order to be a doctor or a lawyer, or to master Italian conversation or shorthand. *Bildning* is a word which, after some years of disrepute, has now been reintroduced to signify a learning process which is less narrowly 'useful' and where the subject's own leanings and interests play a substantial part in discerning what is to be learned. Although the distinction between *Bildning* and *Utbildning* was not often clear cut in the early nineteenth

---

[19] Schelsky, *Einsamkeit und Freiheit*, and Jürgen Kocka (ed.), *Interdisziplinarität: Praxis – Herausforderung – Ideologie* (Frankfurt, 1987).

[20] See *Bildning* in *The Dictionary of the Swedish Academy* (SAOB).

century, in time *Bildning* assumed the German meaning as both a process and the outcome of a process which results in a person of wide orientation and cultivation, who may even possess a keen critical ability.

Bildning was applicable to all forms of education, early as well as gymnasium and university. Its widespread acceptance has in fact much to do with its general connection with the question of Swedish literacy. In Sweden, as in many other European countries, discussions about compulsory primary education were very active in the early nineteenth century. The alphabetism of the Swedish people was already at an astonishingly high level, the result of the efforts of a highly dominant and committed Lutheran State Church (far more dominant than in religiously divided Germany) which had assumed an obligation to take care of the fundamental schooling of common people. A debate occurred, however, between those groups which simply wanted to raise the existing standard of schooling and those which argued that such efforts would only produce *Halvbildning*, that is to say, a half-educated populace not really conversant with serious issues. Such a situation, they said, was politically and socially dangerous.[21] In 1842 Parliament resolved the debate by creating a system of compulsory primary education which spread slowly through the large and sparsely populated country. This reform was parallel to many other fundamental changes in early nineteenth century Swedish society, such as urbanisation (which preceded slowly), the development of business and commerce (industrialisation, however, did not begin until the 1880s), and the increasing political and social influence of the bourgeoisie.

Many changes also occurred in the structure of secondary and higher education as a consequence of the spread of French revolutionary ideas. These resulted in the constitutional changes of 1809 which replaced royal absolutism with mixed government. Well before the constitutional changes of 1809, however, actually as early as the 1680s, members of the bourgeoisie had been penetrating the lower nobility, and the lower nobility itself had been aspiring to civil service careers generally dominated by the higher nobility. After 1809 legislation was passed stipulating that all government offices should be within the reach of every qualified aspirant. While the high nobility was not thereby totally replaced, the opportunity structure was greatly liberalised, putting new pressures on secondary and especially university education and producing changes in the curriculum and examination system.

[21] Nils Runeby, 'Varken fågel eller fisk: Om den farliga Halvbildning' ('Neither Bird nor Fish: On the Dangers of Quasi-Bildning'), in *Vetenskapens träd. Idéhistoriska studier tillägnade Sten Lindroth*, ed. Tore Frangsmyr (Stockholm, 1974), 157ff.

Historically, the university examination system was relaxed, consisting for the most part (as elsewhere in Europe) of a set of 'disputations' where the student argued and defended several 'theses' or perhaps an entire dissertation, which either he or his professor had authored. The standards were low, and the examination itself had little effect on chances for upward occupational and social mobility. Noblemen's sons entered the university as adolescents of fifteen or sixteen or even younger. They were instructed by personal tutors, generally older students of humble origins, visited lectures of their own choosing, and moved on to posts in the military or government without much ado.

Improving the examination system by making it both stricter and more impartial had limited results, but major changes did in fact occur in the course of the nineteenth century. Around 1800, oral examinations became more frequent, difficult, and in most cases decisive for the professional future of the student. Earlier, eloquence and elegance – a courtly style used in conjunction with a scholastic exercise – in the art of defending and attacking different types of academic theses in front of an academic audience had been the main requirement. Henceforth, the capacity to memorise the content of a series of lectures and textbooks became essential. Students themselves regretted the change, but so did many professors, rising in Academic Senate meetings to denounce eloquently the 'examination frenzy'. One of the consequences of a more demanding control system was that the different subjects tended to become much more separated than before, and specialisation started to appear. Each professor began to claim that his subject required more insight and rigour from students than those in neighbouring fields. In short, stricter examinations and specialties went hand in hand.

Evidence for the growth of specialisation and the diversification of the university curriculum can be collected from other areas of academic life, but is particularly apparent from the history of professorial chairs. In the eighteenth century, most professors occupied more than one chair. They started their professorial life in one subject and changed chairs in order to improve both income and status. The most successful ended their academic careers as professors of theology.

The progression from chair to chair was made possible because in some sense the general education of a Swedish academic provided the kind of intellectual flexibility which allowed him to roam from subject to subject, that is, assuming the subjects were reasonably connected in the first place. Thus, a typical career in the philosophical faculty might start with the teaching of Latin poetry, oriental languages, or ethics (all of which were low-paying) and go on to Latin declamation, logic and metaphysics, ending in the first chair in the prestigious faculty of theology, which also carried with it the deanship of a cathedral. Even many professors of jurisprudence began their academic careers in the philosophical faculty.[22]

However, the pattern was different in the medical sciences, where chairholders were likely to remain. The great Linnaeus at Uppsala could not even begin to entertain the possibility of a chair of theology to be bestowed after a migration of three or four chairs. Almost by their very nature technical and practical, and less clearly associated with a general academic education than the subjects of the philosophical faculty, the medical, natural, and experimental sciences lent themselves to specialisation; and professors in these subjects could not easily exchange inferior for more lucrative and prestigious posts.

Nevertheless, even within the philosophical faculty, the pattern of migration so characteristic of Swedish (and German) universities became a rare phenomenon after about 1800. This rather dramatic change, which was not much commented upon at the time, coincided with the introduction of the stricter examination system. The cause of the shift was without doubt the deepening cleavages between most subjects, each of which demanded some unique competence from its chairholder.

It is hardly surprising that the spread of specialisation at the universities is related to the acute interest in *Bildning* and *Bildung* that one encounters in Sweden and Germany in the early nineteenth century. Likewise, those who most fiercely attacked the new examination system in Sweden were identical with those who were most eager to find a new higher *Bildning*. We must not err in thinking that such critics were merely reactionaries in educational or other matters, whose thoughts harkened back to the old university. On the contrary, they were very unhappy with the earlier state of affairs, which according to them was characterised by pedantry and a misplaced predilection for 'useful' knowledge. The leading ideologists of a university *Bildning* were trying to find a new solution to the problem of using education to develop a common fund of knowledge.

Most of them represented the subjects belonging to the group which earlier had formed a philosophical unity. However, in the Romantic period, there were important exceptions. Friedrich Schelling and his followers, who played a very important part in Sweden too, searched for an organic unity consisting of all branches of knowledge, including those of artists. Schelling developed his ideas in a booklet published in 1803 called *Lectures on the Methods of Academic Studies* (*Vorlesungen über der Methode des Akademischen Studiums*), which in fact is one of the most

---

[22] I have studied this career pattern in detail in my book, *Den synliga handen. Anders Berch och ekonomiämnena vid 1700 – talets svenska universitet* (*The Visible Hand: Anders Berch and Economics at the Eighteenth-Century Swedish University*) (Stockholm, 1986), 74–80.

important anticipations of the University of Berlin.[23] Several adherents of
his programme were natural scientists who tried to rescue their own
subjects from the kind of isolation which characterised science in the
eighteenth century. Their remedy was to purge them of their mechanistic,
Newtonian direction, which for nearly a century had heavily influenced the
world picture in Sweden as well as in Germany, and to open them to the
influence of the new organic, romantic philosophy.

Bildning *and Swedish popular education*

There were, however, Swedes like Carl Adolph Agardh who developed
their own ideas of *Bildning*; and while perhaps Romantics, were not
themselves necessarily followers of Schelling. Agardh is particularly
interesting because he illustrates for us what was and perhaps still remains
the substantial difference between Swedish and other intellectual traditions
there at stake, namely, the greater interest in popular education that
continues to this day.

By training a natural scientist, Agardh earned (and retains) international
renown as the 'Linnaeus of algae'. The chair which he held at the
University of Lund combined botany with economics in a way reminiscent
of the very utilitarian Swedish eighteenth-century university practice. He
ended his career as a bishop, and he started to study theology in such an
assiduous way that after some years he became a prolific author. In rare
and personal fashion, he seems to have realised his own *Bildung*
programme.

In his view of the university, Agardh came very close to the original
German ideal represented by Berlin. In the Swedish *Riksdag*, of which he
was a member, he eloquently argued that all vocational training should be
separated from the university. He expressed this view in the debates going
on in the 1830s about the preparation of future clergymen. As in the case
of the famous German theologian Ernst Schleiermacher before him, he
maintained that all professional training should be located outside or at
least at the periphery of the university, the chief educational task of which
was to remain the free, universal, and undirected *Bildung* of its students.

In this debate, Agardh also claimed that Swedish universities had been
destroyed by frequent and unnecessary compulsory examinations, which
only encouraged pedantry inside and served the ends of control outside. In

---

[23] The cited works by Schelling appear in *Sämmtliche Werke*, ed. Karl Friedrich August
Schelling (Stuttgart and Augsburg, 1859), I:5. The *Vorlesungen* have also been published
separately or in other collections dealing with university questions, for example, *Die Idee
der deutschen Universität. Die fünf Grundschriften aus der Zeit ihrer Neubegründung durch
klassischen Idealismus und romantischen Realismus* (Darmstadt, 1956).

Germany, Agardh told the *Riksdag*, there was a sharp dividing line between real university instruction and the examination of future civil servants. This cleavage was necessary since the tasks of research and *Bildung* on one side and practical life on the other were incompatible.[24]

Turning to the question of the curriculum itself, Agardh argued that the value of classical languages was seriously overestimated and the value of the natural sciences greatly underestimated. He did not advocate the study of the natural sciences because of their superior utility – a defence common at the time – but because they were an essential aspect of *Bildning*, and he asked that their position in the curriculum of elementary schools and gymnasium be appreciably strengthened.

Agardh was also a keen supporter of popular education, in his youth being one of those who introduced Pestalozzi's ideas to Sweden.[25] In his old days as a bishop in Karlstad and in this capacity the head of the school system in his diocese, he worked intensely to amend the instruction in science at all levels of schooling, claiming that ordinary people, because they mostly dealt with practical, material affairs, could more easily acquire a knowledge of nature than of human affairs.[26]

The narrowing of the ideal and practice of Bildning

In 1852, after a long series of public debates and royal commissions wherein it was held that the existing higher education system did not correspond either to the scientific or practical demands of the time, all Swedish universities were reformed in a way which corresponded fairly well to what Humboldt and others had brought about in Germany some decades earlier. Research and not just teaching was declared a primary duty of the professors; and in order to receive degrees, students now had to write their own theses. *Bildning* remained, none the less, being regarded as necessary for acquiring flexibility in life, direction, and maturity. The

[24] See the remarks of Carl Adolph Agardh in the debates in the Clerical Estate of the *Riksdag* in 1834 as reprinted in *Handlingar rörande prestbristen i Lunds stift, samt prestbildningen vid Lunds universitet* (*Proceedings Concerning the Scarcity of Clergymen at the University of Lund*) (Lund, 1836), 17ff and 58ff. A special copy deposited in the Uppsala University Library (K138a) is also accompanied by a collection of letters, booklets, and other documents which altogether form the most comprehensive view of Swedish ideas of a university to be found in the early nineteenth century.

[25] Agardh and his friend Martin Bruzelius translated Pestalozzi's *Elementarbücher* into Swedish (published as *Elementar-Böcker* at Lund in 1812). In his introduction to the volume, Agardh interpreted Pestalozzi's ideas in his own way.

[26] Agardh, *Försök till en Statsekonomisk Statistik* (Essay on a Statistical Survey in Political Economy) (Karltad, 1852), I:1, 168. My portrait of Agardh appears in an essay on the relationship between him and the famous chemist, Jöns Jakob Berzelius, and between him and Israel Hwasser, the 'romantic' Professor of Medicine. Forthcoming in a volume on Berzelius edited by Evan Melhado.

problem, as in Germany, was to combine it with a certain emphasis on specialised work. The solution adopted was to institute a series of preliminary degrees for future doctors, priests, and lawyers, which, according to the reformers, would furnish the students with knowledge and skills necessary both for their general cultivation and future profession. Even for those who only studied in the philosophical faculty but intended to be schoolmasters, a compulsory programme of studies was specified.

Philosophy was still central in most preliminary degrees (ethics for the students of law, theoretical philosophy for the others) but also history and mostly Latin. In fact, this system came rather close to what had been practised in the earlier part of the nineteenth century. Still, it is a highly interesting curriculum as it tells us about the current ideas of what a good academic general education or *Allmänbildning* was thought to be. As Wilhelm von Humboldt had already argued, the future State official had to know not only current rules and regulations but also their philosophical foundations. In the same way, the doctor could not be a good doctor without knowing something about the position of nature according to the views of philosophers, and the vicar was in the grip of superstition if he did not base his faith on the solid ground of idealist speculation.

As many notes from lectures given to students preparing their preliminary degrees are preserved, we have a good idea about the education they received. In philosophy, the world was explained in terms of that kind of idealist philosophy which was especially dominant at Uppsala University, whose most important representative was Christopher Jacob Boström (1797–1866). According to Boström, sensorial knowledge was misleading and illusory if not guided in the first instance by thought. External or 'objective' nature played a very limited and secondary part in his system, where everything which really existed only existed in the form of 'persons' defined as entities possessing self-consciousness. The highest person was no less than God, and the second highest was the State viewed as an organic unity. The State, Boström said, was the highest part of the 'official' or 'public' society (*samhälle*), whereas the people as a whole constituted the highest private person or society. The lower private persons were (in proper order) the Four Estates, the municipalities, and families. Boström's social philosophy was strictly hierarchical, and those who occupied an inferior position in his classification could not fully understand those holding a superior one. The higher the position, the higher the intelligence ascribed to it. Altogether, this established the premise that a person lower in rank could never properly criticise one who was higher.[27]

[27] On Boström, see Svante Nordin, *Den Boströmska skolan och den svenska idealismens fall* (The Boström School and the Decline of Swedish Idealism) (Lund, 1981); Christoffer Jakob Boström, *The Philosophy of Religion*, translated with introduction by Victor

The hierarchical philosophy of Boström and his followers almost naturally evoked protests. For other students, however, their doctrine gave some kind of philosophical justification for their own favoured social position. In a period when industrialism, materialism, and other 'enemies' of the traditional university seemed more and more threatening to the self-confidence of future civil servants, it was comforting to hear that in reality those challenges were either illegitimate or mere fabrication.

The historians, who most students also encountered when preparing their preliminary degrees, were much more empirical than Boström, but their instruction was none the less highly idealist. In Latin, another compulsory subject, students had to re-learn what they had learned earlier at school and to improve their skill in translating a Swedish text into Latin.

By and large, this meant that in practice the obligatory university *Bildning* which the students received was highly traditional; but it scarcely fulfilled the subjective side of the original concept of *Bildning* as conceived by Agardh and others. Most of all, the degrees prepared students for a future position far above the social level of most Swedes. The entrenched position of this curriculum in the Swedish university system meant that new and fresh intellectual currents in the late nineteenth century did not substantially influence the degree programme. Intellectual innovations such as Darwinism were of course available to all Swedish students from the 1870s or at least the 1880s onwards, but nothing thereof was said in lectures necessary for the preliminary degrees.

Compared to liberal education in Britain or the USA, the university *Bildning* in Sweden, just as in its counterpart in Germany, had a predominantly intellectual content. In Sweden and Germany, the university assumed no responsibility for the other dimensions of education. Neither the Swedish nor the German university stood *in loco parentis* to undergraduates, and the physical or psychological health of students was a private affair to be handled outside the official boundaries of the university. Residential institutions on the English or American collegiate models did not exist. Students customarily rented separate rooms in the apartments and houses of burghers.

To some extent, the absence of a parietal element in Swedish higher education was attributable to the rising age of undergraduates (although the same phenomenon did not equally affect nineteenth-century ideas of moral guidance in Britain and America). After 1830 age at entrance seldom

Emanuel and Robert Nelson Beck (New Haven and London, 1962); and my book, *Att förändra världen – men med måtta: Det svenska 1800-talet speglat i C. A. Agardhs och C. J. Boströms liv och verk* (*To Change the World – But Moderately: Sweden in the Nineteenth Century as reflected in the Life and Work of C. A. Agardh and C. J. Boström*) (Stockholm, 1991).

fell below eighteen. Many students were, in fact, even older and did not require the kind of personal superintendence associated with younger students. The situation had been somewhat different in prior centuries. Earlier, in the seventeenth and eighteenth centuries, many (and mostly aristocratic) students arrived at the university at a quite young age, and a personal tutor supervised and to some extent watched over them.

But another reason for the absence of a fully developed system of officially recognised residence has to do with the social composition of Swedish universities and of Swedish society generally. Sweden never had a large, broad-based gentlemanly class of wealthy landlords whose wastrel sons, as in England, drove up the social costs of residence. In fact, a 'folksy' tone was already evident in the universities in the seventeenth and eighteenth centuries as large numbers of sons of farming families began to enter the universities. The numbers of them increased substantially in the second quarter of the nineteenth century. Students of humble origin attended the Swedish universities in far greater proportions than in England or Germany, and the so-called 'peasant student' (*bondestudenter*) was a well-known figure at Uppsala or Lund. Such students required lower-cost instruction. Their economic resources were very limited. In the nineteenth century especially, many poor students attended lectures irregularly and only for short periods, having to earn a living as private tutors for the sons of wealthier people living outside the university towns.

Bildning *and* Folkbildning

In 1902, the state of preliminary or first degrees was debated in the Riksdag. According to reformers, the university education of lawyers, physicians, and teachers took far too long. They claimed that future professionals wasted a good part of their lives as students and therefore suggested that preliminary degrees be abolished. In Sweden, they argued, the value of *allmänbildning* or general education was over-stressed. 'Abroad', critics said, having in mind most of all Germany and the other Nordic countries, professional training was just professional training and nothing else.

The advocates of reform were highly influential, the most important of them being Ernst Trygger, Professor of Law at the university in Uppsala and a member of the First Chamber, where he eventually became the leader of the conservatives. After a few years, he resigned his chair and began a career as a State official, obtaining the highest possible appointments, and eventually he was made University Chancellor.

Trygger was the leading proponent of the view that the concept of *Bildning* and the programme of studies following from it was highly impractical. The State, he and others asserted, did not really have any need for supposedly educated people who only possessed a hodgepodge of very general insights. At the university, *Bildning* had become virtually identical with the preliminary university degrees, whose content had dwindled into a rather *jejeune* mixture. Professional education, said Trygger, was the real task of the universities.

Trygger and his adherents were victorious; and after some reports by a government commission, preliminary degrees in the faculties of law and medicine were discarded. In the faculty of the sciences and the arts, a new type of degree specially designed for future secondary school teachers was established. Even there, the importance of general education or *Bildning* was reduced, while professional training was favoured.[28]

Even though for some university teachers the reforms meant a lesser or reduced position for their own subjects, especially for philosophy, whose long-standing privileged status now came to an end, the government changes evoked astonishingly few protests at the Swedish universities. University representatives, it is true, sat on the government commission, but as loyal civil servants they acquiesced in the decisions of the majority. It is also the case that philosophy achieved a special importance in secondary education by becoming an autonomous subject at the gymnasium; but this was meagre compensation, for its role there was decidedly secondary. To the reformers, however, this level seemed to be the correct one for general education. Humboldt's and Agardh's idea that the university should be the place for the free cultivation of mind was far away.

In one respect, the successful reformers in Parliament were wrong. Even before the reform, the position of general education at Swedish universities was somewhat weaker than in neighbouring countries, and after the change it was weaker yet. In Germany, where higher education was the self-evident model for most Swedes, the position of philosophy remained particularly strong. In other Scandinavian countries, the preliminary degree was saved. In Denmark, in fact, this degree lasted until the early 1960s, and in Norway the so-called *philosophicum* still exists!

Seemingly, the conclusion from such facts would be that all the grand Swedish ideas about *Bildning* and *allmänbildning* dating from the nineteenth century were fading away around the turn of the century. Goal-oriented 'useful' professional education was introduced everywhere at the highest educational level. If at the German technical universities, philosophy and history were seen as necessary for the future engineer's educational breadth or *allgemeine Bildung*, the Swedish engineer was

[28] On the commission and its results, see Sven-Eric Liedman, 'Civil Servants Close to the People: Swedish University Intellectuals and Society at the Turn of the Century', *History of European Ideas*, *VIII* (1987).

taught to pay little respect to basic knowledge in the arts and sciences, except for those portions of mathematics, physics, and chemistry deemed necessary for his occupation.

To this, two substantial observations are now required:

Discussions about *Bildning* carried on at least up to the 1950s in Sweden. But now this talk rather unambiguously concerned only education in subjects conventionally regarded as humanistic. It is true that the word *Bildning* really did first of all denote such studies as Greek and Latin, philosophy, history, and literature, but Agardh was far from alone in arguing that the natural sciences (and, of course, mathematics!) likewise had much to do with the process of self-education called *Bildning*. In the twentieth century, when the humanities lost ground to natural science, technology, and after World War II to the social sciences, the case for *Bildning* tended to be only a detail in a broad defensive strategy of protecting support for the humanities. But once upon a time *Bildning* had been a word associated with personal emancipation and dignity and a dedication to public life. By and by the conception narrowed and degraded; it came to mean the preservation of old memories, preparation for the meditative life, and singularly good manners.

We must look elsewhere in Swedish culture and history to find much more of the original vigour of the idea of *Bildning*. It was in fact preserved in the different popular movements so typical of modern Sweden. Most of all, this means the Labour Movement, which includes the trade unions, the social democrats, and, from the 1920s, the communists. The temperance movement was also an important part of the modern history of *Bildning*, especially in the decades just before and after the turn of the century.

In all these popular movements in Sweden, adult education was a central concern, and in Swedish adult education is called *Folkbildning*, which means the *Bildning* of the common people. According to a formerly widespread idea, *Bildning* was important for all facets of social and political life. It was essential for furthering human dignity and was as important in this respect as political rights or influence, social security, and humane working conditions. In fact, all kinds of knowledge were important and desirable. Consequently, in study circles and at folk high schools everything from astronomy to poetry was studied. Cheap books – good novels and solid popular science – were published and widely read, and temperance lodges and local trade unions collected volumes which formed decent libraries open to their members. Here, therefore, the concept of *Bildning* was just as alive and vital as it had been among learned people a century earlier. Of course, the subjects studied were not the same as then. Classics played a much more modest part if at all, as did philosophy. But natural science and technology were always important to the *Bildning* of the workers; the social sciences, economics, and political science were also valued.

Needless to say, a good portion of these studies for the sake of *Bildning* were undertaken out of practical considerations. Many young workers dreamed of being mechanics or even (civil) engineers, and not a few realised their cherished dream. For many, the studies served the political cultivation of the working class and enabled them to undertake such civic responsibilities as chairing meetings, taking minutes, or speaking in public. Many popular guides about such matters were published and widely circulated. In his spare time, the Swedish labourer instructed himself in how to be an efficient committee man.[29]

The upper classes, educated at school and university, did not need adult education to given them self-assurance. Therefore, the idea of compulsory schooling providing worker's children with the same good start in life was an attractive idea. However, disagreements about how to proceed divided social democrats. In the 1930s the Social Democratic minister of education, Artur Engberg, strove for the preservation of the old school system with its sharp dividing line between a compulsory school and a highly selective junior secondary school leading on to gymnasium and university. Of course, Engberg wanted to give the workers' children better opportunities than before to reach the elite school, the preservation of which was still thought necessary for the survival of a traditional *Bildning*. Most of all, Engberg stressed the importance of the ancient classics![30]

After the war, Engberg's programme was less attractive to later social democrats and Swedish society generally. The ideas of a comprehensive school open to all became strong and soon victorious. At the same time, a highly utilitarian view of knowledge became dominant. All ideas of *Bildning* for its own sake – or, better, for the sake of self-cultivation – seemed outdated. Dead languages, history, and literature lost ground rapidly, whereas social science, economics, natural science, and technology assumed a much stronger position. For obvious reasons, German influence, so pervasive for more than a century, weakened drastically, whereas ideas, vogues, and styles from the United States became popular. In many respects, the new comprehensive school, which finally was realised in the early 1960s, was constructed on the American model. Of course, this

---

[29] Ronny Ambjörnsson, *Den skötsamme arbetaren. Idéer och ideal i ett norrländskt sågverkssamhälle* (The Conscientious Worker: Ideas and Ideal in a Sawmill Village in Norrland (1988), 115ff).
[30] See Bernt Gustafsson, 'Socialism och bildning – Artur Engbergs ideologi' ('Socialism and *Bildning* – The Ideology of Artur Engberg'), in *Ideologi och institution. Om forskning och högre utbildning 1880–2000*, eds. Sven-Eric Liedman and Lennart Olausson (Stockholm, 1988).

influence was highly selective, as a comparison of the different forms of general education today makes quite clear.

The young American student receives a general education while an undergraduate in university colleges of letters and science (or arts and science) or four-year liberal arts colleges. The Swedish homologue of general education is, as we already know, *allmänbildning*. According to the official position, *allmänbildning* is provided at the comprehensive school, whereas the gymnasium and university curriculum are predominantly vocational.[31] While historically speaking this may not make sense, the present-day rationale of the distinction is quite clear. From the moment that it was first conceived, the comprehensive school was expected to provide pupils with what in an earlier day the lower classes had to arduously learn as adults. The fact that the stock of knowledge which nowadays is taught at comprehensive school differs substantially from the old radical conception of *allmänbildning* does not change the official position. *Per definitionem*, the comprehensive school furnishes all Swedes with their general education.

Reviving Bildning *at the university*

In everyday Swedish, the words *Bildning* and *allmänbildning* became much less frequently used from the 1940s onwards. When in the 1940s and 1950s they tended to disappear from everyday language, the world *Bildning* had either degenerated into a slogan in a reactionary critique of every endeavour to broaden access to higher education, or it had been merely a reference to a kind of superficial gentility. *allmänbildning*, which once was the catchword for radical popular movements aimed at the important role of the diffusion of all kinds of knowledge among ordinary people, had lost all of its strength and now meant just the activity of collecting a great many bits of knowledge, the intellectual counterpart of stamp-collecting.

But in the 1980s *Bildning* and *allmänbildning* made an astonishing recovery. The words appear to have regained some of their original vigour. Why?

To a large extent, their revitalisation is part of the traditions of Swedish social democracy which adopted *Folkbildning* and *allmänbildning*. While weakened, these traditions nevertheless survive since they are so strongly associated with Swedish politics. Also, the interest in *Bildning* can be viewed as a reaction on the part of some to the ongoing crude

---

[31] See Mac Murray, 'Utbildningsexpansion. jämlikhet och avlänkning. Studier i utbildnings-politik och utbildningsplanering 1933–1985' ('Educational Expansion, Equality, and Policies of Diversion: A Fifty-Year Perspective of the Swedish Educational System'), *Gothenburg Studies in Educational Science*, 66 (1988), 137ff.

disparagement of knowledge as such. Among most politicians and industrialists, research and education are highly valued if economically profitable but not as vehicles of self-cultivation. Art and literature are seen as superficial ornaments – and as objects of investment. Mass media favour exactly the kind of passivity and immediate, thoughtless satisfaction which the old philosophers of *Bildung* and *Bildning* detested so ferociously.

Not a few critics, alarmed at the declining quality of political culture and standards of public debate, fear that unless arrested this decline will inevitably endanger Sweden's unique democratic culture. They notice that as portrayed on television, a political party is not distinguished by its principles and values so much as by the party leader's prevailing media image. Social problems are not treated as central issues to be faced by an informed polity but as some sort of scandalous 'affair' with its special scoundrels and heroes.

In this respect, the background to the revival of *Bildning* seems to resemble what had been happening in the United States in the 1980s, although debate there on liberal education was more intense than in Sweden. But the similarities notwithstanding, there still appear to be substantial differences between the two countries, differences rooted in their distinct social structures and separate national histories. The new Swedish debate on *Bildning* and *allmänbildning* has its roots in the modern development of Sweden. If *Bildning* most of all denoted the cultivation of civil servants in the nineteenth century, *allmänbildning* was a central concept in the popular movements so typical of Swedish modernisation and democratisation. Especially after World War II, a definite solution about how to inculcate *Bildning* and especially *allmänbildning* seemed to be found in the establishment of the new comprehensive school.

The comprehensive school was especially attractive to those who still believed in the original idea of *Bildung* that learning and knowledge derived from a combination of objective and subjective factors. Ideals of knowledge existed objectively, as it were, but in striving to gain them, an individual expanded his own self-awareness and over time developed into a unique human being. This was a life-long or continuous development (and hence has some affinities with American 'continuing' education, as adult university extension programmes have been re-christened). The goal was no less than the older goals of *Bildning* and *allmänbildning*, and these, in their historical derivation, appear to mean much more for individual growth than the English phrase 'general education' connotes. Those who embraced the comprehensive school as the twentieth-century purveyor of nineteenth-century ideas of personal development naturally deplored the widespread notion that the value of an academic subject could only be determined by a direct and narrow utility aimed at the pupil who was facing a concrete life situation. They also rejected the idea that the importance of an academic subject was measured by its supposed intrinsic difficulty. According to this attitude, only two kinds of subjects could ever exist, 'hard' and 'soft' ones. The former were essential for the practice of a profession like engineering or medicine, or for the performance of a skilled trade. Subjects like history, geography, and literature, the old arts and humanities subjects generally, were 'soft' and hence dispensable.

But however exhilarated are the present-day supporters of *Bildning* about the possibilities of the comprehensive model of schooling, they have had to face the competition of their old enemy from the nineteenth century. The supporters of *Utbildning* have refused to leave the comprehensive schools to them. The quarrel or debate between two different conceptions of knowledge has gone on in Sweden since the nineteenth century, as we have seen, as indeed it has gone on in England and especially the United States, and, making allowances for the different conceptions of general education, in broadly similar ideological fashion.

The common difficulty is in finding a way to make ideals of general education or self-cultivation or breadth of outlook operative in the highly specialised and highly technical world of the late twentieth century, of discovering a way to gain a perspective on the scattered fields of human knowledge as a possible opening to wisdom and creativity. To the old exponents of *Bildung*, the study of philosophy seemed to offer such perspective. Later on in the nineteenth century, history was the favoured medium. In this century, not a few have claimed that sociology has the capacity to offer integrated and comprehensive views.

But despite a flurry of interest in the 1980s, the discussion about a unifying discipline seems outdated in the Sweden of today. The reputation of sociology has reached a nadir. An interest in philosophical questions is increasing, but more philosophers are themselves highly specialised. Perhaps to many, an historical perspective, especially on science and on political ideologies, is a correct and possible approach.

But no one disciplinary solution appears to be sufficient for Sweden, and certainly the 'traditional' American liberal education panacea of a hodgepodge of self-contained modules, some electives, some requirements, is not compatible with the Swedish school or university system. In Sweden the training of a doctor, an engineer, or a teacher starts immediately after arrival at university; he or she has no preliminary undergraduate studies to encounter before career training commences.

However (and predictably), one American experiment has attracted Swedish attention, and that is the 'core curriculum' as advocated at Harvard in the Henry Rosovsky Report of the 1980s. At the University of Lund, the first steps towards such a curriculum have been taken. It is even called a 'core curriculum' in Swedish, a fact which must be seen as the sign of the faulty knowledge of Swedish intellectual history. Of course, what is intended is a revival of the old Swedish preliminary degree, the Norwegian *philosophicum* of today. This also seems to be the most appropriate Swedish name.

It does not seem sensible to argue that a new Swedish *philosophicum* would offer any solution to the problem of *Bildning*. In the full sense of the word, *Bildning* presupposes a free choice. In this respect, the American elective system seems more acceptable than a core curriculum, but only as an idea, not as a curriculum composed of a huge list of modular fragments of what in Sweden would be wholly autonomous course subjects. The Swedish choices would more properly resemble the English single-subject courses – history, philosophy, physics, astronomy. All to a certain extent could be made available throughout higher education, even in the professional faculties.

It may be objected that these disciplinary subjects still remain specialties. Of course, this is true. But at the same time, every subject has its perspective-opening traits, which make it a candidate for *Bildning*. It contains theories and puzzles which are connected with still more encompassing theories and puzzles. It raises questions which are linked to still broader questions. One may say that each subject has its philosophical, i.e., epistemological, logical, ethical, and aesthetic dimensions. Similarly, if a field of study has a future, it also has a history; and this history cannot simply be handed over to the historian, since the historian needs the assistance of the practitioner of the field in question. In many respects, a subject is an enclosed world, functioning as a society in miniature. It is, as Burton Clark says in his contribution to this volume, a 'small world'. But every subject also has a social context or set of wider relationships that must be studied and understood, and there are neighbourly disciplines on its borders requiring attention, not to mention neighbours with whom relations are still in need of cultivation. Furthermore, an academic subject needs resources from outside, and its practitioners are consequently part of a much larger universe of institutions and social arrangements. Approached in this way, a single-subject university curriculum becomes a broad and integrated education. The whole topic is indeed worthy of attention from the sociologists of knowledge.

There is also the question of whether a 'general' curriculum is, in the present Swedish context, rather too elementary for university work. These are difficult questions, but we must at least avoid one common error. General knowledge only appears to be 'elementary' when contrasted with specialised knowledge as represented today in the disciplinary organization of universities. To this, I would say that all the subject matter which we now look at as general knowledge is not truly elementary. It is a product not only of pedagogic considerations but also of bold abstract generalisations made in the past combined with theories and empirical work. Why not try again to use the single-subject curriculum – paradoxically – to devise a general education to produce men and women who are *bildade*?

This, I maintain, is what we have to do to revive the old ideal of *Bildning* or *Bildung*. I am not sure that such a revival is feasible in the actual Swedish higher education system, in which the central State bureaucracy still plays an all too important part and where the influence from industry is rapidly growing. But at least it is a remarkable fact that the old, encompassing concept of *Bildning* has been recently revived. According to this concept, to be *bildad* does not mean to know a little about everything, but to be able to reflect, in a personal and responsible way, on fundamental problems which meet in all branches of knowledge. The reappearance of this concept must indicate some kind of need in today's higher education, a demand for an Isis to return from Byblos with the body of the once-venerated Osiris.

A related discussion has started up in Sweden about *allmänbildning* in primary and secondary education. Of course, this discussion involves an even more encompassing idea of general education. However interesting, it does not belong to this presentation.

Part 2

The State, the university, and the professions

3 The transformation of professional education in the nineteenth century

Rolf Torstendahl

Introduction

Concepts

The problem of this chapter is mainly descriptive, but to solve the descriptive task a theoretical basis had to be laid. One part of this basis concerns professions, another science and education. A few initial considerations are consequently necessary concerning both aspects.

It is not possible to write an article on professional education in general in the nineteenth century. There was not one single type of professional education, nor was there any single profession that we could label 'archetypical'. Many different routes led to professional standing: apprenticeship, university courses, and specialised technical institutes all played a role in creating a professional society. Furthermore, when dealing with Scandinavia and the European Continent it is necessary to rely on a definition of the term 'profession' which is different from English language usage, for in the parts of Europe which are not English-speaking the concept 'profession' is not of domestic origin, though now imported and used in sociological discourse.

'Professions' are, generally speaking, 'knowledge-based groups'. These groups, furthermore, are defined in terms of their identification with their particular knowledge base and found their market strategy on their exclusive access to this particular kind of knowledge. There are two main scholarly approaches to the definition of professions.[1] The first may be called 'essentialist' in that it tries to pinpoint those properties that are meant to be 'essential' or characteristic of all professions. This approach is therefore *a priori*. A second or *a posteriori* approach can be termed 'strategic'. It deduces professional values from the conduct or actions of

---

[1] Rolf Torstendahl, 'Essential Properties, Strategic Aims and Temporal Development: Three Approaches to Theories of Professionalism', in *Professions in Theory and History: Rethinking the Study of the Professions in Europe and North America*, ed. Michael Burrage and Rolf Torstendahl (London, 1990).

professional groups in various social circumstances. For empirical analysis, good reasons exist for combining both approaches. Thus, we can say that in order to be a professional group, a knowledge based group must rally around a body of abstract knowledge and use a protective strategy. Finally, I have also suggested – agreeing with arguments put forward by Michael Burrage, Konrad Jarausch, and Hannes Siegrist[2] – that a historical dimension is necessary for the analysis, for clearly professionalism has not been the same at all times but has changed as social circumstances have changed.

The occasional references which are made in this chapter to centuries prior to 1800 and also to Britain should not detract from my main concern here which is Scandinavia and Continental Europe during the nineteenth century. It is important, however, that the history of professionalism in Britain (or England) not be represented as a norm, as has often been the case in accounts of occupational differentiation on the British and American scenes. Rather, the educational development on the Continent and in Scandinavia during the last century will be analysed against the comparative backdrop both of earlier developments in Continental Europe and Scandinavia, and of the British development.

Minimum demands and optimum norms

In order to discuss changes in criteria of adequacy and scientificity in historical research, I have introduced the concepts of minimum demands and optimum norms.[3] However, they apply equally well to disciplines other than history. Here I also want to apply them to scholarly activities in general, as well as to professionalism as such, i.e., to the body of abstract knowledge which I want to make a part of the presuppositions for the constitution of a profession.

Minimum demands are the requirements which – at a certain time and in a certain social environment – become indispensable if a particular kind of knowledge-based activity is to be regarded as having a scholarly character. Occasional deficiencies in regard to minimum demands may be excused but never long accepted.

Optimum norms are the guidelines acknowledged or adopted by a community of scholars – a group, a 'school', or the proponents of a

---

[2] Konrad H. Jarausch, Hannes Siegrist, and Michael Burrage, 'An Actor-based Framework for the Study of the Professions', in Burrage and Torstendahl (eds), *Professions in Theory and History*.

[3] Torstendahl, 'Minimikrav, opimumnormer och paradigm i historisk vetenskap', in *Filosofiska smulor tillägnade Konrad Marc-Wogau* (Uppsala, 1977), 24–33; Torstendahl, 'Historiska skolor och paradigm', *Scandia*, 45 (1979), 151–70; Torstendahl, 'Minimum Demands and Optimum Norms in Swedish Historical Research 1920–1960. The "Weibull School" in Swedish Historiography', *Scandinavian Journal of History*, 6 (1981), 117–141.

'paradigm' – in order for the contributions to a discipline to be considered 'interesting', 'fruitful', 'rewarding', or 'promising'.

While minimum demands are normally concerned with logic and method, optimum norms are normally concerned with the cognitive core of the discipline. There are links between these two sets of rules, but they are sufficiently dissimilar to make it possible to distinguish clearly between them in most cases. Scholars within a certain field will normally agree that adherence to some particular method and means of analysis is necessary and indeed minimal in order for a contribution to be acceptable as a disciplinary one in the first place. However, this in and of itself does not make all such contributions equally important. The best kind of contributions can only be evaluated by relating them to another set of normative ideals, i.e., the optimum norms. These two sets of rules may be transferred to the study of professionalism as well, since there must be some abstract knowledge involved in constituting a profession according to the definitional criteria set out above.

Both in humanistic scholarship and in natural science, minimum demands as well as optimum norms are bound to change over time. Similarly, professional minimum demands and optimum norms change with time and the social environment. Obviously this fact has far-reaching implications for professional eduction, the subject matter of this chapter.

Professional education as a mainstream of university education before 1800

Much rhetoric to the contrary notwithstanding, university objectives were professional in learning from the very beginning. They were designed to assure that groups of people would be given a training which would enable them to cope with problems in certain defined fields of practice of particular concern to princes and churches. Thus, bluntly put, universities were called upon to provide the manpower needed for the purposes of mental and bodily welfare. Of course, this was not their sole duty, but it was certainly one of their principal tasks, and one which was favoured by many worldly and spiritual powers.

The knowledge of how to teach and to cure soul and body

In the high Middle Ages the educational emphases in universities shifted from grammar and logic to dialectic, and philosophy and law replaced rhetoric in the scholarly world.[4] Both dialectic and philosophy were

---

[4] Marjorie Reeves, 'The European University from Medieval Times with Special Reference to Oxford and Cambridge', in *Higher Education: Demand and Response*, ed. William Roy Niblett (London, 1969), 61–84.

rigorously controlled so that they did not jump the fences limiting their pastures, and this guardianship was exerted by theology in abstract terms and by some theologians over others because there were thinkers who might violate the norms set by orthodox theology. For several hundred years theologians played this role: they taught men how to lead a proper life in order to save their souls. They guarded the true faith against all deviation. But first and foremost they taught the clergy what *they* should teach.

In this type of two-step teaching we recognise much of what has been the case in later social settings where the secondary practitioners of the teaching have been regarded as professionals. In the medieval university there was no very great chasm separating theology and law. Professors in both fields largely elaborated the norms separating right and wrong. The worldly application of legal teaching made it an important field in the eyes of State and clerical authorities alike. A third specialty developed in medieval universities was medicine. It was the learned heritage of Greek science and was more deeply marked by library dust than by empirical observations.[5]

Two basic points must be made here. In medieval society knowledge was highly utilitarian. All three main branches of knowledge taught in universities – theology, law, and medicine – were types of useful knowledge and cultivated precisely for their utility. However, on the other hand, it must be emphasised that during these times there also existed a *canon* of learning, a body of theoretical knowledge, to which the practical uses were more or less directly related. And there existed a devotion to learning with the explicit intention of searching for the truth, even though this truth was expected to be found in the interpretation of texts rather than in the exploration of the physical world. The heritage of the medieval university system was thus to organise curricula for practical men from essentially theoretical sources.

Administrative competence from the sixteenth century to the eighteenth

It may be argued that the civil service was and is a field where professionalism cannot be properly exerted, if *Leistungswissen* – applied, 'effective', or achievement-oriented knowledge – is taken as one of the essentials (in an essentialist definition) of professionalism. If this is so, then the competence of civil servants would be measured by another standard called *Herrschaftswissen*, the knowledge of how to govern. But in my

[5] Randall Collins, *Sociology Since Mid-Century: Essays in Theory Cumulation* (New York, 1981).

opinion such a view limits inquiry into the problem of professionalism and hampers the advancement of the theory of this subject. Elsewhere I have tried to show how civil servants in the nineteenth and twentieth centuries developed interesting varieties of professional action strategies, though other kinds of strategic patterns also existed.[6]

Thus the education of civil servants under all circumstances deserves special attention in the history of professional education. The obvious parallel, the Church and the spiritual career, should also be mentioned in spite of the fact that the Church was never a 'pure' bureaucracy. The Church possessed religious responsibilities which made its servants look also at those dimensions of experience outside the sphere of relevance for civil servants and later professionals. The education of ecclesiastical administrators from the early Middle Ages onwards must, however, be mentioned, if only because of their schooling in ecclesiastical law as well as in theological matters.[7]

Studies in law became a prerequisite for a career in the gradually developing civil service of the sixteenth century. There were other gates to be passed through as well – in several states in Europe a noble origin was, if not necessary, at least of great help. What is important for our analysis, however, is the kind of education that was required and the importance of a growing demand for practical experience as well. Nils Runeby has pointed out that four phases can be observed in the establishment of a specialised layer of civil servants. In the first phase, some civil servants used for special tasks already possessed a requisite specialised education. In the second phase, the State undertook to provide the specialised education that was needed. The organisation of regional universities – consciously meant to serve a specific geographical area in contrast to the old universities with their European-wide recruitment of students – was a means to this end, and a result was the first stage of the German *Juristenprivileg*, the exclusive right of law students to enter the civil service which had its counterpart, only some decades later, in Sweden. Runeby has also emphasised that the important period of internship in the *Reichskammergericht*, a kind of supreme court, must be seen as a predecessor of the Swedish system of a compulsory period of practice in the court of appeal before the trainee was regarded as qualified for joining the service.[8] In a

---

[6] Torstendahl, 'Essential Properties'.

[7] Wilhelm Sjöstrand, *Pedagogikens Historia* (Lund, 1954), I, especially 49–53. It must be observed that canonical law was regarded as a fundamental teaching duty of any new university. See Sten Lindroth, *Svensk lärdomshistoria: Medeltiden, reformationstiden* (Stockholm, 1975), 126–37, especially 133.

[8] Nils Runeby, 'Mandarinernas uppkomst. Framväxten av ett kompetensbestämt ämbetsmannastånd: en exempelsamling', in *Bördor, Bönder, Börd i 1600-talets Sverige*, ed. M. Rivera and R. Torstendahl (Lund, 1979), 302–8. Noticeable among his references are

114   *Rolf Torstendahl*

third phase, a combined education of theory and practice was made a *de facto* prerequisite for certain positions. Finally, in a fourth phase, this prerequisite was also made into a formal one.

Especially interesting is the fact that there was an intimate relation between universities and the practical purpose of a civil service. Universities were even founded with this explicit purpose in mind. Further, a combined theoretical and practical education was established where the prospective civil servants received theoretical training at universities, followed by practical training outside of the university, and then the combination of the two gradually was made into a condition for entry to a civil service career.

It is hardly necessary to go into detail here about the close links between practical purposes and university education that became dominant in the eighteenth century. Administrative 'science' became a new wide-ranging field extending from the study of the economy of cultivation to political economy. It had intimate connections to the earlier 'cameralist' knowledge derived from the half private, half public possessions of European princes and was combined with an interest in the mechanisms behind demographical change.[9] A concern for practical use became even more evident in many of the natural sciences which developed rapidly and which were thought to be relevant for much of everyday life, not least for the advancement of agricultural production.[10]

*The rise of science from the Renaissance to the eighteenth century
– the amateur ideal*

Of course there was always something of a scientific spirit at the universities. The long-standing privileged position of bodies of useful knowledge in university settings is by no means inconsistent with this fact. Many studies have provided evidence of the scientific and critical mind in

W. Bleek, *Von der Kameralausbildung zum Juristenprivileg. Studium, Prüfung, und Ausbildung der höheren Beamte des allgemeinen Verwaltungsdienstes in Deutschland im 18. und 19. Jahrhundert* (Berlin, 1972), and B. Distelkamp, 'Das Reichskammergericht im Rechtsleben des 16. Jahrhunderts', in *Rechtsgeschichte als Kulturgeschichte. Festschrift für Adalbert Erler zum 70 Geburtstag*, ed. Hans J. Becker *et al.* (Aalen, 1976). For the Swedish system, see David Gaunt, *Utbildning till statens tjänst. En kollektivbiografi av stormaktstidens hovrättsauskultanter* (Uppsala, 1975).
[9] Sven-Eric Liedman, *Den synliga handen. Anders Berch och ekonomiämnena vid 1700-talets svenska universitet* (Stockholm, 1986), 126–50; and Lindroth, *Svensk lärdomshistoria: Frihetstiden* (Stockholm, 1978), 91–145.
[10] Many examples of this reasoning can be found in *Enseignement et diffusion des sciences en France au XVIIIe siècle* (Paris, 1964), and in Lindroth, *Kungl. svenska vetenskapsakademiens historia 1739–1818* (Stockholm, 1976), I, and *Svensk lärdomshistoria: Frihetstiden* (Stockholm, 1978). It is important to notice the role of the royal and princely academies and societies for the development of a link through publications and propaganda between universities and the use of science.

individual researchers through the ages of antiquity to the eighteenth century. This is not a matter of controversy.

The points to be made here go in two other directions. First, the development of scholarly thought from the twelfth century onwards and the rapid growth of science from the sixteenth century forward took place without any encompassing ideology of the university as a place for – and only for – free scientific inquiry. It was taken for granted that the university should serve other purposes as well. On the Continent and in Scandinavia it was assumed as a matter of course that the State, which provided the necessary means for the existence of universities, could legitimately demand from them the educated people required for its special needs.

Second, in the early modern era and throughout the seventeenth and eighteenth centuries, scientists and humanists of different branches did not form exclusive university circles separate from those of other educated people. The educated amateur, for example the *dilettante*, was welcome to partake in scholarly and scientific work in all European countries. It was taken for granted that learned men could recognise and appreciate legitimate intellectual work without paper qualifications and certificates. There were indeed certificates, the *magister diplomata*, but they served their purpose mainly in the civil service and opened few doors in the scholarly world where only writings in the form of printed texts, then as now, were valid. The amateurs of these times operated on a universal scholarly level which in many respects puts them on a par with the later world of learning. The differences in the function of 'permitted' arguments and 'permitted conclusions' are important but will not be developed here.

The rise of 'the scientific university' and the professionalisation of academic research

In the nineteenth century a major change took place in the university system. What was more or less a universal European university system up to the late eighteenth century consisted of several different parts. During the course of the nineteenth century those parts came to be emphasised in different ways in different national contexts. Actually – this is not the customary viewpoint – universities had started to become parts of national systems even before 1800, but it is the case that nationally constituted networks were the dominant ones by the end of the nineteenth century. This development leaves the impression that different university ideals existed in different countries and has certainly been interpreted as such.[11] The

---

[11] Joseph Ben-David, *The Scientist's Role in Society: A Comparative Study* (Englewood Cliffs, NJ, 1971), and Björn Wittrock, 'Dinosaurs or Dolphins? Rise and Resurgence of the Research-Oriented University', in *The University Research System: The Public Policies*

interpretation is of course partly a question of point of view; but I will argue here that obvious differences notwithstanding, at a general level the European universities moved in the same direction, i.e., they were all influenced by the same new ideas, though to a varying extent.

One of the reasons for the prevalence of explanations in terms of national university traditions is attributable to the close link between modern nation-states and the universities' role in underpinning a sense of national culture and identity. When universities became linked to one another within the boundaries of the nation-state, some fields of study as well as a more general self-understanding of the role of universities tended to acquire a very national orientation. Thus German universities claimed to guard a German cultural heritage, while the old British universities maintained their traditions and national heritage, as did the French. However, 'national tradition' in this context most often refers to the content of certain cultural disciplines, e.g., history, literature, and art, where styles and assumptions are expressed in the language that are themselves the most visible signs of national differences. But that is not the same thing as saying that the principles for establishing knowledge in any discipline were different in different countries, or that the relations between disciplinary knowledge and society-at-large were fundamentally affected by such differences. Indisputably, tertiary education established new links with society in the nineteenth century. Changes and reforms were of several kinds: one took place within the existing universities themselves, but a second consisted of the establishment of new types of educational institutions, quasi-universities, or specialised institutes which did not have a recognised university standard or notable feature.

Humboldtian ideas and ideals

As noted, there exists a common understanding that the national universities of Europe became distinct from each other at the beginning of the nineteenth century. The unique feature of the German university, for example, was thought to be its special emphasis on 'educating' students, meaning that the universities were less interested in preparing students for professional competence.

In a very well-argued article, Peter Moraw has questioned the conventional view of the Humboldtian influence on German university culture.[12] There is, he argues, a difference between the actual teachings of

---

of the Home of the Scientists, ed. Björn Wittrock and Aant Elzinga (Stockholm, 1985), 13–37.

[12] Peter Moraw, 'Humboldt in Giessen. Zur Professorenberufung einer deutschen Universität des 19. Jahrhunderts', *Geschichte und Gesellschaft*, 10 (1984), 47–71.

the Humboldt brothers, Wilhelm and Alexander, and the conception of a university ideal attributed to them as summarised by the slogans 'unity of research and teaching' and 'loneliness and freedom', the latter being rendered by M. Riedel as 'loneliness, freedom, and society'.[13] In Moraw's view, the usual depiction of the Humboldtian ideal of a university as a place which focuses its interests on scholarly purposes (*Bildung*) rather than on professionalism or vocationalism (*Ausbildung*) is really a retrospective construction. Because scholars have been preoccupied with talking about the overall conflict between these two orientations, they have failed to perceive other kinds of important differences in German university history, such as those between the Humboldts' own University of Berlin and Germany in general, differences that fundamentally affect our understanding of the relative positions of *Bildung* and *Ausbildung* in German higher education. For one thing, Germany was not a nation-state until about 1870, and, for another, Berlin's influence was not as strong in many parts of German-speaking Europe in the earlier decades of the nineteenth century as it was later to become.

Moraw's examination of the influence of the Humboldt brothers on the university in Giessen shows both how little changed to begin with and how many other influences were also at work. Traditionally, Giessen had recruited the majority of its professors from a closed circle of kin which Moraw calls a 'university of families'. The Humboldt brothers undoubtedly had influence over the Prince, but when they recommended the appointments of F. G. Welcker and J. Liebig to him, they did not actually stray very far from the usual pattern of kinship recruitment. They did not go so far as to adopt the policy of making professors compete for positions as suggested by their own ideology of academic and intellectual freedom. Only gradually during the course of the nineteenth century did the recruitment of professors become more consistent with the model of free competition. Furthermore, when it finally adopted the new appointments model, the administration of the University of Giessen not only had the 'humanist ideals' of the Humboldt's in mind: it also wanted to incorporate the successful realism in applied chemistry introduced by Liebig. The Giessen example shows how models mixed in Germany.[14]

An actual university in Germany like the one in Giessen thus combined old practices and new ideals, and in its shaping of university culture

---

[13] The older standard picture of the Humboldt university is found in Helmut Schelsky, *Einsamkeit und Freiheit. Idee und Gestalt der deutschen Universität und ihrer Reformen* (Düsseldorf, 1971). Most influential outside of Germany has been Fritz K. Ringer, *The Decline of the German Mandarins* (Cambridge, MA, 1969). A good first-hand analysis of Humboldtian neo-humanism in Germany and mid-century changes in the concepts of research and science is given in Charles E. McClelland, *State, Society, and University in Germany 1700–1914* (Cambridge, 1980), 101–232.   [14] Moraw, 'Humboldt', 65–71.

resorted to more than one ideal. The 'Humboldt university', if in fact there was one, was certainly not the *quintessential* German university.

In Germany, as elsewhere, universities were influenced most of all by the branching off of new disciplines during the nineteenth century. The differentiation of disciplines[15] and, more or less consequently, the specialisation of research was a fundamental trait, which made some universities look more 'Humboldtian' after a period of time than they did before, though this development was by no means just a German process.[16]

While there seem to be good reasons for accepting a view of historical development within the nineteenth-century universities in line with what have been thought of as 'Humboldtian ideals', this was also true of other national universities in Britain, France, or America. There is hardly any evidence to show that it was uniquely and particularly a German development. Furthermore, as universities everywhere underwent a common process of rapid differentiation and specialisation, there is no reason to believe that this outcome owed more to the Humboldtian ideals held by an idealised republic of erudites than to a conception of the usefulness of knowledge.[17] The latter, in fact, was inherent in the very institutional structure of universities.

Professional scientists, humanists, and social scientists

The development of a new university culture which favoured specialised research stimulated science and learning in many disciplines. History was one of them. Leopold von Ranke made himself a name in the history of learning for his immense empirical research as well as for his methods (where I think his renown is not equally well justified)[18] and for his analysis of the driving forces in history, the role of the State and the periodisation

---

[15] Fundamental information on this differentiation is provided in *The Transformation of Higher Learning 1860–1930*, ed. Konrad Jarausch (Chicago, 1983), especially the essays by Sheldon Rothblatt, Peter Lundgreen, James McClelland, and Jurgen Herbst.

[16] Jarausch discusses the differentiation from a comparative point of view in 'Higher Education and Social Change: Some Comparative Aspects', in *The Transformation of Higher Learning*, 9–36. This perspective is generally more derived from Burton R. Clark than from neo-humanist ideas. See his 'Academic Differentiation in National Systems of Higher Education', in *Comparative Education Review*, 22 (1978), 242–58, and further elaborated in *The Higher Education System: Academic Organization in Cross-National Perspective*, ed. Burton R. Clark (Berkeley, 1983).

[17] The term 'usefulness of knowledge' is taken broadly and with different uses in mind as advocated by Liedman, 'Integration and Higher Education', in *Disciplinary Perspectives on Higher Education*, ed. Rune Premfors (Stockholm, 1987).

[18] On methodological precursors, see Herbert Butterfield, *Man on His Past: The Study of the History of Historical Scholarship* (Cambridge, 1955 and 1969), 32–61. See also Torstendahl, 'Leopold von Ranke's historiografiska betydelse', in *Historievetenskap som teori, praktik, ideologi*, ed. Torstendahl and Thorsten Nybom (Stockholm, 1988), 25–38, for a fuller argument on this point.

of history. In his discipline he undertook pioneering work in several respects. But he was not alone. In a culturally determined discipline like history there are always national heroes in different countries. Gibbon, Macaulay, Carlyle, and Acton in Britain; Guizot, Thiers, Thierry, and Barante in France all, in different ways, contributed to the advancement of history. Of course, there were several minor stars in Germany besides Ranke, and there were national celebrities in Sweden, Denmark, Holland, and Austria as well.

What made Ranke special in his field was, first, the wealth and originality of his thought and, second, the establishment of a definite 'rule system' in which his students were trained and through which they became recognised scholars. This rule system does not refer exclusively to methodology in a strict sense, as Ranke himself illustrates. His importance was primarily in the field of theoretical analysis, and what his students learned from him was mainly how to analyse historical events in the light of intellectual tendencies and political relations.[19] His importance was even more pronounced after a couple of generations when the so-called Rankean renaissance disseminated his teaching in a new – and distorted – manner. His methodological holism with its subjectivist traits – the fundamentals of which were the development and spiritual content of super-individual entities – was replaced with a neo-Kantian and Diltheyian methodological individualism.[20] But these were incorrectly regarded – and have been so ever since – as just a variation on Rankean teaching!

Ranke's rule system made him the founder of a 'school' in history. His students attempted, more or less successfully as students do, to apply the same type of analysis based on the same type of presuppositions. Insofar as Ranke was recognised as a master of his discipline, they tried to follow in his tracks and even to imitate him. Of course, they wanted to do something that had the same high value in historiography as Ranke's work, which was regarded as 'optimal'. The normative system deciding

[19] Karl Heinz Metz, *Grundformen historiographischen Denkens. Wissenschaftsgeschichte als Methodologie. Dargestellt an Ranke, Treitschke und Lamprecht* (Munich, 1979), especially 75–98 on the fundamentals of Ranke's analysis. On Ranke as a teacher, see especially Günter Berg, *Leopold von Ranke als akademischer Lehrer* (Göttingen, 1968). On Ranke in general, see Ernst Schulin, *Die Weltgeschichtliche Erfassung des Orients bei Hegel und Ranke* (Göttingen, 1958); Rudolf Vierhaus, *Ranke und die soziale Welt* (Münster, 1957); and George G. Iggers, *The German Conception of History: The National Tradition of Historical Thought from Herder to the Present* (Middletown, CT, 1968), especially 80–9.
[20] For methodological individualism in Dilthey, see Lars Udéhn, *Methodological Individualism, A Critical Appraisal* (Uppsala, 1987), 8–9; for Dilthey's statements on Ranke, 100–1. There is a vast literature on *Historismus*, but the importance of the concepts of development and individuality are widely recognised. See Otto Krogseth, *Den tyske historismen. En idéhistorisk undersökelse av den tyske historismens utviklingshistorie* (Oslo, 1984). On the Ranke renaissance, see Hans-Heinz Krill, *Die Rankerenaissance* (Berlin, 1962).

which concepts were fruitful, which theories were valid (or 'true') and which standpoints historians ought to take regarding the moral content of history – that system was derived from Ranke's teaching and constituted a system of optimum norms.

Methodology in a strict sense has another type of importance which is different from theories and conceptual schemata. The treatment of the sources and the techniques for determining accuracy or validity in old histories made a tremendous advance in the nineteenth century. Historians started to develop a methodology which was only vaguely related to the theoretical content of different historical schools. These methods and techniques – refined in different ways which cannot be shown here – became necessary and indispensable. They were adopted as a 'minimum' requirement for historians no matter which school of history-writing was followed – whether the 'old' Rankean, Droysen's, or Treitschke's school, Erslev's school in Denmark, or Halvdan Koht's school in Norway. A basic agreement on such minimum requirements was also fundamental for the establishment of national and international associations of historians. Historians were expected to recognise the validity of a set of fundamental methodological rules which were independent of the theoretical claims of any single school of thought. There seems thus to be an important difference in the role of the recognised minimum demands and the sets of optimum norms that historians use.[21]

Not only did historians display this ambiguity in their scholarly equipment. Minimum demands and optimum norms apply also to T. N. Clark's discussion of 'patrons and clusters' in the French university system, a reference to the circles of scholars gathered around a leading thinker or prominent figure.[22] Patrons had their optimum norms or special notions of excellence which were transmitted though the clusters of the French university system. At the same time, the development of a more broadly constituted notion of minimum demands made recognised progress in the social sciences. This change took place simultaneously with, but was unrelated to, the new optimum norms of different patron-related 'clusters' which we can discern in different disciplinary settings. The minimum demands continued to spread independently and ultimately became standard scholarly equipment in particular professional groups, the French statisticians for example.[23]

Although the two sets of norms develop in an uncoordinated fashion, there does occur an interplay between them that is fundamental to our

[21] See Torstendahl, 'Minimikrav', 'Historiska', and 'Minimum Demands'.
[22] Terry Nichols Clark, *Prophets and Patrons: The French University and the Emergence of the Social Sciences* (Cambridge, MA, 1973), 66–92.
[23] *Ibid.*, 122–46; 162–201 for the Durkheimians.

understanding of the rise of professional scholars and social scientists. Training in method alone had been sufficient for forming good civil servants in earlier times, and 'schools of thought' may be discerned with more or less accuracy in earlier university systems (Wolffianism in philosophy is an example). But only the combination of the two – of a widely recognised set of methods of fundamental principles, the minimum demands, and varying sets of prerequisites for the fruitful analysis of society and men – the optimum norms – made it possible for scholars to close their ranks to the amateurs and, at the same time, to maintain their differences on really important matters.

The process of professionalisation of scientists shows national or structural peculiarities in diverse national settings. For example, the French emphasis on Paris and on research institutes affiliated to the university (rather than on disciplinary departments within the university) made this organisation of studies in Paris the model for several French provincial universities, and they consequently were dependent upon verdicts of their work from Paris. Scientific progress in general depended upon approval from the central university, and the provincial universities tended to become satellites in a national scientific production system centred on the capital.[24] But even if that was a peculiar type of national university system, it has to be emphasised that all European countries acquired their own systems deviating from each other in some respects.

In the professionalisation of scientists, including social scientists and the humanists, there was also another aspect. They developed a dual status as university teachers as well as scientists. As teachers they defined their social identity in relation to an institution, their university, as scientists in relation to knowledge or science and learning. The two were, of course, intertwined. Higher education asked for teaching which required special gifts and knowledge from its performers. This was one of the arguments of the dons when they professionalised in Oxford and revolted against the ecclesiastical influence there,[25] but it is interesting that in Oxford, as elsewhere, it is hard to find a clear dividing line between the purely scientific argument and the educational. In Oxford, as in France under the Second Empire, remuneration was related less to scientific quality than to teaching,

[24] Victor Karady, 'Teachers and Academics in Nineteenth-Century France: A Socio-Historical Overview', in *Bildungsbürgertum im 19. Jahrhundert*, I, ed. Werner Conze and Jürgen Kocka (Stuttgart, 1985), I, 458–494; Terry Shinn, 'The French Science Faculty System, 1808–1914: Institutional Change and Research Potential in Mathematics and the Physical Sciences', in *Historical Studies in the Physical Sciences*, 10 (1979), 271–332; and Clark, *Prophets and Patrons*. The unequal share in resources and responsibility in the French national university system is hardly visible in university policy as analysed by Paul Gerbod, *La condition universitaire en France au XIXe siècle* (Paris, 1965).
[25] Arthur J. Engel, *From Clergyman to Don: The Rise of the Academic Profession in Nineteenth-Century Oxford* (Oxford, 1983).

and teaching was not always linked directly to scientific achievement.[26] The complications of this combination were particularly felt in new universities and specialised institutes, which could not bestow upon the eminent researcher the same status as enjoyed in the old universities.

It is important to realise that the professionalisation of university teachers and scientists was a process which in the main occurred independently of the formation of professionally educated groups of various kinds in the early nineteenth century. Previous scientific activities had not been professionally closed. Rules were gradually formulated that made it difficult for non-academics, 'practitioners', and dilettantes to establish themselves as 'real' scientists, especially social scientists and humanistic scholars. Professional status in the world of academia was slowly permeated by two sets of closure mechanisms. One of them related to scientific activity and referred to the interrelationship between minimum demands and optimum norms. The social scientist or humanist showed that his (and later her) application of technical method was in accordance with the theoretical outlook for one 'school' or the other. The second type of closure referred to the university and made university teaching and scientific practice the only proper training for academics. These two types of closure became intimately interrelated. Ranke the teacher is impossible to distinguish completely from Ranke the thinker.[27]

The professionalisation of science as a process within the university as a whole occurred at approximately the same time in the different countries in Europe and in the United States. Nevertheless, this does not mean that it was a rapid change. Different disciplines have different histories, and what happened slowly in the cultural disciplines, such as history from the 1840s to the 1890s and sociology from the 1860s to the 1920s, may have occurred more rapidly in the natural sciences. But in all disciplines the relation to the educational conditions served to underpin a secular process of discipline-based professionalisation.

This process meant one important thing for the relation between universities and society at large. The link became more tenuous. It was less possible than before for the outsider to maintain a standpoint in scientific questions without being casually dismissed as an 'amateur' by the 'real' scientists, as a mere antiquarian or journalist by historians, and it became more and more difficult for the outsider to go straight into the university as a teacher in scientific matters. Universities became professionalised by cutting most of the strings which had tied them to the earthly powers and by emphasising their primacy in everything related to science *in abstracto*.

[26] George Weisz, *The Emergence of Modern Universities in France, 1863–1914* (Princeton, 1983), 55–89, and Engel, *From Clergyman to Don*, 139–55, 257–85.
[27] Berg, *Ranke*.

However, the earthly powers in most European countries were well aware of the situation and held on to the most vital string, economic support. The demonstrated or asserted self-reliance in scientific matters on the part of the universities presented no real danger to governments either in terms of the content of teaching or in the output of students with degrees and diplomas as long as universities were not self-supporting. Most of them were not.[28] In fact, a 'social contract', *de facto* if not *de jure*, was obviously agreed upon in Western European countries between the self-governing universities and the State. While professional autonomy in scientific and educational matters was generally recognized, universities had to continue to supply the State with the educated professional practitioners who were needed in society and for special tasks in public administration.

An analysis of this social contract is relevant for understanding the subsequent tensions occurring between the professionalised academics in the university and professionalised practitioners outside, but such an analysis falls outside the scope of the present overview. Suffice it to say that the 'professional university' seldom returned to the original social contract. Facing new outside pressures and demands, the academics who were not 'professionalised' began to think of their universities as autonomous and separate and not necessarily as places for the professional education of practitioners. The university drifted towards an idea of itself based on a feeling of seclusion from the world, and this idea of the 'true' university as uncontaminated by usefulness slowly spread. A counter-trend was, however, also strong.

The rise of 'applied science'

At the same time as scientists formed their own identity through rules for correct and optimal scientific reasoning, high-level education received new tasks. Society had need for new competencies, especially in the growing sector of the industrialised economy, but also, it ought to be remembered, in the reformed agriculture sector. Veterinarians, agricultural engineers, agronomists, and industrial engineers (bearing different titles in different languages) were categories for which a demand arose parallel to the growth of a modern capitalist economy. These occupations were later followed by accountants, economists, business managers, to give a few examples, all emerging in the nineteenth century if coming into their own only in the next

---

[28] Asa Briggs, 'Development in Higher Education in the United Kingdom: Nineteenth and Twentieth Centuries', in *Higher Education: Demand and Response*, ed. Niblett (London, 1969), 98, contends that Oxford and Cambridge accepted no grants before the University Grants Committee was set up in 1919. This seems to be an overstatement, but the Oxbridge colleges and a few other universities were richly endowed.

century. At that time some quite new service professions also emerged, such as psychology, social work, and journalism.

It is important to note that as education for these purposes was new, there was no self-evident link with the university. Consequently, professional education for new purposes mostly started elsewhere, in specialised schools, institutes, and network systems. It would be wrong, however, to conclude that a university link was out of the question from the start. On the contrary, some of the proponents wanted to integrate such new forms of education on a grand scale with the traditional university, others wanted to make them parallel to the university but on the same level – partly out of distrust towards the traditional university – and still others aimed at an education which was not thought of as comparable to the traditional university education at all. Engineering education, which will be considered more closely below, provides an example of different solutions both to the connection and strain between new teaching demands, content, and traditional university organisation and to the problem of the relationship between different levels of professional education in new as well as traditional institutions.

Gradually, new types of technical education were incorporated into national education systems when bridges were created to secondary schools. Organisationally these schools became linked up to universities and to each other. The higher education systems were, it must be remembered, national ones for all practical purposes. Organisational solutions varied, but they were all more or less well-adapted responses to the challenging demands for a specialised labour force inherent in modern capitalist society. The 'professional' solution – if this term is given its theoretical import and is not only used as a linguistic device of the English language – meant that the labour force in turn used the mechanisms of the capitalist economy for its own benefit. There is, thus, no clear line separating actual needs in the economy from demands for professional qualification and competence.

From these premises attention will be paid to the formation of technical education in some European countries. Examples will be taken from the literature on the French, British, German, Swiss, and Swedish educational systems. The last is best known to me from primary sources, even though I have done occasional research on parts of the German, French, and Swiss systems of technical education. For British engineering I rely only on secondary sources.

Technology and engineers

There were two important roots of technical education in most European countries in the nineteenth century. One of them was the demand from the State for a labour force for specific needs, especially in communications (roads, bridges) but also in mining (with origins in the legal *regalia* conceptions) and construction in general. The other root was in the developing industrial economy and in capitalist agriculture.

Of these two roots, the second one was dominant. However, most technical schools were eager to benefit from the prestige of the École polytechnique, which was the paradigm case of a school for the training of civil servants. But at the outset only a few schools were explicitly founded to provide both the State and the private economy with their need for technical expertise. For many of them the hybrid form of mission developed gradually. This even occurred in the case of the École polytechnique by virtue of the fact that many of its students chose to go into private business rather than to enter the application schools for the civil service, a phenomenon which has become known as *pantouflage*.[29] As for the Royal Institute of Technology in Stockholm (the KTH or Tekniska), none of its first graduates became civil servants. Both the École and the Tekniska were State schools: supported by the State and provided with curricula and tasks by the State, but they went in totally different directions.

It is not surprising to find that engineering schools which were intended to produce civil servants emulated existing traditions for the education of civil servants, being especially influenced by the models for legal training. Also, it is not astonishing that they had to establish their education at a level with normal university education, even though in many cases they were not formally part of the same university education. In these respects the technical schools that had their origins in the labour markets of the industrial economy are more interesting and problematical. How and when did it become imperative for these schools to give their education an 'academic' slant and to conform to standards set by the universities or by the State for the universities? If just to prepare labour for the immediate needs of industry, this was not necessary.

Other causes must be sought for the development of the professional engineer in the nineteenth century and the education tailored for him. The academisation of engineering has been analysed by Manegold.[30] Our

[29] Terry Shinn, *Savoir scientifique et pouvoir social. L'École polytechnique 1794–1914* (Paris, 1980), 93–7, 167–9.
[30] Karl-Heinz Manegold, 'Zur Emanzipation der Technik im 19 Jahrhundert in Deutschland', in *Wissenschaft, Wirtschaft und Technik. Studien zur Geschichte*, ed. Karl-Heinz

interest is directed primarily at professional education in 'high-level' institutes. The institutes have been selected for detailed analysis rather for reasons of available material than objective interest.[31] Four of them, the precursors of the Technische Hochschule (TH) Berlin, the precursor of the Royal Institute of Technology in Stockholm, the École Centrale des Arts et Manufactures (ECAM) in Paris, and the Eidgenössische Technische Hochschule (ETH), or Swiss Federal Institute of Technology in Zurich, were all successful institutions in their national settings. The first three also belonged to the first generation of high-level institutes, having been started in the late 1820s. They were not, however, the first to teach civil engineering. The originator in many ways was the École polytechnique, which has been excluded because of its close links to the civil service.[32] Another initiative more important in its ideological framework than in its actual teaching effects was the imperial school in Vienna for which Johann Joseph Prechtl published a plan in 1810 and which he was able to open in 1815. Both his plan and his remarks on engineering show his interest in the teaching of a special technical method. He wanted to establish technology in its own right, and he was also determined to secure a standing for the institute comparable to that of a university.[33] Prechtl's ideas come close to those which will be analysed in the formation of the four schools selected.

The Institute of Technology (KTH) in Stockholm

The Swedish Institute of Technology – it took half a century to make it 'royal' and to establish by government statute its standard as on a par with the universities – was chartered and started its teaching in 1826.[34] It was the outcome of initiatives from the Riksdag. The most important among the initiators was Lieutenant General Bengt Erland Franc-Sparre. Due to his background (he was a baron and a member of the Estate of Nobility in the Riksdag) and his profession he could not have been expected to favour the new bourgeois elements in society. In fact, he was most interested in the conditions for economic progress, and as a former head of the military engineering corps he was well acquainted with and interested in the professional application of science.

Manegold (Munich, 1969), 379–402, and Manegold, *Universität, Technische Hochschule und Industrie. Ein Beitrag zur Emanzipation der Technik im 19. Jahrhundert* (Berlin, 1970).

[31] For a fuller presentation of different types of institutions within an analytical framework, see Lundgreen, 'Differentiation in German Higher Education', in *The Transformation of Higher Learning*, ed. Jarausch, 149–79.

[32] On the École polytechnique, its organisation, teaching, recruitment of students, and the careers of students, see the important analysis in Shinn, *Savoir scientifique*.

[33] Manegold, 'Emanzipation', 384–6.

[34] On the beginnings of the Tekniska, see generally Pontus Henriques, *Skildringar ur Kungl. Tekniska Högskolans historia* (Stockholm, 1917), I.

Franc-Sparre's projected institute for the main branches of economy in Sweden was remarkable in its scope and design. It comprised three main branches: one for agriculture, one for mining, and a 'technical and mechanical central institute'. He was convinced that all these economic activities could and should be made more 'scientific', and it was self-evident for him that the manufacture of industrial products was dependent upon 'science'.[35] What is less self-evident is what he – and many other of his time – really meant by science, as the professional usage of scientific terms and procedures had not yet become stabilised either in Sweden or anywhere else. However, Frank-Sparre did not intend research to be conducted at his projected institute. Only useful knowledge was to be taught there, and nothing else.[36]

I have followed, in an earlier work, the transformations that Franc-Sparre's ideas underwent in parliamentary committee and State administration before the Institute of Technology became a reality.[37] Here it may be sufficient to jump to the presentation that the head of the Institute, Gustaf Magnus Schwartz, gave of the work there when he was attacked by the chairman of the governing board and criticised in two successive authorised investigations. In 1834 he argued that professors tended to devote their time to non-useful book-learning and neglected 'practical matters'. If the Institute was to be concerned only with knowledge of natural laws and such things, it would cease to be 'technical'.[38] Eleven years later Schwartz argued that many people had the false idea that there is nothing between the two extremes represented by the sciences, on the one hand, and the practice of handicrafts and industries, on the other. There was, he said, another point of view. 'All measures which are taken in industries and handicrafts where natural forces are used for special purposes have been systematised according to these purposes and their general tendencies. In this way a system of artificial means has been formed which has a rather wide scope, and it is known under the name of technology.' Technology was guided by problems, not by theorems. 'Through a methodological registration of results, experience has created its own practical theory, which has been brought about through analogies and by induction. This practical theory is technology or experience systematised.'[39]

Schwartz was a remarkable man with uncommon views. The results of the Institute under his leadership were less remarkable. This was the reason for the investigations, where the critics had formulated conceptions of

[35] Torstendahl, *Teknologins nytta. Motiveringar för det svenska tekniska utbildningsväsendets framväxt framförda av riksdagsmän och utbildningsadministratörer 1810–1870* (Uppsala, 1975), 44–6 and 56–7.
[36] *Ibid.*, 57.   [37] *Ibid.*, 57–61.   [38] *Ibid.*, 65.   [39] *Ibid.*, 71ff.

practical utility contrary to those of Schwartz, and the second of the two investigations led to his resignation in 1845. The scientists, more and more articulate in their professional points of view, got the upper hand, and the Institute had to base its teaching on their conception of science. Thus arose a link, in the content of the teaching, between the Institute and the universities. Its reputation was, however, damaged from the perspective of the universities, and it took a few decades to prove that it was a top-level educational institution in its field with teachers and students on a par with the universities. But it took additional decades more before research in the KTH was allowed to lead to doctoral dissertations, as was normal in universities.

What is most remarkable about the controversy over the Institute of Technology are the two different conceptions of practical knowledge, of technology *in abstracto*, standing sharply against one another. Schwartz represented a line of thought which may have had much sympathy among practitioners in industries and businesses but which was defeated none the less. Its main thrust was that practical knowledge, when systematised, becomes technology, and that science was not technology.

The École Centrale (ECAM) in Paris (1829)

The problem of the relation between theory and practice, or different conceptions of science and different conceptions of technology, was by no means limited to Sweden. In 1729 Bernard Forest de Belidor, in his book *Engineering Science (La science des ingénieurs)* had complained about a lack of interest in practical matters in the world of learning, and a century later Louise-Marie-Henri Navier, trying to make mathematics fruitful for the science of the strength of materials, also found too little relation between theory and practice in the scientific world. Both these examples are mentioned by J. H. Weiss in his investigation of the first decades of the École centrale des arts et manufactures.[40] Like Schwartz in Sweden, Auguste Comte, in a lecture unknown to Schwartz, had defined engineers as an intermediate class between the scientists in a proper sense and the 'effective directors of productive enterprises'. It was the mission of engineers to 'organise the relation between theory and practice'.[41] In Comte's world, however, this engineering knowledge ranked clearly below scientific theory-building. His view on the ranking of this type of knowledge was thus quite different from Schwartz's, although both tried to typify engineering as a form of intermediate knowledge which had some methods in common with science without sharing its overall objectives.

[40] John Hubbel Weiss, *The Making of Technological Man: The Social Origins of French Engineering Education* (Cambridge, MA, 1982), 92ff.   [41] *Ibid.*, 94ff.

In the École centrale this was also a central theme. Weiss says that the phrase 'industrial science' (*la science industrielle*) best expressed the unity and coherence of the educational programme of its founders. It was repeatedly asserted, in the programme of the school, that industrial science was the heart of all courses in the school. Jean-Baptiste Dumas, one of the first and most important teachers there, stated that industrial science embraced 'the study of matter and of force, of everything that had weight, that vibrates, that changes'.[42] When it came to teaching and textbooks, however, Dumas made no secret of his opinion that a rather theoretical basis was necessary: 'my intention has not been to describe the practice of the arts, but to clarify the theory of them' (as he says in Weiss's translation). Weiss also concludes that incorporated into the basic premises of industrial science was the thesis that there could be no separation between 'pure' chemistry and the work of the engineer, entrepreneur, or agronomist whose activities involved chemical processes. Practical arts were based on some 'theory' which the engineer needed to understand, and the future belonged to those who could replace trial-and-error procedures with scientific knowledge.[43]

The Gewerbeinstitut in Berlin

In 1821 Christian Peter Wilhelm Beuth, who in a leading position in the Ministry of Finance played a crucial role in promoting the freedom of economic, industrial, and trade activities in Prussia after the Napoleonic wars, opened a technical school of two classes in Berlin. Its task was 'not only to bestow on the concerned manufacturers and craftsmen a general culture and an insight into the matters which are necessary for every craftsman but also to give to them the preparatory knowledge [*Vorkenntnisse*], which are necessary for the practice of a technical occupation,[44] according to the instructions issued by Beuth. In this manner he seems to have made a distinction of importance between, on the one hand, craftsmen's knowledge and, on the other, preparatory knowledge of a more general kind, which obviously meant a rather elementary teaching in the natural sciences. He persisted in the same idea when he widened the scope of his technical school in 1826 and reformed it into the Gewerbeinstitut.

Beuth had three objectives in mind in his policy for the stimulation of industry and handicraft. First, he wanted to expand technical schools, meaning technical schools in a broad sense including vocational training

---

[42] *Ibid.*, 97.   [43] *Ibid.*, 115ff.
[44] Hans J. Straube, 'Christian P. Wilhelm Beuth', in *Abhandlungen und Berichte* (Deutsches Museum Munich) (Berlin, 1930), II: 5, 120–3.

generally. Second, he wanted manufacturers and industrial people to have more schooling than they had. Third, he wanted private interests to join into associations for the promotion of industry and technology.[45] As could be expected from a person in his position, he was more of an organiser than a theoretician, but he maintained one fundamental idea on the schooling of technicians that became important. It was most evident when he criticised the schools that were already at hand when he started his career. According to Beuth, they were all too academic in their manner of teaching. Lectures were given, but those attending could not profit from them because they lacked an understanding of the fundamentals of the subject. This convinced Beuth that all technical education presupposed a scientific schooling that had to be given in ordinary classroom teaching.[46] Thus, in all his reforms of the lower technical education as well as in his directions for the *Gewerbeinstitut*, he carried through a teaching programme that made scientific training the basis for all technical subjects. Technology was thus not to be a teaching subject in its own right but had to be preceded, and understood, through scientific learning. In a way Beuth's programme was thus the opposite of that of Schwartz, who wanted technology to be taught in its own right undisturbed by science. However, even Beuth's programme meant that technology was singular, even if it could not be taught or understood without science. Technology did not follow directly from scientific teaching but had to be added.

Comparatively speaking, the richly endowed Gewerbeinstitut soon flourished, and good teachers were recruited. One of them in the following generation was Franz Reuleaux, who was asked to come to Berlin in 1864 after eight years at the ETH. In Berlin he became the *Director* of the Gewerbeakademie that was created in 1866 through a merger of the Gewerbeinstitut and the Bauakademie and also became the first Rector of the Technische Hochschule Berlin as it was called from 1879.[47] It is most enlightening to compare the views on technology which Reuleaux advanced with those of the 'founding fathers' of technological schools half a century earlier.

Reuleaux is well known for his *Kinematik*, but he was not the first one to try to systematise mechanics. Monge, Willis, Laboulaye, and Redtenbacher had done so before him. Their presentations stopped with rather simple typologies, that is to say, they were simple in basic principles but complex as to the objects that were taken as typical for the main forms.

---

[45] *Ibid.*, 117. His faith in bourgeois thrift for the economic growth of Prussia was strong and clear. Hermann Fernholtz, *Beuth: Deutsches Bürgertum vor 100 Jahren* (Berlin, 1931), which contains long, illustrative quotations.   [46] *Ibid.*, 128–35.

[47] Carl Weihe, 'Franz Reuleaux und die Grundlagen seiner Kinematik', *Abhandlungen und Berichte*, 14: 4 (1942), 81–104.

Reuleaux went the other way round. He wanted to go to the simple forms in order to be able to construe the more complex from the elementary ones. Thus, his typology is a sophisticated model of elementary mechanical force transformations and their linking relations. He tried to make his *Kinematik* a basic of technology in general, but his technological ideology is worth analysing even apart from that effort.

Reuleaux gave to technology a scientific theory of mechanics. He could 'explain' through this theory a mechanical force transformation as a complex of certain elementary forms and certain of their defined relations. Only with Reuleaux and his contemporaries did technology receive the standing that Schwartz in his time had hoped to accomplish by a short-cut. Technology had acquired its own theories. Through Reuleaux it was no longer what Beuth established in Berlin, a subject dependent upon science for its self-understanding. It became a science (or several sciences, possibly) in its own right. This served as a major starting point for the secular process of the scientification of technology.

The ETH in Zurich

The Eidgenössische Technische Hochschule in Zurich was founded in 1854, or a quarter of a century later than the three other schools dealt with here. There was a plan that arose under French domination of the Helvetian Republic to start an institute of a true polyscientific kind as early as 1798. Its aim was to be the training of doctors, artists, and engineers as well as judges, clear-sighted lawmakers, and ministers. Philipp Albert Stapfer, the leading minister and the most important spokesman for the proposal, had obviously been impressed by the educational innovations achieved by the French Republic. The most interesting feature of his plan was, however, the obvious collection of various kinds of professional training in one institute planned as a national institute for the Helvetian Republic in a way that had no precedent in any of the other educational systems in Europe. When the Parliament brought the issue up in 1799, the time for such proposals rapidly ran out: new wars put an end to them and later to the Helvetian Republic.[48]

The establishment of a common Swiss educational system in the Federation of cantons recreated after the Napoleonic Wars was fraught with administrative, linguistic, and cultural difficulties. When these difficulties were slowly overcome, the Federation very thoroughly investigated the matter before a polytechnical school was instituted. The

[48] Gottfried Guggenbühl, *Geschichte der Eidgenössischen Technischen Hochschule in Zürich, Eidgenössische Technische Hochschule 1855–1955* (Zurich, 1955), 13–15.

commission that was to deliberate on the precise form of the school decided, after paying tribute to the École polytechnique,[49] to take the polytechnical school in Karlsruhe as its real model.[50] This school had been founded in 1825, but in 1833 it was re-directed at the instigation of the minister in Baden, Karl Friedrich Nebenius, towards trying to influence industry through the education of industrially knowledgeable men.[51] Nebenius had stated that 'the education of the productive classes is quite as important for the State as the proficiency of its civil servants'. He wanted technical education to fulfil three tasks: first, to make already proven methods generally known; second, to establish practical applications for theoretically known methods; third, to make it possible for 'the productive classes' to establish new knowledge through proper observation without unnecessary and expensive trials.[52] The idea that technological education should aim at 'the productive classes' was an ideal which was picked up in Zurich, but Nebenius' key ideas, that technology was above all a question of a set of 'methods', left no imprint. Explicitly, the commission had started with projecting an institute that would educate civil engineers, manufacturers, mechanics, chemists, and teachers in the relevant disciplines. Later on in the deliberations, it was agreed that Swiss needs should be especially regarded in the teaching of technical skills for the construction of roads and railways, waterways, bridges, but also in industrial mechanics and chemistry.[53]

The Swiss school was not created with the purpose of realising something that was revolutionary in thought or practice. The original idea in the discussions leading up to the establishment of the school in 1854 was to create something that would be manageable and useful. There was no ambition to elaborate a new educational ideology for the school. Rather, the Swiss school was consciously drawing on the experiences of the 'practical' Karlsruhe by emphasising education for the needs of industry rather than for a civil service. Of course this has to do with the timing of the

---

[49] Manegold is of the opinion that the École polytechnique was important as a model for both ETH and the German polytechnical schools. He refers explicitly to the mathematisation of practical problems as one influence. Manegold, 'Emanzipation', 381. Historians are, in general, divided in their opinion. Wilhelm Schlink believes that while certain influences of the École polytechnique on Karlsruhe and Munich are discernible, the origins of German polytechnics are not French. Wilhelm Schlink, 'Entstehung und Entwicklung der deutschen Technischen Hochschulen', *Das Akademische Deutschland*, 1 (1930), 429, 431–2. Franz Schnabel thinks that ECAM was the model for Karlsruhe, but Weiss considers ECAM itself to have been generally influenced by the École polytechnique. Franz Schnabel, *Die Anfänge des technischen Hochschulwesens* (Karlsruhe, 1925), 37. Weiss, 'Making of Technological Man', 13–16.

[50] Guggenbühl, *Eidgenössische Technische Hochschule*, 30–5.

[51] Schnabel, *Anfänge des Technischen Hochschulwesens*, 37.

[52] *Ibid.*, especially 35–40.

[53] Guggenbühl, *Eidgenössische Technische Hochschule*, 34–7.

initiative. The commission, and later the leadership of the school, could draw on the experiences in the many polytechnics that had been established from the 1820s onwards in Germany, Austria, and France. Ideas had already been tested, and some workable curricula was in operation. Many unworkable concepts had failed and were already discarded, as had indeed happened in Stockholm even with the original plan. Thus the ETH was established at the right moment. Its design was perhaps less bold than that of many others but at the same time considerably more successful than most of them.

Change and conformity in engineering education

It is important to make clear that the three oldest of the engineering schools mentioned changed in varying degrees from their beginnings. In Stockholm and Berlin the different 'practical' standpoints were abandoned for other technological ideologies. While the Technological Institute in Stockholm did not get another strong ideologist after Schwartz, someone who could replace his 'systematised practice' with a consistent view of a core alternative, Berlin had its most brilliant theorist on the content of technical teaching in Franz Reuleaux. But in the 1850s, even before Reuleaux came to Berlin, a gradual development in Germany called *Akademisierung* had taken place within the Berlin Gewerbeinstitut.[54] When it was renamed Gewerbeakademie in 1866, it had already reformed its teaching from the classroom drill that Beuth favoured to conform with the freedom for students that characterised German universities. At that time the polytechnic schools had begun to designate themselves *technische Hochschulen*, and they were renamed such in the 1870s. As already mentioned, this was also the time for the creation of the famous Berlin Technische Hochschule (1884) situated in Charlottenburg.[55] The process of 'academicisation' also meant a standardisation of more rigorous entrance requirements, as well as standardised examination for diplomas. Both these steps were taken by State authorities only after an active campaign from the German association of engineers, the Verein deutscher Ingenieure (VDI) and an association of architects.[56] Obviously, this was only part of a very clear

---

[54] On this process and the concept, see Manegold, 'Technology Academised. Education and the Training of the Engineer in the Nineteenth Century', in *The Dynamics of Science and Technology*, ed. Wolfgang Krohn, Edwin T. Layton, and Peter Weingart (Dordrecht, 1978), 137–58.

[55] Hermann Boost, 'Technische Hochschule Berlin-Charlottenburg', in *Das akademische Deutschland*, I, 461–4; and Reinhard Rürup, 'Die Technische Universität Berlin 1879–1979: Grundzüge und Probleme ihrer Geschichte', in *Wissenschaft und Gesellschaft. Beiträge zur Geschichte der Technischen Universität Berlin 1879–1979*, ed. Reinhard Rürup (Berlin, 1979), 10–12.   [56] Schlink, 'Entstehung und Entwicklung', 442–8.

exclusionary strategy for professionalisation, where the aims of professional groupings corresponded well with those of the State.

When Reuleaux came to Berlin, the school already occupied a formal place in the State educational system and possessed privileges almost on a part with the universities. A total equality with the universities, however was only attained in 1899 when Kaiser Wilhelm II found occasion to bestow on the Technische Hochschulen the right to confer the honour of 'Doktor-Ingenieur' to the students who qualified for the title.[57]

As regards privileges, Sweden followed closely the model given by Germany (as it did in many matters during this period). Thus the Institute of Technology was made both royal and a *Hochschule* (*högskola*) in 1877 and was awarded the ceremonial right to confer the degree of doctor in 1927.

The four schools that we have taken into consideration here underwent a similar development of academicisation and accordingly rose in status. At the same time they contained differences of a peculiar kind. If we identify three dimensions, one regarding ideology, one regarding mission or programme, and one regarding integration into a university system, we will find that a considerable change took place in the nineteenth century.

First, in Berlin and Stockholm it was necessary to change the prevailing ideology from 'practical' with its implied opposition to technology to 'academic' science. In Stockholm this also meant that science finally was accepted as the bulk of the curriculum. Important engineering theorists, such as Ferdinand Redtenbacher, Karl Karmarsch, and Franz Reuleaux, helped to form a scientific body of theorems and conclusions connected with scientific theory which allowed technology to be regarded more and more as a part of a very abstract, perhaps, but also a highly respected academic disciplinary culture.[58] Neither in Paris nor in Zurich was any such change necessary, because in Zurich science as such had been accepted from the beginning. In Paris the concept of 'industrial science' had been guiding teaching for a long period and had its front direction not against science (conceived as a mathematical formulation of technology) but against a French university system deprived of many types of professional education.

Second, all four institutions started out with a programme for educating industrial men and managers of private enterprises rather than public servants (even though some public duties obviously were taken into account when the curricula were formed for the ETH); but all of them, except ECAM, changed their policy in this respect during the nineteenth century. In some courses public service objectives even predominated,

[57] Rürup, 'Die Technische Universität Berlin', 19; Schlink, 'Entstehung und Entwicklung' 448-9.   [58] Manegold, 'Emanzipation', and 'Technology Academised'.

although the vast majority of the students continued to start and mostly also complete their careers in the private sector.[59]

Third, as regards integration into a national university system, other differences are apparent. Again, Zurich stands out as the technical school with the fewest number of breaks in its development. It was rather well integrated into the system of the Swiss universities when it was started. Social sciences and humanities formed part of the school programme, and a leading humanist, Jakob Burckhardt, was one of its professors. Furthermore, Zurich was designed to be an educational institution corresponding to a Federal university. By contrast, Berlin and Stockholm had to fight for their standing and only gradually acquired recognition from universities and government authorities as being equivalent to universities. Nevertheless, they both tended in this direction. ECAM in Paris, on the other hand, did not acquire a position as a university, nor did it strive for it, though it gradually became officially recognised and State-sponsored instead of being a private institution.[60] This, of course, has to do with the university system in France and the standing of the professional schools or *grandes écoles*. It was more attractive for a specialised school to become one of the favoured specialised schools, or even better, one of the great ones, than to become either part of a university or just parallel to one. But this also meant that the École centrale never became a true university-like teaching institution, and links with academic careers outside of ECAM itself were weak.

Finally, what is important is that whatever their national differences, all four schools provided a good basis for the professionalisation of the engineering occupations. But this professionalisation itself could not take place until there was a demand in industry or in public administration for engineers as salaried employees. The market for self-employed prac-titioners on a consultant basis, a kind of engineer that has continued to exist all along, was (and has been) too small to form a basis for a professional standing equivalent to that of private doctors in late eighteenth and early nineteenth century. The fact that there were some associations of engineers – especially the VDI – is not conclusive evidence of professionalisation in and of itself. Since engineers differed in standing, independence, and aspirations, they were not able to form a comprehensive organising strategy before the end of the century. Earlier, the various educational systems were the principal determinants of professional

[59] Torstendahl, *The Dispersion of Engineers in a Transitional Society: Swedish Technicians 1860–1950* (Uppsala, 1975), and 'Career Mobility of Engineers in France and Sweden', in *Technical Education and Social Mobility* (Bern, 1986), 32–47. (Section B12 of the Ninth Economic History Congress).
[60] Michalina Vaughan, 'The *Grandes Écoles*', in *Governing Elites: Studies in Training and Selection*, ed. Rupert Wilkinson (New York, 1969), 93; Weisz, *Emergence*, 25.

policies and standards. These systems may have shared some common fundamental goals, but the examples of KTH, ECAM, TH Berlin, and ETH show that specific national histories and content also caused them to diverge from one another. Thus they may be said to have achieved common goals but in quite dissimilar ways.

A note on the British education of engineers

Already in the middle of the nineteenth century there was an established conviction in Britain that the Continent had overtaken them regarding the education of engineers. The famous chemist, Lyon Playfair, was soon speaking for many others when, in the early 1850s, he argued for an improvement in the training of engineers.[61] In order to give a balanced judgment of the British system, twentieth-century scholars have tended to emphasise, on the one hand, the importance of practical education on the shop floor and, on the other hand, the science education that became institutionalised in Britain during the nineteenth century.[62] Recently still another position has emerged. It has been argued that there were in fact a number of major teaching institutions in Britain that gave instruction in engineering, from the London University's constituent or affiliated colleges and Durham and Cambridge University, to new 'university-level institutions in London and the provinces' and to vocational schools.[63] Perhaps these developments have been under-rated in the previous literature, even though it still holds true that most of the high-level education that was arranged in Britain in order to improve matters was science education rather than engineering education.[64] From the present perspective, however, it is still important to observe that in Britain no national standard for the teaching of professional engineers came into

[61] Donald S. L. Cardwell, *The Organisation of Science in England* (London, 1957 and 1980), 60 (for Babbage in Berlin), 86–92 (for Playfair and State action).
[62] *Ibid.*, 58–61; Stephen F. Cotgrove, *Technical Education and Social Change* (London, 1958), 11–59; Michael Argles, *South Kensington to Robbins: An Account of English Technical and Scientific Education Since 1851* (London, 1964), 1–44. On shop floor education, see Sidney Pollard, *The Genesis of Modern Management: A Study of the Industrial Revolution in Great Britain* (London, 1965), 104–22, 126–33.
[63] Thomas N. J. Hilken, *Engineering at Cambridge University 1783–1965* (Cambridge, 1967); A. Rupert Hall, *Science for Industry: A Short History of the Imperial College of Science and Technology* (London, 1982); but primarily Robert Fox and Anna Guagnini, 'Britain in Perspective: The European Context of Industrial Training and Innovation, 1880–1914', in *History and Technology*, 2 (1983), 133–50, and Fox and Guagnini, 'The Flexible University; Some Historical Reflections on the Analysis of Education and the Modern British Economy', in *Social Studies of Science*, 16 (1986), 515–27, from which the references to Hilken and Hall are taken.
[64] Torstendahl, 'Engineers in Sweden and Britain 1820–1914: Professionalism and Bureaucratisation in a Comparative Perspective', in *Bildungsbürgertum im 19. Jahrhundert*, ed. Conze and Kocka (Stuttgart, 1985), 545–9.

effect in the nineteenth century. There seem to be two reasons for this. First, no prestigious technical school was established to offer or represent a national model of engineering education in general. Second, as engine operatives were also called 'engineers', the word depreciated. It was hard to conjure up a status-filled image of engineers with it, or use the designation 'engineer' as a strategy for professionalisation.[65]

Concluding remarks on 'applied science' education

Historians and sociologists of education have often simplified matters for themselves by discussing either the supply of or demand for technicians and engineers and have taken for granted that educational policy in technical matters must follow some predefined rationality in this respect. It is certainly possible that a policy has been rational; but it is not at all clear which postulates that rationality follows.

At least three quite different possibilities for rationality in the policy of technical education are demonstrated in the European scene from the nineteenth century. First, there is the British policy which was slow to create high-level schools as an instrument of technical education, and which responded to an internal market demand by restricting the emigration of technical experts and technically experienced manpower generally.[66] Second, the French policy (with the exception of the École polytechnique) and still more the German policy may be taken as examples of a decision which tended to develop education at all levels, not least the highest, as a response to a demand for technical competence in the labour force.[67] Third, there is a policy demonstrated in Sweden (and also partly in Germany) for government to try to influence demand by creating a more industrialised and thus more technically developed economy by increasing the supply of engineers and other people with technical schooling. There does not seem to have been one obvious policy for technical education. Furthermore, the effectiveness of a specific technical education policy is always difficult to assess, as the results or consequences have not usually followed very clearly from the initial or stated intentions.

Certainly a simple functional model for societies at large[68] tells us little

[65] This argument is a little more developed in Torstendahl, *ibid.*

[66] David S. Landes, *The Unbounded Prometheus: Technological Change and Industrial Development in Western Europe from 1750 to the Present* (Cambridge, 1972), 147–9.

[67] Weiss, *Making of Technological Man*, 8–13, contains an apt discussion of this problem. See also Landes, *The Unbounded Prometheus*, 147–51.

[68] 'All societies, no matter how simple, strive to solve their various functional problems, both universal and organisationally specific. One such problem is the management of the "total selection process"...All societies strive to provide their personnel with sufficient kinds and amounts of technical and diffuse skills so that the solution of still other problems can

when confronted with historical alternatives. But we are also not greatly helped by a thesis that assumes the autonomy of the educational sector:[69] it is evident that technical education has not developed totally by itself.

Different conceptions of technology – as systematised practical knowledge, as industrial science, as applied natural science – were combined with different policy intentions in forming the professional education of engineers. Nowhere, however, were the group interests of the engineers as professionals a driving force in the process in its initial phases in the first half of the nineteenth century. Engineers were not regarded as professionals and had not yet formed a policy of their own – that is one reason for this. But neither had State institutes or private schools articulated or adopted the idea of using paper qualifications as a means of excluding entrants to engineering occupations. It was a discovery – or an invention – later on, around 1880, when engineers became employed in great numbers in industrial production as salaried employees.[70]

Conclusion: professionalisation and the transformation of higher education in the nineteenth century

The renewed emphasis on professional education in the nineteenth century was of course related to the rise of industrial and agrarian capitalism. However, it is important to remember that there are also vital continuities between the new developments and the centuries-old tradition of professional education in universities. Ever since the middle ages universities had provided society with a variety of utilitarian services, training priests, lawyers, physicians, and civil servants. Numerous linkages between the universities and their special educational concerns, political interests and the State, and groups that were or became 'professional' existed, and all of the parties played a role in the development of the modern professions.

In the nineteenth century a systems transformation took place in higher education on the Continent and in Scandinavia. Professional education played a vital role in this transformation, and in the process it was itself transformed. Some forms of professional education retained but also re-negotiated their relationship with the university. Clergymen, lawyers, and

be attempted and, at least in large measure, met.' Earl Hopper, 'Educational Systems and Selected Consequences of Patterns of Mobility and Non-mobility in Industrial Societies: A Theoretical Discussion', in *Knowledge, Education, and Cultural Change*, ed. Richard Brown (London, 1973), 21.

[69] See such writers as the soviet sociologist Friedrich R. Filippov, 'Social Structure and Systems of Education', in *Education in a Changing Society*, ed. Antonina Kloskowska and Guido Martinotti (London and Beverly Hills, CA, 1977).

[70] Torstendahl, 'Engineers in Industry 1850–1910: Professional Men and New Bureaucrats, a Comparative Approach', in *Science, Technology, and Society in the Time of Alfred Nobel*, ed. Carl G. Bernhard, Elisabeth Crawford, and Per Sörbom (Oxford, 1982), 253–70.

doctors continued to be educated there, and their educational grounding in scholarship and science kept its fundamental character. However, as 'professions', their conception of what was proper learning and preparation changed as advances in science and scholarship occurred, especially in medicine.

What has been argued here is that there were two changes in higher education that led to a transformation of the university system. One of these changes was that new professions arose which had no traditional linkage to the university but rather to the despised business sector outside. Technical education is the paragon example, but business education also provides some interesting additional information. The other change was the professionalisation of all scientific and scholarly work.

The professionalisation of scientific work within the university relied on the codification of a minimum demands systems for the methodology of different disciplines, on the one hand, and on the formation of schools of thought that provided optimum norms to direct the search for fruitful problems on the other. The combination of minimum demands and optimum norms established exclusive boundaries around groups of scholars and scientists, setting them apart from other groups that were not regarded as having the requisite values and qualifications. As this was also combined with university teaching where scientific closure was joined to academic teaching practices, the professionalisation of universities was more or less completed. Thus, only professors could decide what was acceptable (minimum demands) and promising (optimum norms) scientific work, and with these new measurements they dictated the terms of admittance to the ranks of teachers at the university. In this respect, the quest for university autonomy was successfully pursued.

The new professions in their turn had their own promoters and supporters both among politicians and the higher echelons of the civil service and among people active in commerce and industry. Consequently, they were allowed to establish their own technical schools, and a number of these were actually on a par with the universities and resembled them in their standard of teaching and staff recruitment. Within these schools, leading theorists who were not always eager to get too close to universities formed their own ideology of useful knowledge. This was turned into different shapes by Prechtl in Vienna and Nebenius in Baden, two of the first leading politicians to take up the idea, and by Schwartz in Stockholm, Beuth in Berlin, and Dumas in Paris. These figures wanted to form, in one way or another, a practical science that could give backbone to the curricula of the new institutions and allow them to stand up to the haughtiness of the universities. Professionals were henceforth trained in these technological institutions according to a set of minimum demands and optimum norms that did not completely coincide with those of any traditional academic discipline.

Towards the end of the century the gradual transformation of science and professional education had reached a new stage with new mutual relations. Science had become an esoteric activity which called for specialised schooling into the minimum demands and one of several sets of optimum norms in each discipline. Professional education in engineering (and gradually also in economics and business administration) became more and more 'scientific'. This process meant three things. First, even in special, technical disciplines a core of theorems was formed which provided a basis for a theory-defined disciplinary field. Second, connections to 'authorised' scientific theories were gradually established in the theoretical parts of technical disciplines which linked them up to a common and coherent body of scientific learning. Third, also in the technical disciplines, a scientific professionalisation process took place, quite corresponding to that of the traditional university disciplines, which meant that the experiences of the 'productive classes' on the shop floor were not included in the category of acceptable scientific, technical work. Technical practice and technical theorising were no longer equivalent in the engineering schools.

These changes meant that a parallelism was created between technical education and university education, a parallelism that held so many similarities that integration itself was not far away. In Germany it was nearly there, and elsewhere only a few decades had to pass before integration was complete, that is to say, whenever integration was perceived to be desirable. In France, as was earlier noted, a parallelism was created that actually excluded integration.

Of course, the transformation followed here wherein professional education was being established at the same time as traditional science was being professionalised was not a final phase in the history of changes in higher education. In the twentieth century two new issues were to arise in the world of higher education, both with policy ramifications. One was Sate intervention, which came in waves after 1890 and eventually brought new forms of dissension into the university. The State could be viewed and used as a powerful support for the independence and standing of science, certainly of importance when science became involved in an on-going international competition for national prestige. But this powerful ally could also make science subservient to ideals quite alien to itself, for example, by giving higher priority to utility than to theoretical innovation. Achieving a balance has been a main question for the twentieth century.

The other new issue has been the concept of higher education itself. What is the relation between science as such and higher education? Must higher education only reflect 'science'? Different answers to these questions have also meant different approaches to the newer forms of professional education that have been brought into existence. Do these forms require a scientific relationship? The integrative ideology of higher education in the twentieth century, through conceptions of 'tertiary education' and 'multiversity', tries to bridge the gulf between university and professional education at the same time as it puts an end to the echoing, in university education, of science alone. Professional education for 'social needs', whether there is a scientific basis or not, is, however, a story that belongs to the twentieth century.

4   From practice to school-based professional education: patterns of conflict and accommodation in England, France, and the United States

Michael Burrage

Introduction

Histories of education usually assume that the extension of educational opportunity is a good thing. Consequently, they rarely spend much attention assessing its opportunity costs or regretting what it may have replaced. Not unreasonably, they assume that the alternatives were probably unpleasant: ignorance, unfulfilled promise, dead-end manual labour, and a less attractive way of life. The history of education therefore has an in-built, Whiggish disposition. Elitists and obscurantists may block the advance of schools, but light eventually triumphs over darkness. In the history of primary and secondary education, this Whiggishness may do no great harm. In the history of professional education, however, we must be more cautious, for professional schools often displaced or discredited alternative practice-based forms of professional education. There are, therefore, opportunity costs and another side of its history, the side of the losers, of the viable, traditional institutions directly under the control of practising professionals. Like all losers' history, it remains largely unwritten.

Of course, practitioner-controlled professional education has not been entirely displaced. As internship, it remains an integral part of medical education, and in other professions, under other names, it remains significant. Indeed, if we were somehow to add to it all the spontaneous and casual transmission of professional knowledge and skills 'on the job', it might still be the most common form of professional education. Nevertheless, over the long run, these practitioner-controlled forms of education have been overshadowed and displaced by school-based professional education. They are adjuncts and supplements to formal training rather than alternatives to it. The role of pupil, clerk, or probationer has a somewhat indeterminate, uncertain status compared with the universally acceptable role of student. In the modern world, it is the university or professional school diploma, rather than the practitioners' say-so, that certifies competence and provides the decisive qualification for professional practice and status. Nowadays, would-be professions invariably acknowledge the fact by seeking, above all else, to have their future entrants certified by a university qualification.

Prior to the acceptance of the contemporary consensus, and following the admission of theology, medicine, and law into the medieval universities, practising professionals organised in defence of their own distinctive vision of what professional education should be, refused to admit that the really important knowledge of their professional practice could be better transmitted in academic institutions, and often resisted the transfer of their educational responsibilities to universities. Control of professional education therefore had, by one means or another, to be prised from their grasp; and even after this had been done, practitioners often launched counter-attacks to try and hang on to, or retrieve, some element of practice-based professional education.

Modern systems of professional education are the outcome of these struggles and conflicts which begin in the late eighteenth century and continue through to the twentieth century, sometimes the late twentieth century. There were three main participants: the practitioners, the State and the universities. Since their behaviour was often affected by wider political events, these conflicts did not follow the same course, or have the same outcome, in all modern societies.

The aim of this chapter is to identify, outline, and compare some of the conflicts which shaped three kinds of professional education – law, medicine, and engineering – in three societies: England, France, and the United States. It will begin with what seems to be the extreme case of formidable practitioner power, English barristers, and compare them with French advocates and American lawyers. After pausing to identify some major inter-professional variations that seem to be relevant in this context, it will then consider in what ways, and with what modifications, the variations detected among lawyers might also apply to doctors and engineers, and whether in fact one can identify systemic, national patterns. The chapter concludes by considering the uses of a comparative investigation of this kind. In a postscript, I try to define what practitioners were fighting for, to reconstruct, one might say, the losers' view of professional education.

Barristers disdain the conventional wisdom: England

To grasp the peculiarities of the professional education of lawyers in England, one must go back to the very beginnings of the English State. Rather than imposing royal laws, the Norman and Angevin kings of England allowed their judges to adapt, amend, and reconcile local customs. From this piecemeal, protracted process of adaptation and amendment, the English common law emerged. Since this law was created and written by legal practitioners, rather than by royal officials or university scholars, the judges were also left to determine the education requirements for legal practitioners.[1] In the twelfth and thirteenth centuries, they delegated this responsibility to the practising advocates who appeared before them by refusing to hear anyone who had not been called to the bar of one of the four Inns of Court into which these practitioners had organised themselves.

From this time until the Court and Legal Services Act of 1990, the four Inns have remained responsible for the education and certification of would-be barristers. In the fifteenth and sixteenth centuries, the Inns organised readings, moots and bolts which had led some historians to describe them, at this time, as legal universities.[2] This seems, however, a rather misleading label since there were no full-time teachers, no curriculum, no courses, no exams, and no degrees. The Inns are perhaps better seen as practitioners' clubs and their system of pupillage as an apprenticeship. The student was educated by living among, dining with, listening to, mooting with, watching, and occasionally assisting, practising barristers. In Dickens' day, the judges continued to recognise their own responsibilities for the training of barristers and reserved a special bench in their courts for student barristers. Occasionally, the judges would point out interesting aspects of a case to any students who happened to be present.[3] However, the main responsibility rested with the Inns.

In the mid nineteenth century, this form of professional education was savagely attacked in the House of Commons as slapdash and inadequate. In 1846 a Select Committee compared the Inns' provisions unfavourably with the university-based legal education of other European societies as well as the United States. The committee was astonished to discover that the Inns never examined any of their students and concluded that they provided no legal education 'worthy of the name'.[4] It proposed that there

---

[1] This line of argument draws on the comparative analysis of the formation of English and French legal institutions in John P. Dawson, *A History of Lay Judges* (Cambridge, MA, 1960), 42–93, 293–301.

[2] William Holdsworth, *A History of English Law* (London, 1924), II, 506–8.

[3] William Holdsworth, *Charles Dickens as a Legal Historian* (New Haven, 1929).

[4] Brian Abel Smith and Robert Stevens, *Lawyers and the Courts: A Sociological Study of the English Legal System* (London, 1967), 64–5.

should be an entrance examination for admission to the Inns, that law courses be provided either in a newly-created college of law, or in the universities, and that there be a final examination before the call to the bar. The Inns do not appear to have been unduly persuaded or moved by these criticisms. Six years later, in 1852, they responded by establishing a Council of Legal Education. This was given the task of organising voluntary lectures by practising barristers for students of the Inns. In 1872 the Council introduced a final examination before a student was eligible for call to the bar.[5]

Criticisms of the Inns and attempts to reform legal education continued off and on in the Commons until the closing years of the century but to little avail. The professors of law at Oxford and Cambridge took no part in the debate and were apparently content with their medieval inheritance which allowed them to provide a part of the professional education of the civil lawyers who appeared in the ecclesiastical courts. Even after the judicial reforms of 1875, which abolished the 'civilian' profession, Oxford and Cambridge professors of law never sought to challenge the Inns' control of the education of the common lawyers. They gave lectures on Roman law, international law, jurisprudence, and constitutional history but hardly referred to the law used by practising English lawyers.[6] This self-denying ordinance suggests that the system of professional education devised by the Inns, which infuriated radical members of Parliament and which seemed to outside observers inadequate, archaic and bizarre, in fact rested on assumptions about the proper jurisdictions of universities and practitioners' corporate bodies which dons and barristers shared.

The new University of London was rather less influenced by such assumptions and rather more anxious, than either Oxford or Cambridge, to increase its student numbers. Between 1884 and 1904 it therefore made four separate proposals to establish a school of law jointly with the Inns. Desperate to obtain the Inns' approval, the University made humiliating concessions which would have given effective control of the curricula, of appointments, and of examination to the Inns. In the end, however, the Inns remained unconvinced and rejected all proposals.[7] The attempt to relocate English legal education, and to create university law schools comparable to those on the Continent, or in the United States, therefore came to an end and was not resumed until after World War II.

The survival of an essentially medieval system until the mid twentieth

---

[5] *Ibid.*, 63–71.
[6] *Ibid.*, 165–8. After noting that English Law was 'ill-provided for', a later Oxford professor observed that this was of little importance since the Inns' Council of Legal Education provided lectures in London. Frederick Henry Lawson, *The Oxford Law School* (Oxford, 1968), 31.   [7] Smith and Stevens, *Lawyers and the Courts*, 172–7.

century was plainly not the result of widespread public support. There never has been an identifiable public opinion on the training of lawyers in England, but most parliamentary or informed comment was hostile.[8] Nor can it have much to do with nineteenth-century *laissez-faire* theories of government since it long predated and long outlived them. One must therefore infer that the unwritten agreement between the practitioners and the universities about their legitimate spheres of action must also have been endorsed by the State. Judging by their actions, it was based on this cardinal principle: that neither the State, nor any other body, has any right to interfere in professional matters, including the way they choose to educate their future members, except on the request, or with the express consent, of the profession's own representatives.

The reform of the Inns' educational provisions in the second half of the twentieth century tends to confirm this argument. Since the sixties, the formal element has steadily increased, and the informal, casual, un-organised practitioner-controlled component declined. Virtually all entrants now obtain a degree, in most cases a law degree, then take a one-year, full-time course organised by the Council of Legal Education at the Inns' own School of Law and finally serve a pupillae which now lasts a year.[9] In appearance, therefore, training for the English bar has become more like the American or other European systems and squares with 'modern' notions of what professional education should be like. Its arrival at this 'modern' destination is, however, curious since none of the major participants changed their traditional stance. The State never intervened to impose what it considered the proper form of legal education. The universities never asserted their competence or interest in professional education, and although public criticism persuaded the Council of Legal Education to provide formal, mandatory courses, the bar remained in control of the system and was not forced to abandon their traditional view of a proper professional education.

The most significant cause of change was that entrants to the bar themselves were increasingly convinced that a university degree, and specifically a law degree, was an appropriate and sensible way to embark on a legal career. It was therefore the private, voluntary decisions of school and university students that, more than anything else, changed the professional education for the bar. Practising barristers evidently remain

---

[8] For examples from the 1950s, see *ibid.*, 446–7. The authors observe 'the benchers paid no more attention to such criticisms than their predecessors had done for over a century'.

[9] In 1949, 57 per cent of those called to the bar had a university degree and 40 per cent of those called had a law degree, while by 1980, 93 per cent of those called were graduates and 78 per cent of those called had a law degree. Richard L. Abel, *The Legal Profession in England and Wales* (Oxford, 1988), 319, 308–9, 406. For the current rules of admission of both barristers and solicitors, see pp. 33–64 and 137–68.

less than wholly convinced. Until 1979, it was not necessary to have any kind of university degree to practice at the English bar. It is still not necessary to have a law degree.[10]

There is no need to recount the history of the much larger, junior branch of the English legal profession, the solicitors, since in essentials it is very similar. They were no less attached to an apprenticeship form of professional training than their seniors at the bar and only expressed any interest in a university-based professional education when they thought it would entail joint education with the bar. A university-based education, in other words, would have been acceptable to the solicitors if it brought with it the status advantage of association, or equality, with the bar. By itself, the solicitors evidently believed that a university-based education offered them no advantages, either in terms of status or anything else.

One episode from their history is worth recalling for the light it sheds on this latter point. The solicitors' professional association, the Law Society, tended to respond to public criticism of their training methods rather more readily than the Inns, no doubt because its membership was scattered across the country and it therefore required statutory support to enforce its authority over its members. They were consequently more energetic in organising formal courses for articled clerks and, at the turn of the century, had contracted with a number of the new civic universities in the Midlands and North to teach courses for their examinations.

At first, these universities welcomed this new source of students and income. However, as time passed, the universities became less dependent on Law Society's patronage, and their teachers evidently tired of giving lectures around the curriculum imposed on them by the Law Society's examinations. They sought, therefore, to make their courses more intellectually-demanding and exciting. The annoyance of the Law Society at these innovations first surfaced during the inter-war years. After World War II it complained repeatedly that the universities were not preparing their students either for their professional examinations or for legal practice. The universities paid little heed to these criticisms, and in 1952 the Law Society therefore carried out its oft-repeated threat and withdrew all of its students from the universities. It then went 'down market' and negotiated contracts with technical colleges and other educational institutions, including private commercial crammers, that it could control and supervise more easily.[11]

The severance of the link with the universities after fifty years,

---

[10] Though those without must now complete a one-year 'academic stage' at City University or the Polytechnic of Central London. General Council of the Bar of England and Wales, *A Career at the Bar* (London, 1987), 11.

[11] Smith and Stevens, *Lawyers and the Courts*, 177–8, 349–55.

demonstrates that, like the bar, English solicitors at that time still rejected the accepted modern view that professional education is best provided in a university. Both branches of the English legal profession evidently had their own view about what professional education should be and had little faith in the universities' ability to provide it. The episode also suggests incidentally, that whatever may have been the case in their earliest days, the civic universities had assimilated something of the Oxbridge view that professional education was not really their business.

Since the 1952 divorce, there has been a steady, student-led rapprochement between the Law Society and the universities. Just as increasing numbers of intending barristers decided for themselves that it would be sensible to take university law courses or law degrees before entering one of the Inns, those intending to become solicitors increasingly did the same.[12] No doubt they were prompted to do so by peer pressure and peer comparisons, especially after the expansion of the number of university places in the sixties. In any event, the pressure did not come from the universities or from the State, though it was the introduction of student grants by the State that enabled entrants to go to university before taking articles. The profession merely responded to these student preferences. Their own preferences are indicated by the survival of a practice-based route into the profession that still enables non-graduates to enter the profession and qualify in the same period of time as graduates.

Reversing the imperial legacy: French advocates

To trace the course of the struggles over legal education in France, one must, as in the English case, first refer to the early formation of the State. French kings were less inclined than their English cousins to exercise their authority through community institutions, or to adapt the customary law of the territories they conquered or acquired, and instead sought to impose royal justice, royal judges, and royal law. As a result, they preferred investigative, inquisitorial, written legal procedures that required vast numbers of university-trained judges and legal officials. They also seem to have been more reluctant to entrust professional education to self-governing bodies of practitioners. From the twelfth to the sixteenth centuries royal decrees regulated both the conduct and the admission

---

[12] In 1949, 36 per cent of those admitted as solicitors were graduates, 42 per cent of whom had a law degree, while in 1979 the proportion of graduates had increased to 90 per cent. In 1978, 76 per cent of graduates admitted had law degrees. The Law Society, *Annual Statistical Report* (1989), 3.

requirements of advocates, and whilst these provided for a practitioners-controlled *stage*, they also insisted on a law degree.[13]

How far these rules were enforced in practice is impossible to say but in the seventeenth and eighteenth centuries under the protection of the judges of the parlements, advocates were able to make their orders into self-governing corporate bodies, which elected their own presiding officers, *bâtonniers*, and maintained their own system of professional education requiring every would-be advocate to serve a *stage* before admission to their *tableaux*.[14] During the eighteenth century this practice-based *stage* was a far more significant period of professional training than the law degree. There is a wealth of evidence to show the decline of the law teaching in the universities, and it seems reasonable to suppose that this decline was a direct result of the way practitioners emphasised and enforced their own rival practice-based professional education.[15]

Both kinds of training, the university degree and the *stage*, were swept away by the Revolution, along with the orders of advocates, their *bâtonniers* and *tableaux*, all in the name of equality and the sovereignty of the people. For more than a decade, therefore, there were no advocates in France, only *hommes de loi*, no regulation of legal practice and no kind of professional education.[16] The reconstruction of French legal institutions began under the Consulate and Empire. It was the work of State officials, most of them legally trained, but under the eye of Napoleon and completed without reference to any organised body of practitioners. They established a system of professional education which rested entirely on formal training at newly created law schools whose diploma constituted a licence to practice and required no additional practice-based *stage* or apprenticeship. In 1810, however, when the reconstruction of the courts had been completed, the law schools had been opened, and most of the codes promulgated, Napoleon finally acceded to the petitions of former advocates and permitted the restoration of the *ordres* along with all their old institutions, including the *stage*.

[13] For a resumé of royal regulation of the French bar over this period, see M. D. Dalloz, *Répertoire de Législation, de Doctrine et de Jurisprudence* (Bureau de la Jurisprudence Générale du Royaume, Paris, 1847), 460–1.

[14] The best description of these institutions on the eve of the Revolution is to be found in Lenard R. Berlanstein, *The Barristers of Toulouse in the Eighteenth Century, 1740–1793* (Baltimore, 1975). There were, however, certain differences between Paris and Toulouse. In 1756 for instance the Paris bar raised the length of the *stage* to four years. In Toulouse, it remained two years.

[15] Laurence W. B. Brockliss, *French Higher Education in the Seventeenth and Eighteenth Centuries, A Cultural History* (Oxford, 1987), 77–82, 106–7.

[16] The best account of their destruction and reconstruction is Michael P. Fitzsimmons, *The Parisian Order of Barristers and the French Revolution* (Cambridge, 1987).

Napoleon clearly did not intend these restored orders to exercise all the prerogatives of their *ancien régime* predecessors, or that they should once again be *les maîtres des tableaux*. He therefore made all their actions subject to the approval of his State prosecutors, the *procureurs généraux*. However, under subsequent regimes, in the absence of any express prohibition, but with the support of the judiciary, they successfully reasserted their absolute right to control admission to the *stage* and their absolute right to determine who should be deemed to have successfully completed it.

This surreptitious restoration of the primacy of the *stage* as a requirement of admission to the bar and as a form of professional education came to an end in the later years of the Second Empire. Under the regulatory framework imposed on the profession by Napoleon I, all the decisions of the orders were reviewable by the courts. In 1867 the Lyons court of appeal decided that the orders could not continue to exercise an absolute discretion without any explanation or review of their decisions and must henceforth admit to the *stage* anyone who had obtained a law school diploma. They were also required to give reasons, which were reviewable by the courts, why someone was deemed to have failed the *stage*.[17] After this decision, the *stage* could not operate in the old discretionary, particularistic, and informal manner. In law at least, school training became, as Napoleon seems to have intended, the decisive hurdle and qualification of professional legal education in France and the *stage* its practical supplement.

There is no evidence, prior to World War I, that the orders ever responded to this setback. Since they were primarily concerned with the regulation of the bar and still without a national organisation, it would probably have been difficult for them either to agree on a national policy or to lobby in its support. Or it may be that the loss of control did not concern them too much, since it was still extraordinarily difficult to establish a practice as an advocate without a private income and some form of sponsorship.[18] After World War I, however, their circumstances and attitude had evidently changed. The Association Nationale des Avocats formed in 1921 began to voice complaints about the inadequacy

[17] This jurisprudence is reviewed in Henri Buteau, *De la Profession d'Avocat à Rome et de l'Ordre des Avocats* (Paris, 1895), 181–201.
[18] Edmond Rousse, for example, who became *bâtonnier* of the Paris order in 1870, completed his *stage* in 1845 but did not begin to earn a satisfactory living for a further fifteen years, during which time he was heavily dependent upon one of the stars of the Paris bar, Chaix d'Est Ange. See Edmond Rousse, *Lettres à un ami* (Paris, 1909), I (1845–1870), 11–12, 21, 26, 89, 112, 139, 179–180, 224, 287, 314, 323. For evidence that such obstacles were still common at the end of the century, see Association de la Presse Judiciaire, *The Paris Law Courts: Sketches of Men and Manners*, trans. Gerald P. Moriarty (London, 1894), 51–2.

and irrelevance of the 'cultural' training provided by the law faculty. The issue was discussed at their meetings in Tunis in 1927, Rheims in 1928, Algiers in 1930, and Versailles in 1931, when it was resolved that a practical, professional training, or *préstage* under the joint supervision of the bar and the law faculty should be inserted between the completion of the *licence* and the *stage*, leading to a *diplôme d'aptitude professionnelle*.[19]

Having obtained the support of the Paris order and the conference of provincial *bâtonniers* for these proposals, the ANA began to lobby for political support. In November 1930 the government agreed to one of their subsidiary proposals to systematise the relationship between *patron* and *stagiaire* by requiring 'a certificate of diligence and morality' at the end of the first year before *stagiaires* were entitled to proceed to the second. They were unable, however, to obtain any further reform before the outbreak of war. In 1941, however, for reasons that have never been documented, the Vichy regime gave them exactly what they wanted and required an additional year of practical training leading to a *certificat d'aptitude à la profession d'avocat* (CAPA).[20] It was thus no longer possible to pass from the *licence* directly, as of right, into the *stage*. Advocates had obtained a new means of controlling entry to the profession and joint control of an additional, practice-oriented period of training.

After the war all Vichy legislation was repealed, but since the ANA was able to show the 'republican pedigree' of the CAPA, it survived. In the immediate post-war years, there was little need for the profession to worry about their numbers since the profession had been much reduced by the war, and there was no rush of applicants after it.[21] In the sixties, however, the numbers wishing to enter the profession increased rapidly, and the CAPA became an effective means of restricting entry.[22] The advocates, however, found it increasingly unsatisfactory; for although they participated in the examination of students, the actual instruction was given in the faculty and it had therefore become, in their view, too academic, 'un enseignement purement magistrale... Il laisse subsister de bons élèves qui seront peut-être mauvais avocats. Il n'exerce aucun contrôle sur cette sorte de sens clinique, ce jugement sûr, ce mélange de bons sens et d'équilibre qui sont les qualités premières de l'avocat.'[23]

They therefore campaigned for reform of the system and were

[19] Jean-Baptiste Sialleli, *Les Avocats de 1920 à 1987*, L'Association Nationale des Avocats, La Confederation Syndicate des Avocats (Paris, 1987), 73. [20] *Ibid.*, 74–80.
[21] Which led some commentators to speculate about the counter-attractions of more modern, technological professions; see Andre Toulemon, *Barreaux de Paris et Barreaux de province* (Paris, 1966), 97–105.
[22] Roland Dumas, *Les Avocats* (Paris, 1977), 17–18, 71–8; Association Nationale des Avocats, *Au Service de la Justice: La profession juridique de demain* (Paris, 1967), 17–18.
[23] *Au Service de la Justice*, 16–17.

rewarded in 1971 with the creation of new *centres de formation profes-sionnelle* attached to each court of appeal, rather than the faculties, and in 1981 with an additional mandatory year of study. Thus the law school graduate must now take a highly competitive exam to enter a *centre de formation professionnelle*, receive a year's professional training, 'primarily oriented toward private practice...taught mostly by lawyers with apprenticeships taken with lawyers or other legal professionals', than take the CAPA, and finally serve a two-year *stage*.[24]

The post-revolutionary history of French advocates' efforts to preserve a practice-based professional education falls into three acts. In the first, with the support of the judiciary, they were able quietly to restore their traditional *stage*. In the second, which began with the decision of the Lyons court of appeal in 1867, the *stage* remained but was no longer a means of controlling entry to the bar. In the third phase, which began in the inter-war years when advocates organised as a pressure group, they were eventually able not just to install new barriers on admission but also to extend the practice-based component in the training of future advocates. The new centres are, it is true, schools and not wholly under their control since they are half-funded by the State. Advocates do, however, control the curriculum. The bar no longer has to accept whomever the professors of the faculty of law choose to send them.

Law schools exploit a market: the United States

In the colonial period, the role and expectations of American universities with respect to professional education were little different from those of Oxford and Cambridge, that is, they provided law lectures merely as part of a liberal education as part of the education of a gentleman. Professional education remained practice-based and practitioner-controlled. This English pattern continued for some time after the Revolution, probably because, like Oxford and Cambridge, the universities were aware of the presence and scrutiny of the bar and deferred to the practice-based education it controlled.[25]

The electorates and legislatures of many of the new states were, however, unwilling to continue with an English-style profession. Some state

[24] Anne Boigeol, 'The French Bar; The Difficulties of Unifying a Divided Profession', in *Lawyers in Society*, II (*The Civil Law World*), ed. Richard L. Abel and Philip S. C. Lewis (Berkeley, 1988), 275–8.
[25] Albert Z. Reed, *Training for the Public Profession of the Law*, Bulletin No. 15, Carnegie Foundation for the Advancement of Teaching (New York City, 1921), 120–2, 134. Edward Potts Cheney, *History of the University of Pennsylvania, 1740–1940* (Philadelphia, 1940), 158–60.

legislatures had first sought to regulate its affairs rather more energetically than the colonial authorities, but attacks on the profession as 'aristocratic', 'unrepublican', and 'undemocratic' which had begun during the Revolution continued thereafter. At the beginning of the nineteenth century a number of states reduced or abolished bar admission requirements. In Massachusetts, the heartland of bar associations, popular attacks on the profession had been successfully resisted for several decades, but in 1835 it too succumbed to the opponents of an organised bar. The repeal of bar admission requirements led to the disbanding or collapse of all existing bar associations with the partial exception of that in Philadelphia.[26] Until 1870, there were no bar associations in the United States and hence no practitioner-maintained system of entry and training. Over this period most American white adult males could prepare themselves for legal practice just as they wished, though in a few states they might have to prove before a judge that they had some acquaintance with the law.

And so, for a while, the United States realised the dream of many critics of the professions. There was little to distinguish the lawyer from the layman. Apart from a few formalities, anyone who called himself a lawyer was one. The result does not appear, however, to have been quite as the critics anticipated. In the absence of an organised bar, the universities started to offer professional training courses leading to a diploma. In the absence of any credential from the bar, these law school diplomas were the only means by which a trained lawyer might try to distinguish himself from an untrained one. Diplomas therefore became a marketable credential, and the universities rushed to exploit the market. Between 1840 and 1860, one new law school was founded every year.

Thus the rise of the law school diploma in the United States was not, as is sometimes suggested, the result of attempts by bar associations to raise the status of their membership but rather of the exact opposite, the absence of any practitioner association to provide professional education and certify those it thought competent to practice as lawyers.[27] The contrast with English experience corroborates this argument, for there the practitioner associations survived and flourished, and school-based legal

---

[26] Partial because it seems to have sought to recruit or regulate only an elite of Philadelphia lawyers, not the bar as a whole. For further details and references, see Michael Burrage, 'Revolution and the Collective Action of the French, American and English Legal Professions', *Law and Social Inquiry*, 13 (Spring, 1988), 246–9.

[27] Collins, for instance, saw the rise of the law school diploma as a coincidence of the interests of upper class bar associations, university professors, and the 'newly-consolidated business elite'. This overlooks the rapid growth of law schools prior to the revival of bar associations and that the oldest upper class associations, in Philadelphia and New York City, first tried to hold on to, or revive, clerkship as the primary admission requirements. Randall Collins, *The Credential Society* (Orlando, 1979), 151–9.

education languished. In the United States, the abolition of bar admission requirements and the subsequent collapse of bar associations left the law schools free to devise professional education without seeking the approval of, or making concessions to, any organised body of practitioners. In short, it left them free to create and exploit a market for professional education, which they did at a fairly rapid rate before the Civil War, and much more rapidly after it. In this market, university degrees, legitimated by states through the process of chartering universities, had a decided advantage over the certificate of a completed clerkship or the diplomas of private, commercial law schools. However, at the end of the century private schools began to open up new markets for themselves in immigrant communities and amongst blacks and women.[28]

When practitioner associations began to revive in the Eastern states in the last quarter of the nineteenth century, their first thought, naturally, was to try to re-instate clerkship to its former pre-eminent role as a professional qualification. Opening this campaign, the first of the revived bar associations, the Association of the Bar of the City of New York, scored an immediate triumph. In 1871 the New York Court of Appeals reinstated a two-year compulsory clerkship which reduced the law degrees to an optional professional qualification and meant law school graduates enjoyed no advantage over those who entered clerkship immediately after leaving school. The triumph, however, was short-lived. Six years later, the court responded to the protests of the schools and reversed its decision.[29] After this setback, practising lawyers, who were by this time organising bar associations in many states, sought new ways of re-establishing their control of professional education.

One strategy was to create schools which they themselves controlled, in which the 'professors' were practitioners, with courses which were oriented to the day-to-day requirements of practising lawyers and readily combined with office training. Although there is no evidence of diffusion of this form of practitioner-controlled professional education from England, they were in effect endeavouring to create in-house institutions similar to the courses of the Inns' Council of Legal Education and the Law Society. Schools of this kind were established in a number of American cities at the turn of the century, usually in direct competition with those providing the more academic professional education that the practitioners evidently found so unsatisfactory. Few of them survived as a distinctive alternative form of professional training for very long.[30]

[28] Reed, *Training*, 396–402.   [29] *Ibid.*, 259–63.
[30] *Ibid.*, 398–9. For a detailed account of the transformation of the practitioner-oriented schools at Marquette, see William R. Johnson, *Schooled Lawyers: A Study in the Clash of Professional Cultures* (New York, 1978), 133–53.

A second strategy was to try to use bar examinations which were usually administered by practising lawyers, to control law school curricula. Schools in many states were, however, able to circumvent this obstacle by persuading the legislature to grant their graduates exemption from the bar examinations, to obtain a so-called 'diploma privilege'. Moreover, the bar examination was a double-edged weapon, and when used too vigorously provoked renewed attacks on the bar association.[31]

The third strategy, that of accreditation of law schools, was borrowed from the medical profession who used it with devastating effect before and during World War I to eliminate inferior medical schools. It could not be used in quite the same way by bar associations since state legislatures, on whom the strategy depended, were reluctant to increase bar admission requirements much beyond the reach of a fairly substantial proportion of the population.[32] Over the long run, however, the American Bar Association's constant pressure has helped to raise the admission requirements. By the 1960s most law schools required a first degree before admission and most law school degrees took three years.[33] But this is hardly a demonstration of practitioner power. The accreditation strategy was in any case only adopted as a second or third best substitute. It has not enabled practitioners to limit the numbers entering the profession. It has not given them any control of the content of professional education and appears to have led them to abandon or forget the original goal of their reconstructed associations – a practice-based professional education.

Why other things aren't equal: inter-professional contrasts

While the nature of the struggle was roughly the same, the variations in the power of the three main participants meant that its course and outcome were quite different. To put it in a nutshell, professional education in England has been dominated by practitioners, in France by the State, and in the United States by the universities. The legal profession is not, however, typical or representative of other professions, and there is no reason therefore to suppose that the struggle over medical or engineering education simply replicated those of legal education. If they had, the

[31] In 1878, reflecting on the 1871 decision of the New York Court of Appeals and the attempts by the revived bar associations to make bar examinations more difficult, Harvard's Dean Langdell issued a blunt warning that, 'if this was to be the result of the so-called efforts to raise the standard of legal education, Harvard's interest lay rather in the direction of opening the profession to all the world'. Reed, *Training*, 255–6, 260.

[32] John Richard Woodworth, 'Some influences on the Reform of Schools of Law and Medicine, 1890 to 1930', *Sociological Quarterly*, 14 (1973).

[33] Richard L. Abel, 'United States: The Contradictions of Professionalism', in *Lawyers in Society*, I (*The Common Law World*), ed. Richard L. Abel and Philip S. C. Lewis (Berkeley, 1988), 191–3.

national patterns would be self-evident, and there would be little to investigate. The next step in the analysis, therefore, is to identify differences between these three professions that are likely to be relevant to the kind of conflicts and relationships we have already encountered. Two seem especially important; the first separates medicine from law, and the second distinguishes engineering from both.

Doctors differ from lawyers because invariably they have been willing to acknowledge that school-based education by lectures, demonstrations, and experiments should have a place in their professional education. It is not difficult to find lawyers who think that the study of the law within the universities is irrelevant to the practice of law, but it is difficult to find any body of orthodox, licensed medical practitioners who believe that knowledge of their calling might be acquired solely by practice or by informal and personal transmission from practitioner to apprentice. This difference may have been reinforced by the advent of scientific medicine in the late nineteenth century when academic researchers were able to prove the uses of their work for medical practice, but it long pre-dates it. Lectures in the French medical faculties of the *ancien régime* were, to take one example, well attended, in contrast to those of the law faculties.[34] Moreover, French surgeons and pharmacists at the time both recognised that the advance of their professions depended, to some degree at least, on the provision of a formal academic component to their professional education. School-based training, therefore, began within the two professions themselves.[35] Conversely, neither the Paris faculty nor Oxford and Cambridge claimed that medical education should be entirely academic and entirely school-based.

The relationship between practical and academic knowledge, and between practitioners and professors is therefore quite different in medicine and law. Medicine has, in fact, established an unusual relationship with universities in as much as it is the only profession apart from the Church and the academic profession itself that has been able, or allowed, to bring its subject-matter and institutions into the university. It would be startling to find a court with detention cells and handcuffed prisoners whose fate was really determined by a trial in a university court. And obviously it

---

[34] Brockliss, *French Higher Education*, 441–3.
[35] Surgeons in Paris had begun to organise lectures and demonstrations in the seventeenth century. Toby Gelfand, *Professionalizing Modern Medicine: Paris Surgeons and Medical Science and Institutions in the Eighteenth Century* (Westport, 1980), 32–6, 44–127. For pharmacy, see F. Prevet, *Histoire de l'Organisation Sociale en Pharmacie* (Paris, 1940), 102–10. This consistent variation between the two professions has never been explained. It may be that medical and surgical apprentices quickly realised that in the ordinary course of their training they might encounter a limited range of disease or traumas, while law students, attending trials or reading law reports, never felt similarly deprived.

would not be practicable to construct real bridges and power stations on campus, or to conduct a real company audit, but it is not at all remarkable to find a surgical amphitheatre or a hospital within a university.[36] Hence, while teachers of other professionals have to pretend to devise academic replicas of the real world, the medical school can easily combine school and practice-based education. The medical school professor can be both a teacher and practitioner. The student can also be an apprentice. The relationship between academic medicine and medical practice is therefore, to some degree, collaborative; and whilst this does not preclude conflicts of interest between academics and practitioners, or variations in the extent to which practitioners may control medical education, such conflicts and variations are likely to be less pronounced than in legal education. A wholly practice-based education, such as that of the English bar in the nineteenth century, or a wholly school-based education such as that of American lawyers after the collapse of their bar associations, is improbable.

As we extend the comparison to include engineers, we must expect to encounter further variations from the professional education of both lawyers and doctors, since engineers differ from them both in one major respect: they have usually been salaried employees. In the earliest days of English and American engineering, civil and mechanical engineers were commonly employed on a fee-for-service basis like that of barristers and solicitors. They evidently valued this status and made attempts to retain it, though only an elite of consulting civil engineers were able to do so. Since then, the vast majority of engineers in both centuries have been salaried. In France, as we shall see, engineering began as part of the State administration, so even the elite of the profession were salaried from the beginning. Engineers may therefore oblige us to introduce a fourth major protagonist into the analysis, employers, and it is reasonable to suppose that they may have influenced the subsequent form of professional education. Bearing these inter-professional variations in mind we may now try to extend the analysis and see if we can discern a larger pattern, or any elements of a larger pattern embracing three professions in these countries.

Practitioners assert their rights: doctors and engineers in England

The comparison of the professional education of lawyers revealed one striking and distinctive characteristic of English legal education: the early

---

[36] The University of California at Berkeley is surely rather exceptional in having a shaft and adit under its campus which, until 1953, was used for the instruction of mining engineering students.

formation of a practitioner association which assumed, or was allowed to assume, control of professional education and qualification. This same characteristic appears again in medical education. The College of Physicians was formed in 1518, and, after the renewal of its charter and various signs of royal favour from Charles II, began to use the prefix 'royal'. The surgeons organised as a separate branch within the United Company of Barber-Surgeons in 1540 but emerged from it in 1745 and obtained a royal charter in 1800. The London Society of Apothecaries obtained their independence from the Grocers' Company of the City of London in 1617 and in 1815 began to examine and licence general medical practitioners throughout the country. Collectively, these three bodies are the institutional foundation of the modern English medical profession.[37]

The most significant difference from the Inns of Court regulation of legal practitioners was that the College of Physicians consisted entirely of the graduates of Oxford and Cambridge. This corroborates the expectation that doctors would be more likely than lawyers to acknowledge that professional education required some element of formal schooling. However, the Oxford and Cambridge degrees constituted only a condition of admission to the college. Promotion within the college, from licentiate to member to fellow, constituted a practice-based and practitioner-controlled ladder of higher medical degrees. Apothecaries and surgeons had emerged form the crafts and therefore from a long tradition of practice-based education, though in the late eighteenth and nineteenth centuries both were increasingly likely to serve their apprenticeships in hospitals and to combine them with formal lectures organised either by private schools or by the hospitals. All three professions therefore had, in different ways, combined school and practice-based training. The key question to consider here is how the balance between the two changed during the emergence of the modern English system of medical education and the respective roles of practitioners, universities and the State.

The two ancient universities made efforts in the seventeenth and eighteenth centuries to reform their medical teaching, but their part in medical education was not much more significant than in legal education.[38] They were content to continue through the nineteenth and the first half of

---

[37] For an overview see Robert S. Gottfried, *Doctors and Medicine in Medieval England, 1340–1530* (Princeton, 1986), 9–51; Frederick N. L. Poynter, 'The Influence of Government Legislation on Medical Practice', *The Evolution of Medical Practice in Britain*, ed. Frederick N. L. Poynter (London, 1961), 1–36.

[38] In 1770, for instance, Oxford amended its statutes in an effort to encourage the use of the recently opened Radcliffe Infirmary for medical students, but they preferred to transfer to Edinburgh or to private schools run by physicians and surgeons in London hospitals. Frederick N. L. Poynter, 'Medical Education in England since 1600', in *The History of Medical Education*, ed. C. D. O'Malley (Berkeley, 1970), 239.

the twentieth centuries within their medieval jurisdiction, providing the
arts degree required by the Royal College of Physicians and a first medical
degree. For clinical training their graduates either went abroad, enrolled in
one of the private schools run by practitioners in London, or entered one
of the London hospital schools, where they joined students who had
entered these schools upon completing secondary education. Cambridge
only established a medical school by associating with Addenbrooke's
Hospital in 1946 and Oxford with the Radcliffe Infirmary in 1968.[39]

Once again, the decisive confrontation between practitioners and academics for the control of professional education took place at the
University of London – it long dwarfed all the other schools put together,
and London established the model for the relationship between practitioners and universities which provincial universities deviated from in
only minor respects.[40] Although it had failed in its attempts to establish a
school of law, it had from the very beginning incorporated hospital schools
run by practitioners – both University and King's Colleges included such
medical schools when they were founded. The University continued to
affiliate with existing teaching hospitals, and by World War II had
accumulated thirty-four medical teaching institutions of one sort or
another. Many provincial universities had affiliated with a single local
hospital school in a similar manner.[41]

At first glance, this presents a startling contrast with legal education, and
it is difficult to believe that they can be part of the same pattern of
professional education when there is a total absence of professional law
schools (as distinct from law departments) and a superabundance of
medical schools. How could there be a greater difference between two
kinds of professional education?

In fact, the key element of the English pattern, practitioner power, will
explain both. Barristers and solicitors rebuffed the university because they
already controlled admission to and training for their professions and
because they considered the university had nothing further to offer them.
Doctors, by contrast, acknowledged that the university did have something

[39] Newman emphasises the reforms at both universities in the first half of the nineteenth
century. However, these did not embrace clinical training. Charles Newman, *The Evolution
of Medical Education in the Nineteenth Century* (Oxford and London, 1957), 122–30;
Poynter, 'Medical Education in England', 242–3.
[40] Which are specified by the indefatigable Abraham Flexner, *Medical Education in Europe,
A Report to the Carnegie Foundation for the Advancement of Teaching*, Bulletin No. 6 (New
York, 1912), 205–15.
[41] Archibald Edmund Clark-Kennedy, 'The London Hospitals and the Rise of the
University', in *The Evolution of Medical Education in Britain*, ed. Frederick N. L. Poynter
(Baltimore, 1966), 111–20.

to offer them and were therefore more willing to cooperate. However, since they also controlled admission to and training for their profession, they could dictate the terms of this cooperation, and repeatedly did so.[42] Affiliation of London teaching hospitals with the University therefore left the teaching hospital intact and its consultants, or their associations, in cÕntrol of appointments, curricula, teaching methods and examinations. After the Medical Act of 1858, the newly-created General Council of Medical Education and Registration (GMC) was given supervisory powers over all medical education. Although this was a State body exercising statutory powers, it never sought to define a State interest that was at odds with those of the practitioner associations. It was in fact dominated by the representatives of these associations and therefore enabled them to control medical education in the name of the State.[43]

Outside or inside the universities, medical education in England therefore remained under practitioner control. Observing it just before the First World War, Flexner decided that it was essentially an 'apprenticeship', that the medical student was 'handled like a schoolboy learning a trade'. The core of his training was 'actual and continuous participation…in the care of the sick'.[44] As a result, he found that medical education had signally failed to coordinate clinical and laboratory training, so the medical sciences remained in an ancillary, supplementary or what he termed an 'instrumental' relation to medicine and surgery. Since in his view a medical school required 'the adoption by the clinic of the methods and conceptions of physiology and other sciences', he was forced to conclude that 'a medical school … is not to be found in Great Britain'.[45] He was also left wondering in what sense the University of London was a university, since 'it examines … students whose teaching it does not furnish or control; it federates without internally directing, a variety of institutions

[42] The relationship was rarely an amicable one. As a result of the efforts of the Royal College of Surgeons, the University of London degrees in surgery did not give the right to practice surgery and did not do so until World War I. Throughout the nineteenth century, the royal colleges toyed with the idea of creating their own rival university. Rosemary Stevens, *Medical Practice in Modern England: The Impact of Specialization and State Medicine* (New Haven, 1966), 20.

[43] It consisted of one representative from each of the fifteen professional corporations of the United Kingdom, one from each of the universities whose degree constituted a licence to practice, five elected by universal suffrage amongst registered practitioners, and five nominated by the crown. After observing its work on the eve of the First World War, Flexner concluded that, 'It cannot mark out a curriculum or overhaul a school. Over neither school nor qualifying body does it possess direct compelling power … The licensing bodies thus actually determine the course of study … the Council has influence rather than powers.' Flexner, *Medical Education*, 267. For a more recent but similar characterisation see Poynter, *History of Medical Education*, 243–4.

[44] Flexner, *Medical Education*, 202, 208.   [45] *Ibid.*, 113, 192.

of incongruous character ... its medical schools are mere private ventures, affiliated but not transformed by the nominal university relationship'.[46]

After the First World War, the medical schools became more dependent on public funds from the University Grants Committee and, after the Second, from funds from the Ministry, later from the Department of Health. Funds were commonly distributed to them via the universities, which presumably increased their power to control or reorganise medical education at the expense of the practitioners. By 1965, however, there was little indication that they had tried to use this means of control. Stevens concluded that medical schools 'continued to be regarded as adjuncts of the particular hospitals from which they sprang – particularly the London schools, which stand on the same site as the hospitals, isolated from the university, and bear the hospital rather than the university name'.[47] One suspects in fact that strong practitioner representation on the GMC, which remained the final authority in matters of medical qualification, was still providing a means by which practitioners could use State authority to protect themselves against demands for change from other public bodies, as well as the universities.[48]

Until the sixties therefore, there was a decided resemblance between medical and legal education in England, since both had been shaped by powerful practitioner organisations rather than by the universities. There were two major differences, the first being that lawyers had remained outside the universities, either ignoring them or negotiating teaching arrangements with them, while the medical profession worked from within. The second major difference was that the State – via the GMC, the UGC, the Ministry of Health and its successors – has been more actively involved in medical education. However, these State agencies have never been used to re-shape the form or content of medical education or to dislodge the practitioner associations from their control of professional qualifications. In the 1970s, the University of London came under severe financial pressure to rationalise and merge its medical schools and has now reduced them to just nine, but there is no more recent evidence to determine how far such mergers and closures have reduced practitioner control of medical education or shifted the clinical bias of medical education or significantly increased the power of the universities relative to their medical schools.[49]

---

[46] *Ibid.*, 216.
[47] Like Flexner, Rosemary Stevens refers to medical school training as 'apprenticeship', and her brief references to the substance of medical education echo his observations. Stevens, *Medical Practice*, 171, 178, 324.   [48] Stevens, *Medical Practice*, 175–178.
[49] Poynter, *History of Medical Education*, 246–8. Reflecting on the mergers of the 1970s and 80s, Negley Harte observed, 'Having for long pushed the University around, the medical schools now found themselves pushed around by the University'. However, he presents no

In engineering, the beginnings of professional education follow exactly the same pattern as lawyers and doctors: practising civil engineers began to form associations long before the universities expressed any interest in offering degrees in engineering and long before the State recognised that it had any interest in the number or quality of engineers. The Society of Civil Engineers formed in 1771 began, like the Inns of Court and many other professional associations, as a dining club, but in 1818 its successors were granted a charter by the Privy Council as the Institution of Civil Engineers. The charter enabled them to perform regulatory functions with respect to admission and training in the manner of the Inns of Court. They were later followed by other kinds of engineer, the mechanicals in 1847, the gas engineers in 1863, the electricals in 1871 and through the turn of the century by many more.[50] And all of these bodies adopted the now-established practitioner-controlled route to a career in engineering via apprenticeship, which consequently became the accepted one in the eyes of entrants to the profession. A degree long remained merely an optional preliminary, just as it had for lawyers and doctors.

Engineering institutions, however, could not exercise the same degree of control over the training of their future members. Nor could they offer them any comparable protection in the labour market. The Inns and royal colleges both controlled work-settings and work jurisdictions within which only those whom they had certified could practice. The engineering institutions merely provided credentials. It was up to the employers of their members to decide what significance should be attached to them. There are no historical studies which would enable us to determine what significance employers did in practice attach to them and whether they reserved certain positions or certain kinds of work for those who had obtained them. The only thing one can say is that British employers never used their potential power to interfere in the process of professional qualification, never sought corporate membership or corporate control of professional bodies, never proposed another form of qualification, never even expressed a collective preference between membership of a professional institution and university degrees.[51] Thus, although we anticipated that employers would participate

---

evidence to suggest that the University was able to exercise any additional powers over the internal government of the schools. Negley Harte, *The University of London, 1836–1986. An Illustrated History* (London, 1986), 272–8.

[50] There are now seventeen professional associations for engineers. Geoffrey Millerson, *The Qualifying Associations* (London, 1964), 227–30.

[51] The proliferation and rapid growth in the membership of the professional associations suggest that they were serving some professional need other than that of learned societies. Between 1860 and 1910, membership of the big four alone – civil, mining, mechanical, and electrical – grew from 1300 to 23,910 compared with just under 20,000 in the United States and 7000 in France. Peter Lundgreen, 'Engineering Education in Europe and the USA,

in the shaping of the professional education of engineers, in Britain they have never done so, at least in an organised or collective way. Evidence from two English manufacturing firms in the 1970s indicates that they were then still reluctant to do so. Qualifications either from the institutions or the universities helped to obtain promotion for those who held them but were not essential qualifications for any particular job. These employers had no preference for one or the other, though the engineers themselves were strongly in favour of practice-based learning and highly sceptical of the utility of a university degree, even the minority who had obtained one.[52]

From their foundation until the 1960s, engineering institutions believed that, like the bar, they did not really need the added credibility or legitimacy of a university degree. Although the formal component of their admission requirements, consisting either of part-time courses at technical colleges or of exemptions for university courses, increased in the inter-war and post-war periods, it was, once again, the entrants to the profession who provoked the decisive shift to a school-based education. Just as would-be lawyers in the sixties increasingly decided to take law degrees, so would-be engineers also increasingly opted to qualify themselves with an engineering degree. In 1971, after a great deal of public criticism, the engineering institutions finally decided to become 'all-graduate'. Since then, the institutions have combined school and practice-based qualifications. Membership of the major engineering institutions requires a relevant university degree and four years of industrial 'training and experience'.[53]

Engineers' long indifference to university education appears to have been a catastrophic miscalculation in terms of defining and protecting a work jurisdiction for their members, in terms of public acceptance and status, and in terms of their solidarity as a profession.[54] The bar could afford to disdain the overtures of the universities; engineers evidently

1750–1930: The Rise to Dominance of School Culture and the Engineering Professions', *Annals of Science*, 47 (January 1990), 70.

[52] Of those called 'engineers' in these two firms, 54 per cent qualified by a Higher National Certificate or membership in a professional association, 27 per cent by a degree alone, 5 per cent by both and 16 per cent by craft apprenticeship, a General Certificate of Education or a technician qualification. Peter Whalley, *The Social Production of Technical Work: The Case of British Engineers* (Albany, 1986) 42–3, 50–4.

[53] For the origins of the Ordinary National Certificate and Higher National Certificate, see W. H. G. Armytage, *A Social History of Engineering* (London, 1961), 257; Robert Smith, 'Access and Recruitment to Engineering', in *Education for the Professions: Quis Custodiet...?*, ed. Sinclair Goodlad (Guildford, 1984), 105–13.

[54] For empirical evidence to support these propositions, see Whalley, *Social Production*, 42–3, 50–4; Allan Silver, 'Is There One Politics of the "New Middle Class?": Engineers in England, France and the United States', unpublished paper, April 1989, 13–14.

164   *Michael Burrage*

could not. For the moment, however, it is important only to note certain similarities between the three professions for, despite the differences between them, they appear to follow a reasonably consistent pattern.

The first step, in each case, was the emergence of associations of practitioners which recruited a substantial, or representative, proportion of the profession. These were then granted, by custom or charter, power to control admission to, and thereby education for, professional practice. Having delegated its powers in this manner, the State subsequently declined either to interfere in professional affairs or to recognise any public interest that took precedence over the interests of the practitioner associations. The universities similarly accepted that professional education and qualification were primarily a matter for the organised bodies of practitioners. And even though private employers controlled the professional practice of engineers, they too deferred to the prerogatives of professional associations.

The transition to school-based training did not, therefore, flow from any deliberate policy decision of the State, the universities, or employers. The transition to school-based medical education in the early nineteenth century was by the practitioners' own choice and under their control, at least until the 1970s. Over the greater part of this period, legal and engineering education had remained practice-based. The main pressure for change seems to have come from entrants to the two professions in the 1960s who opted for a university qualification prior to that provided by the practitioners. The State was indirectly involved, since it financed university expansion and student grants that made this possible. The universities were also involved only indirectly. They were beneficiaries of school-leavers' decisions, since it was the preferences of would-be lawyers and engineers that defined a role for them in both kinds of professional education which the practitioners were subsequently forced to acknowledge. In both cases, however, the practitioners' associations remained the important certifying agencies. The national peculiarities of this 'system' of professional education will, however, emerge more clearly when we have examined the other two.

Adversaries and dependants of the State: French medicine and engineering

It is no surprise to learn that the State played a greater part in the development of legal education in France than in England. Indeed, the more surprising fact to emerge from the account of the development of French legal education was the continuing resistance of practitioners, or more precisely, the orders of advocates. Before the revolution, their *stage* constituted *de facto* the significant qualification for legal practice before the higher courts, while after it, even though the law schools had been decisively reformed, rehabilitated, and legitimised by the Napoleonic regime, the orders of advocates were none the less able to preserve, and in recent times even to increase, the practice-based element. The orders of advocates, however, are known to have an exceptional, even unique, degree of autonomy and solidarity. As we consider medical and engineering education, it is of some interest therefore to discover whether medical and engineering associations reacted to or countered State initiatives in a comparable manner and whether they were able to exercise a comparable influence on professional education.

Under the *ancien régime*, medicine was, like law, organised and regulated by the corporate institutions of its constituent professions, though only the physicians enjoyed a high degree of autonomy. They were organised into nineteen faculties of medicine, and hence there was no in-built conflict between professors and practitioners. The university was not a separate institution but the basis of practitioner association. Surgeons and pharmacists were both organised as craft guilds and therefore trained mainly by apprenticeship. Both were supervised by the faculties of physicians. However, as we have already noted, in the decades prior to the Revolution, both were moving towards a school-based professional education. In the mid eighteenth century, royal support and sponsorship had enabled Paris surgeons to escape faculty control and to establish their own courses at hospitals, their own schools, and their own learned society, the Academy of Surgery, established in 1731. Paris pharmacists clearly intended to do likewise and in 1787 created a College where lectures were to be given for students and practitioners.[55]

During the Revolution, the corporate bodies of the medical professions suffered the same fate as the orders of advocates, though the revival of medical education preceded that of legal education by more than a decade. Three *écoles de santé* were established in 1793 to supply *officiers de santé* to the revolutionary armies.[56] In so doing, the Revolutionary State merged the previously separate professions of medicine and surgery and instituted clinically or practice-based education by linking these new schools to hospitals. These innovations were incorporated in the Napoleonic reconstruction of medical institutions which converted the *écoles de santé* into medical faculties of the Imperial University. State action therefore

---

[55] Professional institutions prior to the Revolution are surveyed in Matthew Ramsey, *Professional and Popular Medicine in France, 1770–1830: The Social World of Medical Practice* (Cambridge, 1988), 18–46.

[56] For a narrative of the main events, see David M. Vess, *Medical Revolution in France, 1789–1796* (Gainsville, 1975).

created a new system of medical education, one which bridged school-based education of physicians and the clinic-based education of surgeons long before any other society had tried to do so. Practitioner associations were illegal and had therefore played no part in these reforms.

Although these institutional innovations of the revolutionary period constitute a critical breakthrough in the history of medical education, and although they, more than anything else, explain French leadership of world medicine during the second quarter of the nineteenth century and brought students from all over Europe to study in Paris, subsequent developments suggest that they did not become a securely institutionalised part of French medical education. During the nineteenth century, successive reforms were necessary to try and ensure adequate clinical training for medical students. At the beginning of the twentieth century, the Paris faculty was engulfed in waves of protest by practitioners calling for reform of medical education which led to the closure of the faculty every year between 1906 until the outbreak of the World War. Attempts to devise an acceptable medical school curriculum continued in the inter-war years and were resumed after the Second World War, culminating in the Debré reforms of 1958 which supposedly merged academic and hospital careers and established university hospitals, though this measure required still further amendments in the sixties.[57] Evidently, the revolutionary design was, in some respect, either flawed or incomplete or unworkable. The development of medical education in France therefore had a long second act, during which various attempts were made to stabilise or realise the pioneering innovations of the revolutionary era. To understand this second act, we will have to examine these innovations more closely.

To begin, we may observe that, although the Revolutionary State had bridged school and the clinic, it had not integrated them. The universities did not own or control the hospitals. The two institutions were invariably physically separated from one another and remained under separate government departments: the faculties under the Grand Master of the University and later the Ministry of Public Instruction, the hospitals under the *Assistance publique*. Coury calls it a 'duumvirate', but they were not of equal power or status. The medical faculty alone awarded the doctorate degree and the licence to practice and whilst its professors were also hospital doctors, their status derived more from the former rather than the latter. And the faculties and the clinics were not left to themselves to work out a satisfactory working relationship since both were subject to rigorous and detailed State control by their respective departments.[58]

[57] For an overview see Charles Coury, 'The Teaching of Medicine in France from the Beginning of the Seventeenth Century', in O'Malley (ed.), *History*.
[58] *Ibid.*, 164; Flexner, *Medical Education*, 220–3.

The second point to note is that the bridge between academic and clinical training was not equally available to all students. The real beneficiaries were the elite of students who were successful in the *concours* for the *externat*, which usually lasted for two years, and the even tinier elite who succeeded in the *concours* for the *internat*, usually of four years.[59] The vast majority of students who were destined for medical practice had to obtain their clinical training during their degree. Since arrangements for ward teaching were poor, lectures in the faculty, on which students were examined, became much the most important part of their education. Attempts were made to correct this widely recognised drift to the lecture hall. In 1841 students were required to serve a one-year *stage*, and in 1862 this was extended to two years, though since no provision was made for the supervision and grading of students during their *stage*, medical education still centred on the 'oratorical exposition of theoretical advances' by the professors of the faculty.[60]

Thus, although the Convention and the Empire had intended to provide a new kind of medical education which combined school and practice-based training for all doctors of medicine, in practice it only provided a satisfactory, indeed over-generous clinical training for a select few and left the rest to fend for themselves. Indeed, we may infer that the innovative system of medical education of the revolutionary period had in fact become something else. It was not primarily a system of medical training at all but a system for the selection and training of an elite of the medical profession who would be eligible for State appointments. Selection as an *externe* and *interne* were the two essential preliminary steps. They led to an appointment as hospital doctor and eventually, for those who had passed the *agrégation*, to a university chair and the host of semi-official medical appointments that were in the gift of State officials.[61] In sum, the precocious innovations of the revolutionary period had been diverted from ordinary medical practice to the service of the State.

Finally, to understand the continuation of the system, one must recall that there was no way, during the three authoritarian regimes which followed the Revolution, in which practitioners collectively could exert a

[59] Coury, 'Teaching of Medicine in France', 166, suggested that 'the proportion of interns nominated in relation to registered candidates is about one in eight', though his figures for 1967 suggest it was even then closer to one in thirteen.

[60] George Weisz, 'Reform and Conflict in French Medical Education', in *The Organization of Science and Technology in France 1808–1914*, ed. Robert Fox and George Weisz (Cambridge, 1980), 80–94.

[61] Jacques Léonard, *La vie quotidienne des médecins de Province au XIXᵉ siècle* (Paris, 1977), 123–8. Léonard describes the system of elite selection as one of concours, coptation, and nomination, and briefly describes it in *La médicine: Entre les pouvoirs et les savoirs* (Paris, 1981), 188–90.

continuing influence to prevent this re-direction of medical education. The *loi Le Chapelier* of 1791, which had outlawed all forms of professional association, was not repealed until 1892. Although innumerable salons and learned societies sprang up in Paris under the Directory, these usually centred around the discoveries or theories of some notable professor or clinician. They were therefore discussion circles or learned societies, usually rather sectarian not representative associations, and did not concern themselves with the problems and grievances of ordinary medical practitioners.[62] In 1845, ordinary practitioners were finally permitted to convene a representative national congress which was such an unusual event that it is aptly described as the 'states-general of medicine'. Its main resolutions, moreover, were little more than a call for the *ancien régime* in medicine. First, they wanted the *officiers de santé*, the semi-doctors or physician assistants, to be abolished. Second, they wanted the restoration of self-governing corporate institutions to regulate medical practice. Finally, and most importantly in the present context, they demanded a much greater role for the practitioners in medical education. Specifically, they proposed that practitioners should be represented on the juries that nominated professors and examined doctoral candidates, that hospital appointments should be temporary, that they and all other State medical posts should be open to all doctors, and that all doctors should have the right to teach medical students on the premises of the medical faculty. This last proposal was, in effect, a call for the restoration of apprenticeship.[63]

The congress disbanded. There was, however, no means by which the profession could continue to press its demands. The system only began to change under the impetus of larger political events: defeat in the Franco-Prussian War, the fall of the Second Empire and the eventual establishment of the Third Republic. These threatened the continuation of the system in two ways. First, defeat provoked a profound loss of elite confidence in French institutions and a critical examination of many, including medical education. The view that eventually prevailed was that German superiority in this sphere depended on their facilities for laboratory research. For eight years (1876–84), the State therefore tried to make French medicine more 'scientific' by pouring funds into the science faculties of the universities and the laboratory facilities of the medical schools and by financing the creation of new clinical chairs. In the same spirit, professors of the medical faculties considered ways in which the scientific content of medical education might be increased and eventually decided on two solutions:

---

[62] Edwin H. Ackerknecht, *Medicine at the Paris Hospital, 1790–1840* (Baltimore, 1967), 40–62.

[63] Léonard, *La medicine* 207–8, 213–17; George Weisz, 'The Politics of Medical Professionalization in France, 1845–1848', *Journal of Social History*, 12 (1978), 1–30.

first, the creation of a new research-based doctorate, to prepare the way for full-time research appointments; second, the introduction of a preparatory year of science for all medical students which would be taught in science faculties.[64]

In formulating these plans, the professoriate together with the Ministry of Public Instruction had ignored the practitioners, as they had been able to do for so long. However, the Third Republic had also legalised professional associations in 1892 and thereby created a new kind of medical politics in which practitioners were at last able to play a part. Practitioners had in fact begun to form semi- or extra-legal associations in the later years of the Second Empire, but their new legal status obviously made it easier for them to recruit members and to publicise their concerns about the overcrowding of the profession, about excessive specialisation and, above all, about the unsatisfactory training in practical therapeutic techniques.[65] Medical education, therefore, faced pressure from opposite directions: from the elite that it should become more scientific and from the practitioners, that it should become less academic and more oriented to the needs of medical practitioners. The stage was set for violent confrontation.

In 1893 the preparatory science course was introduced.[66] This decision infuriated and mystified the practitioners. It did nothing to redress the long-standing academic bias of medical education, in fact, made it still more pronounced. However, since their associations had been legalised only in the previous year, and since they were mollified by the abolition of the *officiers de santé* included in the same legislation, they took no action. In 1906, however, when the government promulgated a decree, the first step towards the establishment of the research-based doctorate, the practitioners were much better organised. On this issue their hostility to the faculty coincided with that of another group of medical practitioners, the hospital doctors who had not passed the *agrégation*. In a sense, these hospital doctors were themselves something of an elite, though since they were not eligible for faculty appointments, decidedly below that of the faculty professoriate. And they also had a grievance against the State, since they received no official recognition or fees for their supervision of the students' clinical training. These two aggrieved groups were joined by a third, the students, who had long complained of the facilities for

---

[64] Weisz, 'Reform and Conflict', 80–94.

[65] There is no longitudinal data on medical unionisation but various kinds of evidence indicate that it had increased rapidly from the late 80s. In 1910 a leading journal, *Concours médical*, claimed that 57 per cent of the profession was organised. George Weisz, *The Emergence of Modern Universities in France, 1863–1914*, (Princeton, 1983), 361–2.

[66] Though certain preliminary measures to make practical work in the sciences compulsory had been taken in 1878 and 1879. Coury, 'Teaching of Medicine in France', 162.

their clinical and laboratory training, and these enlisted the support of many other students whose grievances had nothing to do with medical education.[67]

The 1906 decree provoked the annual protests which closed the medical faculties. They were usually prompted by student invasions of lecture halls, or attacks on some especially unpopular professor, and often incited or accompanied by practitioners. In the wake of the protests, the practitioners' associations held three national congresses. They nominated 'committees of vigilance' to prosecute their demand for the abolition of the *agrégation* and for a longer, more practical medical training based on the hospital and under practitioner control. In time their protests led to the revising of the curriculum, improving clinical training, and lengthening medical training by a year. They also prompted recognition of the teaching by hospital doctors and the transfer of State supervision of medical education from the Ministry of Public Instruction to a newly-created council of medical studies.[68] The question which had initially provoked the protests, of finding an acceptable balance between the lecture hall, the laboratory, and the hospital, remained to be addressed in subsequent decades.[69] In 1935, the preliminary year in the faculty of sciences was abolished in favour of a preliminary certificate, but in 1960 it was reintroduced and merged with the first year of the medical degree. In 1963 it was again organised separately; and three years later a sixth year, to be spent entirely in the hospital, was added to the degree. An internship, in other words, was finally provided for all students, a reform that might be said to fulfil the revolutionary promise and bring the second act to a close.[70]

The politics of medical education in France obviously followed a quite different form, but we may none the less note certain points of resemblance between medicine and law. Both doctors and advocates sought to reverse the school bias of the system created for them during the revolutionary era and to defend or preserve a practice-based element within it. Their freedom of action was for long limited by differing kinds of State control, the advocates by strict regulation of their corporate institutions, doctors by outright prohibition. Elite segments of both professions had moreover been co-opted by the State judges and *procureurs-généraux* in the law and by professors in medicine. Both therefore had to mobilise their members

[67] Weisz, *Emergence*, 352–63.
[68] *Ibid.*, 363–8. Flexner, *Medical Education*, 227–30, counted 'forty witnesses, not an unusual number', at one bedside clinic at the Hôtel Dieu but nevertheless suggested the problem of providing systematic clinical training had been solved.
[69] Little had been done by the time Flexner observed French medical schools in 1912. Flexner, *Medical Education*, 113–44, 231–2.
[70] Coury, 'Teaching of Medicine in France', 158.

against an alliance of the State, the university, and the elite of their own profession. Both eventually have had some measure of success. Was there, we may now ask, a comparable reaction and mobilisation amongst French engineers?

To grasp the peculiarities of French engineers, we must first recall that they only began to emerge as a recognisable occupation in the seventeenth century, that they were almost exclusively employed by the State and therefore had no history of independent corporate organisation similar to that of the legal or medical professions. Instead, in the seventeenth and eighteenth centuries they were organised as *corps* within the State, a *fonctionnaire* profession one might call it. As a result, the formation of school-based education did not entail a transfer to a separate institution or a take-over by a separate group of full-time specialists but grew out of a reorganisation of traditional practitioner-controlled training. The École des Ponts et Chaussées, for instance, established in 1747, was merely the conversion of the drawing office of the *corps* into a school.[71]

Although there were no corporate bodies of the engineers for the revolutionary assemblies to destroy, they were none the less suspicious of its corporate esprit and exclusiveness and initially placed them under the control of locally-elected *directoires*. Threatened by war, however, the Convention demonstrated that the education of engineers was still a high priority for the French State and created the Écoles des Travaux Publiques in 1792 which shortly afterwards became the École polytechnique. The importance of engineering education was further confirmed by Napoleon and every subsequent regime, all of which established similar professional schools as they needed them or complemented them by 'post-graduate' *écoles d'application*. These institutions were subsequently recognised as *grandes écoles* and as such have remained at the pinnacle of the French higher education system to this day.[72]

If the English barristers represent the extreme of practitioner power and self-government, then French engineers may be said to represent another extreme, the complete absorption of professional practitioners into a system of education, employment, career, and status – all of which were structured by the State. It therefore limited the opportunities for a rival, practitioner-controlled system of engineering education to emerge. The private sector tended, in fact, to take the State institutions as a model. Thus the manufacturers who thought the training provided by the École

---

[71] Jean Petot, *Histoire de l'Administration des Ponts et Chausées, 1599–1815* (Paris, 1958), 144–5.

[72] Their foundation is outlined in Peter Lundgreen, 'Engineering Education in Europe and the USA, 1750–1930: The Rise to Dominance of School Culture and the Engineering Professions', *Annals of Science*, 47 (January, 1990), 36–41.

polytechnique inappropriate for their firms supported the establishment of the École Centrale des Arts et Manufactures in 1829, but they soon conceived it as a sort of private sector École polytechnique. Thirty years later, it voluntarily came under State control and obtained recognition as a *grande école*.[73]

The enclosure of the engineering profession within the State meant that they adopted an unusual and distinctive form of practitioner association. In the 1840s students of the Centrale made several attempts to create a Société des Ingénieurs Civils along the lines of the Institution of Civil Engineers formed some twenty years earlier in England. Their teachers blocked the plan among other reasons because the students wished it to include *non-Centraux* in its membership. However, during the brief interlude provided by the Second Republic, it was formed none the less, and though mainly consisting of *Centraux*, was to some degree a professional association. Subsequently, however, French engineers organised mainly as alumni associations, rather than as a profession, and perhaps for this reason never formulated a distinctive practitioner ideology or defined a collective practitioner policy towards the engineering schools as a whole.[74]

In the twentieth century, French engineers have been free to form or join trade unions, but they have still declined to organise as practising engineers and have instead preferred *cadre* unions, which is to say that they preferred to organise on the basis of their status at their places of employment rather than on the basis of their occupational or professional identity. Their trade unions are therefore not well-placed to voice specific practitioner discontent with their system of professional education. The evidence suggests that they do not have any. Silver reports, on the contrary, that the French engineers in his study stressed the value of abstract knowledge as taught in the *grandes écoles* and frequently mentioned the *polyvalence*, or versatility, that it had given them, that is, the capacity to take charge of any problem from a managerial perspective. Even more revealingly, the French tended to identify their fellow *cadres* as their friends and that fully one-third of their friends were drawn either from those they met during the *cours*

[73] John Hubbel Weiss, *The Making of Technological Man: the Social Origins of French Engineering Education* (Cambridge, 1982), 1–25, 219–43.
[74] *Ibid.*, 86, 207, 303. Lundgreen reports that *Centraux* originally made up only 40 per cent of its membership and that originally 'its uniting principle was ... the exclusion of all state engineers'. It complained about 'false engineers', presumably *Polytechniciens*, who trained as engineers but were actually administrators and never practised as engineers. Lundgreen, 'Engineering Education', 40, 74, 194–5. Terry Shinn, 'From "Corps" to "Profession": The Emergence and Definition of Industrial Engineering in Modern France', in *The Organization of Science and Technology in France, 1808–1914*, ed. Robert Fox and George Weisz (Cambridge, 1980), 194–6, 183–208.

préparatoires which preceded their entry to the engineering schools or from the schools themselves.[75]

There is little indication among French engineers of the kind of practitioner dissatisfaction that we encountered among the advocates and the doctors. The three French professions therefore show three different responses to the academic domination of their professional education. While the advocates tried to encroach on the schools' prerogatives unobtrusively, and the doctors, having been long obliged to remain silent, incited a 'revolt' in the streets and lecture halls, the engineers seem to have willingly embraced it. Engineers are thus the deviant profession and pose an interesting problem. Why is it that they have been able to avoid the estrangement between school and practice that is commonly found among advocates and doctors?

There are several possible reasons. Bearing in mind that their schools originated in eighteenth-century work settings and were organised as separate institutions rather than within universities precisely to prepare students for State service, it is possible that the kind of education they have provided has been less academic, less removed from everyday working practice than that provided by professional schools located within universities. Moreover, some of them are *écoles d'application* and have very specialised vocational goals. It may be that engineering education in France is well integrated with engineering practice and hence has been able to avoid the disorientation and re-socialisation that often accompanies the transition from school to the workplace. Accounts of the formal, abstract, and theoretical curricula of the École polytechnique and of the Centrale, however, make this rather difficult to believe.[76]

It seems more plausible to look for an explanation to the unique combination of roles performed by the French State which has, as we have seen, not only organised and controlled engineering education, but employed their graduates and also, more than elsewhere, been the final arbiter of their professional status. Hence, whether or not the schools have been integrated with engineering practice, they manifestly have been integrated with the engineering labour market and the careers of elite engineers. Their diplomas promise, if not guarantee, high income, career advancement, and elite status. The advantages their graduates enjoy in these respects over the non-qualified *ingénieurs maison* and the technicians who work under their direction provide daily reminders that they have reason to be grateful to their old schools. It may be that these schools have been preparing their graduates less as practising 'hands on' engineers than

---

[75] Silver, 'Is There One Politics of the "New Middle Class?"', 13–14.
[76] Terry Shinn, *L'Ecole Polytechnique, 1794–1914* (Paris, 1980), 52–60.

for a mid-career transition into management. For this reason they might be better compared, not with the engineering schools of British or American universities, but with war or staff colleges of their armed forces. Like the latter, they not only prepare their students for elite roles but indicate that they have already been accepted into them. As a result, loyalty to their *corps*, to engineers with a similar educational background, similar employment prospects, and similarly high status has displaced the interests and loyalties that engineers elsewhere share by virtue of their common knowledge and from which a practitioner ideology, and practitioner resentments, develop.

Triumph and setback for the universities: doctors and engineers in the United States

Like the lawyers, doctors of the colonial and post-independence period were on their way to becoming a self-governing profession. In a few colonies their societies were granted licensing powers and, subject to certain limitations, post-revolutionary legislatures continued this policy.[77] Like doctors elsewhere, they did not try to discourage or block the development of medical schools, though they did try to control it and ensure that it complemented the practitioner-controlled apprenticeship system. Initially, this was not a particularly difficult task since the medical school faculty usually continued in private practice and often saw their courses as no more than part-time additions to apprenticeship training. Nevertheless, there were identifiable conflicts of interest in the early nineteenth century as practitioners sought to defend their control of admission to medical practice and refused to recognise medical school degrees as equivalent to the medical societies' licence.[78] Both medical societies and medical schools were, however, soon overwhelmed by another kind of medical practitioner, the irregular self-styled doctors who obtained widespread popular support for their campaign against any kind of State-backed licence. In 1824 Maine repealed legislation regulating admission to medical practice. Illinois did so in 1828. Eight more states followed in the 1930s, four in the 40s, and three in the 50s. In 1849, the newly-formed

---

[77] William G. Rothstein, *American Physicians in the Nineteenth Century: From Sects to Science* (Baltimore, 1972), 74–84.

[78] Harvard fought for nearly a decade for this right. Some schools were able to affiliate to a university, in their own or another state, which had obtained recognition for its degree. One Maryland school, founded under the auspices of the state medical society, eventually persuaded the legislature to grant it a charter as an independent university and in this way escaped practitioner intervention in its affairs. For these and other examples and further references, see Richard Shryock, *Medical Licensing in America, 1650–1965* (Baltimore, 1967), 1–60.

American Medical Association claimed that only New Jersey and the District of Columbia had any laws regulating medical practice.[79]

The sentiments behind these attacks were similar to those that had already destroyed the legal profession and the effects of the repeal of medical licensing were also the same as the repeal of bar admission requirements. Legislatures might destroy the licence but the medical school degree remained, and the demand for this credential therefore increased. To meet it, the number of medical schools also increased. As they did so, they were compelled to try to increase their enrollments by lowering their entrance requirements, by allowing transfer with 'advanced credit' from competing schools, and by setting curricula that were not too demanding for the students. The medical practitioners' societies did not disband or collapse as the bar associations had done. Those that survived, however, were small, unrepresentative bodies that could hardly control the schools.[80] There is therefore a basic similarity between law and medical schools in the United States in that state legislatures, by repealing admission requirements and undermining professional associations, gave them the freedom to create and exploit the market for their diplomas.

Significant differences between the two professions began to emerge in the last quarter of the nineteenth century when both began to reorganise and tried to re-establish practitioner control of professional education. The lawyers, briefly at least, saw clerkship as an alternative to a law school education. This was not an option for the medical societies. Lawyers could readily contemplate a legal profession and professional education without any school component. The physicians could not. The primary concern of the AMA was to raise the standards of medical education. By so doing, they could limit the numbers entering the profession and then to exercise some control over the schools, pushing some distinctive practitioner concerns, such as the provision of clinical training and the defence of the role of the general practitioner against excessive specialisation.

The AMA's efforts to raise the standards of admission to medical schools and the standards of teaching within were triumphantly successful, at least during the decisive decade of 1910–1920.[81] Thereafter, however, it seems to have had rather little influence on the content of medical education. Most accredited schools shared its concern about the provision of internships and residencies, so this was seldom a source of dispute after 1920.[82] The remaining issue closest to the heart of the organised practitioners was to prevent the proliferation of specialties and to defend

[79] Rothstein, *American Physicians*, 328–39. Shryock, *Medical Licensing*, 24–31.
[80] Rothstein, *American Physicians*, 63–84, 101–24.
[81] James, G. Burrow, *Organized Medicine in the Progressive Era* (Baltimore, 1977), 31–51.
[82] Rosemary Stevens, *American Medicine and the Public Interest* (New Haven, 1971), 151.

the status and role of the general practitioner. However, the alliance the AMA had put together to support its accreditation campaign could not be re-deployed to control the development of postgraduate specialties or to prevent the appearance of newly organised specialty boards.[83] In the end, practitioner hostility towards specialties was simply overtaken by events: by students who continued to opt for specialty qualifications, by patients who preferred to consult specialists, and by the organisation of hospitals into specialty departments. By the 1940s, the AMA itself was dominated by specialists, so this was no longer a major issue. The most the AMA could then do was to try to see that there were residencies for would-be general practitioners and that they were not subsequently denied hospital privileges.[84]

Apart then from the decade of 1920–20, organised medical practitioners have not been able to exercise any more influence over medical schools than lawyers over law schools. The distinctive characteristic of American medical education is that the university has been able to organise it just as it wishes without regard to the wishes of either practitioners or the states. The new model of American medical education which coordinated, in a single institution, teaching of the basic sciences, laboratory research, and clinical training was derived largely from Germany and installed at Johns Hopkins between 1889 and 1893. Neither organised practitioners nor the states had any part in this. The diffusion across the United States was the product of competition between accredited schools rather than of any action by practitioner associations or legislatures. The most one can say is that neither tried to block it.

What, finally, of engineers? The first important fact about the American engineering profession is that it began to organise after the self-governing institutions of the two older professions had been destroyed. It had no model of a self-governing body of practitioners to imitate. It therefore initiated an unprecedented, and indigenously American, kind of profession which began with the foundation of private educational institutions, notably the Rensselaer Polytechnic in 1823 which in 1835 became the first institution in the English-speaking world to award a degree in civil engineering. Harvard followed in 1845, Dartmouth in 1851, and Yale in 1852. By 1880 there were eighty-five private and public institutions offering degrees in civil engineering.[85]

Practising engineers only began to organise some time after a number of schools had been established. Their first association, the American Society of Civil Engineers, was formed in 1867. The second, the American Society

[83] *Ibid.*, 75–172.   [84] *Ibid.*, 302–17.
[85] George S. Emmerson, *Engineering Education: A Social History* (Newton Abbott, 1973), chapter 8.

of Mechanical Engineers, was established in 1880. Engineering schools were therefore able, unlike law and medical schools, to create and exploit their market from the very beginning without ever having to defer to the demands or rules of practitioners' associations. The schools had to counter a strong 'shop culture' but not well-organised bodies of practitioners. On the contrary, practitioner associations were forced from the beginning to acknowledge the schools' role in professional education. Both the civils and mechanicals therefore allowed members to qualify either by 'active professional practice' or by an engineering degree with a reduced period of practice.[86]

Neither of these associations nor any of their successors ever contemplated the creation of a rival, wholly practitioner-controlled system of professional education and qualification on the English model. It would have been quite impossible for them for to do so, however, attached as they were to a 'shop culture'. Engineering schools were already established institutions, and the movement towards school-based education in engineering, as in the law and medicine, was well under way. Hence, when the societies voiced the usual practitioner discontent with 'impractical' academic training, the schools had no reason to respond, other than to answer in kind and discredit the 'shop' culture of apprenticeship-trained engineers.[87]

The failure of the practitioner associations to define a role for themselves in the education and qualification of engineers probably explains the quarrels, protest, and splinter movements that have dogged them throughout their history. Most failed to distinguish the interests of individual practising engineers from those of the corporate enterprises that employed their members and tried, unsuccessfully, to represent them both. The first association, the American Society of Civil Engineers, started out in 1867 as a professional body with a code of ethics and high admission requirements, and it also attached great importance to its journals and learned society functions. When challenged in 1871 by the establishment of the more business-oriented American Institute of Mining and Metallurgical Engineers, the Society began to alter its stance. The American Society of Mechanical Engineers and the American Institute of Electrical Engineers, founded in 1880 and 1884 respectively, 'both tended to be closely allied to business interests and, to a degree... served as trade associations'. All four of these 'founder' societies (as they were called) 'represented compromises

[86] The civils initially required non-graduates to have worked as an engineer for five years and allowed graduates to become members after three. For this and other examples, see Lundgreen, 'Engineering Education', 47–8.

[87] Monte Calvert, *The Mechanical Engineer in America, 1830–1910: Professional Cultures in Conflict* (Baltimore, 1967), 55–72; David F. Noble, *America By Design: Science, Technology and the Rise of Corporate Capitalism* (Oxford, 1977), 27–8.

between professionalism and business interests'.[88] As industrial corporations expanded in the closing years of the century, their employees became increasingly influential within the associations and increasingly used the associations to voice their employers' concerns about the supply and quality of their engineering manpower.

The associations were in no position to resist this corporate takeover since they needed direct and indirect business support to survive.[89] In the early twentieth century there were several attempts to distance the engineering profession from corporate capitalism and to define a more honourable, even heroic, role for the engineer, standing between capital and labour in the public interest, preferably, for many of the dissidents, in the public service. This 'revolt', as Layton describes it, was an entirely domestic affair. It prompted debates within the associations, reform movements within the societies, some of which were successful, and a number of splinter associations, some of which survived.[90] It did not mean the emergence of a strong, distinctive, rival professional view of engineering education.[91]

In the early twentieth century, therefore, the 'practitioner' view of engineering education came by default to be that of the large corporations employing engineers. It was expressed either through the engineering societies, serving as proxies for large corporations, or through the Society for the Promotion of Engineering Education, which had been created in 1894 and established direct organisational links between employers and the engineering schools. Whilst the schools might ignore the views of individual practitioners, they had little choice but to respond to complaints of corporate 'practitioners'. Large corporations could, after all, decisively affect the schools' market prospects either as their benefactors, trustees, or alumni, as their collaborators, as employers either of their graduates or their faculty, or, of course, as potential competitors by providing in-house training facilities. Consequently, from the turn of the century to the outbreak of the First World War a host of 'cooperative' schemes to

[88] Edwin Layton, 'Science, Business and the American Engineer', in *The Engineers and the Social System*, ed. Robert Perrucci and Joel E. Gerstl (New York, 1969), 54–5.

[89] *Ibid.*, 62–3.

[90] Such as the Federated American Engineering Societies founded in 1920 (subsequently re-born as the American Engineering Council) and the National Society of Professional Engineers founded in 1934. Edwin Layton, *The Revolt of the Engineers* (Cleveland, 1971), 58–74, 112–25. See also Noble, *America by Design*, 44, 62–3.

[91] The only policy of these associations unambiguously in the interest of individual practitioners and of little interest to large corporations was reserving certain kinds of work for state-registered engineers. Even though state legislatures were favourably disposed, their assistance was limited to particular kinds of work, usually in the public service. Paul H. Robbins, *Building for Professional Growth: The National Society for Professional Engineers*, National Society for Professional Engineers (Washington, 1984), 235–50, 299.

integrate engineering education and engineering practice emerged. The University of Cincinnati plan to alternate school and employment weekly was adopted by twenty universities and seventy companies between 1907–1919. In 1910 the University of Pittsburg launched a rival cooperative system, and the University of Akron devised 'second shift' and 'night college' plans for engineers in the rubber industry. Elite schools were less inclined to participate in such schemes, though the Massachusetts Institute of Technology also launched various cooperative initiatives of its own – a School of Engineering Practice and special honours and graduate programmes – with a similar intent.[92]

Over the long run, given the engineering industry's determination 'to bring education into some correlation with the business world', given the resources and sanctions at its disposal, and given also the support it received from the federal government during the Second World War for its efforts to fashion an integrated system for the recruitment and training of engineers, the wonder is that the universities were able to preserve any autonomy for their engineering schools.[93] Continuing complaints of engineering employers about the schools suggest that they were in the end able to resist a corporate take-over. Their academic ideals, their links with neighbouring scientific disciplines, and the tradition of curricular in-dependence of universities, even when in receipt of industrial donations, seem to have prevented the same degree of coordination of education and employment imposed by the French State. Engineering schools, we may conclude, have been far more practitioner-oriented than either law or medical schools, though only because in this instance 'practitioners' means not the individual professional engineers but corporate America's major employers.

Conclusion: the uses of comparative analysis

The starting assumption of this analysis was that practitioners have tended to resist the transfer of professional education into academic institutions. In only one of the nine professions examined, French engineers, is there no evidence of any kind of dissatisfaction with the academic control of professional education, and it therefore constitutes the striking deviant case. The aim of the analysis was to see whether, bearing in mind the significant variations between the three professions, one could identify and specify recurring national, systemic patterns in the inter-relationships of the major participants in the development of systems of professional education.

[92] Noble, *America by Design*, 184–202.   [93] *Ibid.*, 206–23.

The evidence suggests that it is not unreasonable to do so. In England, practitioners have dominated the system. The State has, for the most part, merely facilitated practitioner control, while the universities have tended to accept the secondary, supportive role allotted to them. The transition to school-based professional education has therefore been much slower than in the other two countries and in the case of legal and engineering education was the result of changing student preferences. In France, the initiative has always lain with the State, and the Revolutionary State in particular used its power to create school-based professional education, elevating the status and power of the academics at the expense of the practitioners. Advocates and doctors have sought to preserve a practice-based component, both with some degree of success, though since it is rather easier for doctors to do so, the success of the advocates is the more remarkable. In the United States, state legislatures, by responding to popular attacks on the professions and repealing bar and medical association admission requirements, enabled universities to market professional education. Practitioners have only been able to influence professional education indirectly, in cooperation with elite professional schools by means of accreditation. Doctors had most success with this strategy and lawyers rather less. Practising engineers have had no discernible impact on engineering education, while that of their employers has been considerable.

Overall, it would not be too wide of the mark to characterise the three systems as practitioner-dominated, State-dominated, and school-dominated respectively, though as we have observed, particular professions tend to cluster round these national 'norms' rather than reproduce them uniformly. The basic point, however, is that the three systems cannot be understood in terms of an economic or a pedagogic logic since their patterns have all been shaped by larger political events. Beneath the convergence of these three societies towards school-based professional education, the relationships of the major participants in the creation of the system retain quite distinctive national characteristics. If these inter-relationships have been correctly identified, one should be better placed to explain their development and dynamics, as well as their contemporary strengths and weaknesses. That, at least, is the hope of this, as I imagine of every other comparative study: to better understand one institution by comparing it with others of a similar kind.

This point may best be illustrated by the case of English engineers. There is already a sizable literature on this profession, which specifically tries to explain the British failure, from the later nineteenth century to the present day, to educate sufficient scientific and engineering manpower to enable the kingdom to keep abreast of the United States, Germany, and other economic rivals. This literature concentrates almost exclusively on the supply side of educational provision and assumes that the demand for formal, school-based professional education can be taken for granted.[94] It therefore castigates those responsible for the supply failure: successive British governments, universities, academics, intellectuals, and businessmen, none of whom had the wit, vision or imagination to support the creation of new, technologically-oriented institutions, or even to recognise the need. And its last resort is usually to criticise the British character or values.

There is reason to doubt this kind of explanation. In fact, the need was widely recognised.[95] And since the new universities established in industrial cities at the turn of the century were hardly flooded with applicants for their places in science, engineering, or technology courses, and since the larger part of their graduates made careers in teaching rather than in industry, it is clear that something has been omitted from these accounts.[96] This comparative analysis suggests what is missing. England already had a viable and functioning practice-based system of professional education and qualification, a system which was supported by the powerful precedents and overwhelming legitimacy of the legal and medical professions. Moreover, this system was much cheaper for would-be engineers in terms of income foregone than a university degree.

The existence of a practice-based form of engineering education, therefore, provides an alternative, demand-side explanation of Britain's failure to create, or take up, sufficient scientific or engineering degrees at universities. Moreover, this explanation meets the two pre-conditions of any satisfactory explanation of Britain's predicament. First, the alleged explanatory factor, the presence of a rival system of professional education, really does differentiate Britain from other economically more successful countries. None of these countries had a rival practice-based system of engineering education of this kind and none therefore had, like Britain, to dismantle or dislodge an existing system, widely-used and accepted by

[94] A partial exception is Donald S. L. Cardwell's analysis of both demand for and supply of applied scientists in the nineteenth and twentieth century. His key proposition is that demand from within the educational system precedes that from industry. 'Until the universities were producing the professional specialist, industrial demand could not make itself felt – did not, in fact exist – and young men could not enter industrial research in large numbers.' The Humboldt education reforms in the early nineteenth century therefore explain why Germany created many more applied scientists before the British. Cardwell does not mention professional bodies at all. D. S. L. Cardwell, *The Organization of Science in England: A Retrospect* (London, 1957), 188–9, 180–92.

[95] For numerous examples, see Geoffrey R. Searle, *The Quest for National Efficiency: A Study in British Politics and Political Thought, 1899–1914* (Oxford, 1971).

[96] Gordon Roderick and Michael Stephens, 'The Universities', in *Where Did We Go Wrong? Industrial Performance, Education and the Economy in Victorian Britain*, ed. Gordon Roderick and Michael Stephens (Lewes, 1981), 198–200.

engineers and employers, before creating a school-based system of engineering education. Second, this practice-based system is relevant to the problem to be explained since it exercised a direct impact on school leavers' educational and career choices, managers' and employers' preferences and, in all probability, relationships at the workplace. By contrast, explanations which refer to anti-scientific, anti-entrepreneurial or other values not only fail to conduct comparative analyses to show that these values are distinctively British. They usually draw their evidence for the existence of these values from the works of a literary and academic elite and therefore fail utterly to demonstrate how they may have affected behaviour at the workplace.[97]

The argument might be taken a step further and used to explain not only Britain's failure to develop sufficient engineers but also to understand the peculiarities of the British educational system more generally. Throughout its history, the formal university or school-based system has had to accommodate or confront a more firmly established rival 'system' of practice-based education. To ignore it is to overlook an educational experience that English lawyers, doctors, accountants, nurses, carpenters, compositors, electricians, civil servants, army officers, and dozens of manual occupations have shared.

The limited provision of university education in Britain is, for instance, usually explained by reference to the values of the political and academic elite, i.e. again from the supply side. But since over a long period professional associations provided an alternative qualification, and since none of them required a college degree, there was no compelling reason for anyone wishing to enter one of the organised professions in England to obtain a university education. The distinctive educational and licensing roles of practitioner associations in England consequently provides a complementary, and equally plausible, 'demand side' explanation for the small proportion of English school-leavers entering university.

The more recent forms of practitioner-controlled education may also have influenced the character of English schools. There is, at any rate, a certain resemblance between professional and craft institutions and those often thought to distinguish English educational institutions. In the eighteenth and nineteenth centuries, for example, professional apprentices 'boarded' with their masters, and it seems not unreasonable to suppose that the common practice of leaving home to serve an apprenticeship in the home of one's master facilitated acceptance of the boarding principle in English public schools. The institutions of fagging, houses, teams, and

[97] See for instance Martin J. Weiner, *English Culture and the Decline of the Industrial Spirit, 1850–1980*, (Harmondsworth, 1985).

prefects found in the public schools are all based on the assumption that the school is not merely an educational institution but a community with its own distinctive moral order. Hence, a boy did not attend simply to learn but also to become a member of this community. Entering the school required an intensive socialisation by those who already belonged to the community and subordination to their authority in a manner not unlike professional and craft apprenticeship.

Similar collegiate ideals have also influenced the development of English universities; and this, along with the role of the tutor and the tyranny of the single-subject honours degree, also have professional and craft precedents. Squires recently put the point succinctly. The central focus of British university education, the single honours degree, he observed, 'bears all the hallmarks of the traditional apprenticeships: the close relationship between master and servant, the clear demarcation of craft boundaries, the emphasis on learning by imitation, the socialisation into the craft ethic (even the jokes), the stages of initiation and progression, the final Masterpiece'.[98]

Postscript: the loser's vision

In the preceding account we have observed practitioners responding, in different ways, to the advance of school-based professional education: English barristers with aloof indifference to what the rest of the world sees as educational common sense; French advocates unobtrusively restoring their *stage* during the nineteenth century, and energetic lobbying in the twentieth; French doctors reacting with violent protests, while ordinary American doctors and lawyers formed an alliance with the enemy to 'accredit' elite schools. Little, however, has been said to explain their actions and attitudes, of what it was practitioners thought they were resisting or fighting for. Perhaps it was simply money or power and status. Losing control of professional education meant a direct financial loss of practitioners' income from premiums and fees. It also meant losing control of the future size of the profession and therefore of the future market for professional services. It might also have been perceived as a loss of power and status because those who control professional education might be said to determine to a large extent what counts as knowledge or what counts as important and relevant knowledge. New school-based knowledge threatens practitioners.

Until there is more research about practitioners' lives and their reactions to the rise of the schools, we can neither accept nor dismiss any of these

[98] Geoffrey Squires, 'The Curriculum', in *British Higher Education*, ed. Tony Becher (London, 1987), 175.

arguments. For one thing, it is rather difficult to measure the influence of economic self-interest or the desire for power or status on the collective decisions of professional associations. One can only say that they do not seem to be a complete explanation because at times the attempts to maintain practice-based training seem to extend beyond any discernible direct financial, power, or status interest. It is hard to believe, for example, that the elite of the New York City bar who founded the Association of the Bar of the City of New York perceived a significant economic interest in the restoration of mandatory clerkships. Some professions, like the French bar in the eighteenth and nineteenth centuries, seem rather indifferent to their aggregate size. It is easier to find instances where practitioners thought they were losing power and status, especially among French doctors, but British engineers held on to their practice-based system while they were rapidly losing both.

Historical and contemporary accounts of practice-based training suggest another possibility. Originally, virtually every profession, apprenticeship, clerkship, or internship was a kin, near-kin or fictive-kin relationship. Their high rates of self-recruitment indicate that the real kin was usually a significant core. The *stage de papa* was familiar to French advocates after World War II. These rates, being confined to father–son relationships, often understate the full extent of kin relationships. However, even when there was no direct kin tie between master and clerk, they retained a strong kin character. To begin with, they were commonly arranged by a father for his son, and whether with a friend, professional colleague, or stranger, the father remained as a silent party to the agreement. Among English lawyers, until the mid-nineteenth century, the pupil or clerk usually lived at the home of his master and was literally incorporated into his family.

In a real or fictive sense, apprenticeship has to be seen as an extension of kin ties into the labour market. Critical accounts of the drudgery and humiliation of apprenticeships contradict this observation not a bit, no more than accounts of the horrors of family life lead one to doubt that the family is a genuine kin relationship. Whilst one cannot say to what extent this kin element survived when the master–pupil relationship became exclusively work-based, it is certain that it remained quite unlike a normal employer–employee relationship. The pupil or clerk was not paid a normal wage, the relationship with his master was a personal and particularistic one, and neither side could of their own volition change the terms or duration of the articles. Moreover, since the master had been entrusted by the pupil's father with certain parental responsibilities, it necessarily entailed certain moral obligations.

Practitioners' commitment to practice-based education might be best understood by reference to these origins and these circumstances rather than by the standards of school-based professional education. By the latter, it can only seem a primitive and ineffective method of imparting information. For practitioners it was evidently doing other things, of much more importance: instilling respect for one's elders and for their experience, forcing entrants to submit to a period of semi-servitude and therefore making them value membership of the profession that much more. It was also providing cast-iron guarantees about the attitudes, demeanour, and commitment of those who entered the profession.

Judged by these standards, a school-based professional education is, for all its cognitive superiority, a grossly inferior institution. Every year professional schools release among practitioners large numbers of confident young strangers, with pieces of paper certifying that they have acquired some knowledge relevant to the practice of the profession and claiming the right to be treated as colleagues and fellow members of the profession. It is only by assessing schools by the standards of apprenticeship in some such manner that we can begin to understand practitioners' attitudes. We can also, incidentally, understand why practitioners have let their case go by default. If it were articulated, it would be, among other things, an argument for deference, for respect, for discipline, trust and loyalty. In modern democratic society, committed to universalistic criteria of occupational selection and admission, certain things must be left unsaid. If these are to influence decisions, they must do so surreptitiously, by informal, post-entry selection procedures. The public gates to the profession mention only publicly acceptable, universalistic criteria.

The idea that practitioners have been motivated by such moral considerations has been corroborated by an admirable piece of contemporary field research by Bosk which documents the existence of all these 'traditional' relationships and attitudes in a contemporary Californian medical school at the frontier of hi-tech medicine. Bosk spent two years observing and recording the relationships between the 'attendings' or chief surgeons, and their 'apprentices', the residents, interns, senior, and junior students.[99]

Again and again, he discovered that the attendings' reaction to the 'normative' errors of interns and students was far more severe and punitive than their reaction to 'technical' errors. Normative errors were failures to perform role obligations conscientiously. They were committed whenever students were less than prompt, or less than willing, to accept their share of work, of responsibility, or of blame. Technical errors were simply the result of ignorance or lack of experience and elicited only mild, tolerant, 'restitutive' sanctions, a reminder of listen carefully or read an

[99] Charles Bosk, *Forgive and Remember: Managing Medical Failure* (Chicago, 1979).

article perhaps. Normative errors, by contrast, were greeted with heavy sarcasm, with expressions of personal distaste, and resulted in the humiliation of the wrongdoer. Seen as moral failings, they elicited severe and repressive sanctions and, in some instances, marked the end of the student's career in surgery. The evaluation of the students, Bosk concluded, was therefore primarily moral rather than technical. Students were judged by their dedication, interest, and thoroughness rather than by their technical knowledge. Such 'moral' qualities could be assessed in the most humble and most routine of tasks, in a word, by drudgery. Bosk goes on to identify what he calls 'quasi-norms', that is rules invented by, and peculiar to, a particular attending. Transgressions of these norms, 'quasi-normative errors', were deemed to reflect an unwillingness to accept professional authority or contempt for its standards. Regarded as more serious than technical errors, they merited repressive sanctions on the grounds that they were an indication of a full-blown normative failing.

Medicine is, as we noted earlier, the one profession that has been able to incorporate apprenticeship into school-based education, so we cannot treat it as representative. It would not, however, be unreasonable to suppose that the moral concerns of Californian attendings have their counterparts in other practice-based systems of training, indeed wherever experienced practitioners are responsible for the training of new recruits and their admission to the profession.[100] They provide a clue as to exactly what it is that practitioners have been fighting for and why it is that they have often been indifferent to the cognitive or technical superiority of school-based education.

It would not be correct to assume that professions whose education is entirely school-based have abandoned all forms of moral selection and moral socialisation of new members of the profession. Sociologists have frequently discovered that workers, without any formal apprenticeship, maintain informal systems of socialisation and collegial control, and it seems likely that professions with school-based training have devised something similar for the graduates entering their professions. None the less, it seems reasonable to suppose that as practice-based training has given way to school-based education, the moral component of professional education has declined.

This puts the transition from practice to school-based training in a rather different light. It becomes rather more than a transition in teaching methods from the haphazard, and often arbitrary and exploitative, training

---

[100] Numerous examples of the humiliation of apprenticeships, their moral, kin, and filial character, as well as their indifference to overt instruction, are to be found in a series of anthropological studies of apprenticeship in Asia, Africa, and North America reported in *Apprenticeship: from Theory to Method and Back Again,* ed. Michael Coy (Albany, 1989).

offered by practitioners to the more systematic and effective methods of full-time specialists. It becomes, in fact, a struggle between two kinds of moral order, that of schools acting on public and universal rules which demand fair and meritocratic selection and assessment for professional employment, and that of practitioners, whose rules and demands are private and exclusive, seeking only to preserve the moral order of the profession itself. If the schools invariably provided more equal opportunities to the disadvantaged, to the children of manual workers, to ethnic minorities and women, then it would not perhaps be much of a contest. At times, however, school-based education has promoted more restricted entry to the profession, as in American medicine, or created new forms of stratification, as among French engineers, while the practice-based system of English and early American engineers enabled manual workers, at whatever age, to rise into the profession. So the struggle is a real one. To do justice to this aspect of professional education, we might best divorce it altogether from general histories of educational institutions or from accounts of the extension of educational opportunity. We must at least root out and discard their Whiggish assumptions.

Part 3

The ambiguities of university research in Sweden and the United States

5 Universities, research and the transformation of the State in Sweden

Aant Elzinga

Introduction: research and development in present-day Sweden

This chapter deals with the transformation of university-based research in a single country, Sweden. It begins with a general introduction followed by a review of the four phases of the history of the university system. Each of the phases is then dealt with in greater detail.

The focus, however, is on the post-World War II era, especially the recent decades when the universities turned into institutions for mass higher education, becoming part of a larger national system that includes regional vocational schools and colleges. The end result was a country-wide unitary system under a National Board of Universities and Colleges controlled by the State. Its head was the Chancellor of what might be called the 'University of Sweden', which is composed of local campuses.[1] The heads of the local universities and colleges are called Rectors, and they also possess the status of Vice Chancellors in the administratively unified national system. Today there are six universities, thirteen specialised institutions of higher education and fifteen university colleges. The latter are of rather recent date. Most of them derive from 1977 when one of a series of university reforms was implemented. Some of them are specialised around particular lines of higher vocational studies which the government and Parliament (the Riksdag) have decided to place in various regions in the country, often as a stimulus to regional development. Research at the regional colleges is limited, often not being much more than an accumulation of projects connected to the core of the vocational curriculum.

Sven-Eric Liedman, Christer Skoglund, and Björn Wittrock have all given me valuable comments on an earlier draft. I wish to extend a sincere thanks. Sheldon Rothblatt has, in addition to his prodding comments and questions, given generously of his time when applying his elegant editorial hand to enhance the readability of this chapter. For this I am most grateful.

[1] In the seventeenth century each university had a Chancellor who served as an intermediary between Crown and University. As such, Chancellors enjoyed great prestige. The present-day linkage between university and centre, a key feature of the unitary system, can therefore be said to have had a shadowy pedagree.

The colleges are not entitled to award doctorates, nor do they have research positions such as professorial chairs and associate professorships. Some grant-aided research, however, is undertaken on a small scale, and funding from research councils is obtained in competition with larger institutions. In addition, and outside the formal purview of this unitary national system, several towns and cities sponsor local higher education institutions providing more or less practical or narrowly vocational courses.

The six universities include Uppsala, the oldest, founded in 1477, and Lund, dating from 1688. Much newer universities are Stockholm and Gothenburg, situated in the two great metropolitan centres. Their histories differ from those of Uppsala and Lund, which were State institutions from the very outset. By contrast, Stockholm and Gothenburg, founded in the latter part of the nineteenth century, were private institutions. They received State support only later, and not until after World War II were they integrated into the national system of higher education. Two additional universities, one in the north in the city of Umeå and the other in the industrialised region of Linköping, were created as late as 1962 and 1975 respectively.

When one speaks of a university-based research system in Sweden, one means the six universities but also several specialised institutions, most of them prestigious institutions with highly selective student bodies, major research laboratories and strong ties to networks and constituencies outside academia proper. The most famous are the Royal Institute of Technology and the Karolinska Institute, a medical school well known for the quality of its research. Both are in Stockholm. Chalmers University of Technology in Gothenburg is also known for its world-class research; and the University of Agricultural Sciences, with its main location near Uppsala, concentrates on agriculture, veterinary medicine and forestry. Mention should also be made of the far northern University of Luleå, which now boasts of excellence in certain areas in the engineering sciences, and the Stockholm School of Economics, which, however, remains a private institution with huge and growing endowments and a reputation as an internationally leading business school. It lies outside the national unitary system.[2]

Altogether, twelve institutions have been mentioned here. Of course, there are also higher educational institutions concerned with the fine, performing and applied arts. These also form part of the national system of higher education, and efforts are afoot to build up some form of research

[2] Roger Geiger, *To Advance Knowledge: The Growth of American Research Universities* (New York and Oxford, 1986).

potential within them, although there has been some confusion as to what 'research' means in their particular contexts.

On the map one can see that the twelve members of the university-based research system are concentrated in seven locations. The squares on the map show the location of universities; university colleges are represented by black dots in the various regions. An inset shows the density points of knowledge-based industries.

To complete this general orientation, it can be added that between 1866 and 1910, Sweden grew from a population of 5.6 million to about 8.2 million. During that period the nation became highly industrialised, with a third of the population finding their livelihood in industry by its end. In 1940 about 38 per cent of the population were working in agriculture and subsidiary branches, and about 34 per cent in industry. Ten years later the figures were about 24 per cent and 43 per cent respectively.

The first two decades of this century also saw the political breakthrough that was to put Sweden on the map of parliamentary democracies. The rise to power of the Social Democratic Labor Party inspired a particular form of Swedish reformism called the 'Folkhome' (*Folkhem*). This movement embodied the ideals of egalitarianism and a class-free society. Its political programme aimed at developing socialism through parliamentary action revolving around the idea of a mixed economy with welfare politics. This required a strong State not only to protect the weak but to correct income maldistribution. Folkhome reformers believed that a strong State would also curb the worst effects of capitalism by protecting those parts of the population bypassed in the modernisation process. The State was to create an extensive protective net of economic and social security while still using capitalist methods as the primary motor of industry and wealth accumulation. At a very general level, then, the expansion of the university-based research system followed the contours of this development mix of capitalist industrial expansion and welfare policies. Research activity paralleled the growth of Swedish social democracy, and it is not a coincidence that today Sweden is internationally respected for its research in some areas of the engineering sciences, and in medicine and biomedical research.

As a rough indicator of the growth of Swedish science, one can look at the historical increase in the numbers of professors. Today the total number of chair appointments is about 1500 in the whole country – or nearly 0.02 per cent of the population. (In the mid-1930s there were about 400.) This number is nevertheless small in comparison with the situation in some other countries like the United States. This is not only because of the smaller size of the country, but also because the decision to create a new professorial chair is ultimately one that is taken or authorised at the highest

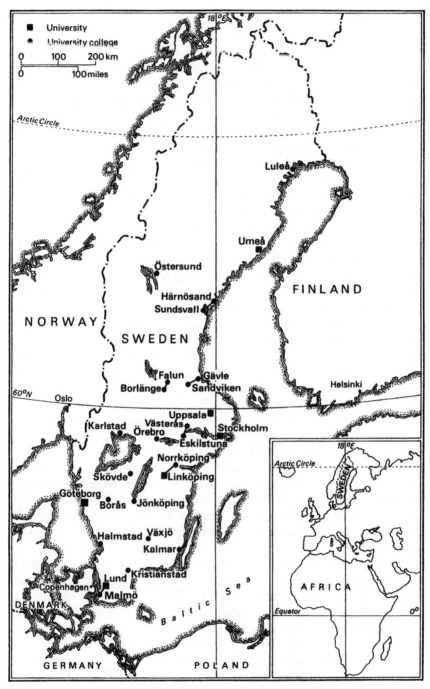

194   *Aant Elzinga*

Map 1 Universities and university colleges in Sweden

levels of government, involving the Riksdag when chairs are being created and the Cabinet when chairholders are being appointed. In this system, professors are higher civil servants. For the most part the State has accepted the recommendations of the professoriate when appointing chairholders. Nevertheless, the creation or contraction of areas of research remains a national policy decision and represents State management of science through control of the top levels of the university research system. Holders of university chairs are formally responsible to and mandated by the State to develop their particular fields of knowledge and train the new generations of scholars and scientists destined to take over and continue their work.

From the late 1960s to the late 1980s, Swedish science policy was based on a so-called 'sectoral principle'. University research was to bear upon problems perceived to be important in the various 'sectors' of social endeavour assigned to particular ministries or associated public agencies: housing, energy, environment, research support to developing countries, transport, etc. Universities, as part of the State system, were the main repositories of all public research, including mission-oriented programmes and projects, and in fact mandated research dominated Swedish science policy during the 1970s. Support for basic research through the universities' own research infrastructure was largely ignored. There was instead a large increase in externally-funded research. Neither Social Democratic reformers nor representatives of the traditional professoriate seriously opposed this policy, the latter sensing, probably correctly, that protests might entail a threat to their established power bases. However, opposition developed in time as serious tensions and problems resulted in the Swedish university system as a consequence of government policy. The authority of the professoriate was eroded, doubts began to circulate as to the proper or true mission of universities, and academic circles began to speak about an identity crisis. The surge of commercial or market pressures in the 1980s, emphasising funding at the university-industry interface, made the general academic situation yet more uneasy.

Expressed in simple terms, one can say that the universities are now facing their most serious challenge. Different vested interests are pulling in different directions. The invasion of external mission-oriented funding tied to political objectives, together with a heavy emphasis on immediate economic gains and suggestions that the universities adopt a more entrepreneurial style of management are viewed by many as a latter-day Trojan horse. Still, the universities have been able to accommodate both external and internal pressures before, and hopefully they will do so today, while strengthening their historic core mission of basic inquiry and independent critical capacity, derived in large measure from the ideals of *Bildung*.

From the universities' point of view, some reason for optimism exists because of the new science policy bill which the government submitted to the Riksdag in the spring of 1990. It is the fourth such bill since 1982. This one draws up guidelines for expenditure and growth in the Research and Development sector for the next three years and even longer in the future. It underscores the real shift in basic science policy which actually began in 1983–4 and which was characterized by a change from short-term economic objectives towards basic research and the strengthening of long-term competence in strategically important areas of R&D. As a result of the shift, some mission-oriented agencies have been closed down, e.g., the Energy R&D Commission. While the National Board of Technology Development (STU) has now been overhauled, others have been transformed into research councils proper with strong peer review influence over the allocation of funds, as in the new programmes for supporting social science and research on higher education. Even more far-reaching, the National Board of Universities and Colleges was dissolved by a new Conservative coalition government in summer 1992.

The tensions and conflicts that have emerged over distribution of support between basic university funding and external funding on the sectoral principle does indicate some resistance by the academy to both State control of research and industrial or private sponsorship and influence over R&D agendas. However, in this complicated situation we also find various tacit alliances cropping up between industrial interests and academics against State domination of the organisational forms in which research is cast. A good example of this is evident from a recent investigation of the rapid growth of private foundations and science parks in the vicinity of universities and colleges. Between 1980 and 1986, no less than sixty such institutions have appeared, most of them without official authorisation from the national review agency that oversees the formation of such bodies. These constitute a source of non-government support for university-based science that could probably reduce academic reliance on public sources. On the other hand, these alliances obviously favour some academic specialties much more than others. They also raise the possibility of a conflict of interest.

Signs of another kind of networking with a different thrust are also apparent. These are linkages between members of the academic community and outside interests or critics who are worried about the penetration of short-term goals into university research and its possible effects on long-term stability and freedom of inquiry.[3]

---

[3] *Stiftelser för samverkan* (Foundation for Cooperation), SOU, 50 (1989) (the commission report).

Transformation of the Swedish university research system since 1919

The transformation of the Swedish university research system can be divided into four phases. The 'pre-war phase' stretches from 1919 to the beginning of the Second World War. It is marked by the relative stagnation and partial isolation of the professors, who, supreme within their own domains, nevertheless possessed little influence over the conditions of knowledge expansion. Still, for obvious reasons, it is a time looked back upon with some endearment. Academic life was relatively simple, government bureaucracy almost non-existent, and the numbers of students and professors few. Loyalty to the system of discipleship was great. Based on personal bonds between teacher and student, it extended downward into the gymnasia which supplied universities with undergraduates.

The second phase began during the war and continued until about 1965–9. It was a period of growth in university science, the creation of government-funded research councils (on the model of other countries, especially Britain) for additional funding over and above faculty grants, and a general expansion of infrastructural arrangements. In short, it was a phase in which supply-side policies of science dominated, to include support for several megascale projects associated with military and atomic energy interests. The style of politics at the interface between the professorial oligarchy and the circles of government was relaxed, epitomized by Prime Minister Tage Erlander's personal relations with a number of prominent scientists of his own generation. Major decisions were made in small collegial groups or in research councils where outstanding scientists rubbed shoulders with leaders of industry, government, and public agencies.

A third phase, starting in the mix-sixties, but clearly taking form in 1969 when Olof Palme became Prime Minister, was dominated by State-driven demand-side policies, by what has been termed a 'radical rationalism' in planning and State intervention, and a more aggressive style of politics at the conjunction between government and the academy. It was during this period that the Social Democratic Labor Party set about its quest to proceed from political and social democracy to economic democracy. This entailed an effort to create the ways and means of directly effecting economic growth through such industrial policies as the introduction of workplace democracy and the accumulation and use of capital generated by a system of employee savings. The system proved ineffective, nor were the proposals popular. Nevertheless, the radical bureaucratic rationalism of the period greatly affected science and academic policy. These were the years when the 'famous' university reforms or 'U68' were introduced.

They consolidated the unitary national system of mass higher education which had been forming since 1959. Attention to advanced research was now being crowded out by a technocratic and egalitarian tunnel vision that tied undergraduate programmes of study to a reformed secondary school system and subjected them to forecasts of future labour markets needs.[4] Terms such as 'post secondary educational institutions' came into usage (as elsewhere in Europe) and the label 'high school' (*högskola*) was applied to all higher educational institutions, including the research universities. These were also the years when the principle of sectoral science policy was introduced, bringing with it a proliferation of sectoral research funding agencies – over fifty during the decade of the 1970s.

Paradoxically, during six of these years, that is, from 1976 to 1982, Sweden was not governed by a Social Democratic government but by what is commonly known as a 'bourgeois' coalition of three parties to the right of the Social Democrats. However, occupying a weak parliamentary position, the new government took it upon itself to implement both the system and the set of policies which it had inherited. One member of the coalition, the Liberals, actually favoured many of the higher education reforms of the previous ministry, but at this time the ideal of a rationally organised society was probably generally popular in Sweden.

The fourth phase, in which we presently find ourselves, may be said to have its origins in the science policy bill of 1984 when basic research was once again recognised as a strategic resource essential for national industrial development. In part the rationale for emphasising basic research lay in the nature of the new and emerging technologies considered important for the country's long-term competitive strength in a global market. Micro-electronics, bio-technology, and advanced industrial materials are all areas in which high technology is intimately dependent upon basic research, and therefore most countries have been establishing science parks and making other attempts to set up 'silicon valleys' and 'silicon glens' (Scotland) as channels through which industry monitors and exploits the most advanced forms of university-originated research.

Another factor encouraging the changeover to a science policy of management rather than prescription was the realisation that the previous technocratic phase with its extremes of trying to earmark and steer research became so obviously counterproductive that even politicians and leading decision makers in public agencies had to retreat from the sectoral science policy in its most mechanical expression. But they have not abandoned the principle. Thus today we see a combination of supply-side

[4] See Bo Lindensjö, 'College Reform, a Study in Public Reform Strategy', in *Studies in Politics*, no. 20, Department of Political Science, Stockholm University, 1981 (in Swedish).

and demand-side policies, synthesized into what I shall later describe as a science policy of 'orchestration' involving both ends of the decision-making continuum.

Having indicated some of the main characteristics of each of the four phases into which the history of the Swedish university research system may be categorised, it now remains to sketch out some of the outstanding events and features in more concrete terms. To do so I shall proceed from past to present, ending with a discussion of the situation today when Sweden puts 3.1 per cent of its Gross National Product back into R&D, with a level of investment of about $6 billion, 70 per cent of which is private sector money mostly going back into product and industrial process development in the laboratories of a handful of multinational companies. Altogether it is estimated that some 75,000–90,000 people are in one way or another involved in research and development. In person-years the figure is about 55,000. The number of scientists and research engineers is held to represent an effort equivalent to about 27,000 person-years, perhaps a little less. In 1985 the total number of university research staff in all disciplines was about 7,600 persons, of which the greater proportion – about 5,000 – were research assistants supported by project funding, the remaining 2,600 comprising those with positions as associate professor, research associate, or professor, the latter about 1,500 in size. The universities had 17,000 registered graduate students distributed over all academic fields and disciplines, but only a third of them recorded as being full time. Tenured academics still only make up a small portion of the cadre of civil servants which in Sweden today number about 250,000 State employees, a figure which includes schoolteachers, police, customs officers, and railway workers.

In global terms Sweden's investments in R&D represent about 1 per cent of the world total, a small amount. In terms of output, however, the country's scientists in several areas of research, particularly in the natural and medical sciences, account for considerably more than this, at least if one takes indices of citation frequencies as a reflection of actual performance.

The inter-war years

As already noted, during the early nineteenth century Sweden only had two universities, the ones in Uppsala and Lund. Uppsala was established in the Roman Catholic era and suffered so severely in the early phases of the Reformation that it was closed down. Opening again in 1595, it was refounded as a Protestant bulwark against papal influence. It was only during the reign of Gustavus Adolphus in the 1620s that the University received major financial support from the Crown. In the following decades Sweden's momentary rise to the position of a European great power, especially in northern Europe, provided Uppsala with the opportunity of supplying the expanding realm with recruits for the Royal State's civil and clerical administration. The next Swedish universities to be founded accompanied a policy of territorial expansion across the Baltic. The University of Dorpat was created in Estonia in 1632. Åbo Academy in present-day Turku was established in 1640 and was lost in 1809 when Czarist Russia took control of Finland. The existing University of Greifswald on the edge of the Baltic in northern Germany was annexed and remained under Swedish sovereignty until the end of the Napoleonic wars. Nearer to home, Lund was established in 1668. The latter was a very deliberate step to bring the newly occupied, formerly Danish province of Scania under the cultural hegemony of the Swedish crown. Lund was endowed with land and property and began life with about twenty professors of Danish, Swedish, or German background. Its immediate task was to educate new generations for the Lutheran priesthood and provide the Crown with civil servants.

The re-established Uppsala University started with eight professors and an agreement which ensured an income from property held in the surrounding countryside. In 1620 the Crown decreed that the needs of law and medicine required the creation of additional professorial chairs, and the Royal connection provided, as mentioned, a generous gift. In the centuries following, Uppsala remained economically self-sufficient until 1830, increasing the number of professorships and adding inquiry into natural philosophy to its mandatory task of educating priests and civil servants. Nevertheless, universities in Sweden as in most countries were places for the dissemination of learning rather than centers of original investigation; and neither by history, organisation nor ethos were they equipped to participate in the systematic development of new knowledge. The main focus of work for a higher degree was the 'medieval' act of defending a thesis at a public disputation rather than original work as in the writing of a dissertation. However, even when the writing of a dissertation became part of the requirements for earning a doctorate, the professors customarily claimed the credit. In the empire of knowledge, the professor was lord of his disciplinary fief. A first change came in 1852 when new statutes promulgated for both universities specified that candidates for the degree of *magister* had to write and publicly defend a dissertation, which could be presented in either Latin or Swedish. The statutes also required some form of research, or at least publication (often in the form of lectures) as well as teaching to be part of a professor's obligations, indeed, a condition of his employment. The German idea of *Lernfreiheit* had made its appearance.[5] It is possible, therefore, to date the professionalisation of academic life from this point. Professors were now more than just civil servants.

In 1876 the large and omnibus philosophical faculties at the two universities were sub-divided into two sections, one for the humanities and one for mathematical and natural sciences. This reflected a process of cognitive differentiation and the emergence of the natural sciences as an important cultural element and potential productive force of significance for industry. In 1873 women obtained the right to qualify for university degrees, an indication of the beginnings of a process of educational egalitarianism.

The institutional arrangements developing in this way were hardly those normally associated with the model of a research university. Indeed it was not until 1916 that 'research' was actually mentioned in the statutes of the universities, and by that time there was already a great deal of research-related activity outside universities themselves, mostly in connection with industrial and commercial developments. Two technological institutes, one in Stockholm and another in Gothenburg, started up in 1827 and 1828 respectively. The former was reorganised into the Royal Institute of Technology in 1876, and gradually expanded with close links to industry. The Chalmers Crafts School, called the Chalmers Technical Institute between 1914 and 1937, also grew into a scientific institution incorporating a research mission. Its higher division was turned into a technological college in 1937, and two years later the Swedish State provided a common set of statutes for both Chalmers and the Royal Institute.

During the years immediately before World War I, there were scarcely 1,000 engineers with advanced education employed in Swedish industry. Most of them had received their higher education outside the country, often in Germany. Industrialists lobbied and campaigned through the Industriförbundet (the Swedish Association of Industrialists) and the Royal Swedish Academy of Engineering Sciences (founded in 1919) to develop the kind of science they preferred. In one early (1913) Industriförbundet publication a future attitude is already apparent, the author observing that,

successive attempts to plant engineering sciences into the universities have failed, since these institutions do not provide an environment in which the technical sciences can thrive and develop their own characteristics, i.e., practical application and rational economic connections ... There are only two ways to go, either: to unite the whole technological college with the university and thus ensure an independent and free development of engineering education within it ... or: to continue to let the

[5] See the contribution of Sven-Eric Liedman to this volume.

universities and the technological colleges be separated and expand the latter in a way that meets the demands of the coming century.[6]

As it turned out, Swedish higher education did in fact follow the second course, and the universities remained separated from the technological colleges and higher professional schools. Thus they also to some extent remained outside the transformation taking place in Sweden after the First World War, a process of modernisation and democratisation in the wake of rapid industrialisation. It was not until the Second World War that the universities seriously began to be brought into this process, the impulse coming strongly from outside academia. The groundwork was laid through the historic compromise between labour and capital that took form during the 1930s. The Social Democrats began a term of power that with some exceptions continued for half a century. In their long-term vision, science was a productive force and an important ingredient for human welfare. Leading politicians and industrialists could accordingly agree that co-operation between State and industry in order to advance the economy should certainly include the realm of science. Ernst Wigfors, a long-term Minister of Finance, expressed it thus: 'If natural resources are one of the building blocks on which people build their welfare, discoveries, technical, and organisational innovations are the other,'[7] He envisioned cooperation especially in two areas:

1) the exploitation of natural resources, requiring risk capital in order to discover and utilize such resources, with the State providing backup investments to prevent the temptation to secure immediate gain;
2) the application of new technologies through the introduction of different institutional arrangements allowing private industry to benefit from State-owned and controlled research institutes and laboratories without university interference.

The title of the book in which Wigfors later republished his essay is called *From Class Struggle to Cooperation* (1941). His was the perspective that obtained in the era to come. When his message was proclaimed, the world of the universities still belonged to the nineteenth century. It was a world in which chairholders still reigned supreme and ancient scholastic customs and rites still predominated. Certainly the universities were important as halls of learning and scholarship, and Swedish scientists had an excellent reputation in certain fields. The founding of the Nobel Prize

---

[6] Cited by Aant Elzinga, 'Science Policy in Sweden', *Forskning och politik i Sverige, USA och Soviet* (Science and Politics in Sweden, the Soviet Union and the USA), ed. Ronny Ambjörnsson, Gunnar Andersson, and Aant Elzinga (Stockholm, 1969), 127.

[7] *Ibid.*, 131 and for further detail on the facts and figures that follow, see pp. 131–2.

furthered international interchange and the maintenance of high standards. In the 1930s there were solid achievements in physics and chemistry,
and the State contributed to the establishment of a cyclotron in Stockholm
in 1938 to be used mostly for medical purposes. Biochemistry was also
successful. But outside the natural and medical sciences, the traditional
system contained only a handful of real research environments, and to a
large extent the 1930s were marked by relative stagnation and the isolation
of universities from mainstream developments in society. Total state
allocations to the universities and colleges increased only very slowly in
this period, rising from 2 million Swedish kroner in 1914, to 2.5 million ten
years later, 4.4 million in 1934–5, and 5.5 million in the last years before
the end of the decade. (The krona was worth about eighty times its present
value.) But in terms of the percentage of budget for cultural activities
generally, this was actually a relative decline. After 1935, in fact, the
allocations to research institutes outside the universities even began to
exceed all grants to the universities. It is estimated that the total support for
R&D during the decade 1934–44 was more or less constant, being about
0.09 per cent of the GNP. Despite the new visions that were developing,
research was for the most part still regarded as a luxury affordable in good
years but expendable in lean years.

When Wigfors first became Finance Minister in the Social Democratic
government, he suggested that twenty-four scholarships be earmarked for
especially talented young researchers. The minister responsible for higher
education opposed the number, believing that so many such scholarships
would be too revolutionary a reform for the academic world. Even the
subsequent introduction of a smaller number met with lukewarm support,
combined with outright resistance.

Those who came to the universities were few and privileged. Educated
in Swedish gymnasia, their teachers possessed higher academic degrees
in specialized disciplines. Urban Dahllöf in his study of the ecology
and career-value of postgraduate studies has shown how certain school
subjects were favoured over others in determining the award of doctorates. During the fifty-year period between 1890–1939, 185 persons
qualified for PhDs in history, while disciplines like statistics or education,
lacking a similar market for specialist teachers, only produced 20 PhD's
each during this entire time. In the natural sciences, Swedish universities
produced 137 PhDs in chemistry, a relatively large number, accounted for
by the fact that chemistry did have a place in the school curriculum since
it was an area in which Swedish industry expanded.[8] But the subject

[8] Urban Dahllöf, *Fasta forskartjänster vid universitet och högskolor i Norden* (Tenured
Research Positions at Universities and Colleges in the Nordic Countries), Report from the
Department of Pedagogy, Uppsala University, no. 60, (1982).

also had a glorious tradition behind it, with names like Berzelius and Ahrenius.

The volume of research at the universities was contingent upon three factors: State support and control over the number of professorial chairs, a specialist labour market created by the demands of the gymnasia and schools, and indirectly to some extent the industrial growth and transformation of the country's economic core. Still, in 1940 there was a slight skewing in favour of the humanities, with the universities counting fifteen chairs in theology, three in Greek, three in Latin, four each in English, German and Romance languages respectively, seven in Nordic languages, seven in history, and four in the history of literature. In philosophy there were six, in education four, geography four, and biology seventeen. Chemistry had ten. The universities were stronger in those disciplines influenced by the work of Linnaeus and Berzelius than in physics (five chairs), mathematics (six) and astronomy (five). The total number of professors in mathematics and the natural sciences in Sweden increased only very gradually, from thirty in 1890 to forty-six in 1920 and to fifty-seven in 1940. In medicine there was an increase from fifty in 1890 to sixty-eight in 1940. If chairs at the technological institutes and agricultural and veterinary colleges are counted, of course one finds a greater number of 'natural sciences' in a broad sense (228) than 'cultural sciences' (130).[9]

The fact is that the universities did not have an organisation that could meet the needs of a major research university. Certainly new disciplines developed as the field of knowledge became more differentiated. However, the numbers of students also increased until the mid-1950s, although very slowly. In view of the relatively small number of chairholders, the increase was possibly detrimental because it required that a larger number of 'new' disciplines be taught, thus cutting into the time available for research. The situation may have mainly affected the natural sciences, for in the late 1930s there was concern about academic unemployment in the humanities. In any case, the professorial mandate was largely to produce educated cadres for the higher echelons of the civil service.

The actual numbers of postgraduates needed for the replacement of the university teaching staff were insufficient, and the possibilities for advancement in this system were few and far between, generally hinging on retirement. When this happened, the ensuing competition between several candidates could of course be very heated, leading to public pamphleteering against one's more successful opponent. There were a small number of docent positions in the system, but these had a limited tenure of

---

[9] *Ibid.* The figures also appear in English as an appendix in Lennart Svensson, *Högre utbildning och staten i svensk historia* (Higher Education and the State in Swedish History) (Stockholm, 1987).

six years. If for one reason or another a chair did not materialise, the alternative was a teaching post at one of the gymnasia. Provided that one kept up research and scholarship, a return to the university was possible at a later date.

A positive feature of this system, often mentioned, is that the students who came to the universities had personal contacts with scholars and researchers. Furthermore, because of the personal bonds existing between teachers in the gymnasia and university professors, some of the gymnasia teachers were deemed sufficiently competent to conduct tutorials at the universities. Torsten Hägerstrand, the internationally renowned cultural geographer, recalls his early studies in this system:

We who started studies in the 1930s were immediately confronted with the ongoing research of the professors and docents. It was instructive to hear the professor take back something one week that he had said in the previous week because new data had come in. We early on were given a little research task the result of which would in due time be ventilated in what corresponded to a little disputation. In some cases we were soon allowed to attend the higher seminars.[10]

Hägerstrand goes on to describe an environment in which the style of critical discussion as learned in the seminar was the central element. Professors questioned their brightest students in order to keep up with new work in their fields. The common gymnasium background of the students not only provided a solid foundation in foreign languages – English, French and German – but also contributed to a shared set of cultural values which transcended disciplinary boundaries and set the students apart as a cultural elite.

Basically the same system of research training was in operation at the two independent university colleges in Stockholm and Gothenburg, although perhaps with less of the scholastic style and traditional rigidity of Lund and Uppsala because of the influence exercised through boards of governors by the industrial and mercantile interests of the cities.

In Stockholm the first lectures started in 1878 were given in the natural sciences in hired rooms. The two first professors were installed in 1881, another four in 1884, and in 1907 a faculty of law and political science was established with five professors, the other faculties having grown in the meantime. While the focus in Stockholm was on the natural sciences, in Gothenburg it was the humanities, the city college starting up in 1891 with seven professors. Gothenburg also featured geography and oceanography, subjects reflecting local trading and marine interests in this major Swedish

[10] Cited in the discussion in *Erövra universiteten åter* (To Recapture the Universities), ed. Gunnar Ström (Stockholm, 1985), 32.

port; yet by 1932 there were only nineteen professors, seventeen docents and 320 students all in all.[11]

The two university colleges enjoyed the patronage of city leaders, and representatives of municipal government sat on the college boards of governors. The State itself began contributing small amounts to the colleges in line with a general understanding of the importance of higher education to society, but it was not until ten to fifteen years after the Second World War that the colleges actually became publicly-supported universities. Gothenburg was accorded the name 'university' in 1954, when it contained two faculties, a philosophical and a medical one. Stockholm first became a full-fledged State university in 1960, and by 1970 had moved from a scattering of buildings in the city to a new location at Frescati in the suburbs near the Royal Academy of Sciences.

Even if the cities had some influence on college studies, the academic infrastructure and environment in 1930s' Stockholm and Gothenburg, as in Lund or Uppsala, did not openly favour or encourage student research interests. As Hägerstrand notes: 'One was not accepted for doctoral studies. One was discreetly invited to continue studies in order to obtain a grade of special honours. We were not so many in a group either, so it was easy after the seminar to go out and talk about general questions.'[12] Tutorials and oral exams were also informal affairs, frequently taking place in the home of the professor where he mostly worked. In the natural sciences, because of laboratory requirements and the beginnings of collaborative research, the teaching style was understandably different.

Despite its lack of an organisation for research in the modern sense, the Swedish postgraduate educational system did have several features that could in principle encourage a belief in the importance of advanced scholarship. The first is the fact that university statutes of 1908 and 1916 connected teaching to scientific research. The PhD thesis came to be regarded as a serious and original contribution to knowledge which had to be published, even if at the candidate's own expense. Second, the system featured a public defence of the thesis, and 'opponents' (the old scholastic designation) functioned like external examiners, thus providing a form of peer review. Third, in medicine and the natural sciences the institution of the Nobel Prize system played a role in promoting quality work. Prominent Swedish scientists had to serve on committees to review nominations, and there was thus an added incentive to monitor and keep abreast of international developments. Sweden could count five Nobel Prize winners

[11] *Statiska Årsboken* (Statistical Yearbook for 1932) (Stockholm); for a more detailed history of the Gothenburg College see Curt Weibull, *Från högskola till universitet* (From College to University) (Göteborg, 1976).
[12] Cited in Ström (ed.), *Erövra universiteten åter*, 22.

in physics and chemistry before 1940. The building of the cyclotron and what is now the Manne Siegbahn Institute for Atomic Physics (originally under the auspices of the Royal Academy of Sciences but until 1992 under the National Board of Universities and Colleges) could be justified in part by reference to Siegbahn's Nobel Prize and his international standing. The other legitimating factor was the link to medicine and the beneficial role of atomic radiation as it was perceived in that context.

Building the base, 1939–1965.

Lennart G. Svensson, in his review of higher education and the State in Swedish history, connects the development of a binary partition of higher education to the basic divisions within Sweden's social structure. The feudal State and aristocratic segments were tied to the two ancient universities. A newer bourgeoisie, demanding entrance into a secularised civil service according to conceptions of individual merit, favoured a different kind of higher education system, one composed of specialised institutes and schools, such as for engineering. While such a two-tiered higher educational system did emerge in time, the city colleges in Stockholm and Gothenburg actually occupied an intermediate position, in the sense that they were less isolated from mainstream trends in society than the State universities.[13]

When industrial interests and Social Democratic welfare visions combined to bring about changes, the basic binary setup was at first left intact. The main thrust of cooperation went towards building up new infrastructural arrangements. The numbers of chairs at the universities increased, research councils were instituted during and after the Second World War, and new facilities and equipment came in to modernise or replace the worn-out buildings in which research was housed during the thirties.

The depression years provided a point of departure for State interventionist policies, while at the same time industry was interested in the State assuming the costs for common services like higher education or research required for the modernisation of society. When the Labour Party came into power in the 1930s, there was thus a basis for convergent interests and an incentive to increase profitability. This in turn was expected to generate revenue for welfare and other common services. However, it was not until about 1967 that a clear break occurred in this compromise between the representatives of capital and labour, and labour

[13] Svensson *Högre utbildning*, 24–5.

assumed a more aggressive approach in accordance with the formula 'from political to economic democracy.'[14]

Sweden remained neutral during the war. Isolation from other countries was one result, and consequently the whole nation was mobilised for the cause of economic self-reliance. Science in particular, together with engineering, was drawn into the object of making the country self-sufficient and strengthening its military potential. This policy not only provided university research with a new lease on life, it also meant the beginnings of a system of planning and budgetary allocations that made individual university faculties only one part of a more comprehensive science and technology effort. The research councils came to play a strategic role. The first such council, the Technical Research Council (Tekniska forsknings-radet or TFR), was introduced in 1942, following an official inquiry into the needs of the engineering sciences. Its board was composed of representatives of both the public sphere and private scientific and industrial interests. The Medical Research Council, created in 1945, represented a different model. The independent role and autonomy of the universities and academic research were emphasised, giving prominence to peer review procedures and the internal criteria of the republic of science. In a sense this policy, as Thorsten Nybom has argued,[15] reflected the strength of the medical research community and its existing organisation, but it also carried out the conviction of those in government that medical research was essential to the underlying aims of the Welfare State. The criteria and goals of basic research dominated, while sectoral welfare interests were also satisfied. A kind of historic contract between scientists and the State resulted, but later, after a shift in policy at the end of the 1960s, the new sectoral research councils did not adhere to the agreement, and mutual trust evaporated.

To a large extent, the policy was repeated in the creation of a Natural Sciences Research Council in 1946, with a small board composed entirely of scientists. A special committee for atomic research was also created, motivated by national military-political concerns. It was transformed into an Atomic Research Council in 1947–8. Immediately after the war, a special institute for military research was also created, *Forsvarets forsk-ningsanstalt* (FOA or Defence Research Establishment). FOA represents a model for the organization of science that departs from the mainstream

---

[14] This is the slogan later enunciated for the 1970s by Olof Palme in connection with the introduction of Employee Funds. For the implications for science policy, see Aant Elzinga, 'Science Policy in Sweden: Sectorization and Adjustment to Crisis', *Research Policy*, 9 (April 1980), 116–46.

[15] Thorsten Nybom, 'Den nya forskningspolitiken: forskningsråden växer fram 1942–1959' (The New Science Policy, The Emergence of the Research Councils, 1942–1959), Department of History, Uppsala University, (unpublished paper, 1985), 13–14.

Swedish pattern with its heavy reliance on the universities and use of research councils to introduce greater flexibility into the growth of scientific fields. The exception is of course dependent on the fact that FOA's research lies in the military and not in the civilian sphere. FOA developed rapidly, having a total staff of about 1500 employees in 1972.

In Agriculture and Housing Construction, research councils were also introduced early on, serving to link research to sectoral economic interests. Particularly difficult was the institution of a special council for the social sciences. This was not a developed 'field' but a mixture of disciplines, some still very young after the war. There was debate concerning the possible function of a social sciences research council, as well as some fear that State influence would likely be greater here than in the more established areas of research. Despite these hesitations, a Social Sciences Research Council was created in 1947, and in the same year a humanities fund was reorganised into a Humanities Research Council.

Clearly the 1940s represented a time of breakthroughs for Swedish research. Apart from the councils, a number of collaborative research institutes were also created, financed on a 50/50 basis between State and private enterprise and serving various branches of industry. University funding, research council funding and the amount of money invested in State laboratories, branch institutes and atomic energy research all increased quite distinctly during the whole period considered here.

Dahllöf's study of the increase in the number of professorial chairs during the entire period 1880–1980 has illustrated how this expansion produced a strong bias towards engineering, natural sciences and medicine but also a remarkable growth in the social sciences, while the humanities tended to become relatively marginalized. Still, even if the humanities were losing ground in relative terms, the number of chairs increased, as is evident from the table. In the forty years before 1980, the number of chairs in medicine increased by a factor of five, and in the engineering sciences by a factor of six. The social sciences, starting generally from scratch, quadrupled their number of chairs in the same period. Table 5.1 gives a rough indication of expansion of various faculty areas.[16]

The bias towards natural sciences and engineering disciplines becomes even clearer in Dahllöf's comparison of Sweden with other Scandinavian countries possessing a smaller and weaker industrial base. By 1980 in absolute figures Finland had the largest number of chaired professors (1,400), followed by Sweden (1,353), Norway (986) and Denmark (753). The per capita density of these research positions puts Sweden next to last,

[16] Dahllöf, *Fasta forskartjänster, ibid.*

Table 5.1. *The expansion of various faculty areas*

Area	Number of Chairs		
	1940	1980	Increases
Law	24	50	2×
Humanities	65	126	2×
Social Sciences	28	118	4×
Medical Sciences	68	372	5×
Agr Sciences	17	54	3×
Forestry	6	42	7×
Maths, Nat. Sciences	57	165	3×
Engin. Sciences	58	302	6×

Table 5.2. *Numbers of first-year registered students (including part-time)*

1960	8,233
1961	9,226
1962	10,745
1963	12,550
1964	15,147
1965	17,704
1966	21,037
1967	26,037
1968	31,220

with 163 professors per million inhabitants after Norway with 240 per million. Sweden is also distinctive in that 77 per cent of its chairs in 1980 were within the natural and engineering sciences, compared to 61–64 per cent for the other Scandinavian countries. Despite the Nobel connections and its own success in obtaining scientific prizes, Sweden has comparatively few chairs in the pure sciences. The applied character that research increasingly took on, then, had become particularly evident by 1980.

Nevertheless, within the universities the power of the professorial hierarchy went largely unchallenged during the immediate post-war period. The main emphasis of science and higher educational policies was on building up infrastructures, and the relationship between senior scientists and politicians in positions of power was quite familiar. In 1962 a Science Advisory Board was created, with direct access to the Cabinet and Prime

Minister. This Board did not, however, deal with controversial matters of atomic or military science.

An important change in the career structure at the universities occurred in 1958 as a result of a proposal by a University Commission appointed by the Riksdag in 1955. Foreseeing a rapid increase in the numbers of students coming to the universities, the Commission proposed the introduction of a new category of university position, the lecturer, whose exclusive task would be to teach undergraduate courses. This further de-coupled teaching from research, even though the lecturers, like professors and docents, needed a doctor's degree in order to receive a permanent appointment and were presumably qualified to do research. In addition, a formula was introduced which automatically tied budgetary allocations to enrolments in a given subject. Lecturers took over basic courses, and the time professors spent with undergraduates radically decreased.

When this reform was implemented in 1958, the number of students registering for the first year of university studies had already leaped dramatically since the previous decade. Until 1948 the number of freshmen at all universities and colleges in Sweden was fairly steady, about 3,500, although Uppsala had reached the 4,000 mark in 1944. By 1955 there were 5,000 freshmen seeking entry into universities and colleges, and by 1959 numbers had risen to 7,600. Table 5.2 provides figures drawn from Mac Murray[17] for the years 1960–8, the latter being the year of the student revolt when labour market and higher educational authorities were having visions of 83,000 new students knocking on the door in the mid-1970s.

This vast increase in the numbers of students entering higher education appeared to parallel the need for a more qualified academically-prepared work force in industry and in the expanding service sectors of the Welfare State. The gymnasia were also being transformed. In 1946 there had been about 7,000 students starting their first year in the gymnasia; by 1960 the figure was nearer 20,000. However, as a result of several reforms, the elite and historic gymnasium system was dismantled and a different secondary educational system with various general and special vocational lines replaced it. Some element of the older merit selection process remained, nevertheless, with the introduction of tracking. As happened in other countries when similar reforms were introduced, the academic streams drew their pupils from the same families which had patronised the gymnasia, while the vocational streams were mainly recruited from non-professional or working-class homes.

[17] Mac Murray, *Utbildningsexpansion, jämlikhet och avlänkning. Studier i utbildningspolitik och utbildningsplanering 1933–1985*, (Expansion of Education, Equality and De-linking. Studies in Educational Policy and Educational Planning, 1933–1985), Gothenburg Studies in Educational Sciences, Report no. 60 (Gothenburg, 1988), 59 and 80.

All in all, however, the changes naturally had repercussions for the universities. The students now coming to the universities were no longer a narrowly-selected but a more broadly chosen elite. A new type of student appeared, still essentially from the middle classes but without a strong academic home life. But these students also encountered a vastly altered university world in the early 1960s. A bureaucratic (if skeletal) apparatus was in place, requiring more paperwork from everyone, and the university had acquired a non-academic staff of guidance counsellors. American-style higher education features were in evidence. The era of mass higher education had arrived.

The introduction of the position of university lecturer to deal with an expanding undergraduate level of studies was the beginning of a serious bifurcation between research and undergraduate teaching systems. At Uppsala the number of ordinary lecturers was 36 in 1965, compared to a tenured research staff of 141 professors and laboratory heads. Ten years later in 1976 there were 132 lecturers and 150 professors. In addition there was a large number of teachers at the undergraduate level who had non-tenured jobs or were paid by the hour. Later university and science policy reforms added further sub-divisions, so that the university today is a place where many different interests have their own structures and pull in different directions.

To bridge over and keep the research and teaching functions together, the 1964 university statutes formally defined an *Inrättning* as the basic academic organisation. *Inrättning* can be translated as 'institution' or 'establishment'. It is a broader term than the English words 'department' or 'institute' which are often deemed its equivalent. 'Institution' refers to the complex of lecture and seminar rooms, libraries, laboratories or academic staff connected to a particular discipline. An 'establishment' is a laboratory or an observatory of independent status. Until 1964 the word *Inrättning* was used informally, being generally applied to larger disciplines containing two or more chairs in the same unit. In the natural and experimental sciences, the word was customarily used to describe a group of related research and teaching activities; but now for the first time a more formal meaning was ascribed.

Gradually the layers of academic administration increased, as new forms of management were introduced into the university governance structure, sometimes as parallel structures. A *styrelse* – executive board or governing body – was placed alongside the 'institution', separating the administrative from the intellectual functions formerly combined in the professorial chair. A 'prefect', reporting directly to the Rector, became the official in charge of the *styrelse*, which was composed of elected representatives of the teaching and non-teaching staff. Above the *styrelse* were other layers of administration: faculty boards, the university board of governors. Under it was the Office of the Rector. In effect, a dual system of university governance was created for the purpose of separating the academic from the non-academic side, but in practice considerable overlapping exists and confusion reigns.

The university changes that were implemented in 1964, 1969, 1977, and 1982 tended increasingly to focus almost exclusively on the teaching functions, while research and research training were more or less depreciated in the eyes of reformers located in the civil service or the National Board of Universities. The perspective taken was essentially an administrative one and did not extend to the actual content of the curriculum. By the beginning of the 1980s what had been created was a vast top to bottom administrative bureaucracy headed by the National Board of Universities and Colleges in Stockholm.

The leitmotif of the University Commission of 1955 was: 'If we live in peace, the men of technology promise us almost a new society in just a few decades. Economists... reckon that the living standards may be double that which we now have'. The general idea was that strongly increased investments in science and higher education would contribute to economic strength and welfare in the entire nation. It was a period of technological optimism. Research and higher education counted as productive factors, on a par with capital and labour. Investment into research and higher education, it was felt, would sooner or later lead to increases in the GNP and standards of living.

There are many more aspects of this period that might be described, but the main point should by now be clear. In Tage Erlander's period as Prime Minister, considerable optimism prevailed, and relations between the academic oligarchy and leading politicians were cordial as they appeared to work hand in hand towards a common goal. In the next period, however, the universities went through a difficult transition whereby they, like the gymnasia before them, were brought into the new Welfare State and tied to the general reform of the primary and secondary systems of schooling in what was now a mass educational system. In this transformation the professors lost much of their historic authority.[18] Research and undergraduate education were further separated, an unstable

---

[18] The point is disputed by some authorities, but Jan-Erik Lane indicates that such was the case, citing such innovations as the unit-credit or modular system which increased the gap between teaching and research by increasing the range of student choice. Modularity may actually have supported the creation of a research mission within American universities, but in Sweden it was bogged down in administrative complexities. Jan-Erik Lane, 'Byråkratiseringen av högskolan fortsätter' (The Bureaucratisation of Higher Education Continues), *Tvärsnitt*, 2 (1986). 56–9.

system of externally funded projects aggravated existing tensions, and one
reform was grafted upon another in hasty succession.

'Radical rationalism' and the decline of the academic oligarchy

In tracing the consequences of the series of university reforms, Lennart
G. Svensson observes that in the process collegial autonomy gave way to a
combination of non-tenured internal and non-academic external influence.
Yet the complicated decision-making structure confuses lay participants.
It also permits the exercise of considerable informal authority, especially at
the lower levels by the professors, which has the effect of at times
hampering the exercise of leadership above.[19]

Nevertheless, it is certainly true that the professorial oligarchy had its
wings clipped. The interesting point is not whether a new elite of
bureaucrats has taken command at various levels. This is patently untrue.
Rather it is the existence of new and different tensions and conflicts within
the system itself that is significant. External funding for research projects
has multiplied, and research has become increasingly policy-driven and
market-related, if not always in form, at least in its overall agenda. The
university has become the home of three types of research, each with its
own governing rationale: basic research, mission-oriented sectoral research, and industrial R&D. Around the latter two, hybrid research
communities have emerged with their own norms and reputational systems
differing from that of the traditional community with its base in the
disciplines. The university reforms were undertaken in order to streamline
undergraduate teaching into quasi-professional study programmes, often
in a way which took little or no notice of the interests of the fundamental
disciplines. These of course continued to exist on the graduate level but at
the undergraduate level were labeled 'single courses' to contrast them with
the newer and fashionable 'study programmes'. In the last few years this
policy has been reversed.

There are many factors responsible for the change from the optimism
and unbridled growth of the immediate post-war period. Economic growth
could not continue as it had, and crises developed, as in the oil shock of
1973 which had its roots in global economic and political problems.
Furthermore, the basic value and assumptions of science were questioned
by representatives of industry, critical students and members of the radical
labour and peace movements. Industrialists were sceptical because studies
carried out by major firms and by the Pentagon in the USA indicated that
basic research did not really contribute directly to product innovation;

[19] Svensson, *Högre utbildning* 53.

students and others protested against the role that science played in 'unjust' warfare and the degradation of the environment. These were trends that appeared in many Western countries at the same time. Within the Paris office for the Organisation for Economic Co-operation and Development (OECD), the 1971 Brooks Report, 'Science, Growth and Society', signalled a new era in science policy, calling for a much closer integration of research with social and political goals. In Sweden, where government certainly intervened to direct a planned mixed economy with a strong welfare emphasis, it was a time when planning was dominated by a 'radical rationalism'. Systems analysis and other methods copied from the military were adopted with the view that large-scale reform programmes and earmarked fields of science could be combined with an organisational form allowing the wide participation of different social and economic interests. The resulting consensus would lead to the transformation envisaged on the drawing boards of planners and dreamers. Such an effort required detailed monitoring, control and steering at the level where innovative activities like research were carried out.

In the field of higher education and research, this 1967 policy of radical rationalism was double-edged. Plans were made to develop the Welfare State and absorb university research into its objectives. But this suggested that the professors stood in the way; and some argued that it was necessary to restrain the academic *baroni*, circumscribe and reduce their power, and open the universities to a new mission that included vocational training, mission-oriented research and decision-making consultancies.

When a new generation of Social Democrats took over the government, the days of informal contacts between academia and politicians ended. The new Prime Minister, Olof Palme, was a leading spokesman for a utilitarian ideology that was now put forward in much clearer and aggressive terms.

Palme's views had been openly and forcefully expressed when he was Minister of Education in the Social Democratic Cabinet. At a gathering of Uppsala students on 25 October 1968, he prepared the way for a more determined State management of higher education by attacking an 'ivory tower' outlook that he associated with the 'Republic of Science'. Bernalism[20] in its Swedish social democratic version had caught up with the professors, and the government and State bureaucrats could play on the student movement's antipathy toward elitism, thereby exploiting the existing conflict at the universities. Among other things, Palme said that

universities were built to educate a very limited elite ... This historically conditioned elite-theory explains why the universities often appeared isolated, a little stuck-up and superior, separated from the development of the rest of society. It also explains

[20] Interventionist views associated with the Cambridge University scientist and marxist, J. D. Bernal, whose *The Social Function of Science* (1939) is the basic text of this genre.

the notion about the autonomy of the universities, the academic republic with its own laws and traditions, which in its defense of its own integrity is forced to turn its barbs outward against those in power and with influence outside its walls.[21]

A student newspaper in Stockholm picked up the signal, commenting, 'Is it not time to pull down the walls and let a little fresh air into the stuffy rooms? And the elite-theory is today already crushed by reality to the extent that only fools can still believe in it'.[22] Olof Palme and his generation of Social Democratic politicians had themselves been trained at the universities. Already in the late 1950s, when the University Commission of 1955 was meeting, many of them had joined Social Democratic student clubs, especially in Uppsala, where they developed far-reaching and concrete plans for bringing the universities more closely in line with the demands of a Welfare State by such measures as opening admissions to the under-represented children of working-class families.

The government assault on the old Swedish academic class took place on three fronts simultaneously. First was the creation of a bureaucratic superstructure serving as an alternative base for decision-making, into which non-university people could be brought at various levels. Second was the introduction of the Swedish variant of the British 'Rothschild principle' of a contractor–buyer relationship between researchers and State agencies dispensing R&D funds – the 'sectoral principle' as defined earlier.[23] During the 1970s a host of special sectoral councils cropped up, each with its own budget for funding R&D relevant to their specific spheres. The largest of these agencies came to be the Board of Technological Development, with objectives that dovetailed with industrial policy.

A third ingredient of Palme's university policy was altering the existing requirements for the doctorate. More stress was placed on coursework as part of the preparation. In the social sciences and humanities, the magnum opus of earlier days, a German-style *habilitation* based on massive and publishable research, was replaced by writings somewhat closer to the North American 'work-in-progress' dissertation. Although these innovations were intended to reduce the time to degree to four years, the combination of coursework and thesis research, plus part-time attendance

[21] Cited in Sten Andersson, 'Från Bologna till Borås. Ett inlägg i debatten om akademisk frihet', in *Vetenskap och vett. till frågan om universitetets roll*, symposium report (Linköping, 1985), 73.   [22] *Ibid.*, 73–4.

[23] Lord Rothschild, *A Framework for Government Research and Development* (London, 1971). The effects of the implementation of the principle in Britain are reviewed by Maurice Kogan and Mary Henkel, *Government and Research. The Rothschild Experiment in a Government Department* (London, 1983). For a discussion of the Swedish version, see Elzinga, 'Science Policy in Sweden'.

(and a residual feeling that the 'dissertation' really ought to be a major piece of work) have actually blunted the effect of the reforms. Four years is also the limit set for graduate scholarship support, even though less than one-quarter of all doctoral candidates enjoyed this subsidy in 1989. In most cases scholarships are being replaced by 'assistantships' which may involve teaching or administrative duties. PhDs acquired before 1969 are still called 'PhDs according to the old order', while those awarded afterwards are referred to as 'new PhDs'. In the natural sciences the newer system was already functioning before 1969.

The university reform of 1977, bringing all higher vocational lines of study into the national higher education system, provided for increased opportunities for research and postgraduate studies in connection with core subjects relating to social work, nursing, physical therapy, or X-ray and laboratory technician training. On one level, the reform represented the continuation of an education policy focusing on applied research and social problems, such as alcohol research, but on another it was a decision to accomodate the aspirations of several semi-professions, particularly the welfare professions, and to upgrade their professional status. Criminology and athletics are examples of other areas where professionalism and Welfare State ambitions coincide, leading inevitably to requests for professorial chairs and other evidence of academic legitimacy. Many more examples could be cited as part of a series of central curricular and funding decisions that provoked serious divisions of opinion within the academic community.

Björn Wittrock and Stefan Lindström, in their critical account of 'radical rationalism' in the 'age of the great programs', have cautioned that

In the modern welfare state public policy cannot have the character of shortsighted groping for solutions and erratic searching for alternatives. It has to be able to take a long term point of view and a comprehensive approach. And it has to be based on systematic thinking that delves into the social problem in its totality, investigates and reviews goals and alternatives.[24]

The 'radical rationalist' approach tried to do this. But by concentrating primarily on the administrative aspect, and by trying to use systems theory and programme budgetting, central government introduced policies that led to serious fragmentation within Swedish society's most fundamental knowledge-producing institutions.

---

[24] Björn Wittrock and Stefan Linström, *De stora programmens tid: forskning och energipolitik I Sverige* (The Time of the Great Programmes: Research and Energy in Swedish Politics) (Stockholm, 1984), 11.

Torsten Husén, renowned for his work in international education and university reform, has reviewed the 'U68' changes, the policy that produced the current Swedish national multiversity system, in this way:

One even pondered in the enquiry [U68] if one should retain the term university or not. The idea was to obtain the same uniform and grey organisation for Kristianstad College and Stockholm University alike. They would be organised in the same way. One didn't consider the fact that research also was done at the universities. In this thick committee report one was prevented from considering research, as if it did not exist. Finally, nothing was said about universities outside the country's borders. The review was monumental in its provincialism.[25]

By 1964 the groundwork was being laid for a bureaucratic system to sidestep, encapsulate, and gradually undermine the existing professional structure. The later defining characteristics of this system was an institution-level network of study programme committees and faculty or sub-faculty boards and supporting administrative staff, with executive committees and prefects reporting through them, surmounted by the National Board of Universities and Colleges with its national-level committees overseeing the entire system within particular areas. These areas are now divided into six sectors for undergraduate studies and ten faculty structures through which resources are allocated across the whole country. The National Board has become a bureaucratic superstructure with corresponding departments and divisions of permanent staff and planning committees on which representatives from the various universities sit, together with persons representing external interests.

Five of the sectors for undergraduate studies cover broad vocational spheres with specific programmes within each:

- education for technical professions
- education for social work and economic and administrative professions
- education for health professions, including both medicine, dentistry, pharmacy and veterinary science and semi-professions like nursing, occupational therapy, physiotherapy, X-ray and laboratory technicians
- education for teaching professions
- education for cultural professions.

In addition to these, there is a system of separate courses and local study programmes falling outside the national unitary system proper. About one-third of all students choose this alternative. Recent criticism, to include that from the National Union of Students, tends to centre on the fragmented and haphazard nature of this curriculum and the absence of anything resembling an 'academic culture'.

---

[25] Ström, (ed.) *Erövra universiteten åter*, 95.

The faculty areas recognised in the science policy bills and annual budget bills at the national level are:

- the humanities faculties of the universities and colleges,
- the theological faculties
- the faculties of law
- the social science faculties
- the medical faculties
- the odontological faculties
- the pharmaceutical faculties
- the mathematical-natural sciences faculties
- the faculties of technology
- the theme-oriented research structure.

The last-mentioned area refers to interdisciplinary studies bearing titles such as 'Water', 'Health' or 'Technology and Social Change'. These began in the 1970s at places like Linköping.

The structure of faculties and undergraduate programme divisions described above was consolidated in 1977. Budgetary allocations to faculty-based research and undergraduate teaching flows through the two sets of channels from the Ministry of Education. A new decision-making layer was also introduced between these institutions and the National Board and the so-called Regional Boards, which are supposed to oversee regional developments and stimulate the growth of a research connection in many of the vocational lines of education. Today this product of the heyday of radical rationalist planning no longer exists, having been removed a few years ago in order to simplify decision-making structures. University policy in the late 1980s moved away from several of its important earlier objectives towards self-regulation and a new spirit of entrepreneurialism.

Sectoralisation

Radical rationalism and bureaucratisation have been the subject of much criticism and debate. Even Olof Palme himself later admitted that it had led to many unintended consequences. Kerstin Niblaeus, who worked with the Science Advisory Board, tells us that by the mid-1980s Palme recognised that too many different decision-making levels had been introduced, and that communication between them was a problem.[26] The recent Prime Minister, Ingvar Carlsson, whose career has been closely allied to Palme's, has ruefully admitted that the Social Democrats regarded all institutions as

[26] *Ibid.*, 127.

essentially units of production, and planned for the expansion of schools, hospitals and so on as if they were factories. The task now was to take consumer preference more into account.[27]

The fact is that the transformation of the universities, incorporating them more closely into the machinery of the Welfare State, generated many problems unanticipated by government. It also introduced a deep-seated transformation in the social and cognitive conditions of university-based research. Fields of research tended more and more to be defined not primarily from an internalist point of view based on disciplinary advances and historical precedents, but from a utilitarian or political perspective. Even in the Natural Sciences Research Council, where peer review procedures were solidly entrenched, the practice of targetting so-called 'strategic' areas of research had an important cognitive effect. Ingvar Lindqvist, General Secretary of the Council in the mid-1980s, noted how new accounting practices introduced a situation whereby it was 'no longer a question of pure science policy but also industrial policy, agricultural policy, energy policy, environmental policy, housing policy, defence policy or even foreign policy'.[28] Thus a science policy incorporating scientific findings and priorities was replaced by all kinds of other radically different sectoral priorities. For example, a $5 million three-year programme to place a research station in the Antarctic in 1989 was undertaken mainly to qualify Sweden for participation in the Antarctic Treaty group and its proposal at the time for an Antarctic minerals convention. Needless to say, this has spurred a considerable amount of activity which can be called 'polar research' but which may well differ from earlier field definitions of legitimate scientific inquiry.

In some cases, external sectoral funding during the last fifteen years dominated whole university research units. In a shift signalled by the science policy bill of 1987, the government urged sectoral funding agencies to take a more long-term approach and also assume responsibility for the expansion of the basic core of knowledge in universities. As yet, the time has been too short to record much progress in this direction. A total of 130 agencies funnel more than half a billion dollars (4.7 billion Swedish Kroner to be exact) to R&D. This is about equal to the entire budget directed to universities and colleges for research via their faculties and research councils. Of sectoral funds, only 21 per cent go to the universities, but of that portion only 1 per cent finances research positions, while 3 per cent goes to projects of more than three years' duration. The remainder

---

[27] Ingvar Carlsson, 'En ny uppgift för socialdemokratin', (A New Task for Social Democracy), *Tiden*, 9 (1985), 486–90.

[28] Ingvar Lindqvist, 'A More Well-defined Science Policy is Needed', *NFR Rådsrapport* (Natural Sciences Research Council – NFR), Part I (Stockholm, 1986).

supports short-term projects[29] predominantly in the technological, natural, and medical sciences. However, a recent evaluation of support for history teaching and research reveals that in a number of universities, history departments received nearly 50 per cent of their funding from external sources, and in two other cases it was over one-third. This is alarming, according to Hans Landberg, the Head Secretary of the Swedish Council for Planning and Coordination of Research, especially considering that the number of research associates has been reduced by one half (from thirty-four to fifteen for history in the whole country) because of the relative erosion of faculty funds.[30] The humanities are of course an extreme case because they have lost ground in the transformation of the State and in its new research policy. If Social Democratic politicians have had anything in common with the industrialists with whom they cooperated in an historical pact of class reconciliation, it is a certain suspicion of the utility of humanistic study. (Erlander was an exception, but not his ministers of finance and industry.) It is only of late that some parts of the humanities are finding themselves drawn into the transformation, but even here it is their possible applied dimension that appears to matter most – artificial intelligence, the design of man-machine interfaces, or export marketing services in countries with Asian or Arabic cultures. Other fields in the humanities were largely ignored, but the new government proposes to change this.

Sectorally-funded research has positive features. Flexibility is one, especially in critical areas of national interest where the rapid creation of new knowledge may be hampered by academic conservatism or disciplinary bottlenecks. Energy research is a good case in point. By the end of the 1970s the budget for energy research was reaching 10 % of total R&D. But a negative side also exists. Examples of serious deficiencies were turned up by an evaluation of the working procedures of the Building Research Council. Peer review mechanisms were ignored in favour of 'relevance' criteria, and project officers arbitrarily awarded sums of up to $10,000 without asking for quality safeguards from contractors. Review and criticism led to the establishment of a Scientific Advisory Board to the Council, which was also a means of re-establishing good working relations with the scientific community.

Generally speaking, the effects of government funding on university

[29] *Svensk sektorsforskning* (Swedish Sectoral Research), a report from the Cabinet Office (Statsrådsberedningen: Stockholm, 1989) (in Swedish). A digest appears in *Dagens Nyheter* (6 February 1989).

[30] *Focus på historia. Sex perspektiv på historisk forskning* (The Spotlight on History. Six Perspectives on Historical Research). Report from the Humanities and Social Sciences Research Council and the National Board of Universities and Colleges, ed. Olof Lindström (Uppsala, 1988).

222   *Aant Elzinga*

research through application of the sectoral principle can be summarised in six points. First, it can be observed that sectoral grants increased at the same time as conventional funding for basic research was either at a standstill or decreased. Support for research shifted towards mission-related projects and applied research, thus weakening fundamental science generally. Second, sectorally funded research encouraged an attitude of opportunism and expediency and biased research at all levels, including that of graduate students and junior researchers, towards work deemed politically or socially useful. An independent research posture was difficult to maintain. Third, with the loss of support, the gaps between disciplinary research and sectoral research widened, which also meant that Swedish university scientists were in danger of losing their connections to the international community of science. Four, sectoral research has proven inherently unstable, uneven, and discontinuous. It changes according to political criteria. It also concentrates resources and therefore a certain kind of competence in the hands of a few senior researchers at the expense of a more broadly-based collaborative or collective effort. Given the relatively small size of Swedish science units, the departure of a senior researcher threatens an entire academic unit with collapse.[31]

A fifth observation is that sectoral-funding encourages the formation of alternative research networks and loyalties centered on officials or project officers in relevant granting agencies. This of course destabilises the academic unit even more, since project officials are tempted to take a proprietary interest in a department's organisation and running. In the literature on the sociology of science, such an effect is called 'de-institutionalisation'. The customary disciplinary bonds are dissolved, both socially and cognitively, and researchers re-group to enter into new reputational arrangements or 'hybrid communities'. These communities are defined around problems not disciplines and are responsive to government departments assigned to housing, energy, social welfare, the environment, and aid to third world countries.

Finally, it may be said that since each government agency has a special interest or priority, alternate research methods, concepts, or programmes are undervalued or disregarded. Blind spots develop in the research

[31] This point is based on the findings of a survey made by the Agency for Energy Research in an evaluation carried out together with the National Board of Universities and Colleges and the Science Advisory Group of the Council for Building Research. The evaluation report refers generally to the state of affairs where senior researchers leave and infrastructures, in part, collapse. *Sectoral Research in the University Milieu*, Report from Högsektprojekt (BVN, Efn, and UHÄ, Stockholm, 1987). For elaboration see Elzinga, 'The Consequences of Evaluation of Academic Research', in *Science Studies* 1 (December 1988), 5–14. (This is a relatively new journal published by the Finnish Society for Science Studies.)

agenda, and whatever is considered the latest word or is regarded as potentially popular is favoured and supported. Newly emerging research areas, as for example in social work, become saddled with cognitive methods or aims that derive from political expedients and not from a tradition of independent-minded inquiry or critical evaluation. In the extreme case, research becomes reactive decision-making and cannot transcend what is currently acceptable. The 'idea' of a university as a source of new ideas or critical thinking is therefore greatly compromised.[32]

A partial retreat and the turn to 'orchestration' policies

In the early 1980s, the negative effects of the 'radical rationalism' in university reform and the sectoral principle were becoming more and more evident, even to decision-makers in responsible positions at various levels in the bureaucracy. The plight of the universities was also a popular topic in the mass media. In 1981, for example, bureaucratistion of the universities was intensely debated in the press, similarly the proliferation of smaller regional colleges with no or little research capabilities. In 1982 the problem of the lecturers came up. The intention was and still is that university lecturers should have a chance to do research. Today all those who were previously associate professors – 'docents' – are consequently lumped together with the lecturers. With the exception of the chairholder, everyone is officially called *högskolelektor*. The idea is to allow appointments at this level to engage in both research and teaching, but in fact this is not possible because of a lack of faculty funds. So the gap between research and undergraduate teaching still remains.

In 1983 the quality of some PhD theses in the social sciences was questioned. As a result, stricter criteria for PhD examinations have been introduced. Some reversions to older practices are the re-introduction of the undergraduate and postgraduate degrees that had been altered or removed entirely from the Swedish university system in the post-war reform period. The *Filosofi kandidat* degree in particular had been attacked by reformers for its presumed elitism since it was the degree taken by undergraduates from gymnasia and was the equivalent of a master's degree in the United States. In its new form, however, the degree will be closer to an American bachelor's degree than to its former self. Similar gyrations have occurred with respect to the postgraduate *Filosofi licentiat* degree, which had been roughly equivalent to the American PhD and was

---

[32] The relevance and accountability pressures of public sectoral missions are not the only innovations affecting the social and epistemic relations of research. As noted in the text, another phenomenon that stands out in the 1980s is the proliferation of industrial parks and research villages.

discarded at the time that doctoral degree requirements changed. It too is no longer exactly the same as formerly, now occupying a position between the undergraduate and PhD degrees; but in both cases the restoration of the old names has symbolic importance in signalling a renewed emphasis on academic quality.[33]

The problem with having so many levels of decision-making, and particularly in the form of Regional Boards, has already been mentioned. This was another issue hotly debated, leading eventually to removal of the boards. The imbalances caused by sectoral funding have been the subject of the science policy bills of 1984 and 1987, although the principle still remains in place. Generally, however, as we enter the 1990s sentiment appears to be running in favour of deregulation.

Other problems being discussed include career mobility at the levels of research associate, assistant professor and associate professor. (The lack of professional opportunities for advancement was made strikingly clear recently in an evaluation of the current state of sociology as a university discipline.[34]) The absence of middle level career positions for researchers within the university system is a major bottleneck, especially because about 60 per cent of the present body of full professors will retire in the next fifteen years. This is one of the reasons why recent science policy decisions specify increasing the number of research associate positions for young PhDs; but most academics agree that the rate of creating such new positions is too slow. Futhermore, while the waiting period for tenure for research associates has been lowered from six to four years, internal funds for such four-year positions are so seriously limited that externally supported research associates are now being created. Finally, new tenure arrangements notwithstanding, in practice advancement on the career ladder from research associate to associate professor, to be then followed by promotion (competitively for a limited number of chairs) to a tenured full professorship still depends in large measure upon external project funding.

Two books published in the early 1980s are revealing for the way in which they describe the tug-of-war preceding the turn to a process of deregulation. One book, an anthology entitled *Erövra högskolan* (Conquering Higher Education Institutions) was issued in 1982, or just about the time a new Social Democratic government returned to office after a six-year interregnum. The contributors are twenty academics from Lund, all of

[33] *Ny examinationsordning i högskolan* (The New Examination System in the Universities and Colleges), Report from the National Board of Universities and Colleges, no. 3 (UHÄ Stockholm, 1989).

[34] *Sociologi i Sverige, forskningsmiljön och organisation* (Sociology in Sweden. Science, the Research Environment and Organization). Report from the Humanities and Social Sciences Research Council, ed. Olof Lindström (Uppsala, 1988).

them members or sympathisers with social democracy. The title refers to the desirability of wrestling universities and colleges from the influence of past elitist traditions and placing them in the service of the labour movement, the people, and the Welfare State. The authors consider the universities to be enemies of democracy and claim they are not open to people in all walks of life. They also maintain that representatives of trade unions sitting on various committees of the State bureaucracy find it difficult to promote their views and ideas. Finally the authors advocate removing the advantages that private industry has in influencing the research agendas and obtaining the first cut of its benefits.

The other book was published in 1986 and contains the proceedings of a symposium held at the Wenner-Gren Centre in Stockholm in May 1984. The symposium brought together participants from various parts of the academic community, the university bureaucracy and government circles. In the main its thrust is quite opposite from that of the first book. It gathers up and focuses the very articulate criticism of the transformation that had taken place. Some participants even spoke of wanting to see a revival of the old style professorial hegemony, or at least spoke of promoting the positive features associated with it, such as the emphasis on excellence, autonomy and the internationalism of the republic of science. The title of the volume, *Erövra universiteten åter* (Reconquer the Universities), captures this agenda. Note that the word 'university' as used in the title is quite distinct from the broader phrase 'higher education institutions' as employed in the first publication.

A second symposium held at the Wenner-Gren Centre in 1987 issued a volume placing the Swedish universities in a comparative international perspective, emphasising issues such as simpler organisational structures and autonomy. Executive leadership was also an issue, and had become a catchword. However, the Swedish word for 'leadership', *Ledarksap*, does not describe an older professorial kind of headship so much as the management style associated with private sector entrepreneurialism. The title of the 1987 volume is *Makt och vanmakt inom universiteten: Autonomi, ansvar och vitalitet*, which may be translated, Power and Powerlessness within the University: Autonomy, Responsibility and Vitality. The key words give an indication of the new winds of decentralisation blowing through the kingdom and reversing the process that began in the late 1960s.

What we are consequently observing in the fourth phase today is a combination of some past policies and ideas joined to present-day reversals, uniting, for instance, a university policy which still relies on the criteria of relevance and accountability, now reinforced by ideas of market discipline, with one that recognizes the importance of fundamental research and greater academic self-governance. As in other countries, the spirit of entrepreneurialism and self-management is sweeping through the universities. With it has come a commercialisation of educational and research ventures and on-going debates over the value of made-to-order courses for business, private sponsorship of research and other academic work and new forms of academic patronage. Science-push and market-pull approaches are being integrated in what might be called a policy of 'orchestration'.

The 'orchestration' principle requires a 'buyer' of academic products to establish a general framework for an activity, identifying certain goals or criteria but allowing the 'seller' to determine how resources are to be used. Funds for travel, salaries and equipment once tightly controlled are now more accessible, and research is allowed to develop along its own lines towards a generally-specified goal. This principle, which has also been incorporated into the science and technology policies adopted by research councils in other countries, is usually called 'strategic research'. It is defined by John Irvine and Ben Martin in their 1984 book, *Foresight in Science, Picking the Winners*, as 'basic research carried out with the expectation that it will produce a broad base of knowledge likely to form the background to the solution of recognised current or future practical problems'.[35] Strategic research lies somewhere between pure or basic science or autonomous research and applied (or tactical) research. Targeted areas are biotechnology, advanced industrial materials, the problems of the aging or polar science. In a way strategic research is based on a paradox. It is an attempt to generate 'guided serendipity' by combining two diametrically opposed principles or outlooks as represented by the OECD's Frascati manual and the sectoral principles of the 1970s. The first, used as a guideline for collecting R&D statistics, divided research into pure, applied, and developmental. The viewpoint was that of science itself looking outward. The second was the viewpoint of the political world outside of science looking inward.

The new unified approach to technical planning and development in 1990 and 1991 is producing amalgamation schemes and reorganisation efforts that are too current and fluid to summarise adequately. One example, however, is the decision, following the science policy bill of 1990, to transfer some of the responsibilities of the National Board for Technical Development (with augmented resources) to a newly created research council for technological research, a body which in fact resembled the old TFR. The National Board for Technical Development has itself now been abolished as a unit in its own right and has become a division in a new

[35] *Ibid.*, 4.

national agency called 'Nutek', or National Board for Industrial and Technical Development. Nutek also contains two former boards, the National Board of Industrial Development (SIND) and the National Board for Energy (STEV).

Another example is to be found in the 1988 Swedish government bill on university policy. In it distinct spheres of responsibility are outlined with different sets of norms. The bill states that 'Government and Parliament are... responsible for the overriding decisions concerning the structure of undergraduate education, its location and dimensions, decided upon on the basis of society's needs, individuals' demands and available resources'. Furthermore, the universities,

with the support of grants for undergraduate education, faculty grants and grants from research councils, [are] to educate and conduct research on the basis of their own programme responsibility. The norms system in this domain is international. The government and parliament further demand that work commissioned by public agencies, municipal councils and private interests be done to a degree that is reasonable.[36]

In this domain the norm to be followed is the fulfillment of the particular contract.[37]

As evidence of a new climate, science parks have cropped up around the universities which function as windows through which industrial firms can monitor the world of advanced research. These and many other institutional arrangements now facilitate university–industry interfacing. So far has this cooperation or market pressure advanced that it threatens to become a new problem for Swedish science policy, overtaking the sectoralisation inherited from the 1970s. For those working at universities, the situation can be confusing. Individual departments are having to cope with a great many layers of quite different kinds of rival academic and research assignments: undergraduate education, research training, basic research, service to public agencies, consultancy, and applied research for private companies, teaching packages to be sold on a private knowledge market, and yet more. Within the university itself the situation is complicated by the presence of several different competing academic value systems. On the one hand there are the traditional professorial values as described earlier, focusing on independent intellectual inquiry and academic self-government, but there also exist the ideologies associated with Swedish social democracy, stressing open access, mass education and

---

[36] 'Reasonable' in this context means that contract work, whatever its source of funding, should not disrupt the normal functioning of academic life or distort the traditional methods of doing science.

[37] *Om formerna för högre utbildningspolitik* (On the Forms for Higher Education Policy) Governmental proposition no. 65 (Regeringsproposition 1988/1989:65).

public service. A third voice now also can be heard. It is especially vocal at the level of the regional college. This voice emphasises the free play of an academic market system but is silent on the pitfalls associated with rapidly changing educational fads and fashions.

From the vantage point of national science policy, the universities remain a strategic asset for economic and regional development. Industry wants high class basic research to gain a competitive edge on the international market. The Welfare State and various subsidiary government agencies want to be able to continue to rely on the universities and the college system for various types of mission-oriented R&D. Four major issues deriving from these competing demands were taken up in the science policy bill of 1987, and they figure prominently also in the bill of 1990.

The first issue concerns redressing the imbalances caused by the sectoral principle. The Social Democratic politicians have not yet had the courage to abandon this principle and allow the R&D funds controlled by various ministries to be transferred directly to the universities via long-term contracts, thus giving prominence to a basic research mission. Just at the moment, however, a change indicating some government flexibility is underway. Humanities and natural science/mathematics faculties have been given funding to see whether they can devise a 'strategic planning function' and thus operate like research councils. Nevertheless, this is not a policy shift but an experiment within the policies of the sectoral principle, and it is initially limited to six years.

It is possible that the new Conservative coalition government taking office in September 1991 after the defeat of the Social Democrats will add to the number of experiments. One possibility is that some of the 'Employee Funds' established by the Social Democrats to allow trade unions a capital reserve to gain influence over the private industrial sector would be shifted towards support for the research and higher education sector. These funds have been anathema to the Conservatives who made their abolition a campaign promise. Use of Employee Funds by the academic research community would doubtless be a welcome short-term injection, even though one suspects that the major benefactors would be the 'hard' sciences not the humanities.

Predictably, the prospect of losing control over research has met with quite strong resistance within ministries and public agencies. Also it is generally felt that university faculties lack the type of policy consciousness and inner cohesion or strength necessary to translate direct funding into research portfolios that accommodate the needs of various public sectors. On the university side there is a certain understandable reluctance to engage in major organisational reforms so soon after a large-scale transformation. At the same time some recent legislation, it is true, has introduced several radical changes into the organisational structure, giving the local boards of governors much more power. These boards already contain a majority of representatives from outside the university, and they are now being encouraged to take unpopular decisions when necessary to cut back on certain fields and stimulate others. From July 1990 they will be able to plan ahead and budget on a triennual basis. All of this is part of deregulation, but it is quite uncertain if deregulation will stretch as far as elimination of the sectoral principle.

The second set of issues involves the relationship between private industry and universities. In its previous science policy bills, the government recognised the dangers involved in letting market forces penetrate more deeply into university-based research. The conflict of interest with the free flow of information, the sensitivity to sudden changes in a profit-driven market, the possibility of a (continued) strong bias towards applied science – all these dangers are now openly acknowledged by government. However, no clear guidelines have been issued for maintaining academic integrity and preserving the university's central mission of encouraging critical thought.

A third issue has to do with the relationship between the research universities and the regional colleges. Strong political sentiment has emanated from the Swedish provinces in favour of creating a research capability within the regional colleges. This of course threatens, as it has in other countries like Australia and the United Kingdom, to erode the binary line. The 1987 science policy bill tried to strike a verbal compromise. But in real terms resources are limited. Nor did the 1990 bill provide any substantial research money for the regional colleges. Furthermore, political pressures may lead to a brake being put on the movement to restore academic integrity to the higher education system, the 'back-to-basics' sentiment as it is sometimes referred to. In passing it might be mentioned here that the type of research council initiative represented by the Swedish Collegium for Advanced Study in the Social Sciences set up in Uppsala in 1985 would not have been likely in the earlier climate. Its creation was made possible by a retreat from the science policies of the previous period. If the sectoral principle was abandoned in the next science policy bill, it would be possible to strengthen basic research, develop initiatives similar to SCASSS and still meet the needs of regional social and economic development.

A fourth outstanding issue, ignored earlier but now of prime importance, is Sweden's relations with the rest of Europe, entailing cooperation with other countries in research and higher education. Currently a portion of the budgets of the basic research councils are earmarked for contributions to such projects as CERN, the high energy physics laboratory in

Switzerland, or to the microbiological laboratory in Heidelberg, and similar intra-European cooperative programmes. Due to the expense of megascale research projects and equipment, we will doubtless see a closer integration of science policies on a Continental plane, a 'Europeanisation' of national science policy. Multi-national firms are certainly interested in research cooperation and forming consortia at the pre-application phase of R&D leading to product innovation. European programmes such as EUREKA are designed to compete with high technology development subsidised by the Strategic Defense Initiative in the United States. ERASMUS is a programme of university-based cooperation and student exchange that has considerable potential. Sweden is involved in EUREKA and became affiliated with ERASMUS in 1991. The prospects and significance of Europeanisation will have to be addressed in more concrete terms.[38]

It is clear that all of these problems have been taken up by the Swedish government from the new perspective of deregulation and orchestration-style policies. The centrality of research as a question of national concern was emphasised by the appointment some years ago of the Minister of Finance, Kjell-Olof Feldt, as Cabinet member in charge of matters relating to science, including the position of head of the Science Advisory Board. Feldt has since resigned from government and was succeeded at the Science Advisory Board by Odd Engstrom, the Deputy Prime Minister. With the demise of the social democratic government in September 1991, he has also been replaced. The slogans Feldt broadcast are quite different from the ones used by Olof Palme twenty years ago. Today the key words are 'initiative', 'quality', and 'internationalisation'. In order to realise these, some of the former authority of the professoriate may have to be restored, the mission of universities will need to be clarified, and the faculties will have to develop their own science policy consciousness at local levels in order to meet the challenge of the various relevance and accountability pressures presently at work. The new government of Carl Bildt also appears to favour this trend.

[38] EUREKA is the European Common Market (EEC) programme designed to stimulate high technology. The original 1985 French proposal for European research cooperation through EUREKA focused on the same six research fields that constituted the core of the Strategic Defense Initiative programme in the United States (opto-electronics, micro-electronics, new materials, super computers, lasers, and artificial intelligence) The later orientation inclined towards a more distinct civilian and industrial profile. See the Government Science Policy Bill no. 90, *Om forskning* (Regeringsproposition 1989/1990:90).

A drift of epistemic criteria?

The transformation of the Swedish universities and research system took place in tandem with the transformation of the Swedish State and the assumption of a different set of social and economic priorities by government. The early Church connection was replaced by a Royal connection and thereafter a Social Democratic connection. The four phases of development discussed in this chapter did not form a process of linear progression. They demarcate very different historical periods, each with a distinct research policy. The transition between phases was never smooth. Controversies and disagreements can be observed in each, but especially during the late 1960s and 1970s when the welfare connection was foremost.

The first phase was marked by relative stagnation for the universities. The second, during and immediately after the Second World War, involved a concentration on building up an infrastructure for developing basic research. In the third phase, encompassing the decade of the 1960s, science policy began to be integrated with industrial and welfare policies under the principle of sectoralization. Finally in the fourth phase, commencing about 1984 with the second science policy bill in Sweden, relevance and accountability pressures continued to increase, but with concurrent recognition that fundamental research was needed for making inroads into future high technology markets. It remains to be seen if this fourth phase spells the end of the sectoral principle in Sweden.

The third and fourth phases can be summarized differently. Sectoralisation and commercialisation came into conflict with the set of disciplinary norms and values found inside academic communities. Sheldon Rothblatt has described the dynamics of this process of external and internal pressures from an historical point of view. He observes of the two kinds of pressures that

The first...consists of demands for a wide range of scientific services for government, industry and the military...The second...derives from the internal constitution of science, from its cultural or value system and from the institutions that scientists have built or have cooperated in building in order to maximize the conditions under which their work is performed.[39]

Michael Gibbons and Björn Wittrock, who cite this observation in their anthology, *Science as a Commodity*, go on to argue that the operation of two kinds of influence, one that attempts to mold science to social need and another that is more concerned with legitimating the pursuit of scientific

[39] Sheldon Rothblatt, 'The Notion of an Open Scientific Community in Historical Perspective', in *Science as a Commodity*, ed. Michael Gibbons and Björn Wittrock (Harlow, Essex, 1985), 21.

knowledge, resulted in the professionalisation of science, giving to the scientific enterprise the institutional shape it now possesses.[40] But when the first influence takes precedence over the second, we obtain what I call 'epistemic drift'.

At one level epistemic drift refers to a shift of focus from internal quality control criteria – e.g., peer review – to external relevance criteria. At another level it refers to a corresponding shift of focus from the logic of problem sets and research agendas determined by the development of theory to those generated by mission-objectives and utilitarian goals formulated outside research. Whereas in the 1960s basic research resources were seen as a font of ideas which could sooner or later lead to practical application, in the 1980s the basic research resources were constantly being assessed from the utilitarian viewpoints fully described in this chapter.

It is the legitimacy of the scientific enterprise as viewed by its practitioners and its status as a self-regulating profession that are being challenged today from two outside sources, one that is rooted in *dirigiste* conceptions of government and the other in the marketplace, both existing at a time when emerging technology clusters like micro-electronics, bio-technology, and advanced industrial materials need to be solidly grounded in primary research.

Foss Hansen suggests that there is a struggle today for control of evaluation criteria, the guidance of research and the premises on which research is based. The several vested interests pull in different directions, towards the market, towards sectoral research, or towards disciplinary loyalties. The scientific community is drawn towards both pragmatism and adaptation, but also exhibits a tendency to close in on itself. The present interest in assessment and evaluation also produces polarities and disagreements according to the type of evaluations being used, e.g., citation indexing, hard data methods or more loosely-applied criteria, or whether the method of evaluation follows along international lines or is influenced by national concerns. To date, international standards appear to have the upper hand; but the differences have affected particular disciplines, for example, sociology and psychology, where real rifts have appeared.[41]

It can be said that whenever the epicentre of strategic problem definition, research, or evaluation and assessment shifts from the scientific com-

---

[40] Gibbons and Wittrock (eds.), Introduction to *Science as a Commodity*.

[41] Hanne Foss Hansen, 'Styrning och evaluering av forskning' (The Steering and Evaluation of Research) (Licentiats Dissertation, Institute for Information and Economic-steering, School of Business, Copenhagen, 1986). See also Hansen, 'Control and Organization of Research: A Case Study of Humanities Departments in Denmark', *Science Studies*, 1 (1988), 15–24; and Elzinga, 'The Consequences of Evaluation for Academic Research', *Science Studies*, 1 (1988), 5–14.

munity, with its traditional norms, systems of training and socialisation, to newly-formed hybrid communities with a different set of priorities, researchers inevitably become more concerned with external than with peer approval.[42] This shift, therefore, is paralleled by a corresponding adjustment in epistemic criteria, which are the measures scientists themselves use to denote the cognitive contents and value of their research projects. Such criteria are not limited to internally generated forms of quality control; they can and do include external opinions respecting relevance. But in the final analysis, such a shift must alter our public image of science and its meaning.

[42] See further Elzinga, 'Research, Bureaucracy and the Drift of Epistemic Criteria', in *The University Research System. The Public Policies of the Home of Scientists*, ed. Björn Wittrock and Aant Elzinga (Stockholm, 1985), 191–220; and 'Large-scale Funding Induces Culture Clash', *Space Policy*, 6 (1990), 187–194, where the case of SDI-research in the US is analysed using the concept of epistemic drift.

6   Research, graduate education, and the
     ecology of American universities: an
     interpretive history

Roger Geiger

The formative generation: the Civil War to 1890

A century ago American higher education was emerging from a generation
of momentous changes. Much of what constitutes the American system of
higher education today took shape and definition in the years between the
outbreak of the Civil War and the last decade of the century. The land-
grant colleges provided publicly maintained higher education across the
entire country. Cornell University, among the earliest of the many major
foundings of these years, showed that agriculture and the mechanic arts
could be taught alongside the liberal arts and sciences. The elective system,
effectively championed at Harvard by Charles Eliot (1869–1909), was
clearly triumphant by the end of the 1880s. It unchained manifold
possibilities concerning what could be learned in college and, just as
importantly, what could be taught. Professional schools blossomed as
expected components of forward-looking universities. Within the arts and
sciences, the disciplines took their modern forms by organising into
professional disciplinary associations. The nature of college-going was
transformed as well between the end of the Civil War and 1890. Higher
education for women attained parity with that of men, whether in separate
colleges or in co-educational settings. Students generally shed the compulsory piety and discipline of the Antebellum colleges, and instead
elaborated an extracurriculum of their own devising, not the least of their
innovations being American football.[1]

Perhaps overshadowing all these changes was the long-awaited establishment of graduate education and research within American higher
education. In the half-century before 1860, Richard Storr has written, 'the

---

[1] Laurence R. Veysey, *The Emergence of the American University* (Chicago, 1965); Hugh
Hawkins, *Between Harvard and America: The Educational Leadership of Charles W. Eliot*
(New York, 1973); Barbara Miller Solomon, *In the Company of Educated Women: a
History of Women and Higher Education in America* (New Haven, CT, 1985), 43–61;
Ronald A. Smith, *Sports and Freedom: The Rise of Big-Time College Athletics* (New York,
1988).

need, as distinct from the demand, for graduate education had been declared loudly and repeatedly'.[2] Increasingly, the inspiration for those who defined this need was the growing prowess of the German universities. The international hegemony of German academic learning and the concrete examples of German university practices presented compelling precedents, not just for American reformers, but for scientists and scholars everywhere. When Yale conferred the first American PhDs in 1861, it was consciously imitating the German degree, in part to spare would-be scholars from having to go abroad.[3] When the Johns Hopkins University was founded in 1876, it was perceived to be, and prided itself on being, a 'German-style' university. This influence continued to grow into the next decade, making the 1880s the high tide of German influence on American universities. The number of Americans studying in Germany continued to swell into the 1890s; but as these ambitious and motivated scholars returned to their home campuses, they would spend the next generation adapting the ideals of German learning to the realities of higher education as they found them in this country.[4] Chiefly, this meant assimilating advanced study and research with the nature of the American college.

Graduate study in the United States is as venerable as higher education itself. At seventeenth-century Harvard students for the master's degree prepared themselves by independently reading in the science of theology and then demonstrated their learning in public presentations. These undertakings were part of the responsibility of the college – in fact only Harvard bachelors were eligible – but they were administratively, pedagogically, and financially separate from what we would call the undergraduate college.[5] This pattern of separateness would endure for two centuries.

Insofar as an actual demand for higher learning existed in Antebellum America, it was pursued outside of the colleges. In the eighteenth century the locus for advanced knowledge was in the learned societies, like the American Philosophical Society founded by Benjamin Franklin. This tradition of the pursuit of learning outside of higher education persisted

---

[2] Richard J. Storr, *The Beginnings of Graduate Education* (Chicago, 1953), 35.
[3] Russell Chitenden, *A History of the Sheffield Scientific School* (New Haven, CT, 1928), I, 70–1, 86–8; coeval German influences in France, for example, are discussed in Roger L. Geiger, 'Prelude to Reform: The French Faculties of Letters in the 1860s', *The Making of Frenchmen: Current Directions in the History of Education in France*, ed. Donald Baker and Patrick Harrigan (Waterloo, Ontario, 1980), 337–61.
[4] Hugh Hawkins, *Pioneer: A History of the Johns Hopkins University*, 1874–1889 (Ithaca, NY, 1960), 127–8, 189; Veysey, *Emergence*, 125–33.
[5] Samuel Eliot Morison, *Harvard College in the Seventeenth Century* (Cambridge, MA, 1936), 69–71, 148–50.

through the first half of the next century and included the establishment of the American Association for the Advancement of Science (1848) and the National Academy of Sciences (1863).[6] Would-be reformers who tried to bring higher learning into the college curriculum met with little success. George Ticknor, for example, was unable to induce reforms at Harvard in the 1820s that would have made the teaching of advanced subjects possible, although he did succeed in raising the level of instruction in his own department.[7] Generally, however, scholarship or research was forced outside of the college. The first approximation of graduate professional training occurred in theological seminaries in the early nineteenth century. The best of these institutions recruited many of their students from among college graduates, became a home for Biblical scholarship, and trained a disproportionate number of future educational leaders.[8] Even more important were the scientific schools that later developed at Harvard and Yale in the 1840s. The Lawrence School at Harvard became the outlet for the scientific studies of a few Harvard faculty. The Sheffield School at Yale was broader, combining both instruction in practical subjects such as agricultural chemistry and advanced studies in science and arts. By being established separate from their respective colleges, these schools trans-cended the limitations of the fixed curriculum. The PhDs awarded in New Haven in 1861 were not the product of Yale College but of the Sheffield Scientific School – even though one of the degrees was in philosophy and another in classical languages.[9]

The very nature of the American college was the chief impediment to the incorporation of the higher learning. The problem – and it only consti-tuted a 'problem' for those who wished this institution to be something different – was the complete adaptation of the 'old-time college' to its singular purpose of forming the minds of young men. According to the accepted contemporary doctrines of faculty psychology, the chief aim of the college training was to instil 'mental discipline' – the capacity to learn.

---

[6] John C. Greene, 'Science, Learning, and Utility: Patterns of Organization in the Early American Republic', and Sally Gregory Kohlstedt, 'Savants and Professionals: The American Association for the Advancement of Science, 1848–1860', both in *The Pursuit of Knowledge in the Early American Republic: American Scientific and Learned Societies from Colonial Times to the Civil War*, ed. Alexandra Oleson and Sanford C. Brown (Baltimore, 1976), 1–20; 299–325. For the decay of this tradition, see A. Hunter Dupree, 'The National Academy of Sciences and the American Definition of Science', in *The Organization of Knowledge in Modern America, 1860–1920*, ed. Alexandra Oleson and John Voss (Baltimore, 1979), 342–63.

[7] David B. Tyack, *George Ticknor and the Boston Brahmins* (Cambridge, MA, 1967), 107–28; Samuel Eliot Morison, *Three Centuries of Harvard* (Cambridge, MA, 1936), 232–38.

[8] Natalie A. Naylor, 'The Theological Seminary in the Configuration of American Higher Education: The Ante-Bellum Years', *History of Education Quarterly*, 17 (1977), 17–30.

[9] Stanley M. Guralnik, *Science and the Antebellum College* (Philadelphia, 1975).

This capacity was best mastered, it was believed, by learning the classical languages, essentially by rote. Such learning was conducted and monitored through classroom recitations. Knowledge under this system was not the end of education, but a means. Only after this salutory preparation would a young man be expected to begin acquiring the rudiments of an actual profession. The curriculum also included a smattering of information about science and society – the 'furniture of the mind' in the words of the Yale Report of 1828, the principal rationalisation of these practices.[10] Over time, these materials were expanded and updated, particularly through a greater inclusion of scientific subjects. But even at those few fortunate institutions possessing sufficient wealth to augment their faculty and their offerings, the superficial character of these subjects was never overcome. Daniel Coit Gilman reported that he was introduced to twenty subjects during his senior year at Yale.[11]

The singular purpose of the old-time college, then, greatly limited its possibilities. Since the aims were identical for each student, so was the curriculum. A single, fixed set of courses in turn precluded advanced or specialised subjects. The requirements of imposing mental discipline upon recalcitrant youths molded the pedagogy of the colleges as well, making them ill-suited for anything else.[12] The colleges nevertheless, in spite of the charges of contemporary critics, largely had the sanction of society. In the population centres of the East, a college education was the accepted prerequisite for professional careers, and those careers were the path to a respectable social status. On the other side of the Allegheny Mountains, the colleges tended to fill an educational void for post-primary instruction. Although their purposes in these locales were more diverse, they still held the promise of social (and geographical) mobility, if not automatic high status. Thus, the upper levels of Antebellum American society largely regarded the colleges as appropriate institutions for the perpetuation of

[10] 'The Yale Report of 1828', in *American Higher Education: A Documentary History*, ed. Richard Hofstadter and Wilson Smith (Chicago, 1961), 275–91; Douglas Sloan, 'Harmony, Chaos, and Consensus: The American College Curriculum', *Teachers College Record*, 73 (1961), 221–51; Jack C. Lane, 'The Yale Report of 1828 and Liberal Education: A Neorepublican Manifesto', *History of Education Quarterly*, 27 (1987), 325–38.

[11] Daniel Coit Gilman, *The Launching of a University* (New York, 1906), 8–9.

[12] The historical critique of the old-time college was best articulated by Richard Hofstadter, *Academic Freedom in the Age of the College* (New York, 1951), 209–61. This critique is now regarded as too sweeping, even though the revisionists focus on rather different issues from Hofstadter's concern with intellectual vitality. See David B. Potts, '"College Enthusiasm!" As Public Response: 1800–1860', *Harvard Education Review*, 47 (1977), 28–42, and Colin B. Burke, *American Collegiate Populations: A Test of the Traditional View* (New York, 1982). For a balanced discussion, see Walter P. Metzger, 'The Academic Profession in the United States', in *The Academic Profession: National, Disciplinary, and Institutional Settings*, ed. Burton R. Clark (Los Angeles, 1987), 123–96.

social position, irrespective of what students actually learned there.[13] Reformers who directly attacked this social institution were largely frustrated: to pursue different purposes usually meant, as in the case of Yale's Sheffield School, to operate on its periphery.

Much of the essential nature of the old-time college persisted after the Civil War. As late as the 1880s, when the classical curriculum was clearly losing its sway, university-builders inspired by the German model saw no place for advanced learning in the American college. They regarded collegiate studies as largely equivalent to what was taught in the Gymnasium in Germany. 'True university work', according to this view, could only commence on the graduate level. Prior to 1890, the chief experiments in American higher education reflected this view. Daniel Coit Gilman shaped Johns Hopkins as an institution in which the emphasis was on graduate education and research, although he realised that prevailing opinion would not allow him to dispense with an undergraduate college. G. Stanley Hall attempted to carry the experiment further by launching a purely graduate institution at Clark University. And William Rainey Harper envisioned the University of Chicago not only as a pinnacle of learning, but also as the capstone of a system of feeder colleges. Unprecedented acts of philanthropy made these bold departures from traditional colleges possible; but the circumstances of American higher education tended to pull them back toward the norm. Graduate students were few in number, and a faculty of specialised professors was expensive to maintain. Clark was not viable as a graduate institution; Hopkins reverted over time to a more traditional (although still small) undergraduate college; and Chicago, the best supported of the experiments, spent the next two generations debating how best to reconcile undergraduate education and the higher learning.[14]

The generation of the American university: 1890 to World War I

The 1890s brought what Laurence Veysey called a 'boom' in university development and with it emerged the standard model of the American

[13] Ronald Story, *The Forging of an Aristocracy: Harvard and the Boston Upper Class, 1800–1870* (Middletown, CT, 1980); Peter Dobkin Hall, *The Organization of American Culture, 1700–1900: Private Institutions, Elites, and the Origins of American Nationality* (New York, 1984); Burke, *American Collegiate Populations*; Potts, '"College Enthusiasm!"'; and for Virginia, Jennings L. Wagoner, Jr., 'Honor and Dishonor at Mr. Jefferson's University: The Antebellum Years', *History of Education Quarterly*, 26 (1986), 155–79.
[14] W. Carson Ryan, *Studies in Early Graduate Education: The Johns Hopkins, Clark University, and the University of Chicago* (New York, 1939).

university.[15] At its centre, still, was the college. Education for utilitarian or professional purposes, however, was largely hived off into separate compartments, at first called 'departments' and eventually known as 'schools'. The proliferation of these professional compartments was an important contribution to the overall growth of universities; in fact, institutions that resisted this trend like Hopkins, Princeton, and for a time Stanford, remained comparatively small. As for research, each type of professional school developed at its own pace. Schools of agriculture, as a result of the experiment stations created by the Hatch Act (1887), developed an extensive research enterprise well before they had an appreciable number of students. Research in medical schools grew markedly after 1900, as the pattern set by Harvard and Johns Hopkins was increasingly imitated at other universities. Graduate study and research in education also had a narrow base, Teachers College at Columbia University (founded 1888) being the outstanding pioneer in this respect.[16] In other parts of the university, however, professional research and graduate education were slower to develop. Arts and sciences nevertheless remained at the core of the American university, and there research and liberal culture – representing, respectively, graduate and undergraduate education – were nevertheless linked. Separate graduate schools were created to minister to the needs and requirements of graduate students, but the 'graduate faculty of arts and sciences' – the title chosen by Harvard in 1890 – was coextensive with the senior faculty of the college. This essential pattern was adopted elsewhere: graduate education and research were inextricably joined with the undergraduate college through the faculty.

The separateness and the connectedness of graduate education and research vis-à-vis the college – this was the situation that bedevilled the first generation of university builders during the decades prior to the First

[15] Veysey, *Emergence*, 263–8. The 'standard' features of the American university were noted by Edwin E. Slosson, *Great American Universities* (New York, 1910), 522. They included high school graduation required for admission; two years of general work in a college of arts and sciences, followed by two years of specialised work; five departments granting the PhD; and at least one professional school. These criteria were taken from a statement by the National Association of State Universities: *Report of the U.S. Commissioner of Education* (1909), 89.

[16] Roger L. Williams, *The Origins of Federal Support for Higher Education: George W. Atherton and the Land-Grant College Movement* (University Park, PA, 1991); Alan I. Marcus, *Agricultural Science and the Quest for Legitimacy: Farmers, Agricultural Colleges, and Experiment Stations, 1870–1890* (Ames, Iowa, 1985); Norwood A. Kerr, *The Legacy: A Centennial History of the State Agricultural Experiment Stations, 1887–1987* (Columbia, MO, 1987). Rosemary Stevens, *American Medicine and the Public Interest* (New Haven, CT, 1971), chapters 2–3; Donald Fleming, *William H. Welch and the Rise of Modern Medicine* (Boston, 1954). Lawrence A. Cremin, David A. Shannon, and Mary E. Townsend, *A History of Teachers College, Columbia University* (New York, 1954); Geraldine Joncich Clifford and James W. Guthrie, *Ed School: A Brief for Professional Education* (Chicago, 1988), 74–84.

World War. The thousands of Americans who earned degrees at German universities had directly experienced a situation in which the advancement of knowledge through research and graduate education was the highest value in university life. German professors had State-funded institutes attached to their university chairs. These institutes provided the resources needed for the conduct of research, made research the central commitment of their position, and permitted them to work directly with advanced students and assistants.[17] Back in the United States all these prerequisites of research – resources, faculty time, and advanced students – were problematic.

At the beginning of this century, the facilities for conducting research in this country were decidedly primitive in comparison to Germany. American professors who incurred extraordinary expenses in their research customarily met them out of their own pocketbooks or sometimes raised subscriptions in the local community. Such arrangements were an obvious constraint, and their inadequacy became increasingly apparent after 1900.[18] By that date the Germans were already using the term *Gross-wissenschaft* (or 'Big Science'); research in the natural sciences required significant ongoing expenditures.

For American faculty, moreover, teaching and research were almost mutually exclusive activities.[19] The burden of teaching undergraduate introductory courses to poorly prepared, often weakly motivated students absorbed most of the time and energy of most of the faculty. American colleges and universities were essentially open to all who met the lenient qualifications. The clientele of the prestigious Eastern colleges was powerfully shaped by self-selection, but even there the actual admissions process was a low barrier. Potential students might qualify on either of two sets of admissions examinations, and then might be allowed to enter with conditions. Failing that, a determined young man might enrol in another institution and then easily transfer. By 1890 most of the state universities had adopted a less complicated scheme by automatically admitting graduates of 'certified' high schools. Standardisation proceeded further when the philanthropic Carnegie Foundation (founded 1906) defined 'units' of secondary school study that any self-respecting college ought to require.[20] None of these procedures did much to discourage the burgeoning

---

[17] Joseph Ben-David, *The Scientist's Role in Society* (Chicago, 1984); Charles E. McClelland, *State, Society, and University in Germany, 1700–1914* (Cambridge, 1980).

[18] Roger Geiger, 'The Conditions of University Research 1900–1920', *History of Higher Education Annual*, 4 (1984), 3–29.

[19] Hugh Hawkins, 'University Identity: The Teaching and Research Functions', in Oleson and Voss (eds), *Organization of Knowledge*, 285–312.

[20] Harold Wechsler, *The Qualified Student: A History of Selective Admissions in America* (New York, 1977).

numbers of secondary school graduates. That group constituted 2.5 per cent of the age cohort in 1880; 6.4 per cent in 1900; and 16.8 per cent in 1920.[21] Before the twentieth century, an ubiquitous concern of American colleges had been finding enough students (as well as retaining them!), and this fact of life had contributed to the basic openess of the system. Not until after the War would a few institutions wrestle with the problem of how to select from an overabundance of applicants. The indubitable fact of American higher education was that many students entered having rudimentary training and much to learn.

Would-be researchers in American universities needed funds for material and equipment, as well as a redefinition of their responsibilities so that they might have the time to utilise these things. Since the support of American institutions was largely tied to teaching, another source of funds was required.

From the time of the establishment of the Hollis Professorship of Divinity at Harvard (1721), it was gifts, and particularly gifts permanently preserved as endowments, that permitted American colleges to do things that were not strictly encompassed in the education of undergraduates. In the nineteenth century, the true research institutes of American colleges – the observatories and the museums – were established in this way.[22] As already noted, it was the burgeoning philanthropy for higher education that had launched the bold experiments at Johns Hopkins, Clark, and Chicago. To university presidents of this era it was axiomatic that research needed its own, specifically earmarked funds if it were to flourish. Arthur Twining Hadley of Yale announced that 'the research of a university should be as far as possible endowed research'. Charles Eliot regularly invited Harvard's benefactors to provide for the needs of research. And Charles Van Hise of Wisconsin envisioned the day when his university's alumni would be numerous and wealthy enough to provide for the institution's research needs with a steady stream of gifts. Most ambitious of all was Jacob Gould Schurman of Cornell, who invited contemporary philanthropists to provide million-dollar endowments for each of Cornell's academic departments.[23]

Another possibility for facilitating research lay with the differentiation of the teaching role. Larger academic departments allowed at least some teachers to be emancipated from the travail of undergraduate instruction. As the universities grew, such differentiation was also accompanied

---

[21] *Digest of Education Statistics, 1985–86* (Washington, DC, 1986), 69.
[22] Howard Miller, *Dollars for Research: Science and Its Patrons in Nineteenth Century America* (Seattle, 1970); Roger Geiger, *To Advance Knowledge: The Growth of American Research Universities, 1900–1940* (New York, 1986), 80–2.
[23] Geiger, *To Advance Knowledge*, 83–7.

through stratification. After the Civil War two-thirds of the teachers in American colleges held the title of professor, but in the first decade of the twentieth century only one quarter would hold that rank at leading research universities.[24] New faculty positions were largely filled with instructors and assistant professors during these years, and these junior appointments were disproportionately responsible for introductory courses. This was the era of autocratic department heads who, like the German mentors with whom many had studied, assigned much of the drudgery to their subordinates. Some considered pushing differentiation even further. After the turn of the century the idea of 'research professorships' became widely discussed. Such positions were actually created for a time at Cornell, Chicago, Wisconsin, California, Indiana, and Ohio State. This experiment was counterbalanced by attempts to create specialised teaching posts. The Princeton preceptors, at least as originally envisioned by President Woodrow Wilson (1902–9), and the tutors created at Harvard by President A. Lawrence Lowell (1909–33), were intended to fulfil such roles. Both these approaches fit awkwardly with the supposed egalitarianism of academic departments. In practice, university leaders generally followed a tacit policy of actively discriminating between assignments for 'teaching men' and 'research men'.[25]

The unification of instruction and research at a high level nevertheless proved to be an elusive goal. Graduate study remained a distressingly minor component of even the foremost universities. As the American PhD replaced the German degree as the norm in this country, the number of doctorates awarded rose above 300 for the first time in 1897, although half of them were awarded by just six universities. But that total did not surpass 400 for another dozen years.[26] Graduate students at the turn of the century typically numbered less than 10 per cent of undergraduates at those few institutions producing the majority of PhDs. Not very many American students possessed the resources or the dedication to devote themselves exclusively to advanced studies. And not everyone thought this desirable. In 'The PhD Octopus', the Harvard philosopher William James penned the most celebrated condemnation of alleged Germanic tendencies toward

[24] Walter P. Metzger, 'The Academic Profession', 123–208, esp. 145; Alan Creutz, 'From College Teacher to University Scholar: The Evolution and Professionalization of Academics at the University of Michigan, 1841–1900', unpublished PhD dissertation, University of Michigan, 1981, 192–218.

[25] Hawkins, 'University Identity', 292–3; Geiger, *To Advance Knowledge*, 72–4.

[26] The six were Chicago, Columbia, Cornell, Harvard, Johns Hopkins, and Yale; however, Penn too was a large producer. These institutions dominated the granting of PhDs until after World War I. See Geiger, *To Advance Knowledge*, 276–7; National Research Council, *A Century of Doctorates* (Washington, DC: National Academy of Sciences, 1978), 7. Before 1900 the number of doctorates was somewhat inflated: Robert E. Kohler, 'The PhD Machine: Building on the Collegiate Base', *Isis*, 81 (1990), 638–62.

pedantry and overspecialisation in American graduate studies. A substantial number of humanists defended an ideal of liberal culture against the growing trend toward specialised erudition.[27]

The fundamental difficulties that beset the infancy of the American university were increasingly overcome after 1900, but not in the ways foreseen by the advocates of the higher learning. American universities received comparatively few endowments for purposes of research, and those they did receive were largely confined to medicine. But they did become decidedly larger and wealthier over the course of this generation, and the undergraduate college was the key to both these developments.

Philanthropy has played a fundamental role in the development of higher education in the United States.[28] Prior to 1900, however, fundraising had been a sporadic and often difficult matter for even the most successful of institutions. After the turn of the century, this picture was altered by developments at Yale and Harvard. The Yale Alumni Fund, which had been started in 1891 in order to collect small contributions, began receiving gifts in such volume that a separate endowment fund was created in addition to the annual donation given to the university. At this same juncture, the Harvard class of 1880 gave $100,000 to the university on the occasion of its twenty-fifth anniversary. Every subsequent class would give at least as much.[29] Substantial magnitudes of gifts thus became for the first time a recurrent and dependable source of income. Both institutions were launched upon a course that would make them easily the country's wealthiest universities; and there was no doubt as to where the money was coming from – the graduates of the college.

The growing affluence of a few universities stood in contrast to the financial constraints facing many others, but it was those few that would lead the way in the expensive business of graduate education and research. The importance of their alumni in this process naturally tended to enhance the importance of the undergraduate college within the university. Although those universities assiduously cultivated the college and its culture, this emphasis was not necessarily inimical to research. As new laboratories and libraries were built, as the size of the faculty was expanded, the inherent capability of these fortunate institutions for supporting research was immeasurably strengthened.

The growth of undergraduate enrolments was a crucial factor for the

[27] William James, 'The PhD Octopus', in *The Harvard Monthly* (1903), reprinted in *Educational Review*, 55 (1918), 149–57; Veysey, *Emergence*, 180–203; Hawkins, 'University Identity', 302–4.

[28] See Jesse B. Sears, *Philanthropy in the History of American Higher Education* (New Brunswick, NJ, 1990, first published 1922); Merle Curti and Roderick Nash, *Philanthropy in the Shaping of American Higher Education* (New Brunswick, NJ, 1965).

[29] Discussed in Geiger, *To Advance Knowledge*, 43–57.

advancement of the leaders among both public and private research universities. At private institutions the tuition paid by the overwhelmingly undergraduate clientele roughly approximated the cost of faculty salaries during these years.[30] More students made it possible to employ more teachers in more subjects. An analagous process occurred in the leading state-supported universities. There, the expansion and extension of undergraduate instruction tended to be rewarded by state legislators with the provision of additional resources.[31] By about 1905 they had grown in size to equal their older and more prestigious private counterparts.

From 1905 to 1915 the major public and private research universities were all approximately the same size – 3,000–5,000 regular students.[32] This was a period of consolidation for American higher education which contrasted sharply with the wide dispersion of resources that occurred throughout the Antebellum years. In 1894 the combined enrolment for the eleven largest research universities (Chicago, Columbia, Cornell, Harvard, Penn, Yale, California, Illinois, Michigan, Minnesota, and Wisconsin) was roughly 21,000; in 1904 it exceeded 35,500; and in 1914 they counted 53,000 students. In 1894 this total represented 15 per cent of all students in American higher education, and from 1904 to 1914 their share constituted 17.5 per cent. This growth allowed the research universities to expand their faculties, to offer new subjects, and to accommodate greater specialisation within established ones. This was a process that Walter Metzger has labeled as 'substantive growth' of the academic profession.[33] At the same time, the increasing affluence of these schools permitted them to lower the teaching burden of faculty. Student–faculty ratios in the first decade of the century declined from 14:1 to 12:1 in state universities and from 10:1 to 8:1 in private universities.[34] In addition, larger and more specialised faculties facilitated a change in the nature of academic departments from the autocratic German model to a collegial, American model. Instead of a single 'head' professor, reigning over subordinates, the American academic department came to have several full professors, together with junior faculty who might aspire to that rank, each individual intellectually sovereign in his specialty. In the American research university all faculty members were expected to be experts on some facet of their field and to contribute to its advancement. This development was crucial for the

---

[30] Trevor Arnett, *College and University Finance* (New York, 1922). Institutional revenues from tuition are given in Geiger, *To Advance Knowledge*, 273–5.

[31] *Ibid.*; Richard Rees Price, *The Financial Support of State Universities* (Cambridge, MA, 1923).

[32] Full-time fall enrollments are given in Geiger, *To Advance Knowledge*, 270–1.

[33] Metzger, 'Academic Profession', 147.

[34] Geiger, *To Advance Knowledge*, 272. See also Metzger, 'Academic Profession', 146–7.

promotion of graduate education and research, but it was principally made possible by the growth of undergraduate education.

Graduate education expanded too, but from quite a small base. It was aided considerably by one of the great unsung inventions of American higher education. In 1899 Harvard received a substantial bequest designated for the general purpose of encouraging research. The university chose to use these funds to create thirty fellowships for graduate students, which included the obligation of teaching half-time. Thus was born the graduate teaching fellow. This was a striking departure from the prevailing pattern, modelled upon German practices, which expected the graduate student to be dedicated exclusively to study. For a time this innovation was controversial – G. Stanley Hall accused Harvard of instituting a 'sweating system'.[35] But the graduate teaching fellow fitted the needs of American universities so perfectly that it soon swept the day. It provided needed support for graduate students, while further relieving scholarly faculty of the much-resented burden of teaching introductory courses. The state universities, with their growing instructional obligations, soon found the use of teaching fellows to be a means for equalising conditions somewhat with their wealthier private counterparts.

By the time of the First World War the American university had evolved a distinctive pattern that was quite different from what had been envisioned by the university purists of the preceding generation. Instead of eschewing the undergraduate college, it capitalised upon its popularity, upon the deep loyalties that it inspired, and upon the possibilities it presented for a fruitful division of labour. The pattern was anything but neat, and the university system still lacked funds for research *per se*; but because this model reflected powerful indigenous trends, it held great potential for the future.

The inter-war generation

The American university truly came of age during the inter-war years. Still in the thrall of European learning after World War I in most major fields, American scientists and scholars had established themselves at the frontiers of knowledge in virtually all fields by the eve of World War II. This accomplishment essentially took place within the universities, where research and graduate education were expanded in scope and made more rigorous in character. During the decade of the 1920s, for example, the production of American PhDs roughly tripled; and in the penurious

[35] Association of American Universities, *Journal of Proceedings and Addresses*, 8 (1906); Geiger, *To Advance Knowledge*, 76–7.

environment of the 1930s, it increased by another 50 per cent. Research is less readily measured, but there can be little doubt that it traced a similar path, accelerating greatly during the 1920s and then augmenting that level of activity further during the Great Depression. Overall, this change was made possible by the strengthening of the universities through their own efforts and through the assistance they received from external agencies.

The 1920s were the key to university development. Starting from the depths of the post-war depression, the decade ended with a flourish that brought American universities the greatest prosperity that they had ever known. Moreover, despite the onset of the Depression, these gains were permanent. Interestingly, they were achieved in two different ways.

In the decade prior to the First World War the public and private universities had been more alike in terms of size and conditions than at any time before or since. After the war their respective developmental strategies diverged.[36] For the state universities the dictum that 'bigger is better' remained in force. By expanding their enrolments, and by utilising increasing numbers of teaching fellows, they were able to have both larger, more specialised faculties, and more graduate students for advanced instruction. The private universities, however, partly in conformance with the preferences of their alumni, restricted their intake and concentrated their growing resources upon a selected group of students.[37] Both strategies were focused primarily upon the undergraduate college, and both succeeded during the 1920s. The image projected by the wealthiest private universities, particularly the group that became identified as the 'Ivy League', was extraordinarily successful in attracting alumni gifts. This affluence permitted the cultivation of both distinguished faculties active in scientific research and a remarkable array of amenities for undergraduates.

The pivotal development of the 1920s, nevertheless, was the interest taken in university research by the great philanthropic foundations, particularly the Rockefeller group of trusts. The turning point for this development occurred in 1922, when Beardsley Ruml became director of the Laura Spelman Rockefeller Memorial, and when Wickliffe Rose was named director of the General Education Board (as well as a newly created International Education Board). For the remainder of the decade these two men would be the chief patrons, respectively, of the social and the natural sciences. Although completely independent of one another, their motives and their actions were closely parallel. Ruml reasoned that an

---

[36] Discussed in Geiger, 'After the Emergence: Voluntary Support and the Building of American Research Universities', *History of Education Quarterly*, 25 (1985), 369–81.

[37] Marcia G. Synnott, *The Half-Opened Door: Discrimination in Admissions to Harvard, Yale, and Princeton, 1900–1970* (Westport, CT, 1979); Wechsler, *Qualified Student*; Geiger, *To Advance Knowledge*, 129–39, 215–19.

adequate knowledge base was lacking for dealing intelligently with existing social problems. The only way to remedy this for the long term, he felt, was to build basic social scientific knowledge, and this could only be done by developing these subjects within the universities.[38] Rose too wished to stimulate basic research in the universities. His thinking undoubtedly reflected a prevailing post-war optimism about pure research leading to technological improvements (or, the 'advancement of civilisation', in the parlance of the day). He also had a long association with the highly successful Rockefeller programmes in public health. Ultimately Rose, more so than Ruml, seemed motivated by a belief in the advancement of science as an end in itself.[39]

Both Ruml and Rose spent the first several years of their directorships carefully assessing their fields and judiciously making grants. Then, in the years before the reorganisation of the Rockefeller trusts, which occurred in 1929, they made grants on an increasingly massive scale. With small staffs and limited knowledge of the actual content of the many fields in which they operated, this was a sensible, although by no means the only, manner of distributing the millions of dollars at their disposal. The largest of their grants provided capital to support various aspects of research, primarily at the leading private universities. This was a strategy, in Rose's words, of 'making the peaks higher'; and this deliberate elitism in fact proved highly effective in terms of allowing the favoured institutions to bring their programmes up to the highest international standards. Grant-making on such a scale, however, was unsustainable for long.

Both Ruml and Rose stepped down in 1929 when their trusts were folded into the reorganised Rockefeller Foundation, which then assumed responsibility for the advancement of knowledge in all fields. Their deeds nevertheless lived on as the Foundation had to meet the commitments they had made, even as its income was shrinking as a result of the Depression. A further reevaluation of the Foundation's activities was needed by 1934, and a scaling back of its grant-making resulted. In both the Social Science and Natural Science Division, a policy was established of supporting specific research projects in strategically chosen areas. The difference from the Rose-Ruml era was that now Foundation research grants were smaller in size and more closely specified; but they were also available to a much larger number of institutions. All of the prewar research universities were receiving foundation support by the end of the 1930s.[40]

[38] Joan Bulmer and Martin Bulmer, 'Philanthropy and Social Science in the 1920s: Beardsley Ruml and the Laura Spelman Rockefeller Memorial, 1922–29', *Minerva*, 19 (1981), 347–407.
[39] Robert E. Kohler, *Partners in Science: Foundations and Natural Scientists, 1900–1945* (Chicago, 1991).   [40] *Ibid.*, 265–357.

248   *Roger Geiger*

Private industry also became a regular supporter of university research during the inter-war years. In contrast with the foundations' role, however, funds from industry tended to support research *per se* and did less to boost the research capacity of the universities. An exception to this generalisation would be the support to graduate students in selected fields. During the 1920s flourishing centres for conducting engineering research for industry emerged at Michigan and MIT, among others. Linkages with university research became commonplace in the chemical industry, electric power, pharmaceuticals, and, through the single firm of the America Telephone and Telegraph Company (AT&T), telecommunications.[41]

The role of foundations, and to a lesser extent industry, transformed the circumstances of university research. For the first time American universities could look to a regular, recurrent source of support for the direct expenses of conducting organised research. A separate 'research company' had emerged, which not only resolved the chief impediment to conducting research on university campuses, but also made the research activities of faculty even more valued for university leaders. This last point deserves emphasis. In a decade in which higher education was dominated by the 'collegiate syndrome' – the pronounced emphasis upon peer culture, athletics, and the extracurriculum in college life – foundation support for research gave tangible backing to the academic side of the university. The academic accomplishments of faculty became a facet of university prestige that universities – although not colleges – could scarcely afford to neglect. This consideration was reinforced in 1925, when Raymond Hughes published the first quality ranking of graduate departments.[42] From that day onward, the academic prestige hierarchy would be measured by attainments in graduate education and research.

The growth of university research naturally had a positive effect upon graduate studies. The handful of universities that regularly received research funding were able to enrol and support larger numbers of graduate students. One facet of foundation support, however, made a crucial contribution to the development of American science – the creation of post-doctoral fellowships. The first 'postdocs' were established by the Rockefeller Foundation and the National Research Council (NRC) in

[41] John P. Swann, *Academic Scientists and the Pharmaceutical Industry: Cooperative Research in Twentieth Century America* (Baltimore, 1988); David C. Mowery and Nathan Rosenberg, *Technology and the Pursuit of Economic Growth* (Cambridge, 1989), 35–97; John W. Servos, 'The Industrial Relations of Science: Chemical Engineering at MIT, 1900–1939', *Isis*, 71 (1980), 531–49; David F. Noble, *America By Design* (New York, 1977). The differing patterns of MIT and CalTech are discussed in Geiger, *To Advance Knowledge*, 174–89.
[42] Raymond M. Hughes, *A Study of Graduate Schools of America* (Oxford, OH, 1925); David S. Webster, 'America's Highest Ranked Graduate Schools, 1925–1982', *Change* (May/June 1983), 14–24.

1919 in an almost accidental way when agreement could not be reached over the matter of founding research institutes. The fellowships were limited to just mathematics, physics, and chemistry. In the first dozen years of this programme, one of every eleven PhDs in these fields was awarded an NRC post-doctoral fellowship, and 80 per cent of these fellows subsequently taught in American universities. Post-doctoral fellowships were soon extended to medicine and biology as well. These awards bolstered American higher education at one of its weakest points – the transition from graduate study to faculty status. These new PhDs, instead of being relegated in the usual manner to extensive introductory instruction, were able to extend mastery of their fields at the most advanced centres of research. Such experience was far more effective in producing first-rate scientists; indeed, these fellows largely comprised the next generation of leadership for American science.[43]

While extraordinary opportunities were opening up for the best and the brightest products of American graduate schools, graduate education in general suffered from a lack of organisation and definition. Throughout the 1920s there were undoubtedly fewer graduate students than university departments would have liked. Thus, even while the colleges were establishing selective admissions, the graduate schools remained open to the brilliant and the plodding alike. Most schools attracted a major portion of their graduate students from among their own recent bachelors. Prominent among this group was always a number of June graduates who had failed to find employment. Many had not compiled very distinguished undergraduate records. Attrition, for this and other reasons, tended to be high. Even at Harvard, one half of the beginning graduate students failed to appear for the second year.[44]

The beginnings of a rationalisation of graduate study did not occur until the 1930s. Harvard imposed restrictive standards upon its incoming students for the first time in 1930. Progress was uncertain, however, due to the lack of reliable criteria for judging applicants and the appetites of academic departments for students. An excess demand for places was clearly the prerequisite to meaningful selection. By the late 1930s this condition was beginning to be met at some institutions. In 1937 Columbia, Harvard, Princeton, and Yale cooperated in the development of the Graduate Record Examination, an effort to improve the standard of graduate admissions.

[43] Nathan Reingold, 'The Case of the Disappearing Laboratory', *American Quarterly*, 29 (1977), 79–101; Fosdick, *Rockefeller Foundation*, 145–6; National Research Council, *Consolidated Report upon the Activities of the National Research Council, 1919 to 1923* (Washington, DC: National Research Council, 1932); Geiger, *To Advance Knowledge*, 222, 235–8; Kohler, *Partners in Science*, 87–104.
[44] Discussed in Geiger, *To Advance Knowledge*, 219–23.

When the rationalisation of graduate education is considered together with the greater financial support for graduate students, the existence of post-doctoral fellowships, and the coeval rationalisation of faculty career structures, a significant transformation becomes apparent. By the end of the 1930s the potential university teacher was subject to evaluative hurdles at recurrent intervals. Selection upon entry to graduate school, discrimination in the award of financial support, post-doctoral opportunities for the most able – all added up to a competitive process that would govern the allocation of the most valuable opportunities for productive scholarship and research. By 1940 this process, which is now taken for granted, was firmly rooted within research universities.[45]

By that date, the conditions just described pertained in large measure to perhaps sixteen institutions – the research universities that to varying extents competed with one another for faculty, sometimes graduate students, and resources from the research economy.[46] To compete in this arena required a level of financial strength that was largely lacking outside of this circle. At least three other institutional types are sufficiently closely related to the research universities to deserve mention. Some relatively wealthy institutions, like Dartmouth and Brown, preferred to emphasise undergraduate education rather than graduate education and research. A second group of institutions had been captured by the late nineteenth-century enthusiasm for graduate education and research but failed to develop the kind of financial strength needed to realise such ambitions. At Northwestern, for example, President Henry Wade Rogers (1890–1900) was constrained by financial limitations from seeking to emulate the established research universities of the East; and in the nation's capital, the efforts of Columbian University (George Washington University) to make the transition to full university status brought the institution instead to the brink of bankruptcy.[47] The state universities, as a third type, presented a full grant of financial and research capabilities. Below the top five – California, Michigan, Wisconsin, Minnesota, and Illinois – significant research efforts tended to be localised within a few departments even in the stronger institutions. Furthermore, when their productive scholars were recruited by other institutions, they were seldom able or inclined to

[45] Cf. Logan Wilson, *Academic Man: A Study in the Sociology of a Profession* (New York, 1942).

[46] These sixteen universities are monitored in Geiger, *To Advance Knowledge*: CalTech, Chicago, Columbia, Cornell, Harvard, Johns Hopkins, MIT, Penn, Princeton, Stanford, Yale, California, Illinois, Michigan, Minnesota, and Wisconsin. They varied widely in the magnitudes of research and doctoral education. The patterns they evinced were naturally evident in other universities but to a lesser extent prior to 1940.

[47] Elmer Louis Kayser, *Bricks Without Straw: The Evolution of George Washington University* (New York, 1970), 147–212; Harold F. Williamson and Payson S. Wild, *Northwestern University: A History, 1850–1975* (Evanston, 1976), 71–84, 93–9.

attempt to match the offered salaries.[48] These last two groups of universities, in particular, expanded graduate education during the inter-war years; however, the sixteen principal research universities, which awarded 69 per cent of doctorates before the First World War (1909), still awarded 54 per cent of them in 1939.[49]

During the course of the inter-war generation the basic pattern of the American university remained intact. That is, the bulk of university resources were derived from its instructional role, but to varying extents some portion of these were utilised to accommodate graduate education and research as well. Maintaining this research capacity became more costly in terms of resources devoted to faculty and facilities during these years; but because of foundation support for university research, it became more rewarding as well. A symbiotic relationship existed between the college and the graduate school that would take on new dimensions after World War II.

The post-war generation

During the three decades that stretched from the end of World War II to the mid-1970s, the American university built rapidly and monumentally upon the foundations that had been laid by the end of the 1930s.

The end of the war brought far-reaching change. A flood of discharged servicemen flocked into the country's colleges and universities assisted by federal aid (the 'G-I Bill'). Most sought bachelor's degrees, but enough persisted through graduate school to double the level of PhD output from 1940 to 1950. University research was increased by an even greater multiple, as the federal government's investment in war-time research became a permanent legacy. The character of that research nevertheless for long caused disquiet among the universities.

The critical technologies of World War II, particularly radar and atomic energy, were such that they could not be put aside with the cessation of hostilities, regardless of the state of international tension. Other lines of research were sustained through the promise of public usefulness. A wide spectrum of war-time research thus continued which resulted in five broad channels of federal support for the university research economy.[50] The first of these, agricultural research, was the only prewar legacy, and it remained comparatively unchanged. The second was research sponsored by the

[48] For example, A. B. Hollingshead, 'Ingroup Membership and Academic Selection', *American Sociological Review*, 3 (1938), 826–33.
[49] *A Century of Doctorates*, 7; Geiger, *To Advance Knowledge*, 276–7.
[50] Discussed in Roger Geiger, *Research and Relevant Knowledge: American Research Universities Since World War II* (New York, forthcoming, 1993).

military services that more or less fulfilled their immediate and particular needs. The responsibilities of the Atomic Energy Commission, which encompassed all radioactive materials, comprised a third and highly important channel. The continuation of war-time medical research by the Public Health Service (the National Institutes of Health) was a fourth channel, one that would in time allow university medical schools to join physics departments as the most research-intensive academic units. All this support, welcome as it was to its recipients, was focused upon specific, rather delimited areas of investigation. Whether this research was basic or applied in character, it chiefly reflected the programmatic needs of its sponsors. For a time after the war there seemed to be no federal recognition of responsibility for a fifth channel – support for the lifeblood of academic science, research intended primarily for the advancement of basic knowledge.

This last channel was to have been filled, according to Vannevar Bush's blueprint for post-war research, *Science – The Endless Frontier*, by a national research foundation.[51] Political wrangling, however, prevented the establishment of this institution during the critical post-war legislative session that produced seminal enactments covering the other emerging channels of federal support – the Atomic Energy Commission, the Office of Naval Research, and the organisation of research in the Public Health Service. The National Science Foundation did not come into being until 1950 and did not have significant funds to allocate until the latter years of that decade. In the interim, the Office of Naval Research became the generous and benign patron of basic academic research. This role, however, was anomalous and consequently temporary. For more than a decade after the war, basic academic research had no secure source of federal support.[52] As a result, complaints about the nature of the post-war research economy were widespread throughout the academic community in spite of the large federal investment in university research. Federal research funds were highly concentrated in a handful of universities, and they were narrowly targeted upon programmatic purposes. Funding was quite inadequate for both basic scientific research and support for sustaining the research capacity of universities.

In the decade of the 1950s, despite the gradual expansion of activities by the National Science Foundation and the large investments of the Ford

---

[51] Vannevar Bush, *Science – The Endless Frontier* (Washington, D.C.: National Science Foundation, 1960); see also Nathan Reingold, 'Vannevar Bush's New Deal for Research, or The Triumph of the Old Order', in *Science, American Style* (New Brunswick, N.J., 1991), 284–333.

[52] J. Merton England, *A Patron For Pure Science: The National Science Foundation's Formative Years, 1945–57* (Washington, D.C., 1982), 45–106; Harvey M. Sapolsky, *Science and the Navy: The History of the Office of Naval Research* (Princeton, 1990).

Foundation, the output of PhDs rose by just 50 per cent. The case was persistently argued for a greater national investment in basic academic research as the seedbed for technology, and in graduate education to augment the inadequate supply of scientists and university teachers.[53] In addition, after the Korean War, for the first time in almost a generation, a buoyant economy appeared to make such an investment feasible. Still, a catalyst seemed to be needed. It came in the form of a small sphere orbiting the earth emitting electronic 'beeps'.

The Soviet launch of Sputnik triggered a massive federal commitment to upgrade the nation's scientific capacity. In this process the federal government met and then exceeded the prescriptions of the post-war critics. In the decade after Sputnik (1958–68) federal support for *basic* research in universities increased by a factor of seven (from $178 to $1,251 million). In just eight years (1960–8) university research doubled in relationship to GNP. The Higher Education Facilities Act of 1963 assisted the construction of $9 billion worth of college and university buildings. And, buoyed by federal fellowships, the nation's output of PhDs tripled during the 1960s, just as it had in the 1920s.[54]

In fact, the developments of the 1960s bear an intriguing similarity to those of the 1920s. In both decades substantial new money became available from external sources for the support of basic academic research; in both cases one result was the enhancement of the value placed upon research within the university. Both decades also experienced substantial enrolment growth – expansive environments that were conducive to institutional advancement. In addition, the gains in both decades, although threatened by subsequent events, proved to be lasting. Given these similarities, the changes of the 1960s nevertheless had a more profound effect upon the ecology of the American university.

In those years for the first time the values and outlook of the graduate school gained ascendancy over those of the undergraduate college for a significant portion of American higher education. This change was apparent to contemporaries. For Talcott Parsons and Gerald Platt the prototypical American university had become dominated by 'cognitive rationality' expressed through 'research and graduate education by and of "specialists"'.[55] Christopher Jencks and David Riesman declared that an 'Academic Revolution' was underway. Instead of the investigative potential of universities being constrained by the nature and extent of the

[53] *Basic Research – A National Resource: A Report of the National Science Foundation* (Washington, DC, 1957); Bernard Berelson, *Graduate Education in the United States* (New York, 1960).
[54] *National Patterns of Science and Technology Resources: 1987* (Washington, DC, 1988).
[55] Talcott Parsons and Gerald Platt, *The American University* (Cambridge, MA, 1973), 106.

undergraduate college, they perceived the graduate schools to be 'by far the most important shapers of undergraduate education'.[56]

To some degree this shifting relationship can be borne out through quantitative changes. Graduate-level education became a much larger component of the activities of most of the major research universities. At private institutions the proportion of graduate students commonly approached 50 per cent; at the much larger state research universities that figure might surpass 30 per cent. If undergraduates were seldom an actual minority on these campuses, they often felt themselves to be a minority interest.

A second important trend was the broadening of the 'Academic Revolution'. Unlike the 1920s, when Wickliffe Rose set out to 'to make the peaks higher', at the beginning of the 1960s the President's Science Advisory Committee recommended that the country needed more peaks.[57] At different times special programmes to develop additional centres of university research were undertaken by the Ford Foundation and by the principal federal agencies that funded research.[58] More important than these explicit programmes was the fact that the conditions tending to restrict the number of research universities no longer obtained in the 1960s. Whereas before Sputnik programmatic federal research funds had been highly concentrated, the sudden abundance of research support and the growing incentives linked with research lured additional universities into meaningful participation in the research economy. Whereas earlier the post-war shortage of scientists had led to their concentration in comparatively few universities, now increasing numbers of research-minded PhDs became available to other would-be research universities. In addition, whereas the availability of research facilities had been a limiting condition favouring the wealthier institutions, now federal support and the general context of growth resulted in up-to-date facilities being built throughout the country. The peaks of the established research universities did not get any lower – in fact most of them continued to rise; but they were joined during the 1960s by other institutions increasingly committed to the advancement of knowledge.[59]

These achievements seemed to augur the fulfilment of the aspirations of America's original university builders: for the first time, American society

---

[56] Christopher Jencks and David Riesman, *The Academic Revolution* (Chicago, 1968), 247.

[57] President's Science Advisory Committee, *Scientific Progress, the Universities, and the Federal Government* (Washington, DC, 1960). This document, known as the Seaborg Report, advocated doubling the number of research universities from the current level of 15–20 to 30–40.

[58] National Science Foundation, *The NSF Science Development Programs* (Washington, DC, 1977); see also Geiger, *Research and Relevant Knowledge*, chapters 4 and 7.

[59] Geiger, *Research and Relevant Knowledge*, chapter 7.

made available ample resources chiefly for the advancement of knowledge. Universities responded with alacrity. Faculty threw themselves into the research puzzles of their disciplines as never before. They trained ever larger cohorts of graduate students to carry these investigations further. If ever German *Wissenschaft* found a home in America, it was during the 1960s. David Riesman and Christopher Jencks wrote at the time that the graduate academic department had become 'autotelic'; and furthermore that 'to suggest that the advancement of a particular academic discipline [was] not synonymous with the advancement of the human condition [was] to be regarded as myopic'.[60] One can readily detect a note of incredulity in their language – a scepticism that this hypertrophy of pure research could prosper, let alone endure, in American universities. Their doubts in this case were not unfounded.

In a quantitative sense the gains of the 1960s were permanent: overall federal support for university research, in real terms, eroded only slightly and temporarily; graduate education continued to expand into the early 1970s; and the number of universities significantly involved with research continued to increase. But the climate of expectations of that era somehow evaporated.

Undergraduates were the first to resist the hegemony of the autotelic graduate department. The student rebellion of the late 1960s was a complex phenomenon, but one of its central themes was the accusation of irrelevance leveled at disciplinary scholarship as reflected in the university curriculum. This was followed in the 1970s by a mass exodus from those disciplines. Students voted with their computer registration cards for vocational subjects of concentration, particularly majors related to business.[61] The reverberations from these developments are still being felt. Universities have had to wrestle with the dilemma of refashioning a curriculum for freshmen and sophomores that would instil more general kinds of skills and knowledge without actually abjuring the edifice that disciplinary scholarship has built.

A second significant change occurred in graduate schools themselves. For the first time in their history they actually ceased to grow. In 1973 almost 34,000 doctorates were awarded; that figure was not surpassed until the end of the 1980s. Even this level of output has only been possible due to a rising proportion of foreign students receiving degrees (from 15 to 26 per cent with much higher proportions in fields like engineering). The principal cause for this stagnation can be readily identified – the weakness in the demand for college and university teachers. Dismal career prospects

[60] Jencks and Riesman, *Academic Revolution*, 250.
[61] Roger Geiger, 'The College Curriculum and the Marketplace: What Place For Disciplines in the Trend for Vocationalism?,' *Change* (Nov/Dec. 1980), 17–23ff.

Table 6.1. *Per cent of total academic R&D by source, 1960–89*

	Federal government	State/local governments	Industry	Institution funds	Other sources
1960	62.7	13.2	6.2	9.9	8.0
1970	70.5	9.4	2.6	10.4	7.1
1980	67.5	8.2	3.9	13.8	6.6
1989	59.9	8.3	6.6	18.1	7.2

also had a disheartening effect upon graduate study itself – thinning the ranks of students and causing self-doubt and anxiety to replace the exuberance that reigned during the 1960s. Even though the market for new faculty has improved of late, and shortages have even emerged in some fields, 4,000 fewer doctorates were awarded to US citizens in 1990 than in 1973.[62] Historically, the two decades of no-growth in doctorates is an unprecedented and somewhat ominous development.

A third significant change since the 1960s also becomes evident in historical perspective. Roughly speaking, throughout much of this century, decades of vigorous expansion of the university research enterprise have alternated with decades of relative consolidation. Thus, the relationship of the 1960s to the 1970s repeated the basic pattern of the 1920s and 1930s, or the 1940s and 1950s. According to this timetable, the 1980s were scheduled to be a decade of renewed growth. After a rather belated start, they fulfilled this destiny. Real expenditures of university research turned up sharply since about 1983. When measured against GNP, university research has attained the levels reached during the halcyon days of the late 1960s.[63] It is noteworthy, however, that the impetus for this upswing has not come from the federal government. The federal portion of total university research funding rose from 63 per cent in 1960 to 73 per cent in 1967. Through the 1970s the federal contribution remained above two-thirds of the total, but by 1989 it had shrunk to just 60 per cent. Industrial funding of university research, which was only 2.5 per cent in 1967, has risen to 6.6 per cent (1989); and the category 'institutional funds' has advanced from 10 to 18 per cent. Moreover, the expectations associated with the expansion of the 1980s nevertheless resemble the 1940s rather than the 1960s.

[62] *Council of Graduate Schools Communicator*, 24 (May–June, 1991), 4–6; Bruce L. R. Smith, *The State of Graduate Education* (Washington, D.C., 1985), esp. 1–83; John Brademas, *Signs of Trouble and Erosion: A Report on Graduate Education in America* (New York, 1984).

[63] National Science Foundation, 'Selected Data on Academic Science/Engineering R&D Expenditures, Fiscal Year 1989' (October 1990), 90–321.

Table 6.2. *Per cent changes in real university R&D expenditures and federal obligations for university research, 1976–86*

	Total	Life sciences	Engineering math/comp. sciences	Other sciences
R&D	59	51	121	45
Federal Obligations	49	42	78	45

Instead of faith in the worth of basic research, the current expansion has been fueled by programmatic goals – by the expansion of military research and development during the first part of the 1980s and generally by hopes for pay-offs in technology transfer to industry that might augment international competitiveness in the relatively near term. Research sponsored by industry has been the fastest growing single component, although still a small portion of the total. The influence of private industry on the research universities is nevertheless larger than its 6+ per cent share of R&D would indicate. Gifts to higher education from private corporations have also been the fastest growing component of voluntary support to higher education, having grown to 20 per cent of the total.[64] When federal sources are considered, the Department of Defense has supplied the principal growth component, having tripled in constant dollars from the mid-1970s to the mid-1980s – a time when total federal obligations for academic research have risen by just 20 per cent.[65] Viewed from the angle of the kinds of research that universities actually perform, the drift toward programmatic research and the relatively restrained growth of research in the basic sciences becomes evident. The interesting disclosure from table 6.2 is that the programmatic shift in research funding is not just a federal policy: non-federal funds have been favouring engineering and computer sciences to an even greater extent than has the government. Philip Abelson, from his unexcelled viewpoint as long-time editor of *Science*, has aptly summarised this change: 'the strong campus bias of the 1960s and 1970s against applications and industry has diminished and will not be reestablished soon'.[66]

---

[64] Council on Financial Aid to Education, *Voluntary Support for Education* (New York, 1989).

[65] *Science and Engineering Indicators, 1987*, 253; National Science Foundation, *Federal Support to Universities, Colleges, and Selected Nonprofit Institutions*, Fiscal Year 1986, 24; Fiscal Year 1983, 44.

[66] Philip H. Abelson, 'Evolving State-University-Industry Relations', *Science*, 231 (1986), 317.

Concluding observations

In the current era, research and graduate education within American universities seems to be influenced by three pervasive trends – the revolt of undergraduates against the autotelic department, the stagnation in graduate studies, and the increasingly utilitarian rationale for university research. Taken together they represent not just a movement away from the ascendancy of graduate-school values that occurred during the 1960s, but also a movement toward an amalgamation of forces and interests that is more typical historically of the American university. The recent spate of public interest in the matters affecting the college and its curriculum is testimony of sorts that the undergraduate college remains the true centre of gravity in American higher education. Since about 1980, campus attitudes about relations with private industry have undergone a transformation, as indicated by Philip Abelson's comment. The protracted anemia of graduate schools of arts and sciences has been compensated in part by the robust health of the graduate-professional schools. These forces, however, are refracted through the American university in different ways.

Martin Trow captured one major facet of this when he wrote of the long-standing unwritten treaty between the State of California and its university: 'we will support your ambitions to be a world-class research university if you will look after our bright children'.[67] In many of our wealthiest private universities there exists a similar unwritten under-standing with alumni that they will support the university's research ambitions if it will also cultivate the highest quality undergraduate college. In both these patterns, then, the research role of the university, particularly a specialised faculty of arts and sciences, has been maintained despite weaknesses in the graduate school by its symbiotic relationship with undergraduate education.

These two patterns, however, do not exhaust the possibilities. In most of the country's metropolitan areas can be found universities that have specialised increasingly in the offering of graduate-professional education. Their mission has been to provide programmes offering a variable combination of intellectual elevation and professional advancement to a clientele that is or recently has been employed in middle-level positions in government, industry, and the non-profit sector. These students frequently comprise the majority of an urban university's enrolments and commonly take some or all of their degree programmes as part-time students. Most significant for this context, these students typically do not aim to devote themselves to *Wissenschaft*. Rather, they seek advanced education in order

[67] Martin A. Trow, 'Reorganizing the Biological Sciences at Berkeley', *Change* (Nov/Dec. 1983), 52, 44–53.

to be more effective leaders and practitioners in an increasingly knowledge-intensive world of affairs. In this type of research university, a somewhat different symbiosis occurs – in this case between graduate-level professional education and faculty involvement with research and scholarship.

Graduate education remains closely linked with research, at least in the PhD programmes of the arts and sciences. But the example of the graduate-service universities underlines the fact that graduate study has also assumed a larger role. It now routinely assists individuals to catch up with the rapid proliferation of specialised knowledge in a variety of fields; and it is frequently utilised by persons seeking professional advancement and/or occupational mobility. These purposes are fully in keeping with the traditions of American higher education. The great success of graduate education and research in the American university over the past 100 years has not occurred because American society accepted very much or for very long the value of learning for its own sake. But rather, universities have of necessity found ways to make themselves both useful and learned at the same time. Entering its second century, this feature of the American university does not appear about to change.

Part 4

Complexity

7   The problem of complexity in modern higher education

Burton R. Clark

The base similarity of modern systems of higher education is that they become more complex. To cope with the unrelenting pressures of complexity, national systems adjust their historic configurations of beliefs, interests, and structures. Hence, to pursue the very nature of this fundamental academic trend, to suggest its more important causes, and especially to seek its compelling effects, is to explore basic modes of evolution. Among the modes of adaptation, we undoubtedly will find some impressive cross-national similarities. But close analysis will surely also reveal large differences that follow from unique national traditions. Guided by the response sets of established orders, nations must necessarily cope with complexity in somewhat different ways. Any theory of convergence that highlights a common drift into complexity, and similar forms of accommodation, will need in time to shade into a theory of divergence that observes individualised national evolutions. In this early analysis, particularly to establish some opening categories, I will concentrate on what seems everywhere operative.

The forces of complexity

With each passing decade a modern or modernising system of higher education is expected and inspired to do more for other portions of society, organised and unorganised, from strengthening the economy and invigorating government to developing individual talents and personalities and aiding the pursuit of happiness. We also ask that this sector of society do more in its own behalf in fulfilling such grand and expanding missions as conserving the cultural heritage and producing knowledge. This steady accretion of realistic expectations cannot be stopped, let alone reversed.

Where among modern nations can we expect a return to the education of a relatively homogeneous 3 to 5 per cent of the age group? Instead,

This chapter is the revised version of a paper presented at the International Conference of the Swedish National Board of Universities and Colleges on 'Higher Education: Creativity, Legitimation, and Systems Transformation', held at Dalarö, Sweden, 1–5 June 1987.

systems slide over the long-run along the track of elite to mass participation (even if some do not slide very well and stall at minor inclines), relating to more heterogeneous clienteles as they include more students drawn from more segments of the populations. Input demands multiply, extending the tasks of teaching and increasing the congruences that must be fashioned if individual desires and institutional capabilities are to mesh.

Secondly, where among modern systems can we expect a return to educating for only governmental elites and several leading professions, the dominant pattern historically in Europe? Instead, as graduates move on to both private and public employment and to a widening range of occupations generally, systems steadily extend their connections to occupational life. On its output side, higher education without doubt is tied to an expanding societal division of labour. Again, the pressure to enlarge the system's bundle of tasks is great, even irresistible.

Thirdly, where among modern systems of higher education can we expect the resident profession to turn away from a widening involvement in the production of knowledge as well as in its refinement and distribution? As a force for enlarging the complexity of higher education, this substantive impulse, embedded in modernity, becomes the steadiest pressure of all. It is driven by the pace set in the international communities of many disciplines, with the biological sciences now the most vivid instance. It is propelled by the disciplinary rewards of specialisation that lead to a Virginia Woolf Society and a Conference Group on Italian Politics. It is promoted by the interests of national governments in the fruits of basic science, and by regional and local economic interests in such useful R & D as the improvement of fisheries in Alaska, oil plant management in southern Norway, and computer services in the cities of northern Italy. The fascinations of specialised research, pure and applied, steadily deepen. Even where a major research sector has evolved separate from universities, as in France and in the Soviet model, university professors seize opportunities to engage in knowledge production and revision within their own shops as well as across the street in the laboratories and offices of the academy. There is no way to keep them away: indeed they are generally the ruling research oligarchs.

With disciplinary linkages operating across institutional and national boundaries, subjects are in the driver's seat. There is quite literally no way to stop the field of history from expanding its boundaries of coverage in time and space and from proliferating its arcane specialties – nor political science nor economics nor sociology nor anthropology. The basic disciplines are inherently imperialistic.[1] Then, too, new specialties, inter-

---

[1] On the basic processes of substantive growth in the academic profession and academia at large, see Walter Metzger, 'The Academic Profession in the United States', in *The*

disciplinary as well as disciplinary, are steadily added. By a process of parturition, they have been and are born out of mother fields: broad approaches to science gave way to such specific scientific disciplines as chemistry, geology, biology, and physics in the early and mid nineteenth century; all-encompassing social subjects gave rise to economics, political science, sociology, and anthropology in the latter part of the century. By processes of importation and dignification, outside endeavours are brought in and lowly fields, new and old, are raised to respectability: modern languages and technology in the past; management and computer science during the recent decades. Such interdisciplinary fields as environmental studies, peace studies, women's studies, and ethnic studies now struggle with varying success to plant a foot squarely in the door of legitimation.

As research both intensifies and diversifies, the academic division of labour accelerates even faster than the rapidly shifting societal division of labour.

Thus, in whatever direction we turn, we confront complexity. If we take research, teaching, and public service as broadly-stated missions of higher education, each becomes over time an elaborate, steadily differentiating set of expectations and tasks. If we pick up on the three categories of general higher education, advanced professional education, and research and training for research that were creatively established in a cross-national perspective by Joseph Ben-David, the outcome is the same.[2] Each is a confused maze. General education can never be whole again, despite periodic efforts to declare its rebirth around this or that person's list of core values and essential subjects.[3] Professional education shades off in endless permutations: from early-childhood learning specialists to international economic planners just within the single field of education; from airport mechanics to secretaries to cosmetologists in short-cycle vocational higher education. As academia trains for both high and low vocationalism, the culture of one outside occupation after another, in an endless stream, intrudes into the higher education system itself. A relevant staff takes up residence within it, directly representing yet another part of the occupational world. Finally, research and training for research, as already emphasised, is the wildest card of all. Virtually without limit, it is a cultivation of the new.

Then, too, when developing societies seek to modernise their systems of

---

Academic Profession: National, Disciplinary, and Institutional Settings, ed. Burton R. Clark (Berkeley and Los Angeles, 1987), 126–47.

[2] Joseph Ben-David, *Centers of Learning: Britain, France, Germany, the United States* (New York, 1977).

[3] See the illuminating assessment of the state of general or liberal education, past and present, by Sheldon Rothblatt in this volume.

higher education, those systems evolve toward an open-ended, ambiguous complexity. Further, when systems in the modern period work out new relations with industry, their tasks multiply. When they seek to accommodate a wide range of local interests by means of regionalisation, utilising different local adaptations, they move further down the road of task diversity.

Therefore, how to handle the complexity of tasks and responsibilities necessarily becomes the root problem of system adaptation. Modern systems must do more and more, invest in the new on top of the new, go from uncertainties to still more uncertainties. How, then, do they face up to the multiplication of tasks? What accommodations produce an organized social complexity that works?[4]

Coping with complexity

The growing diversity of tasks pushes modern systems of higher education towards a number of systemic accommodations. Most important is structural differentiation, an adaptive trend that in its various forms deconcentrates the over-all system. Closely related is the elaboration of academic professionalism, within which academics specialise their interests and commitments in a widening array of subjects and institutions.

Self-amplifying structural differentiation

National systems of higher education have operated in the twentieth century with one type of institution, two or three types, or ten, twenty, or more types.[5] It is now no secret that the more simply structured systems (e.g., Italian higher education today, the Swedish system up to the expansion of the last two decades) have had the greater difficulty in coping with the growing complexity of tasks. Without an arsenal of organisations that are differently competent, they simply expand their one or two main forms – in particular, the national public university – and turn them into conglomerates within which an expanding welter of interest groups fight out all the battles that are involved in doing everything for everyone. Compromises among such competing competencies as undergraduate and graduate studies, practical training and pure scholarship, the humanities

---

[4] For a much-overlooked intensive and extensive modern exploration of the problem of societal complexity, see *Organized Social Complexity: Challenge to Politics and Policy,* ed. Todd R. LaPorte (Princeton, 1975).

[5] See Burton R. Clark, *The Higher Education System: Academic Organization in Cross-National Perspective* (Berkeley and Los Angeles, 1983), 53–62.

and the sciences, are made all the more difficult as the 'have-nots' seek equality with the 'haves'. Vicious circles of interaction are readily generated in which various major and minor interests block one another's development. The need grows for a separation of tasks whereby groups can get out of each other's way and find organised supportive niches. Sooner or later a working agreement emerges, at least tacitly, that the old-line university really cannot do – does not want to do – short-cycle higher education, and hence there is created or allowed to evolve institutes of technology and two-year colleges and other units that pass out first degrees of their own. Sooner or later it becomes reasonably clear that in trying to do well the expanding bundle of tasks involved in the traditional lines of university performance and status, the dominant sector really cannot do – does not want to do – extensive adult or continuing education, especially at less than the most advanced levels, and then we see the creation of an open university or a set of user-friendly regional colleges. Hence, sectorisation, in many country-specific forms, can be seen as a general answer to the overloading of simple structures. If additional types of institutions are not created or permitted to emerge, the all-in-one conglomerates increasingly become nominal forms, political pretences to academic unity, while cramping the organised space within which new units undertaking new tasks must find their way. Bypasses and add-ons are then hard to come by.

Notably, despite the convergencies induced by emulative academic drift, the main university sector itself begins to break up into different types of universities. The rising costs of big social science, big humanities, and big arts, as well as big science, increasingly ensure that money will not be passed around equally. Within the different major subject clusters, and often discipline by discipline, there will be centres of excellence and centres of non-excellence. If not, high costs spread across the system will drive down access to the system at large; *and,* highly talented people who want to sit with other highly talented scholars and scientists, but are not allowed to so concentrate, will flow into the emerging pipelines of brain-drain. As different university combinations develop, statesmanship then includes the elaboration of sub-sector ideologies that blunt invidious comparisons and justify second-best and third-best statuses. Have-not institutions may desire and actively seek a single non-invidious central niche; but complexity reverses the tide and moves them in the other direction. In an evolution that is natural for adaptive species, systems move toward more niches rather than fewer.[6]

[6] On the application of a biological evolutionary perspective to system diversity, see Robert Birnbaum, 'System Arguments for Diversity', in *Association for the Study of Higher Education Reader in Organization and Governance in Higher Education*, ed. Robert

268   *Burton R. Clark*

National systems of higher education have also operated in the twentieth century with control systems that vary from heavily centralised to radically decentralised. It is now no secret among the more centralised cases that the centre cannot hold, that one or more national offices, or academic oligarchies, cannot manage in a top-down fashion the sector of society that is most naturally bottom-heavy in its location of disparate expert judgement and that is most naturally resistant to all-system command. We find curious cross-mixtures of centralising and decentralising imperatives. Centralisation readily captures our attention. After all, the evolution of the British system 1965–1985 is already a classic example ready for the textbooks. Central ministerial control in France, when loosened for a few years by crisis-level resistance of faculty and students, seems to snap back into place like a rubber band that has been stretched too far. Then, too, after the events of the last two decades, Swedish academics are no strangers to *dirigisme*.

But the flow of control is not all one way, and systems strain to accommodate the conflicting imperatives of centralisation and decentralisation. Behind the impulse to decentralise lies the simple fact that the evermore swollen professional underbelly of higher education gives the central cadres a 'knowledge problem' they cannot handle.[7] It is well-known that scientists and scholars grope toward truth by an unending, elaborate process of mutual criticism and discovery. Even with the best academics on top, secure in central offices, they cannot effectively substitute their judgement to short-circuit that process. They will not know what is going on at the bottom, in the many departments, laboratories, and programmes, in sufficient detail to be able to plan science and scholarship effectively. They are not able to miniaturise the social structure of scholarly interaction and change. Since they are unable to recapitulate the understandings of thousands of professional operatives, many thousands of bits of tacit knowledge will escape them, no matter how much they amass information. Then, the adaptive structural response is to engage in a layering of authority. In the nationalised systems, decentralisation introduces a regional or provincial level of institutional grouping and public accountability.[8] The centre is encouraged to devote itself to the

Birnbaum (Lexington, MA, rev. ed. 1984), 411–23. This article is taken from his larger study, *Maintaining Diversity in Higher Education* (San Francisco, 1983).

[7] For a modern treatment of 'the knowledge problem' as viewed by an economist advocating a radical agenda for turning away from planning, see Don Lavoie, *National Economic Planning: What is Left?* (Cambridge, MA, 1985), chapter 3.

[8] Symptomatic is the reaction now (1987) developing in Britain to the centralised powers of the University Grants Committee and the Department of Education and Science: for example,

Eleven northern universities are contemplating a go-it-alone plan that would loosen the

setting of 'a broad outline of policy' or a broad 'framework'. In the federal systems, two levels of government continue to vie for influence; with, for example, Australia now relatively top-heavy, the Federal Republic of Germany a case of balanced federalism, and Canada and the United States still radically decentralised.

Particularly in the large nations, growing complexity tends to call out and/or strengthen regional structures. But even these structures find supervision of other than a most general kind extremely difficult to effect in the face of the individualised professionalism that increasingly characterises the specialties tucked away in hundreds of corners inside the institutions. The institutional levels then become the best hope of the formal integrators: that at the all-campus level, and at a divisional level within the institution, supra-disciplinary gatherings of faculty and administrators can establish boundaries, allocate budgets, maintain some common internal rewards and sanctions, conduct foreign affairs, and otherwise offer some semblance of a civic order – all within the bounds of the broad frameworks established by those higher up the national ranks whose job descriptions call for the construction of guidelines.

Now looming large internationally in the differentiation of structures of control is the havoc wreaked upon unitary ideals and approaches by privatisation. The two largest systems of higher education in the western world, the American and the Japanese, have been heavily shaped by their critically-important private sectors. In the American case, the private institutions have been historically dominant; they presently number 1,500 or about one-half of all institutions, they contain 20–25 per cent of the enrolment, and, in both the four-year sector and the university sector, the leading private institutions set the pace for the public brethren. The top fifty four-year colleges are all private; among the top ten universities, six or seven are private. In the Japanese case, the private sector became *the* vehicle for mass entry, handling 75 to 80 per cent of students. It has a variety that stretches from degree mills to institutions now positioning themselves quite high in the institutional hierarchy. In these two leading cases, in particular the American one, the construction of individual institutional niches is a high art.

Especially outside Europe, the encouragement of private higher education is very much on national agendas. Even in Europe, the matter is more than a passing rumour. The recent major studies by Roger Geiger and

planning controls from London. They are discussing whether to agitate for the creation of a northern regional university council, which would take over the job of detailed nationalization from the University Grants Committee and foster cooperation among the 11.

See 'Northerners Bid to Plan Their Own Universities', *The Times Higher Education Supplement*, no. 753 (April 10, 1987), 1.

Daniel Levy have shown that as analysts bring into view the Philippines as well as France, Brazil as well as Sweden, we find that the pros and cons of privatisation are situationally rooted.[9] There are many forms of privateness – mass and elite, secular and religious, central and peripheral, parallel and divergent in relation to State-supported institutions. In such large cases as the United States, the private sectors may exhibit three or four major types of privateness. Private development has many modern appeals. It can reduce State costs. It often absorbs discontents that otherwise continue to agitate government. It offers alternatives to perceived failures of the State sectors. As part of a broad zig-and-zag adaptation to complexity, private types of universities and colleges may emerge not only in a largely unplanned fashion but also receive support from central officials seeking new paths of development or simply ways to make their own jobs easier.

The tendency to have both public and private sectors in the over-all system can have extremely powerful effects at the institutional level. Competition is likely to be enhanced. *And* individual institutions enhance their viability by diversifying their financial base. Private institutions find their way to public treasuries; public institutions learn that money exacted from private sources is as spendable as funds allocated by governments. As institutions mix multiple public sources with numerous private ones, they create individualised institutional packages. They also strengthen their defences against sources that turn ugly. For institutional autonomy in the late twentieth century there is no more urgent dictum than that of avoiding the situation of all financial eggs in one basket. Multiplying the channels of resource allocation becomes a key form of adaptation.

At the level of institutional structure, one hardly needs to argue the case that institutions, whether nominally specialised or comprehensive, elaborate themselves year-by-year horizontally and vertically: horizontally in more departments, more organised research units (ORUs), and more interdisciplinary programmes (IDPs); and vertically in degree levels and levels of oversight. As example: a strategic planning committee at my own institution is examining its entire academic and business organisation with an eye toward reorganisation that can better position the campus for competitively enhanced strength by the year 2,000. There is much agreement that central bodies operated by the faculty as well as the administration are overloaded, yet at the same time many units on campus are relatively unsupervised. ORUs and IDPs are scattered all over the place, greatly extending the network of basic units that traditionally

[9] Roger L. Geiger, *Private Sectors in Higher Education: Structure, Function, and Change in Eight Countries* (Ann Arbor, MI, 1986), and Daniel C. Levy, *Higher Education and the State in Latin America: Private Challenges to Public Dominance* (Chicago, 1986).

consisted mainly of departments. The ORUs and IDPs are clearly adaptive units, set up to accommodate research interests, and, separately, teaching interests, that are not well supported by the departments. They may report hardly to anyone; or if they have a reporting line, a central official may find that the number of significant units for which he or she is responsible is twenty not ten, thirty-five not fifteen. Then, too, Berkeley and UCLA have had much experience with centralised faculty personnel structures that increasingly become *the* achilles heels of faculty retention, promotion, and long-range development. Central bodies become bottlenecks that turn three-month actions into ones that stretch over nine, twelve, and fifteen months. Institutions that are awake take these phenomena seriously and try to do something about them: notably, by enlarging the central apparatus so that it can subdivide itself; by more clearly separating critical decisions from routine ones; and, most important, by deconcentrating operational responsibility to the divisional level. Who among us cannot report similar problems of coping with complexity inside the university?

At the disciplinary level, it is clear enough that we all confront an irresistible emergence of new subjects that we ignore at our peril and to which we respond by underpinning them with new and varied organisational units. The disciplinary dimension of the system-wide matrix of disciplines and institutions is restless and self-generating, with an expansionist dynamic, as suggested previously, that has cross-national affiliations behind it. International conferences illustrate this dynamic. They encourage the professionalisation within many countries of emergent, multi-disciplinary fields such as 'comparative higher education'. The fields are structurally propped up by a centre here and a centre there, a cluster of semi-organised interested scholars within a university in one country, and a cluster scattered across a half-dozen universities in another. The true believers among us ache for more solid foundations in and among the basic disciplines and the professional schools. In comparative higher education, we measure progress by the firming of small bases in an Hiroshima ORU, an Amsterdam centre, a coupling of a half-dozen researchers in a study of the Italian professoriate that seeks to utilise a comparative perspective. We note the intellectual progress, or lack of it, over the years in successive conferences in Lancaster and Stockholm and in the books and articles produced by second- and third-generation scholars. Who radically differentiates the academic world? We do. As we pursue scholarship, we differentiate structures as well as ideas and literatures.

Self-elaborating academic professionalism

In a current book on the American professoriate, I portray American academics as having evolved from a first to a second and then to a third 'intellectual moment'.[10] In a first stage that spanned the colonial period and even stretched into the nineteenth century, academics in my country were temporary hired hands, tutors taken on for a few years before they went off to other work. Academic positions then gradually solidified into a lifelong occupation, one that developed into a fullblown profession (in the modern sense of the word) on the back of specialisation. The age of the university that supplanted the age of the college, starting roughly in the 1870s, gave the occupation a second intellectual moment in which a semi-integrated professionalism obtained. At its initiation (1915) and during the quarter of a century leading up to World War II, the American Association of University Professors was able to draw upon the leadership of such distinguished scholars at leading research universities as John Dewey, E. R. A. Seligman, and Franklin Giddings at Columbia, Roscoe Pound at Harvard, Richard T. Ely at Wisconsin, and Arthur O. Lovejoy at Johns Hopkins. It could reasonably pretend that it represented the interests of *the* professoriate, even if more academics stayed out than enlisted in its cause.[11]

The third intellectual moment that has developed during the four decades since 1945 is of an increasingly different character. Academic work is not only set apart in the hands of numerous clusters of trained experts who can claim special knowledge, but it is also greatly differentiated by institutional type. This fragmented professionalism puts involvement and commitment at a different level, that of the disciplines and the institutional types, and turns the American Association of University Professors and its several major rival union organisations increasingly into units of secondary and often non-academic affiliation.

Particularly instructive is the night-and-day contrast between the extremes of life in the leading research universities and the community colleges. The two-year units have grown so much that they now embrace one-third of all students (four million by head-count!), and one-fourth to one-third of faculty. Their faculties teach fifteen hours a week, almost entirely in introductory courses, to students many of whom are still performing at the secondary level and who need remedial attention. More students are 'terminal vocational' than 'academic transfer', and even more are non-matriculated adults. Facing a student body that comes and

---

[10] Burton R. Clark, *The Academic Life: Small Worlds, Different Worlds* (Princeton, 1987).
[11] Metzger, 'The Academic Profession', 167–8.

goes on a short time schedule, the institution needs a disposable faculty. As a result, they have turned to part-timers, enlarging their ranks to the point where they outnumber full-time staff. (One-third of the American professoriate is now part-time).

Hence we can observe two broad avenues of deprofessionalisation, or at least a casting of academic work in forms far removed from those of the leading universities: work moves from full-time to part-time, with the part-timers ('gypsy scholars', 'academic nomads', 'freeway scholars') piecing together a livelihood as best they can; and work loses its advanced intellectual content, with 'scholars' becoming 'teachers' who have positions markedly similar to those of American secondary schoolteachers. Discipline matters much less, since few are doing the advanced things in their fields that differentiate the disciplines.

Across the many fields located in the large universities, we find significant differences in workloads and orientations of faculty in the sciences as contrasted to the humanities; and, more broadly, between life in the professional schools and in the letters and science departments. The latter divide is an important schism. One-half of the faculty in the universities is in the professional schools, where work is clinical as well as scholarly, and where it is increasingly set off in the graduate tier, away from the problems of undergraduate teaching. The demands of the professional-practice dimension, and the tension between it and the academic side, have already produced a plethora of additional faculty roles – clinical, part-time, non-tenured, tenured without a salary guarantee – as an internal differentiation that makes the professional schools decidedly differ from the letters and science departments, even as it helps those schools to cope.

In such professional features, as well as in system characteristics, the American case is an extreme one. But in its extremity it is revealing, often exhibiting in relatively stark form what is more muted in other systems. What it helps to reveal in this case is that the academic profession steadily decomposes itself as it responds to the complexities of input and output demands and especially to the substantive imperative of research and scholarship. The profession separates into constituent parts that multiply within its ranks. As it does so, we may intuit, existing controls – professional and bureaucratic – are thrown out of whack. If knowledge is power, then new knowledge is new power, expanded knowledge is expanded power, and fragmented knowledge is fragmented power. Then not only do central administrative cadres have a knowledge problem they cannot handle, they have a control problem that grows steadily larger before their eyes. Power steadily accumulates at the operating levels of the system, shielded from easy penetration by arcaneness and ambiguity in its knowledge foundations. Those who would gather all academics in a unified profession also find that the ground slips from under them. Academic professionalism produces power, but it produces it in a highly fragmented form. The natural self-elaboration of our profession turns it into a mosaic of small worlds, different worlds.

Coping with structural differentiation and fragmented professionalism: what integrates?

So much has been made of the defects of academic professionalism that we overlook its compelling contributions. Academic reform in the United States, centred on a strengthening of undergraduate general education that is purportedly necessary to save the nation, castigates the disciplines for their narrowness. Reform in Sweden has attempted to realign undergraduate education around interdisciplinary clusters that are labour-market defined. In both cases, the drift of recent reform underestimates what focused professionalism accomplishes for faculty, students, and the system at large.

Academic specialisation is one response to the inherent limitations of the human mind. Individuals increasingly cannot expect to cover such major areas as 'the social sciences' or 'the humanities'. It is increasingly odd that we think undergraduate students can and should master such broad domains. As it delineates restricted areas of inquiry and of facts, specialisation – compared to non-specialisation – leads towards mastery and a sense of competence. Most important, specialisation develops a particular kind of structured thinking that we call a discipline.[12] In contrast, theme courses and purportedly interdisciplinary studies typically focus on topics, not intellectual structure. The discipline is treated as a subject matter rather than as a structured method of analysis. Overlooked then is the reality that particular kinds of questions have their own specific systems of analysis. When a question pertains to gross national product, the ways of thinking of physicists and classicists cannot help very much: those of economists can. When a question pertains to Dante's fourth level of Hell, the perspectives of economists become totally irrelevant while the accumulated insights of classicists become relevant. Specialisation has rational bases that are the foundation of the modern academic enterprise.

It is around the modern structures of reasoning that we call disciplines that academics develop their professionalism. Since that professionalism is closely tied to disparate fields, each a self-aggrandising concern, we appropriately portray it as enormously fragmented. But we can also see

---

[12] My formulations in this paragraph have drawn upon Thomas Sowell, 'Recipe for Change on Campus', a review of Ernest L. Boyer, *College: The Undergraduate Experience*, in *The Wall Street Journal* (9 April 1987).

that professionalism is a crucial way in the modern occupational world by which self-interests are hooked to larger institutional chariots. In the normal course of his or her work, a biologist or a political scientist or a professor of literature can simultaneously serve and blend self-, other-, and ideal-regarding interests:[13] one's own achievement; the progress of one's department and one's disciplinary group; and the furtherance of scholarship, the education of the young, and a host of other ideals that give meaning to the academic life. Who in our own invisible college is serving only narrow self-interest? Our colleagues in other specialties are surely doing no less to serve others and to serve ideals, even when they 'selfishly' seek greater monetary rewards, higher status, greater individual and group autonomy, and more power. In an age of specialisation, academic callings will reside basically not in broad theme courses or in labour-market-defined subjects but in the cultural homes that disciplines construct around their individual structures of knowledge and reasoning. Tunnel by tunnel, the disciplines are simultaneously *the* centres of meaning and *the* devices for cosmopolitan linkage.[14]

Further, the disciplines do not simply exist as isolated tunnels, linking individuals in parallel chains that never meet. In coverage of empirical domains, and as modes of reasoning, they overlap. Harold Perkin has described the historian as 'a kind of licensed rustler who wanders at will across his scholarly neighbors' fields, poaching their stock and purloining their crops and breaking down their hedges'.[15] As poachers, the historians have good company: modern disciplines are inherently imperialistic. Anthropologists who use to hanker after lost tribes now turn back on their own advanced societies to pursue domains as they please – the ethnography of the classroom, or the hospital, or the business firm. Sociologists are prepared to offer a sociology of whatever human activity you can think of. You cannot keep economists out of anything, since they are sure they have the keys to the analytical heavens of the social sciences. The boundaries between political science and sociology are so blurred that top scholars in the one can actually be elected to high office in the mainline associations of the other.

We now have at hand a useful vocabulary for conceptualising and elaborating on this phenomenon. Michael Polanyi has spoken of modern

---

[13] The concepts of self-regarding, other-regarding, and ideal-regarding interests are drawn from Jane J. Mansbridge, *Beyond Adversary Democracy* (Chicago, 1983), 24–6.

[14] On the basic role of the disciplines as separate cultures and as communities of knowledge, see the work of Tony Becher as represented by his book, *Academic Tribes and Territories: Intellectual Enquiry and the Culture of Disciplines* (Milton Keynes, 1989).

[15] Harold Perkin, 'The Historical Perspective', in *Perspectives on Higher Education, Eight Disciplinary and Comparative Views*, ed. Burton R. Clark (Berkeley and Los Angeles, 1984), 17.

science as consisting of 'chains of overlapping neighborhoods'.[16] Donald
T. Campbell has stressed that a comprehensive social science, or any other
large domain of knowledge, is 'a continuous texture of narrow specialties'.
Multiple narrow specialties overlap much like the overlap of scales on the
back of a fish. That overlap produces 'a collective communication, a
collective competence and breadth'.[17] When we take this perspective
seriously, the implications for reform are breathtaking. Efforts to fill gaps
between fields, and to bridge fields, by training scholars who have mastered
two or more disciplines are doomed to fail. Such efforts are like trying to
make the Mississippi River run north instead of south: better to go with
the natural flow, and use it. The way to proceed is to make those
organisational inventions that will encourage narrow specialisation in
interdisciplinary areas. The interdisciplinarian must 'remain as narrow as
any other scholar'. The slogan for reform (overdressed in academic
rhetoric) becomes: 'collective comprehensiveness through overlapping
patterns of unique narrowness'.[18]

In a creative essay on how cultural integration may coexist with cultural
diversity in a highly differentiated society, Diana Crane has acutely
observed that the social system of science is an appropriate model:

Contemporary science comprises hundreds of distinct specialties, but each specialty
has connections, both intellectual and social, with other specialties...[C]ultural
integration occurs because of overlapping memberships among cultural communities that lead to the dissemination of ideas and values.

What we find are 'interlocking cultural communities'.[19] As we extend this
formulation to academic fields more generally, we can say that while
modern academia is a system powered by specialisation and hence by
diverging interests, it may also be a system that allows for a collective
comprehensiveness that is integrative.[20] The analytical handle is the idea of
integration through overlap. We no longer need to think that integration
can come only from similarity of function, or common values, or united
membership in a grand corps. We do not need to ask that we all become Mr
Chips, nor that we pull ourselves together around four values and a core
curriculum, nor that we enter a national civil service and join one union.
We can understand that integration can come from the bit-by-bit overlap
of narrow memberships and specific identities, with specialties and

[16] Michael Polanyi, *The Tacit Dimension* (Garden City, NJ, 1967), 72.
[17] Donald T. Campbell, 'Ethnocentrism of Disciplines and the Fish-Scale Model of
Omniscience', in *Interdisciplinary Relationships in the Social Sciences*, ed. Muzafer and
Carolyn Sherif (Chicago, 1969), 328, 330.   [18] *Ibid.*, 328, 331.
[19] Diana Crane, 'Cultural Differentiation, Cultural Integration, and Social Control', in
Social Control: Views from the Social Sciences, ed. Jack P. Gibbs (Beverly Hills, CA,
1982), 239.   [20] Burton R. Clark, *The Academic Life*, chapter 5.

disciplines – and whole colleges and universities – serving as mediating institutions that tie individuals and small groups into the enclosure of the whole. For a realm that is so naturally pluralistic, and for which the future promises an ever-widening complexity of task and structure, a large dollop of pluralist theory is not a bad idea.

This line of thinking pushes us toward the relatively unexplored phenomenon of the associational linkages that academics themselves fashion. My recent study of the American academic profession found that, in the United States at least, the associational structure of the academic profession mirrors the ongoing contest between centrifugal and centripetal academic forces.[21] 'Splinteritis' is everywhere. The country has something in the order of 350 associations that are largely or importantly academic, from the omnibus American Association for the Advancement of Science (AAAS) to the John Dewey Society and the Society for Nursing History. Each major association, be it the American Physical Society, the American Psychological Association, or the Modern Languages Association, finds itself steadily subdividing into numerous major divisions along subject-matter lines, which then divide still further into subsections. As the associations grow substantively, tracking and furthering their respective fields, they incorporate more specialties and sow the seeds of their own fragmentation. If they are not accommodative, even quick on their feet, specialists break away to form their own associations. The American associations are also now subdividing internally and externally by type of institution: e.g., the community college sector has interests so far removed from those of the research universities that instructors in this realm have and are constituting the likes of the Community College Humanities Association, the Community College Social Sciences Association, and more discipline-centred ones in mathematics and biology.

Academics associate voluntarily from the bottom-up. They fashion informal individualised sets of ties on their own campuses. They participate in quasi-formal local, regional, and national groups of a dozen or several dozen people who meet separately or within the programme of the 'monster meetings'. The informal ties link to the quasi-formal, and the quasi-formal to the formal. The small groups connect to large ones that link up in gigantic conglomerates, as when a regional disciplinary association connects to a national one that in turn participates in one or more national and international 'umbrella' associations. Professional associating follows well the many natural contours of academe.

[21] *Ibid.*, chapter 8.

Conclusion

As national systems of higher education seek the means of enhancing flexibility and responding adaptively, in the face of ever-expanding complexity, they undoubtedly can assist themselves through some State targeting. While large countries may permit diffuse coverage of all subjects, small countries undoubtedly have to be selective, opting to invest only in certain fields. State-guided limitations – coercive simplicity – is one way of trying to control complexity. But beyond such planned responses lie more adaptive profession-led and market-led forms of differentiation and integration. These latter forms depend on more spontaneous, unplanned developments.

The profession-led responses on which I have concentrated depend in higher education upon competitive discovery processes. The give-and-take of scientific fields, and other fields of scholarship, are, at the level of the individual, an 'anarchy of production'. But out of a furious turmoil of lower level disorder a higher level order can and does evolve. This more spontaneous road to order depends on the interacting competencies, tacit and explicit, of thousands of individuals. They try to help things along by establishing such bottom-up forms of their own devising as informal, quasi-formal, and formal associations. 'Spontaneous orders' are likely to be central to a fruitful, changing integration, offering a 'mutual co-ordination in which the actions of each participant both contribute a kind of pressure to the actions of other participants, while simultaneously being guided in its own actions by similar pressures contributed by others'.[22]

Associating professionally with one another in webs of relationship that form and evaporate as substantive interests change, academics evolve structures that follow the development of knowledge, rather than the other way around. Flexibility is gained by escaping both from the iron cage of bureaucracy and from the professional iron cage that is wrought whenever close unity among academics is achieved.[23] Specialisation that creates so much freedom, and allows order to follow function, deserves at least two cheers.

The problem of complexity is not without its surpassing ironies. Try as we might to theorise it and to order it in boxes, the idea of complexity implies the primacy of practice over theory.[24] There is an old joke in science

[22] Lavoie, *National Economic Planning*, 67.
[23] On bureaucracy and profession as twentieth-century iron cages, see Paul J. DiMaggio and Walter W. Powell, 'The Iron Cage Revisited: Institutional Isomorphism and Collective Rationality in Organizational Fields', *American Sociological Review*, 48 (April 1985), 147–60.
[24] Harlan Wilson, 'Complexity as a Theoretical Problem: Wider Perspectives in Political Theory', in *Organized Social Complexity*, ed. LaPorte, 281–331, 307.

that research is what I am doing when I do not know what I am doing. As a minor paraphrase, complexity is perhaps what we have to think about when we do not know what to think. Émile Durkheim drew a powerful bead on the problem when he argued that generalisation was a sort of pride, a refusal to accept the personal restraints and social obligations imposed by complexity, while specialisation was an implicit means of adaptation to complexity.[25] This precept for occupational practice can and has been translated into a precept for thinking about politics, the economy, and other social orders: do one's narrow duty and let the complex whole take care of itself. Theory then must not only maintain a modest sense of limits but also deeply appreciate ambiguity.

At the same time, it still seems to remain the case that only general theoretical reflection, together with a sense of history, will enable us to think through the operation and meaning of our complex social institutions in a systematic way. At the least, when we think about complexity in higher education we are driven to return to fundamental exploration of the ways that spontaneous orders develop within and outside of officially-enacted structures. Such an approach is particularly appropriate in the analysis of a major sector of society – higher education – in which a diffuse profession-led specialisation and integration are so clearly the main alternative to bureaucratic allocation and linkage.

[25] *Ibid.*, 315, 331.

8 Comparative perspectives on British and American higher education

Martin Trow

Introduction

It is common knowledge that Harvard College was created on the model of a college of Cambridge University. But we know also that almost from the first moment, American forms of higher education began to diverge from the English model – and that divergence has continued apace over three and a half centuries. Already by the time of the American Revolution the colonies had eight institutions of higher learning, while two were still adequate for the much richer and more populous mother country. And by the Civil War the United States had hundreds of colleges and universities. Four – the two ancient universities plus Durham and London – were all that England had chartered. There were additionally four universities in Scotland, and two – Trinity College, Dublin and Queen's University – in Ireland. Owens College, Manchester had been established as a university college as the first of a number of university colleges which much later were to be chartered as separate degree-granting universities. But while higher education in Britain has continued to grow, it has done so within the firm constraints of central government and its criteria for the chartering of universities and other degree-granting institutions.

The divergence has continued, so that England, while currently moving toward some form of mass higher education, still has a relatively small system of degree-granting institutions – universities, polytechnics, and colleges, with relatively high and common standards for the first degree and low rates of attrition, enrolling the smallest proportion of the age grade, just under 15 per cent of any modern industrial society. By contrast, the United States has the largest and most diverse system of higher education in the world, enrolling some 14 million students in some 3,500

This chapter, an earlier version of which was given at Dalarö, Sweden, in June 1987, arises out of a comparative study of British and American higher education in collaboration with Sheldon Rothblatt. I am happy to acknowledge my debt to him which extends beyond our collaboration.

Comparative perspectives on British and American higher education

institutions, earning credit towards degrees, working at every level and degree of difficulty.

That quantitative comparison, of course, is 'unfair' to the United Kingdom in that it excludes the whole of its Further Education sector, with its 1.3 million students, while it includes the American community colleges, a large part of whose work is in 'vocational' studies that are not of degree standard in Britain (or the US), and much else is which is at or below the standard of British sixth form work or its equivalent. (On the other hand, the American figure also excludes an enormous amount of post-secondary continuing education that is not pursued in degree-credit courses.)

But even if we are not making invidious quantitative comparisons, then it is of some considerable importance for other reasons that in the UK the institutions of further education are not part of higher education, whereas in the US the community colleges are. And that is only one of many significant differences between these two national systems, differences whose nature and origins challenge our understanding.

Thus we can pose the questions: why is it that these two systems, starting from common assumptions and models, evolved in such sharply different directions over the centuries? Or put differently, how can we explain the fact that the United States has developed a large and diverse system of colleges and universities with near universal access to students of all abilities, ages, and interests, where 'any student can study any subject', while by contrast the UK has created a system of universities, polytechnics, and colleges for academically-gifted students, enrolling altogether a much smaller proportion of the post-secondary school age grade, a system marked also by high academic standards, low rates of attrition, deep and close attention to teaching, and distinguished levels of scholarship and research carried on within the universities themselves?

Contrasting sequences

If we place the historical development of two great systems of higher education over two centuries side by side, and perhaps in no other way, we may discover a number of occasions in which the sequences of development in the two societies have differed, and that these differing sequences have on one side their roots in the characteristics of the larger societies, and on the other in a broad range of ramified consequences for those societies. Sequences, for the chronicler of a single society, almost never excite special notice or attention: it is simply the way things occur in time, the way history happens. But there is surprise, and questions arise, when one places two chronologies side by side and discovers that the sequences which seem to be the 'normal' progression in one society did not occur that way in the other. And the questions that arise out of that recognition take a familiar set of forms:

1) Are the phenomena themselves, whose sequences we are chronicling, the 'same' phenomena in the two societies, or if similar, how do they differ?
2) Why do these sequences occur differently in these two societies – and how do we account for those differences?
3) What consequences flow from the fact that these sequences differ?

I want to point to five of these 'sequence reversals' – though there are others in the comparative modern histories of these two societies and their educational systems – to suggest their importance both as sources of subsequent differences between the two systems, and as reflections of prior differences in the basic character and development of the two societies.

1. In America, in Louis Hartz' vivid phrase, the market preceded the society[1] and its institutions of higher education. In the United Kingdom, Oxford and Cambridge (the powerful models for all subsequent higher education), were created in the medieval world before market forces came to dominate social and institutional relations.

2. In America, the presidents of our colleges and universities were present before the creation of a body of teachers and scholars which later became the faculty and even later the academic profession. In the UK, a class of learned men preceded the creation of the university and its leadership; their coming together in fact created Oxford and Cambridge, and over time they came to elect or choose their own institutional leaders. Put somewhat differently, in the UK the academic guilds preceded the modern university; in America the university (initially only the lay board, the president, and a few assistants), came over time to create the academic guilds.

3. In America, for the most part, colleges and universities developed before the emergence of a broad system of upper secondary schooling.[2] In the UK, by contrast, while mass secondary schooling was also a development of the late nineteenth and twentieth centuries, the schools that prepared students for university (when they were not tutored privately at home) were in place all through the modern period, and indeed changes

---

[1] Louis Hartz, *The Liberal Tradition in America: An Interpretation of American Political Thought Since the Revolution* (New York, 1955).
[2] Frederick Rudolph, *The American College and University: A History* (New York, 1962), 281ff.

in the leading secondary schools – the public schools – stimulated change and reform in the ancient universities in the second half of the nineteenth century.[3]

4. In America, the professional guilds have been relatively weak as compared with professional education in the universities; on the whole professional education has created the professions and still gives them leadership. Professional schools and colleges are enormously strong in American universities *and* colleges. In the UK, by contrast, professional education was largely excluded from the universities. There the professional guilds have dominated professional education, often providing the bulk of it themselves through a form of apprenticeship as in law and, to a large degree, in engineering. Even where they do not provide it all themselves, the professions and their organisations continue to be strong in relation to university-based professional education.

5. In the UK (except for Scotland) in the nineteenth and twentieth centuries, the college as a teaching institution, and the federation of colleges as modelled on Oxford and Cambridge and embodied in London and Victoria Universities and the provincial colleges, has preceded the emergence of the university, which granted degrees. Indeed, the 'university' in the UK was and is the degree-granting body, as over against the colleges, which have been agencies for teaching. In Britain the authority to grant degrees is jealously guarded and associated with the granting of a royal charter, but only to institutions which can demonstrate that they can teach and examine to high and common academic standards; it is thus an instrument for quality control of undergraduate education. In the US, 'university' came to mean an institution which offered higher degrees, and especially the doctorate, by contrast with a 'college' which offered only the bachelor's degree. Whereas in the UK the crucial issue was what body taught and what body examined and awarded degrees, in the US these functions were carried out by the same institution, whether college or university. The crucial distinction here was whether an institution was concerned primarily with the transmission of knowledge, or at least equally with the creation of knowledge. The idea of a university as the locus and agency for the creation of knowledge came later in the UK and, it can be argued, never achieved full equality with the teaching function until after World War II. Even then it was restricted to just a handful of universities, and research work centred on the professors. This helps account for the quite different weight and importance attached in the two

---

[3] Sheldon Rothblatt, *The Revolution of the Dons: Cambridge and Society in Victorian England* (1968; Cambridge, 1981).

countries to postgraduate education as compared with education for the first degree.

Let us look at three of these issues a little more closely:

1. America has been, almost since its earliest settlements, a liberal society, whose reliance on free markets and mistrust of central government is built deeply into its structures of society and government, for example in the constitutional separation of powers, in federalism and the continuing power of the states, and in the Bill of Rights. Americans are not embarrassed by the enormous role of markets – and indeed, of commercial considerations – at the very heart of universities. For example, land speculation has been a significant motive in the creation of colleges and universities throughout American history.

By contrast, while the UK has a stronger liberal tradition than most Continental European societies, it never accepted the hegemony of the market over the sphere of high culture. If we set aside the English dissenting academies (which collapsed at the end of the eighteenth century, probably because they could not get charters to give degrees), there was a brief window of liberal – that is, of private local – initiative in British higher education in the nineteenth century, taking form first in the creation of University College, as the first of a group of London colleges that came to compose the University of London. This movement showed greater life in the second half of the nineteenth century with the creation of the provincial universities (Owens College, Manchester, and the subsequent federation in 1880 of Owens, Leeds, and Liverpool in the short-lived Victoria University). Liverpool gained a charter of its own in 1881, and Leeds in 1904. There were also colleges created in Newcastle, Birmingham, and Bristol in the last decades of the nineteenth century, but most of the old civic universities did not gain charters as independent universities – that is, the right to award their own degrees – until the first decade of this century. The creation of English provincial universities in the late nineteenth and early twentieth centuries can be seen as a response to civic pride, to local demands for graduates for local business and industry, as well as for increased access to universities for local youth. But universities in England were, and continue to be, bedevilled by a conflict among different ideas of the university: the university as an instrument for the transmission of the high culture and the cultivation of the sensibilities and character of young gentlemen; the German and later American conception of universities, now regaining strength under severe cuts and pressures from central government, as places for practical, even vocational studies, and service to local business and industry.

The English provincial universities of the late nineteenth century were established by local notables and interests in part to provide trained graduates and services for local needs, though, as always, motives were mixed. But no English university could be established without the enormous weight of Oxford and Cambridge, as models and mentors, having a profound influence on their subsequent development. Indeed, the creation of the provincial universities coincided with reforms at Oxford and Cambridge, which led to their improving the quality of their teaching and a gradual rising of their academic standards.[4] These reforms made Oxford and Cambridge even weightier as models for the new institutions. But above all, Oxford and Cambridge were where England's national elite was educated, and for the provincial universities to seek academic distinction and social status meant moving out of their local orbits and the provisions of services for local needs toward Oxford's and Cambridge's standards and values, in the process becoming less local institutions and more and more part of a national system with common entry standards, common standards for the honours degree, a common academic salary scale, and above all a commitment to national rather than local service. This national system only developed slowly. The creation of the University Grants Committee in 1919 as the agency for the development of a common State budget request and the allocation of the block grant from the Treasury was an important milestone, but the national system had already begun to develop before that, and did not fully crystallise until after World War II.

Nevertheless, it can be said that for the provincial universities, useful practical studies were linked to local ties, local support, and the kind of responsiveness to the market for graduates and services that marks the college and university in a liberal society. There was every motive for these new provincial colleges and universities to forego those ties to their local origins, to flee from their dependence on the market, to find a greater nobility of mission and function (as they saw it) in becoming linked to national public service and the old professions, coming under the benevolent wing of the Treasury and then of the University Grants Committee and its provision of public funds from central government. Indeed, the increasing dependency on the State has been dramatic over the past sixty years, and especially since World War II.[5] In 1920, taking all British universities together, only about a third of their total income came on a direct grant from central government; between 1939 and 1949, that went up to nearly two thirds, and by the mid eighties it was roughly three

---

[4] *Ibid.*, and Arthur J. Engel, *From Clergyman to Don: The Rise of the Academic Profession in Nineteenth-Century Oxford* (Oxford, 1982).

[5] Martin Trow, 'Comparative Perspectives on Higher Education Policy in the U.K. and the U.S.', *Oxford Review of Education*, 14 (1988), 81–96.

quarters.[6] For British universities, to gain support from central government was a liberation from the petty demands and ignoble interests of local government and local trade, we see the very same process occurring today, as the polytechnics, created with strong local ties in ways very similar to the creation of the provincial universities, welcome the severance of their remaining dependence on local government and local industry as central government assumes their whole direct support.[7]

The American contrast is well known: dependence almost from the beginning on markets of various kinds, and the need to provide services and products for those markets, have shaped every aspect of the subsequent development of our system of higher education. This is a force whose importance can hardly be exaggerated. We can look at this orientation to the market in two ways: on one hand as an outcome of the absence of stable and assured support for our colleges and universities from the State (or states) or established Church has forced them to look for support from a multiplicity of other sources, notably student tuition and fees, contributions from alumni and other friends, and especially from wealthy benefactors and institutions. A constant concern for financial survival and resources for development and growth engendered a steady sensitivity to the needs and interests of this varied support community, reflected in the enormous diversity of activities and services that our institutions have provided. The other side of the coin shows the relative autonomy of our colleges and universities, even formally 'public' institutions, from direct control and management by agents of state or central government.

The force of markets on American colleges and universities has also greatly increased the power of the student as consumer, and that in turn has driven the curriculum to meet the students' interests, which in turn often reflect the interests of the job market. It also forces the colleges and universities to shape their curriculum to the realities of the primary and secondary schools, whose preparation the students bring with them. If our colleges and universities, for example, were to try to maintain a high and common standard for entry, as in the UK, many of them would have no students at all. So the great diversity of entry standards, of curricular offerings, and of standards for the degree are all indirectly related to the

---

[6] Michael Shattock, 'The Last Days of the UGC?', *Minerva*, 25 (1987), 471–85; Thomas William Heyck, 'The Idea of a University in Britain, 1870–1970', *History of European Ideas*, 8 (1987), 205–19; Peter G. Moore, 'University Financing 1979–1986', *Higher Education Quarterly*, 41 (1987), 25–41.

[7] It was not until the late 1970s and 80s of this century that British universities began to have second thoughts about their near total dependence on central government grants, and only under the most severe financial pressures and constraints have the British universities – or at least some of them – begun to cultivate anew their local ties and seek out local missions and services in the hope of gaining local financial support. There is, under duress, what may be a new rebirth of liberal perspectives in the British universities.

need to attract students who ultimately support the institutions in large part through their fees or generate support from state authorities by way of enrolment-based budgetary formulas.

If entry into markets implies sensitivity to the preferences of the buyers, it also suggests competition among the providers. Most American colleges and universities (though not all) were relatively poor at their founding (and some for long periods thereafter), and could only survive by finding ways to serve various constituencies which provide their support – students, benefactors, religious denominations, state and local governments, more recently business organisations and federal governmental agencies, in various combinations. But the habits of service do not disappear with affluence and security. And that is because our colleges and universities are also competitive with each other for distinction and prestige – nationally, regionally, or in some functional category. And in the pursuit of distinction and relative status, affluence provides no security. A college or university – even the richest – always needs more: another science building, higher faculty salaries, another chair in a new subject, more residence halls, and so on. So even our wealthiest colleges and universities act as if they were poor, always engaged in fund-raising, continually cultivating new friends and supporters, public and private, seeking always to find new ways of serving old and new constituencies in a constant exchange of service for support. The forms of service, as of support, are many and various, and the connections between them are often subtle, indirect, and delayed (though equally often simple and direct, through the cash nexus). In the UK it is the most desperate university, Salford, whose budget was cut most deeply in 1981–2, which has been the most energetic. Among American universities, the richest ones are also the most successful at fund-raising – Harvard, Stanford, Princeton, the Massachusetts Institute of Technology – and among the colleges, their elite counterparts – Amherst, Swarthmore, and the like. They raise money so as to compete academically, and they also compete in how much money they can raise. And all with no embarrassment. That, too, is of long standing.

But however strong these market forces may be, they are not all-powerful, and part of the history of American higher education has been of the tension between the 'popular' functions of these institutions, the services they perform for other institutions in society and for the vocational interests of students and their future employers, on the one hand, and the 'autonomous' functions, those that arise out of the intellectual life of the subjects that are taught and studied in the colleges and universities, on the other.[8] Some colleges and universities have been

[8] Trow, 'The Public and Private Lives of Higher Education', in *Daedalus*, 2 (Winter 1975), 113–27.

able to provide a measure of resistance to the powerful demands of the market, asserting their own inherent logic and integrity, refusing to be pressed into some kinds of public service or subordinating 'liberal' to 'vocational' studies in their curriculum.[9] Most successful in this have been the private colleges and universities with large endowments and those state institutions that have been able to count on substantial private support sources and a multiplicity of other support. All those factors reduce the direct influence of student preferences or governmental directives and give the autonomous functions of the institution a measure of room to survive and in some places even to flourish.

So institutional autonomy, the ability of an institution to defend its own character and mission, is, I suggest, a function less of sheer wealth than of the multiplicity of sources of support. This can be shown over time in the US, and events in the UK since World War II, and especially since 1970, also support this thesis.[10] But there the direct intervention of central government into the private life of the universities – what they teach and study – has had to overcome the traditions of autonomy rooted in the models of Oxford and Cambridge and their centuries of self-governing and endowed colleges. Those traditions were institutionalised in 1919 after World War I in the University Grants Committee, which the Thatcher government of the 1980s abolished and replaced with another body, the Universities Funding Council (UFC) consisting of lay members and directly responsive to central governmental policy. But the process associated with the movement from a system of elite to a system of mass higher education is still underway there, and the outcome is uncertain.

2. I have said that in the United States, for the most part, colleges and universities developed before the emergence of a system of public secondary schooling. One consequence was that our colleges and universities all through their history have had to do considerable remedial work to bring students even up to the not-very-demanding standards that they have imposed. The continuing weakness of their links to the secondary schools has meant that most American colleges and universities have not been able to assume any general standard of accomplishment and have had to teach students of widely varying ability and preparation. That has had consequences for their curriculum, methods of instruction, and requirements for the degree.

One result of the emergence of higher education before secondary schooling over the greater part of the United States, and of the scarcity of what Europeans would call upper secondary education even to this day, is

---

[9] Trow, 'Elite Higher Education: An Endangered Species?', *Minerva*, 14 (Autumn 1976), 355–76.   [10] Trow, 'Comparative Perspectives', 81–96.

that throughout our history, much of what colleges and universities do would seem to Europeans (and Britons) to be more appropriate to the upper secondary schools. The whole idea of general education – the non-specialised introduction to the main branches of learning which characterises the first two years of almost all American higher education – is in Europe completed in secondary school, and indeed in the UK at age 16, before entry into the upper secondary school, the sixth form. In addition, there is the enormous variety of student services provided by our colleges and universities – health centres, centres for remedial studies, for academic counselling, psychological counselling, career counselling, learning centres, and many more – all staffed by professionals or semi-professionals employed directly by the university. The elaborate facilities for sports and games, both intramural and intercollegiate, also staffed by professionals, certainly must remind Europeans of the spirit of school rather then of university, as do the many staff people who look after student residence halls. Everywhere we find counsellors and older students providing a certain measure of adult – and institutional – presence in situations where students in the Universities of Paris, Stockholm, or Rome, or the British universities, would be astonished to find it.

This psychological climate of prolonged immature dependency, that is to say, the climate of the school, was more pronounced in American colleges and universities twenty-five years ago than it is today. Political and legal challenges to the concept of the college standing *in loco parentis* have reduced the weight of the institutional authority in the American students' extracurricular life. But the universities' presence in extracurricular life is still large, and indeed has grown over the past two decades as student service staffs have become more highly professionalised and have spun off sub-specialties, professional associations, annual meetings, journals, and special post-graduate degrees that are virtually new professional credentials. All this activity now falls under the rubric of student services; no longer retaining the authoritarian overtones of a dean of students enforcing rules, representing the college or university *in loco parentis*, it has assumed the character of technical services rather than moral guidance. But these services inevitably have a moral dimension, and link the student to the institution more closely than is common in Europe.

In the UK, by contrast, public, private, and grammar schools had co-existed for centuries with Oxbridge, though many upper class students had been tutored privately for the universities – a much rarer pattern for the United States. But in the crucial middle years of the mid nineteenth century, the Arnoldian reforms in the leading public schools had an impact on the universities through their graduates, the moral force of their headmasters, and the establishment of close links between the sixth form in these public schools with the universities which made that avenue almost the only way into higher education, an avenue marked by many tied scholarships and strengthened by the Cambridge and Oxford entrance examinations.[11]

In important respects the secondary schools in the United States have been extensions of primary education upward, in their forms of teacher training and credentialling, in their structure, governance, and finance, and in the status and qualifications of the secondary school teachers. By contrast, in the UK, as in most other European countries, upper secondary education (both public and private) has been an extension of the universities downward, both in the character (and in the UK, the specialisation) of studies and teaching and in the origins and education of the sixth form teachers, university-trained scholars who might, in more expansive times, have held university posts. Again the exceptional patterns in the US are illuminating: one thinks of the significant role of the selective preparatory high schools and streams in the public sector in the 1920s and 1930s, with PhD's as department heads, before the great post-war expansion drew such people out of the high schools and into the colleges and universities.

It is hard to think of any fundamental way in which American secondary schools have influenced American colleges and universities, except by the weakness of their curriculum and teaching, or, as in most of our history before the turn of this century, their near-total absence. There is of course one outpost of the schools in our colleges and universities, and that is the departments and professional schools of education. But that linkage has inhibited the integration of schools of education into the university and prevented them from gaining the relatively strong and independent status of other professional schools in the university. As Burton Clark has suggested[12], the fundamental organisational, political, and normative characteristics of public secondary schools in America have a strong 'bias toward mediocrity' and are in this respect fundamentally different from the organisational characteristics of American colleges and universities.[13] Indeed, one important characteristic of the educational system of the United States is the enormous contrast between its public secondary schools, which are arguably among the least effective major institutions in society, and its colleges and universities, which are among its most successful and effective. The differences in organisation, character, and

[11] Rothblatt, *Dons*.
[12] Burton R. Clark, 'The High School and the University: What Went Wrong in America', Part 1, *Phi Delta Kappan*, 66 (1985), 391–7.
[13] Trow, 'The National Reports on Higher Education: A Sceptical View', *Educational Policy*, 1 (1987).

quality between American secondary schools and its colleges and universities have many consequences for both the schools and the colleges.

This is all very much by way of contrast with the UK and other European societies where, as I have suggested, the preparatory upper secondary schools have, over time, become extensions of the universities downward into the schools. But that allowed the maintenance of high and common entry standards, which replaced money and social status as the chief constraint on the expansion and democratisation of access to British universities as they slowly became meritocratic in this century. By contrast, the looseness of the articulation of our schools and colleges, the weakness and variability of secondary education in the US, all contributed to the ease of access to the latter, since no general level of secondary school achievement could be either expected or examined. That meant in turn that admissions criteria (beyond, in this century, a high school diploma) would be for many of our colleges and universities almost wholly lacking, and for others highly variable.

Indeed, it also helps explain the continued variability of achievement and ability among the entering class within any specific college or university, even those thought to be 'selective'. And this variability of preparation, and the extraordinary diversity of ability, achievement, and motivation among the entering students, all have tended to force on the colleges and universities the virtues of the elective curriculum, and that in turn depended on the primacy of the autonomous modular course, taught and examined by the same college or university instructor at whatever level of standard that he or she could achieve, or the students allow. This modular course structure which began to be introduced into American higher education after the Civil War is a crucial structural characteristic of the American organisation of teaching and instruction, with a broad range of implications for other aspects of the life of our institutions and the curriculum.[14]

3. I have been pointing to a series of questions which, I suggest, arise with special force and clarity from a comparative and historical study of inverted sequences in the development of our systems of higher education. Another such question is why the professorship – the chair – never assumed the overwhelming importance either in the UK or in the United States that it did on the Continent, and particularly in Germany and German-influenced systems.

The chaired professor, often also directing his own research institute, was (until the major 'reforms' of the 1960s) the central figure in most

---

[14] Rothblatt, 'The Idea of the Idea of a University and Its Antithesis', *Conversazione* (Seminar on the Sociology of Culture, La Trobe University, 1989).

European universities, in both the Humboldtian and Napoleonic systems. Indeed, in a sense the professors *were* the university; they dominated its intellectual and scholarly life, they elected its deans and rectors, and shared with politicians and officials in the ministries the governance and direction of the university. And remnants of this system survive to this day, diluted by the great increase in their numbers and the presence on internal governance committees of representatives of non-professorial teaching staff, students, and other staff members. But neither the UK nor the US has ever given the chair-holding professor such enormous authority and power in their universities. The reasons for this in the two countries are quite different. In the case of the US, the absence of a large class of learned men throughout much of our history meant that almost without exception our colleges and universities have been created by a group of laymen who selected a president to actually direct and manage the day-to-day life of the institution,. And this founding body and its successors (now the governing body, the lay board of trustees, or 'regents') together with their chosen agent (the president), have occupied the leading positions of authority and power in American colleges and universities, and still do.[15] While the academic staff – the 'faculty' – in a few leading universities and colleges have managed to persuade their boards to delegate to them a substantial measure of authority over the academic life of the institution, that authority is almost always exercised through academic bodies (usually 'Senates') consisting of all the members of the academic staff, or at least all the tenured ones, and further is actually exercised in steady consultation with the president and his senior academic staff – the academic vice-president, provosts, deans, and department chairs. There were few great scholars present at the birth of American colleges and universities and no room for them to exercise great powers when they finally did emerge through the development of their academic disciplines.

In the UK, the power of the professors was constrained in the ancient universities not by a lay board and powerful president, as in the US, but by corporate bodies of academics – the fellows – who are the governing bodies of the Oxford and Cambridge colleges and have been since their founding. These bodies have retained the egalitarian democracy (within their own elite membership) of medieval guilds of masters and have little room for the hierarchical and authoritarian rule of professors of the traditional European universities. While the professorial chair-holder has had a much more powerful position in the provincial universities than in

[15] The decision of the Supreme Court in the Dartmouth College case of 1819 confirmed their authority – and the inviolability of their charters – against challenge by state authorities. See Jurgen Herbst, *From Crisis to Crisis: American College Government, 1636–1819* (Cambridge, MA, 1982).

Oxbridge, the enormous influence of Oxford and Cambridge as models for the others, and the experience of most English professors as students or fellows in Oxbridge colleges, along with other factors, has inhibited the emergence of a dominant 'professoriate' at any English university comparable to the power of chair-holders on the Continent. And the differences between professors in Oxbridge and elsewhere have been declining with the introduction of rotating and even elected headships of departments in the provinces.

The emerging shape and nature of the academic profession in the US and UK pose an interesting contrast. Of particular interest is the evolution of an academic profession and career in the US after the Civil War, marked by their familiar academic ranks of today – instructor, assistant professor, associate professor, 'full' professor – in which it came early to be assumed that the ordinary career rank would be full professor and that every new instructor could *expect* to become a full professor *somewhere* as the predictable outcome of competent service, rather than of extraordinary scholarly achievement as in the UK and the Continental countries.

There are several questions here:

1. When did the crystallisation of this academic hierarchy occur in the US, and with what variations among different institutions?
2. Why did the academic profession develop in this way, as nowhere else?
3. What have been the consequences of this set of arrangements for academics, and for their institutions?

A tentative answer to the second question, of why the profession developed this way, can be suggested in the following terms. The relative ease with which American academics could achieve the rank of professor may be oddly related to the relative poverty of American institutions. Academics in the US were paid in part in rank and title, rather than in money. Since professors collectively did not have much power (for reasons already discussed), the existing ones did not and could not resist further diluting the status of the rank by adding to its numbers.

This raises the question of the enormously greater role of individual 'exit' over 'voice' in the higher levels of the academic profession in the US and the organised weakness of the guild as an instrument of 'voice' as compared to the individual exercising his own power in the academic marketplace.[16] 'Exit' of course is a function of the market for academics, which in turn is related to the sheer numbers of competing institutions. 'Exit' as a threat scarcely exists as a serious way for European academics

[16] Albert Hirschmann, *Exit, Voice, and Loyalty* (Cambridge, MA, 1970).

to improve their situation in their own institutions, though to be called elsewhere may be, and often is, a step in an upward progress. But that 'call' (or in our language 'offer') is rarely met by the home institution in the competitive way familiar to American colleges and universities.

One consequence of this arrangement in the US has been to increase the importance of an individual's own scholarly distinction and reputation and slow the development of academic unions. If one's professional fate is so much more a function of one's own research work and reputation, this greatly reduced for American academics their sense of a shared life fate in the same rank, institution, or system which is the main motivation for the development of academic unions. And not surprisingly, faculty unions in the US are found for the most part in the non-research institutions whose faculty are least able to exercise the power of threat of exit as a way of improving their own situations. And so they turn more to 'voice' through a union than to exit or threat of exit as a way of strengthening their positions. This fact has clear consequences for the governance of institutions, both those full of research academics and those with non-research oriented teaching staffs.

But there are other consequences of a normal career linking instructor to full professor as well. The absence in the US of a distinct body of junior non-professorial faculty who will never be professors, as found in the UK and on the Continent, is a factor in the anticipatory socialisation of all academics in American colleges and universities to common norms. If most instructors and assistant professors see themselves as full professors in the future, they are less likely to want to reduce the power and prerogatives of that status to which they realistically aspire. (But this does not apply to the growing body of part-time and 'temporary' faculty in many American institutions, excluded from the 'tenure-track', a reserve army that buffers these institutions against the vicissitudes of the market.) On the Continent, of course, the changes in university governance since the mid-1960s have been marked by sharp conflicts between the professoriate and the 'junior' academic ranks. This is less visible in British universities, perhaps because British academics inherited the relatively egalitarian ethos and governance structures of Oxford and Cambridge, and also because the roughly 40 per cent of all academics currently in the 'senior' ranks (professor, reader, senior lecturer) make achievement of those ranks a reasonable expectation for most junior staff (though one would guess a source of bitterness and resentment for the minority who do not make it).

Events, challenges, and contrasting patterns of response

Such questions as the above, which arise out of a comparative perspective, can be multiplied in number and extended in treatment. But there is another level of analysis which looks toward a more comprehensive statement about the intrinsic nature of these two systems, their internal development, and their evolving relationships with other groups and institutions in their societies.

Let me return to the question of why it is that the United States, alone among modern nations and in sharp contrast to the United Kingdom, had a system of mass higher education already in place 100 years ago, before it had the numbers that we associate with mass higher education. As a result of its structural and normative precocity, the great expansions of the twentieth century have not required any fundamental change in any of the basic structural, organisational, or normative features of American higher education and its component parts; those features were already in place, ready to accept the growing numbers that would pour into them in this century, and especially rapidly since World War II. It was as if the system had been created in anticipation of growth, and to some extent that seems to be true. So much in the history of the United States has been predicated on the assumptions of growth: its location of towns and cities, its infrastructure of roads, canals and railroads, its very conception of itself.[17]

But we cannot make too much of the 'intentionality' of higher educational policy; much of the premature readiness of the American system of higher education, before its movement to mass and then to universal access, was the result of the way the system was already being created and growing in the period between the Revolution and the Civil War, and some of its characteristics were foreshadowed before that. It is, I believe, possible to show the marked similarities in origins, organisation, and behaviour of American colleges created in 1815, 1870, and 1960. The continuities in their character and structure are striking, even if changes in the undergraduate curriculum over time are large and the research function almost wholly missing from the pre-Civil War colleges.

We must root this discussion in the literature of theories of American exceptionalism, theories which try to explain the differences between the American experience and that of most other advanced industrial societies. And this discussion must at least make reference to diverse approaches to this concern for exceptionalism; Louis Hartz' focus on the role of the market in American life;[18] Potter's on the role of general affluence and

[17] Daniel J. Boorstin, *The Americans: The National Experience* (New York, 1967).
[18] Hartz, *Liberal Tradition*.

wealth in the American experience;[19] Turner and his critics on the influence of the moving frontier;[20] Lipset on our historical experience as 'the first new nation', and on the economic and political forces that resulted in our being the only industrial society that never developed a strong socialist movement and tradition;[21] and above all Tocqueville's classic analysis of American democracy and the enormous weight it has placed on the quality of condition, on individual opportunity and achievement, and on the highly-developed propensity of Americans to create and join private associations to accomplish all kinds of purposes.[22] Each of these (and other) broad perspectives on United States history has its implications for the character and functions of American colleges and universities. They are by no means mutually contradictory or incompatible, and one task is to show how together they and other aspects of the American experience, and not least our experience as a country of immigrants, had consequences for American colleges and universities, which in turn have reacted back upon other aspects of American life, other American institutions.

Similarly, there is a rich literature on English 'exceptionalism' – on the unique features of its history and culture which have distinguished it not only from the US, but from other European nations. Among these surely are the social and political consequences of its revolution in the seventeenth century, its pioneering role in the industrial revolution, the continuing social and political roles played by its aristocracy, its steady extension of the concept of citizenship, and the evolving cultural role of its several social classes. British and American colleges and universities were affected in part by characteristics of their internal life and structure – as in the ways they were chartered, or the forms of the academic profession and career that evolved on both sides of the Atlantic. But they were also shaped by characteristics of their societies and social structures, as for example in their contrasting patterns of access, or the different provisions they have made for engineering and other technical studies within the university.

Surely one unique aspect of American higher education has been the character of the 'policy' of the federal government toward higher education over the past 200 years. One might start with the early land grants, even before the Constitution was ratified, built into the Northwest

---

[19] David M. Potter, *People of Plenty: Economic Abundance and the American Character* (Chicago, 1954).

[20] Frederick Jackson Turner, *The Frontier in American History* (New York, 1920). See also Richard Hofstadter and Seymour Martin Lipset (eds.), *Turner and the Sociology of the Frontier* (New York, 1968).

[21] Martin Lipset, *The First New Nation; the United States in Historical and Comparative Perspective* (New York, 1963).

[22] Alexis de Tocqueville, *Democracy in America* – many editions since the original publication in 1835, but see the one translated by George Lawrence and edited by Jacob P. Mayer and Max Lerner (New York, 1966).

Ordinance. But five other milestones over the past two centuries define a pattern of relationships between the federal government and American colleges and universities.

First are the efforts made by George Washington and his immediate successors to establish a university of the United States and the failure of those efforts. That precluded the emergence of a 'capstone' institution able to establish national norms and standards, and thus constrain the proliferation of colleges and universities. Second is the Supreme Court decision of 1819 in the case of Dartmouth College which confirmed the right of private groups and bodies to establish colleges and to retain control of them in the face of efforts by state and local governments to take them over and operate them as public institutions. This ensured the survival of the many small private colleges which have characterised American higher education ever since. Third is the Land Grant (Morrill) Acts of 1862 and 1891, which provided federal money first to the states and then to the colleges themselves for the creation of institutions and pro-grammes devoted to a combination of liberal studies and the agricultural and mechanic arts; it did so with very few administrative controls or regulations. Fourth is the G.I. Bill of Rights which provided free tuition and support for over two million veterans to attend some form of post-secondary education after World War II, and became the model for later forms of federal support for student aid, and in particular, the legislation passed in 1972 providing general student support for higher education in the form of grants and loans to individual students which they could take to accredited institutions, rather than grants to the institutions themselves. And fifth is the growth of federal support for science during World War II, and the establishment of the National Science Foundation and the National Institutes of Health after the war, with their support largely taking the form of direct grants to individual scientists through a peer review process organised by the federal funding agency.[23]

I might have added to that list the Hatch Act of 1887, which funded the land-grant colleges directly (rather than through the states), and the federal programme after World War II that provided higher education with science buildings, instruments, and aid to libraries. In each case the decision of policy contributed to the diversity and complexity of American higher education, a diversity and complexity of character, mission, academic standard, and access. In each case public policy tended to strengthen the competitive market in higher education by weakening any central authority that could substitute regulations and standards for competition. It accomplished this by driving decisions downward and

---

[23] The National Institutes of Health also support a good deal of in-house research.

outward, by giving more resources and discretion to the consumers of education and the institutions most responsive to them; it increased the power of the states in relation to the federal government, as in the Dartmouth College case and the Hatch Act; and of the students in relation to their own institutions, as in the G.I. Bill and the Higher Education Act of 1972.

By contrast with the pattern in the United States where decisions at the centre have tended to strengthen the principle of competition between institutions and within various markets for students, support, and faculty, the British pattern has been a continued tendency to impose constraints from the centre, and more recently to strengthen the direct role of central government in a way that begins to resemble the *dirigisme* of Continental countries in respect to their systems of higher education. We can see this from the establishment of the universities of Durham and London in the first third of the nineteenth century. In both cases, central government exercised a tight control over the granting of their charters and the conditions under which degrees could be awarded. We also see the role of central government in the Oxbridge reforms of the 1860s and 1870s, the introduction of civil service examinations, the effects of these on the university honours degree examination, and the establishment of the provincial universities and their slow transformation and incorporation into a national system between 1880 and 1925. The creation of the University Grants Committee (UGC) in 1919 provided an instrument for mediating the role of central government in the life of the universities where the central element of control over their establishment and the standard of first degree had already been put in place. The British pattern was also visible in the character of their Veterans' Act of 1944, and the marked difference between that legislation and its counterpart in the United States, the G.I. Bill.[24] Post-war expansion in Britain took the form of the establishment of colleges of advanced technology (CATS) and their incorporation in the 1960s into the university system; the creation of new 'plate glass' universities in cathedral towns, small by American standards and only marginally different from the older provincial 'red-brick' universities; and the establishment of the polytechnics in the 1960s as a 'public sector' side by side with the universities but separate, though maintaining (at least in principle) the same standards for admission and the same high level for the first degree. All of this expansion was marked by (a) tight control over growth, (b) a strong commitment to the maintenance of high and uniform academic standards for the first degree, and (c) the rhetorical encouragement (and actual discouragement) of diversity in the forms and content

[24] Trow, 'Comparative Perspectives', 81–96, and 'The Robbins Trap: British Attitudes and the Limits of Expansion', *Higher Education Quarterly*, 43 (Winter 1989), 55–75.

of British higher education. Since the middle 1970s we have seen a pattern of budget cuts by the central government, a steady increase in the influence of central government on the decisions of the individual universities, and the decline and disappearance of the UGC as a buffer between central government and the universities.

But this chapter has tried to show that the differences between the British and American systems of higher education go deeper than the dramatic events in the UK of the last decade and the quite different kinds of criticism directed at American colleges and universities, and especially at undergraduate education, in the last few years.[25] A broad comparative and historical perspective may help us better understand recent developments in both countries.

[25] Trow, 'National Reports'.

Part 5

The ironies of university history

9   The modern university: the three transformations

Björn Wittrock

Introduction

The university is, together with the Church, the most time-honoured of all present-day macro-societal institutions. Yet arguably it is also the most innovative. It is the source of our ever-growing technical mastery of nature and of the meaning we attribute to that mastery. Bits and pieces of university-based knowledge constantly trickle into the daily discourse of society, provide information and ammunition for public debate, and, more fundamentally but also more inadvertently, for basic reconceptualisations of societal order.[1]

Modern social science emerged in a university environment as part of the efforts of individuals to understand the wide-ranging effects of industrialisation, urbanisation, and deep-seated social change. This process of change also posed questions as to the nature and possibility of a cultural identity beyond the limited experiential horizons of traditional rural society. There was also a close link between the new social sciences and a general societal concern about the formation of new political and cultural institutions to cope with the changing social conditions. One important part of these institutional transformations focused on the shaping of more effective representative and administrative institutions in the new and reformed nation-states, but another was directly concerned with public affairs, such as new social policies to help solve the so-called social question, *die soziale Frage*.[2]

Yet for all the innovative capacity of contemporary universities, the research function is relatively new. It is co-terminous with the nineteenth-century transformation of universities from institutions for the trans-

---

[1] See e.g. the different contributions to *Social Sciences and Modern States: National Experiences and Theoretical Crossroads*, ed. Peter Wagner, Carol H. Weiss, Björn Wittrock, and Hellmut Wollmann (Cambridge, 1991).

[2] *Ibid.*, and also the contributions to *Discourses on Society: The Shaping of the Social Science Disciplines*, ed. Peter Wagner, Björn Wittrock, and Richard Whitley (Dordrecht, 1991), and *Social Knowledge and the Origins of Social Policies*, ed. Dietrich Rueschemeyer and Theda Skocpol (forthcoming).

mission of a received body of knowledge to generally immature adolescents into research-oriented institutions, the 'axial' institutions of the modern world.[3] Still, even after decades of strenuous efforts to streamline universities into efficient bureaucracies and enterprises, or make them into arenas for the fair participation and co-determination of all conceivable parties concerned – or to fix upon them one or another organisational ideal assigned high priority by reform-minded politicians and trustees – many of the governing principles bear a surprising resemblance to features which already existed in medieval precursors to the institutional dinosaurs of the present. Even in a thoroughly reformed university system such as that of Sweden, there are vague, and sometimes not so vague, memory traces from past centuries. These are names and rituals or recurring practices strangely frozen in time as – to use Sven-Eric Liedman's Nordic metaphor – 'frozen ideology', except the practices are not really frozen but rather constantly repeated, 'reinstantiated' – as the sociologists would have it – and thus part and parcel of a warm, living community. Uppsala still has its *konsistorium*, its *Rektor magnificus*, its doctoral 'disputations', its student 'nations'; and much to the surprise of the rationalistic reform bureaucrats of the 1960s and 70s, the old disciplines refused to disappear in favour of 'study programmes' and 'single courses' but easily outlived these publicly force-fed neologisms in the private life of academic institutions.

All of this makes for a confluence of different streams of institutional thought and legacies which have made the study of universities a starting point for the intellectual exercises of many a leading sociologist of organisations, but a starting point which most of them, despite familiarity, have quickly preferred to leave behind. Instead, they have chosen to move on to other fields where organisational practices are less likely to resist efforts at creating clear, and not overly historically trained, classificatory systems – systems, one might add, less likely to be inhabited by objects of inquiry with an uncomfortable habit of constantly talking back, thereby always threatening to upset the best laid scholarly schemes.

Similarly, not only the medieval universities but also many of their nineteenth- and twentieth-century descendants may basically have depicted themselves as independent legal bodies, as corporations being older

---

[3] Harold Perkin, 'The Historical Perspective', in *Perspectives on Higher Education: Eight Disciplinary Perspectives,* ed. Burton R. Clark (Berkeley, 1984), 17–55. See in addition Lawrence Stone, 'Social Control and Intellectual Excellence: Oxbridge and Edinburgh 1560–1983', and Stuart Hampshire, 'Comments', both in *Universities, Society, and the Future,* ed. Nicholas Phillipson (Edinburgh, 1983), 3–30 and 30–6. Also Roger Geiger, *To Advance Knowledge: The Growth of American Research Universities 1900–1940* (New York, 1986), and Björn Wittrock and Aant Elzinga (eds.), *The University Research System: The Public Policies of the Home of Scientists* (Stockholm, 1985).

than and independent of the absolutist states of early modern Europe as well as the modern nation-states. Yet, as pointed out by many observers, the true ancestors of today's universities are certainly not their medieval precursors.[4] Rather, the emergence of the modern university is by and large a phenomenon of the late nineteenth century. It is only in this period that universities are resurrected as primary knowledge-producing institutions and that the idea of a research-oriented university becomes predominant. It is only too obvious that this institutional process is intimately linked to another one, namely the rise of the modern nation-state whether in newly-formed polities on the European continent, such as Italy or Germany, or through the reform of older State organisations, such as France or the United States of America.[5]

From this perspective, far from being detached from the basic societal and political transformations of the modern era, universities form part and parcel of the very same process which manifests itself in the emergence of an industrial economic order and the nation-state as the most typical and most important form of political organisation.

In historical perspective, then, having been exposed to the ruptures of largely discontinuous societal processes, universities exist with layer upon layer of quite divergent legacies, yet somehow they have also succeeded in preserving a strong element of continuity amidst all the change. Given this basic feature of universities, there is little reason to be surprised by a corresponding divergence of analytical traditions in analysing them. Research on universities is but a name for a cross-current of different

---

[4] See Peter Scott, *The Crisis of the University* (London, 1984), or Everett Mendelsohn, 'Science, Power and the Reconstruction of Knowledge', in *Knowledge and Higher Education: A Series of Colloquia*, ed. Gunnar Bergendahl (Stockholm, 1983), 49–71, for eloquent statements of this point. It should, however, be noted that there has recently been some discussion as to the validity of what might be termed the standard view about the relative insignificance of the universities in the Scientific Revolution. See Mordechai Feingold, 'The Universities and the Scientific Revolution: The Case of England', in *New Trends in the History of Science*, ed. Robert Paul Willem Visser, *et al.* (Amsterdam, 1989), 29–48, but also the rejoinder by H. Floris Cohen, 49–52.

[5] Terry Nicholas Clark, *Prophets and Patrons: The French University and the Emergence of the Social Sciences* (Cambridge, 1973); Charles E. McClelland, *State, Society and University in Germany, 1700–1914* (Cambridge, 1980); Pierangelo Schiera, '"Science and Politics" as a Political Factor: German and Italian Social Sciences in the Nineteenth Century', in *Discourses*, ed. Wagner *et al.*, 93–120; Rolf Torstendahl in this volume; Peter Wagner, *Sozialwissenschaften und Staat: Frankreich, Italie, Deutschland 1870–1980* (Frankfurt-on-Main, 1990); George Weisz, *The Emergence of Modern Universities in France, 1863–1914* (Princeton, 1983); Wittrock and Wagner, 'Social Science and State Developments: The Structuration of Discourse in the Social Sciences', in *Social Sciences, Policy and the State*, ed. Stephen Brooks and Alain Gagnon (New York, 1990), 113–37; Wittrock, Wagner, Wollmann, 'Social Science and the Modern State: Policy Knowledge and Societal Transformations in Western Europe and North America', in *Social Sciences and Modern States*, ed. Wagner *et al.*, 28–85.

intellectual traditions. Furthermore, almost none of these traditions has the study of universities as a primary focus.

Thus, to intellectual historians, universities and other scholarly institutions are certainly not the main theme of analysis. Rather they tend to emerge as the more or less explicit, more or less tacit, institutional backdrop to accounts of ideational transformations, whether the theme is the Scottish Enlightenment, the French Revolution, or the intellectual foundations of the modern nation-state in Germany, or, for that matter, Sweden.[6] To the sociologists of science as well as to the sociologists of education, both being but sub-professions within the wider context of sociology as a whole, studies of the institutions of higher education have traditionally been, at best, a small sub-field. Thus in standard volumes from the 1970s such as those of Robert Merton and the one edited by Ina Spiegel-Rösing, there are but a scattered handful of references to universities.[7] In political science and in the burgeoning fields of policy and management studies, higher education is just one amongst a plethora of different policy areas and certainly not the most prominent one.

In practice, much of higher education research has evolved as a correlate to the political and administrative concerns inherent in the processes of university reform and expansion. This is true both of the situation at the time of the birth of the modern research-oriented university in the late nineteenth and early twentieth century and during the rapid expansion of the higher education system of Western countries in the 1960s and early 1970s. It is true today as well when universities are seen once again as crucial to the long-term build-up of competence within broad fields of knowledge in ways which neither easily correspond to the traditional disciplinary demarcation of academia itself, nor to the schemes of narrowly utilitarian university planners in the age of great policy programmes and a

---

[6] Nicholas Phillipson, 'Culture and Society in the 18th Century Province: The Case of Edinburgh and the Scottish Enlightenment', in *The University in Society, Europe, Scotland, and the United States from the 16th to the 20th Century*, ed. Lawrence Stone (Princeton and London, 1974 and 1975), II, 407–48; Johan Heilbron, *Het ontstaan van de sociologie* (Amsterdam, 1990) – English edition under preparation with Polity Press, Cambridge; Schiera, '"Science and Politics"'; Fritz Ringer, *The Decline of the German Mandarins* (Cambridge, MA, 1969), 'The German Mandarins Reconsidered' (University of California, Berkeley: Center for Studies in Higher Education, Occasional Paper No. 20, 1981), and 'Differences and Cross-National Similarities among Mandarins', *Comparative Studies in Society and History*, 28 (1986), 145–64. Also Sven-Eric Liedman, 'Institutions and Ideas: Mandarins and Non-Mandarins in the German Academic Intelligentsia', and 'Reply' (to Ringer), *ibid.*, 119–44 and 165–8.

[7] Robert K. Merton, *The Sociology of Science: Theoretical and Empirical Investigations* (Chicago, 1973); Ina Spiegel-Rösing (ed.), *Science, Technology and Society* (London, 1978). This fact has been pointed out by Simon Schwartzman in 'The Focus on Scientific Activity', in Clark, *Perspectives*, 199–232.

shaken perhaps but still strongly-held belief in the virtues of a 'radically rationalistic' policy process.

Circumstances of this kind may well be conducive to an enlightened dialogue between higher education scholars and a broader public. In many ways, this seems to have occurred on more than one point in this century. Emile Durkheim's lectures at the Sorbonne on the evolution of educational thought were, of course, of the utmost importance given the role of teachers as the bulwark of republicanism in turn-of-the-century France.[8] However, they also represent, in the words of a modern observer, an analysis where '[t]he significance of history for sociological explanation, in fact, is accentuated more explicitly...than in any other of Durkheim's major works'.[9] Much the same close links between a broadly interpreted policy relevance and intellectual advancement can be found in studies of Durkheim's German contemporaries such as Max Weber and Friedrich Paulsen.

When some decades later major university reformers such as Abraham Flexner in the United States or Gunnar Myrdal in Sweden expounded their views, their proposals were based on careful historical and sociological overviews and reflected the same scholarly stance that they wished to see advanced in the university systems they addressed.[10] In recent decades also, theoretically oriented social scientists such as Talcott Parsons, Neil Smelser, and David Riesman in the United States, Pierre Bourdieu, Michel Crozier, and Alain Touraine in France, Jürgen Habermas and Renate Mayntz in Germany and Olsen, Allardt and Hernes in Scandinavia, have time and again broached key themes in the study of higher education. Yet, it is equally true to state that these fortuitous instances are far from representing a strong tradition of sustained scholarship. Rather, the opposite would seem to hold true for social science research on universities and higher education.

[8] Emile Durkheim, *L'Evolution pedagogique en France*, 2 vols. (1938); English translation in one volume, *The Evolution of Educational Thought* (London, 1977).

[9] Anthony Giddens, *Durkheim* (London, 1978), 76. See also *Durkheim on Politics and the State*, ed. Anthony Giddens (Cambridge, 1986) as well as Terry N. Clark, *Prophets*; Roger L. Geiger, 'The Institutionalization of Sociological Paradigms: Three Examples from Early French Sociology', *Journal of the History of the Behavioral Science*, 11 (1975), 235–45; Viktor Karady, 'Strategies de réussite et modes de faire-valoir de la sociologie chez les durkheimiens', *Revue francaise de sociologie*, XX (1979), 49–82; Peter Wagner, *Sozialwissenschaften*. The texts by Geiger and Karady as well as an excerpt from T. N. Clark also appear in German translation in Wolf Lepenies (ed.), *Geschichte der Soziologie, Studien zur kognitiven, sozialen und historischen Identität einer Disziplin* (Frankfurt-on-Main, 1981), II, 137–262.

[10] Abraham Flexner, *Universities: American, German, English*, (Oxford, 1930); Second edition with an introduction, 'Remembering Flexner', by Clark Kerr, 1968 (Flexner's book was published in German in 1932); Gunnar Myrdal, *Universitetsreform* (Stockholm, 1945).

Whatever tradition of theoretically-informed research might be followed, its evidence is precarious and its performance erratic.[11] At almost
any point in recent decades, it has represented little but a trickle of
scholarship in a sea of useful but often quite narrowly policy-oriented
evaluations, management, and implementation studies.[12] As a consequence, the domain of more broad-ranging higher education research has
largely been inhabited by historians rather than by sociologists, anthropologists, or political scientists, not to mention economists. This volume
itself bears strong testimony to this fact.

Needless to say, there is every reason for social science to welcome a
situation when, once again, the importance of adopting an historical
perspective is strongly emphasised in the social sciences.[13] Simultaneously,
however, a momentous process parallel to that of restoring an historical
perspective has occurred in contemporary social science and social theory.
It is the rediscovery of agency after some decades when either theories
about more or less atomistic individuals or else about practically actorless
systems, with or without a functionalist garb, have been the predominant
modes of analysis. In recent years a whole range of theories have been
advanced which all aim at overcoming the dualism of traditional theorising
with its chasm between abstract, actorless structures, and a free-floating, if
structurally limited, single human being.[14] However, these developments in
social theory have had but the scantiest impact on higher education
research which is still largely, if often just tacitly, premised on a systemic-
functional analysis.

In this chapter I shall try to demonstrate, not by rhetoric but by example,
that this situation can indeed be corrected. I believe that it is possible to
pursue theoretically-informed empirical research on the university as a key
macro-institution of modern society. Such research should not be
conducted in the tradition of functionalism which tends to begin with
empty abstractions and afterwards gradually fills up with exemplifying

[11] Of course, the work of the Carnegie commission on higher education, where scholars such
as Clark Kerr and Martin Trow played a crucial role in the 1960s and 1970s, set the agenda
for higher education debate and still represents an unsurpassed model of policy-oriented
scholarship on higher education. See e.g. *Teachers and Students: Aspects of American
Higher Education*, ed. Martin Trow (New York, 1975). The Carnegie Foundation has
long been active in higher education. It is worth noting that two of Flexner's detailed, oft-
cited reports on medical education (1910 and 1912) were commissioned by the Foundation.
[12] The perseverance and broad-mindedness of Burton Clark's and Martin Trow's respective
programmes for the promotion of higher education as an academic field in its own right
stand out in a field which is only all too often characterised by centrifugal tendencies and
nationally parochial orientations.
[13] This point has been effectively made by several prominent sociologists in recent years,
most consistently perhaps by Piotr Sztompka.
[14] For a delightful selection of essays elaborating some of these points, see Anthony Giddens,
Social Theory and Modern Sociology (Cambridge, 1987).

elaborations that never allow room for the actual inhabitants of the social universe, human beings with mind and memory, living and moving in actual places at particular times. Nor should it be guided by a free-floating principle, an 'idea' of the university, just as abstract and disembodied as the rule systems of functionalism and their 'instantiations'. Instead, an effort will here be made to take seriously both the ideational element, the beliefs, as well as the institutional settings with their rules and norms, and enforcing and enabling practices, without losing sight of the simplest fact that ideas and institutions are always situational and are neither disembodied nor mindless. This basic position informs the analysis throughout, but I hope it will not get in the way of the evolving argument about the path of development of the modern university since the early nineteenth century.

The development of universities will be analysed in the three critical periods of transition, which comprise the focus of this volume as a whole. These periods are: first, and mainly serving as a background for most of the contributions to the volume, the period of the crisis and rebirth of the idea of the university at the turn of the eighteenth and nineteenth centuries; second, the emergence of the modern research-oriented university in the late nineteenth century; and third, the current period of reappraisal in the wake of the experiences of a less than all-successful planning euphoria on the one hand and rapidly growing streams of demand – and often enough also support – from government, industry, and the educational system at large.

This historical analysis will then be reviewed comparatively. Finally, the three periods of transition with their institutionally-oriented analysis will be related to a discussion of comprehensive notions of a university, as such notions have evolved in conjunction with the transformations of the university itself.

The actual empirical focus on three periods of transition is justified both in terms of the actual events of institution building and in terms of the range of existing scholarship. It requires concentration on what might be called the coming of age of modernity in the period of full-scale industrial development and urbanisation in the second half of the nineteenth century, and on the present period of – what for want of a better term and with the deliberate avoidance of any loose talk of 'postmodernism' – might be called late-modernity. However, such a delimitation unavoidably detracts attention from the period of the birth of modernity in the late eighteenth and early nineteenth centuries. Koselleck called such a period a *Sattelzeit*. It was a period of pivotal change when a traditional form of life, governed by the narrowly delimited 'spaces of experience', was followed by one in which identity and authority had to be redefined in the wake of deep-seated societal changes and where attention tended to be focused on 'horizons of expectations'. Similar notions about the late eighteenth and early nineteenth centuries as a 'great transition', to use Steven Turner's expression, have been advanced by other scholars, including Michel Foucault in *The Order of Things* and Friedrich Meinecke.[15] In recent years there have been some studies which focus precisely on the interaction between ideational, institutional, and societal developments.[16] Yet the precise implications of a 'great transition' for an analysis of the interplay between scientific activities, the institution of the university, and the wider society still require elaboration.

The great transition and the resurrection of the university

In the history of science, the eighteenth century has often been regarded 'as a tiresome trough to be negotiated between the peaks of the seventeenth and those of the nineteenth century; or as a mystery, a twilight zone in which all is on the verge of yielding'.[17] The same general perspective seems to be the dominant one whether discussion is on the development of discourses on nature and natural history or on human society and its historical development. Standard accounts are dominated by the French and Industrial Revolutions, but the intellectual side tends to be depicted in terms of the late Enlightenment or pre-romanticism. This means that intellectual and scientific developments in these eras are not taken seriously in their own right. They tend to be described either in terms of Herbert Butterfield's 'Whig interpretation of history' (1931) or Roy Porter's 'tunnel histories' of individual disciplines where 'precursors' are neatly arranged to fit a present-day image of the achievements of the past. Figures

---

[15] For an interesting discussion of Foucault's never fully elaborated concept of *episteme* and a comparison of that with Thomas Kuhn's concept paradigm, see George S. Rousseau and Roy Porter (eds.), *The Ferment of Knowledge: Studies in the Historiography of Eighteenth-Century Science* (Cambridge, 1980), 212, 257 and 290.

[16] See R. Steven Turner, 'The Great Transition and the Social Patterns of German Sciences', *Minerva*, 25 (1987), 56–76, and 'University Reformers and Professorial Scholarship in Germany 1760–1806', in Stone (ed.), *The University in Society*, 495–531; Randall Collins, 'A Micro-Macro Theory of Intellectual Creativity: The Case of German Idealist Philosophy', *Sociological Theory*, 5 (Spring 1987), 47–69. See also *The German Enlightenment and the Rise of Historicism*, ed. Peter Hanns Reill (Berkeley, 1975). More recently, Laurence Dickey has analysed the German Enlightenment, specifically Hegel, in terms quite compatible with the general themes of Reill but more critically towards Peter Gay's analysis of the European Enlightenment. Gay is unwilling to see the close links in the German context between Protestant pietism and Enlightenment philosophy. See Laurence Dickey, *Hegel: Religion, Economics, and the Politics of Spirit, 1770–1807* (Cambridge, 1987); Also Keith Tribe's review in *Journal of Modern History*, 62 (September 1990), 645ff of James Van Horn Melton, *Absolutism and the Eighteenth-Century Origins of Compulsory Schooling in Prussia and Austria* (Cambridge, 1988).

[17] Rousseau and Porter, 'Introduction', *The Ferment of Knowledge*, 2. I am indebted to Peter Hanns Reill for calling this quotation to my attention.

who do not neatly fit into these schemes are then disregarded and cast aside, their intellectual projects being but dead-ends and deviations from the high road towards progress and reason.[18]

Much the same signs of relative neglect recur in studies of the institutional development of universities. Thus Turner has pointed out how 'traditional histories have always regarded the eighteenth century as an era of institutional and intellectual decline for the German university system'.[19] Clear exceptions to this picture, such as the development of the life sciences at Göttingen (see, for example, Sven-Eric Liedman's discussion in this volume of Blumenbach and his concept of *Bildungstrieb*) have often only been seen as the exceptions which confirm the rule. Even in such an internationally leading institution as Edinburgh, 'things were beginning to go wrong' around the turn of the century.[20] Yet, as argued by Peter Hans Reill, Johan Heilbron, Turner and also Liedman, this conventional interpretation may suffer from a certain tendency towards 'Whiggishness'. It is, for instance, clearly the case that distinctions which were later taken for granted in the intellectual worlds of, say Germany and Scandinavia, such as those between the nomothetic natural sciences and the ideographic cultural sciences, were of exactly such a type as late-nineteenth-century scholars were refusing to accept. It is, of course, also a time when mechanistic metaphors predominant in an earlier period tended to be superseded by those of biology and of notions such as vital forces and when biology, history, and linguistics become crucially important to the scholarly enterprise in general.

Similarly, the type of organisation of knowledge which became the accepted pattern in the course of the nineteenth century in Germany – and increasingly in the universities of other countries as well, in Sweden quite explicitly so from the 1850s onwards – was not so much superior to but rather fundamentally different from the conceptions guiding the professors of the preceding generations. As argued by Turner, 'what distinguished the "old universities" of the later eighteenth century from the "new universities" of the nineteenth century was not their differing assessments of the professoriate's obligation to learning. It was rather their different visions of scholarship itself... By 1835 much professorial learning had

---

[18] Herbert Butterfield, *The Whig Interpretation of History* (London, 1931); Porter, 'The Terraqueous Globe', in *The Ferment of Knowledge*, ed. Rousseau and Porter, 285ff. See also Stefan Collini, Donald Winch, and John Burrow (eds.), *That Noble Science of Politics: A Study in Nineteenth Century Intellectual History* (Cambridge, 1983), 4ff.

[19] Turner, 'University Reformers', 495.

[20] Stone, 'Social Control', 21. See also Phillipson, 'Culture and Society', and 'The Pursuit of Virtue in Scottish University Education: Dugald Stewart and Scottish Moral Philosophy in the Enlightenment', in *Universities, Society, and the Future*, ed. Phillipson, 82–101.

312   *Björn Wittrock*

narrowed into disciplinary channels oriented toward research, discovery, and specialization.'[21] With these remarks in mind, Liedman's account of Agardh in an earlier chapter can be read as an almost archetypical account of the career and vision of a professor of the 'old' generation, although in this case in a Swedish rather than German setting.

However, regardless of how the intellectual transformations of the first decades of the nineteenth century are interpreted, it is undeniably the case that the turn of the century is a period of major institutional restructuring in the university world of Europe. As pointed out by Sheldon Rothblatt and Lawrence Stone, this is a period when the old universities of Oxford and Cambridge began 'slowly to put part of their house in order'.[22] In the German context, the creation of the new university in Berlin in 1810 as a direct result of an effort at major national reform in the wake of Prussian defeat and occupation in the encounter with Napoleonic France has been the object of an endless stream of studies. The Humboldtian example as a precursor of later developments is certainly open to different interpretations.[23] It is, however, clear that in the latter part of the nineteenth century the University of Berlin came to be the unquestioned model for university reformers from the United States in the West to Japan in the East. It is equally clear that links existed between the late-nineteenth-century achievements of German universities and the institutional developments in the period around the preceding turn of the century.

The partial resurgence of Oxford and Cambridge in the English context occurs at the same time as the demise of universities in the French setting. In the German states, over forty universities existed in the latter half of the eighteenth century, a number far larger than could be found in any other part of Europe. Roughly half of them had to discontinue their activities in the period of the revolutionary and Napoleonic wars.[24] The close ties between universities and government in the German principalities made institutional restructuring all but inevitable in a period of major political turbulence and realignment.[25]

[21] Turner, 'University Reformers', 531.
[22] Stone, 'Social Control', 22. See also Sheldon Rothblatt, 'Failure in Early Nineteenth-Century Oxford and Cambridge', *History of Education*, 11 (1982), 1–21.
[23] Joseph Ben-David, *The Scientist's Role in Society: A Comparative Study* (Englewood Cliffs, NJ, 1971), and *Centers of Learning: Britain, France, Germany, United States* (New York, 1977); Walter P. Metzger, 'Academic Freedom and Scientific Freedom', *Daedalus*, 107 (1978), 93–114; Perkin, 'Historical Perspective'; Ringer, 'The German Mandarins Reconsidered'.
[24] A comprehensive analysis of this development is given in Thomas Ellwein, *Die deutsche Universität. Vom Mittelalter bis zur Gegenwart* (Königstein, 1985), and Collins, 'A Micro-Macro Theory', 58ff is useful.
[25] Turner, 'The Great Transition' and 'University Reformers', and Collins, 'A Micro-Macro Theory', discuss the implications of State-university relationships for the social position of German academics, as does McClelland, *State, Society, and University*. Marc

However, if a challenge to existing institutions in this period was inevitable, the outcome of the restructuring process certainly was not. Alternatives existed, and at least two broad institutional paths of development were possible. One of these was being pursued in the French setting. Universities were superseded as the primary vehicles for technical, administrative, and educational training by special institutions known as *grandes écoles*. Actually, some of these institutions had been founded during the *ancien régime*; but in the revolutionary situation, survival of the new regime and the urgent need for talent proved to be a strong incentive for the creation of more *écoles*. Most notable perhaps was the École polytechnique, founded in 1794 to supply the Revolutionary army with artillery officers. This foundation was followed in the next year by the establishment of the École Normale Supérieure, a school which has subsequently played a crucial role as a republican, not a clerical training ground for teachers and an intellectual elite.[26] On other European countries corresponding objectives were met in a different way, and academies of science were the chosen instruments. These were institutions which had been set up all over Europe in the course of the eighteenth century.

In the German context, the crisis of the universities led to similar thinking, and some reformers were even able to draw on a tradition associated with strong figures like Leibnitz. The head of the Berlin Gymnasium argued that the universities should be abolished,[27] and as late as 1806 a member of the Prussian government, von Massow, made similar suggestions. However, in the important, if brief, period of fundamental reforms in Prussia in the wake of military defeat and foreign occupation, a group of reformers in a more or less uneasy discourse alliance with towering figures of radical German idealist philosophy, Hegel most

Raeff, *The Well-Ordered Police State: Social and Institutional Change Through Law in the Germanies and Russia*, 1600–1800 (New Haven, 1983), is an interesting study of German and Russian developments in the eighteenth and nineteenth centuries in the context of the interventionist absolutist state and its demands for various types of knowledge. For another interesting comparison, this time of French and German developments in the eighteenth century and especially for an overview of the intellectual and institutional background of the Prussian Enlightenment, consult Reill, *The German Enlightenment*, and also Catherine B. A. Behrens, *Society, Government and the Enlightenment: The Experiences of Eighteenth-century France and Prussia* (London, 1985).

[26] For an overview of French developments in the late eighteenth and early nineteenth centuries, see Johan Heilbron, *Over het ontstann van de sociologie*, and 'The Tri-partite Division of French Social Science: A Long-Term Perspective', *Discourses*, ed. Wagner *et al.*

[27] See the preceding note for relevant works. For an overview Eginhard Fabian, 'Die lange Geburt einer Wissenschaftsmetropole 1789–1870', in *Wissenschaft in Berlin: von den Anfängen bis zum Neubeginn nach 1945*, ed. Hubert Laitko *et al.* (Berlin, 1987), 96–171; and Herbert Scurla, *Wilhelm v. Humboldt. Reformator-Wissenschaftler-Philosoph* (Munich, 1984).

prominently, elaborated a scheme for the rejuvenation and reform of the university. It was to be a centre of learning and teaching with wide but also clearly circumscribed limits of autonomy and self-government.

The reformers were a coalition of aristocrats, such as Hardenberg, Humboldt, Stein, and Scharnhorst, and idealist philosophers of a more or less pronounced pro-revolutionary bent – in the 1790s Fichte, Hegel, and Kant must certainly be included in this category. In this particular historical setting, the coalition proved strong enough to at least momentarily overcome the traditional discourse alliance of the preceding century between the cameralist and mercantilist governments of absolutist monarchy on the one hand and the aristocratic high culture of the academies and salons on the other.

There can be little doubt that radical German philosophy helped resurrect the very notion of a university at a time when the university in Europe had been more threatened than perhaps at any time before or afterwards. But for the philosophical efforts of Fichte, Hegel, and Schleiermacher, the efforts of the Humboldt brothers and vom Stein are hardly conceivable. The old Friedrich Meinecke described this as the 'Golden Goethe Age' bestowed upon the German people by a miracle.[28] Goethe himself, however, had the deepest misgivings about the university in Berlin. Even Wilhelm von Humboldt could only bring himself to express a highly conditional approval of the plan to establish a university in a residential capital. Futhermore, he was successful in this endeavour largely by virtue of the fact that the Prussian government had left Berlin for fear of the proximity of French troops, which for a time even occupied the city, and was administering the truncated remainder of the country from the distant province of East Prussia. In a strange way this situation is vaguely reminiscent of Scottish intellectual life 100 years earlier when the highest aristocracy had left Edinburgh for London after political power had moved South and the Scottish Parliament had been abolished. It was in this situation that an alliance was gradually formed between the 'rump establishment' left behind in Edinburgh and reformist intellectual circles on terms very different from those in other parts of Europe. Intellectuals joined clubs and societies and other sociable environments on a much more equal footing with the notables than almost anywhere else.[29]

When the first plans for a new university in Berlin were being drawn up, Wilhelm von Humboldt had been abroad for years, first in France and

---

[28] In Friedrich Meinecke, *Die deutsche Katastrophe* (1946) – in English as *The German Catastrophe* (Boston, 1963).

[29] This process has been described in detail by Phillipson in the works cited. For a recent comparison of Enlightenment developments in Scotland and Prussia, see Robert Wuthnow (ed.), *Communities of Discourse: Ideology and Social Structure in the Reformation, the Enlightenment, and European Socialism* (Cambridge, MA, 1989), 228–64.

Spain and then as the Prussian ambassador to Rome. Fichte – subsequently the first elected rector of the new university – and Schleiermacher had been advertising the need to establish a new institution for years, and Humboldt's predecessor in the ministry for education and culture, von Beyme, claimed that he had been solidly behind the idea of a new foundation for just as long. The fact, however, is that von Humboldt himself was always in a highly precarious position *vis-à-vis* the Prussian government. In 1809 vom Stein was no longer a member of the Cabinet in which Hardenberg remained the only real reformer. Together with a small group of sympathetic spirits in the Ministry of the Interior, Humboldt was able to devise an effective plan for the creation of a new university within a few months in the spring and summer of 1809. With great sensitivity and diplomatic skill, he was able to get royal approval despite deep suspicion on the part of large circles at court.

However, Humboldt's direct involvement with the establishment of the new university was over in less than a year's time, after which he resumed diplomatic service, increasingly pessimistic about the possibilities of safeguarding the interests of enlightenment and national emancipation in the face of mounting pressures for restoration and conservative hegemony in Germany and Europe alike. The fact that conservative circles were able to prevent his appointment to the government later, even when he was by far the most experienced Prussian diplomat and had served as his country's representative at the Congress of Vienna, says something about the fragile nature of his position.

The irony, pointed out by many historians, is of course that the Humboldtian university, inspired by holistic thinking in broad historical cultural categories and informed by a type of philosophy which rejected narrow-minded specialisation, turned out to become the ideal and archetypical home for scientific activities which were, if anything, based on opposite conceptions. The assumptions behind modern scientific thinking are that the historicity of idealist philosophy is at best an impossible dream, and that the distinction between the natural and cultural sciences, a distinction fundamentally alien to late-eighteenth- and early-nineteenth-century science and philosophy, is necessary and valid.

The 'great transition' from the late eighteenth century up until the 1830s evolved on three different but interconnected levels. On the cognitive level, the late eighteenth-century challenge to mechanistic and compositional thinking in favour of organismic and holistic reasoning produced a wave of scholarly, literary, and philosophical activities strongly parallel to the upheavals of the revolutionary restructuring of Europe. These were then gradually superseded by new forms of disciplined and mathematical thinking which were capable of overcoming the pitfalls of earlier formulations and provided more promising research programmes than the often simultaneously vague and overambitious ones of historical and idealist philosophy.[30]

This emerging new 'epistemic regime' entailed a new *social organisation* of science.[31] The professional scientist eventually replaced the learned amateur. Instead of the broad-ranging generalist, there emerged the specialist scholar. Simultaneously there were efforts in the new industrial civilisation to find new applications for knowledge. This led by reaction to the birth in the 1840s of the concept of 'pure science', which implied that the rest of science was not 'pure' but contaminated.[32]

At a third level a new epistemic regime also entailed a new *institutional organisation* and a divergence of national paths which, in spite of the secular processes of industrialisation, scientification, and bureaucratisation which, among others, Rolf Torstendahl has rightly emphasised in his contribution to this volume, came to lead to significantly different organisational patterns for institutions of higher education and scientific activities.

Whereas the cognitive changes, rooted as they were in processes of elaborating and overcoming the legacies of various scholarly traditions, nevertheless are part of the discourse of larger societal-cultural transformations, the institutional changes in Continental Europe were intimately linked, and inevitably so, to the fate and demise of various principalities and states, that is, to the dominant macro-political institutions of the given societies.

[30] Heilbron, 'The Tri-partite Division of French Social Science', 73–92, has highlighted the crucial role of August Comte in laying the foundations for this new epistemic regime, a role possibly more significant than creating the concepts of sociology or positivism. It is important to see, however, that there are also continuities between the German Enlightenment tradition and the gradual overcoming of organistic thinking within natural science. Frederick Gregory, 'Kant's Influence on Natural Scientists in the German Romantic Period', in *New Trends in the History of Science*, ed. R. P. W. Visser *et al.*, 66, observes that

Kant's strongly mechanistic philosophy of natural science not only equipped those who preferred it with a respected means of opposing Schelling's organic philosophy of nature, but it also, through its restricted but steady focus on the phenomena of experience, reinforced reverence for the empirical labors of *practicing* scientists... As *Naturphilosophie* was transformed into unabashed German idealism, the Kantian position appeared more and more viable as the appropriate philosophy for a natural scientist. The Kantian lamp was by no means extinguished during the Romantic Period: but it only began to burn brightly again after mid-century.

[31] I am greatly indebted to Johan Heilbron not only for suggesting this 'neo-Foucaultian' concept but also for many conversations on different aspects of intellectual and institutional change in the period of the great transition in late-eighteenth- and early-nineteenth-century Europe.

[32] As noted for example in Mendelsohn, 'Science', 59ff, a key role in this process was played by the Cambridge philosopher, William Whewell.

The complex interaction of intellectual and institutional developments formed the background against which the whole concept of *Bildung* evolved. This concept, which perhaps should not so easily be translated as 'general education' or the like but rather, and more literally, as 'formation' or even 'imagination in the process of realisation', was constituted within the framework of the historicist and organicist thinking of the period of the great transformation. It reflected broad efforts to come to terms with a period of fundamental change. The University of Berlin was the institutionalised form of *Bildung*, and together they represented an attempt to recreate and reinvigorate national culture after the traumas of military defeat and political disruption. *Bildung* therefore was an heroic effort to overcome the socio-cultural disembeddedness inherent in this situation and to 're-embed', as it were, a re-created national culture in a reformed polity. The university should, in the words of Humboldt, be 'the summit where everything that happens directly in the interest of the moral culture of the nation comes together'.[33] It should, as Frederick Wilhelm III argued, 'regain for the State in the realm of intellectual activities what it had lost in the physical realm' (*um dem Staat auf geistigem Gebiet wieder zu gewinnen, was er auf physischem verloren hat*).

Statements like these may sound like little more than high-flying rhetoric detached from the administrative and political realities of the world, but such a characterisation would be a gross misreading. Rather the statements drew on a powerful, if not predominant, line of thought in public discussion in a highly practical and politically-oriented advocacy for reform. Humboldt himself was, of course, quite familiar with both contemporary German philosophy and with German university life at large. He and his brother Alexander had begun their academic studies at the Prussian University of Frankfurt an der Oder (at the present-day border between Germany and Poland) in October 1787. It was a youthful experience which left both with an unpleasant picture of the German university as pedantic, lifeless, and unimaginative, without intellectual merit, something to be abhorred and avoided. They stayed only until April

---

[33] Wilhelm von Humboldt, *Ueber die innere und äussere Organisation der höheren wissenschaftlichen Anstalten in Berlin, unvollendete Denkschrift, geschrieben 1810 (vielleicht 1809)* – first published 1896 and reprinted in Ernst Anrich (ed.), *Die Idee der deutschen Universität, Die fuenf Grundschriften aus der Zeit ihrer Neubegruendung durch klassischen Idealismus und romantischen Realismus* (Darmstadt, 1956). This volume contains 'the five foundational texts', by Schelling, Fichte, Schleiermacher, Steffens, and von Humboldt. The quotation from Humboldt's *Denkschrift* can be found on page 379 in the volume. The whole text by von Humboldt is reprinted in pp. 379–86. This unfinished text, perhaps the most discussed document in the modern history of universities, is by far the shortest of the five classical texts. It breaks off immediately after a brief sketch of the relationship between the University and the Academy of Sciences and before a discussion of the role of the Academy is to commence under the heading, 'On the Academy' (*Von der Akademie*).

1788. Wilhelm then went to the Hannoverian University of Göttingen, where Alexander followed him in the next year. Founded in 1736, Göttingen was probably the leading German university in the field of natural science, and together with Leiden and Edinburgh, was certainly one of the intellectually liveliest of European universities.

As an experienced high-ranking administrator, Humboldt did not entertain any romantic notions about university professors, whom he described as a group of people invariably inclined towards petty internal controversies. Most fundamentally perhaps, the Humboldtian scheme entailed a decisive break with a type of university which was and to some extent still is prevalent in the English universities but which early on in their history American colleges replaced with a system of strong presidential leadership. It involved the elaboration of a delicate balance of power which was intended to secure that the intellectual freedom of teaching and learning, the *Lehrfreiheit* and *Lernfreiheit*, was safeguarded not only from political incursions and violations but equally from narrow guild-like interests within academia itself.

Thus Humboldt insisted that the professors of the new university of Berlin be appointed by the State and not by the university:

The appointment of university teachers has to be exclusively reserved for the State, and it is surely not a good arrangement to allow the faculties to exercise more influence on that... because in the university, antagonism and controversy are healthy and necessary, and the clashes which arise between the teachers through their work may also inadvertently affect their perspectives.[34]

These strictures reveal that Humboldt was nothing if not a practical reformer. He had a clear vision of the needs of the Prussian State – indeed of all Germany – as also reflected in such subsequent curricular developments as *Juristenprivileg*, i.e., the requirement of a law degree for civil servants.

There was also a close link between these institutional and societal events, the notion of *Bildung*, and the 'invention' of the new cultural community of the nation as a partly real, partly imagined community of cultural-linguistic commonalities and legacies. This community came to achieve real prominence because increasingly it came to be postulated as the proper basis of both political and cultural identity in a Europe where the authority of tradition, after the decades of revolutionary and Napoleonic wars, could never again rely on received or unquestioned acquiescence.[35]

[34] *Ibid.*, 385.
[35] For an interesting discussion of the notions of dis-embedding and re-embedding, see Anthony Giddens, *The Consequences of Modernity* (Cambridge, 1990) and Peter Wagner, 'Liberty and Discipline. Making Sense of Postmodernity; or Once Again towards a

Thus the idea of *Bildung* exerted a profound influence on the key institutional event represented by the rebirth of the university in this period. However it also came to constitute a key component of academic ideology and self-understanding in Continental Europe and Scandinavia. It became an equally prominent if uneasy, not to say incompatible, part of the academic culture of discipline, specialisation, and research from the 1830s onwards. In this context, *Bildung* as discussed by Liedman earlier in this book, came to take on a whole set of new meanings with increasingly attentuated links to the conceptual universe in which it had emerged. It is, perhaps, particularly ironic that the notion of *allgemeine Bildung*, sometimes, as Liedman notes, came to be associated with a kind of superficial polish essential for becoming a member of the upper classes. In Humboldt's notion, *allgemeine Bildung* referred precisely to those features of the formation of the character of a person which could not and should not be defined in terms of a particular social or occupational position.[36] *Allgemeine Bildung* began life as a revolutionary educational idea within the occupational structure of a thoroughly regulated economic and social order, and it was never intended to merely sanctify and legitimate that order.[37]

Rise of the research-oriented university in the modern-nation State

There is a perennial debate about the real significance of the resurrection of the university in the Humboldtian guise for the later development of scientific activities. Thus it has often been argued that 'despite rather than because of the Humboldtian ideal, the German university became the embodiment of the specialized research-oriented ideal and the model for the progressive system of higher education in other advanced societies'.[38]

Sociohistorical Understanding of Modernity', unpublished paper, Princeton Institute for Advanced Study, 1991.

[36] See also Ellwein, *Die deutschen Universität*, 115ff. Hartmut von Hentig complains about the pettiness of current conceptualisations in German higher education policy, 'Verständigung und Verantwortung. Allgemeine Bildung: Ueber die kleinkarierte Behandlung eines grossen Themas', *Sueddeutsche Zeitung* (June 27–28, 1987).

[37] The allusion to Goethe's influence on the idea and development of *Bildung* in relation to universities to be found in such historians as Meinecke does have some substance. Goethe initiated an intellectual relationship with Wilhelm von Humboldt in 1794 which lasted until the poet's death in 1832. Humboldt needed Goethe as a sounding board, for he considered Fichte much too utopian and only gradually did he learn to collaborate with Schleiermacher.

   Actually, because Berlin was not an intellectual centre in his own day, Humboldt would have preferred Halle (Friedrichs-University) to be the major Prussian university. But Halle belonged to the new pro-French kingdom of Westphalia.

[38] Perkin, 'Historical Perspective', 34ff.

Similarly, time and again, it has been pointed out that the connection between the philosophical idealism and radicalism of the generation of thinkers who inspired Humboldt and other aristocratic reformers in early-nineteenth-century Germany and the scientific pre-eminence and productivity of late-nineteenth-century German universities is, at best, a highly tenuous one.[39]

To formulate the problem of influence and descent in these terms is 'Whiggish'. The conceptions of scholarship and scientific work which became the predominant ones in cognitive terms around the 1840s and in institutional terms in the following decades were radically different from those of the earlier periods. Thus the major long-term impact of the Humboldtian reforms was not the preservation of a particular conception of appropriate scientific specialisation but the resurrection, or rather better, the creation of an autonomous institutional setting for intellectual activities which later came to be co-terminous with the modern research-oriented university.

Within this setting, Humboldtian philosophical idealism functioned as an accepted idiom of academic self-understanding, especially in late nineteenth-century Germany. But the type of disciplinary organisation of science and scholarship which gained prominence in the course of the nineteenth century was virtually the antithesis of the unified conception of knowledge characterising idealism in its original phase. This does not mean that idealism was unimportant. What it means is that idealist philosophy served institutional rather than cognitive purposes. In Ringer's somewhat hard-nosed prose, it was 'a tactically sound defence of the autonomy of science, which certainly aided the emergence of the modern research university in nineteenth-century Germany'.[40]

Needless to say, the generations of 'German mandarins' would probably have tended to make the same point in a different terminological guise. The elderly Meinecke did so in 1946 in *The German Catastrophe* when he tried to explain how the golden 'Goethe-age' could have led to the disasters of the power-driven 'Bismarck-age' and the total demise of civilisation in the 'Hitler-age'. When speaking of the nineteenth century, he outlined a historical landscape of slow, then almost imperceptible but in the end irreversible and disastrous decline:

About the middle of the nineteenth century and later it was the high aim of German culture to preserve from this pressure and from its coarsening and deteriorating effect the sacred heritage of the Goethe period – an almost miraculous gift bestowed upon the German people – and at the same time to support strongly what

[39] Ben-David, 'The Scientist's Role', 117ff.
[40] Ringer, 'Mandarins Reconsidered', 21.

seemed vital and fruitful in the demands of the new masses. There was to be a synthesis of intellect and force, of the intellect-building and the state-building factors, and therewith of culture, state and nation. In this synthesis, however, there was a slight preponderance on the side of the new ideas of power and nationalism. Such was the painstaking purpose of a group of intellectual leaders in Germany who are customarily known as the 'classical liberals' and who at the end of the fifties found their organ in the *Preussische Jahrbuecher*.[41]

To someone like Meinecke, with Johann Gustav Droysen as his teacher, the intellectual landscape of increasing specialisation, the material landscape of increasing industrialisation and urbanisation, and the political landscape of the shaping of new powerful nation-states of late nineteenth-century Europe could not be anything but a threat. The best that could be hoped for – and a hope that soon proved to be vain – was a 'silver-age', an uneasy synthesis of intellectual growth and – in the words of Meinecke – 'the Prussian state with its monarchistic-militaristic structure' and 'the higher bourgeois class which was partly oriented towards capitalistic acquisition, partly towards its interests in *Bildung*'. Yet is was in precisely this industrialising, modernising, State-reforming world of the late nineteenth century that the modern university took shape.

It is important to see, as forcefully argued by Torstendahl, that the general features of this process of increasing scientific specialism and professionalism were pervasive and largely independent of a specific national or institutional context. However, it would be a gross misreading of the process of university development to subsume all the different institutional paths under the label of a broad functional evolution, adaptation, and differentiation. Sweeping functionalist generalities are utterly unable to account for the real process of creating and restructuring institutions against the backdrop of particular intellectual, cultural, and institutional traditions which in decisive fashion have altered the shape of modern universities.

In this process of the reform and reconstitution of intellectual institutions, the German universities, and in particular that of Berlin, served as the undisputed international model for university reformers. In Germany itself, as in many other parts of Continental Europe, the rise of the research-oriented university was largely coterminous with the formation of a modern nation-state. Universities came to be key institutions both for knowledge production and for strengthening a sense of national and cultural identity. As pointed out by scholars such as Liedman and Torstendahl, there was a high degree of national and institutional self-consciousness on the part of university representatives in this period.

---

[41] Meinecke, *German Catastrophe*, 9.

Thus there is a deep tension between a universal development towards scientific specialisation on the one hand and an increasing emphasis on the particular role of universities in constituting key institutions in particular national contexts on the other. The duality of this development can neither be captured in terms of a broad functional-evolutionary account, nor through a minute historical account of the peculiarities of individual institutions in different countries and contexts. What is required is an analysis which is sensitive to institutional and intellectual traditions in particular cases, yet is able to show how the specific features are constituted and reconstituted by university reformers in the wake of a much more general development across the Western world at particular historical junctures. Such an analysis is the more urgent since university reformers and spokesmen themselves have tended to be highly conscious of the argumentative uses of university history. Time and again, proposals for reform have been bolstered by reference to the achievements, past and present, of a given university system.

A good case in point is provided by the leading German university historian at the turn of the century, Friedrich Paulsen, who was fully aware and proud of the exemplary role of German universities. His contribution to the German volume presented at the 1893 university exhibition in Chicago is typical of the tone of the time:

France has just started to forge its separate faculties into real universities; and England seeks to reconstitute university education from its fragmentation into the different Colleges. Up until now some of the most distinguished American universities have perhaps been the most successful in terms of implementing the German unity of scientific research and scientifically based education.[42]

This German self-consciousness was mirrored in the efforts of university reformers in other countries. Even in the case of France, a country with a tradition for the organisation of research and higher education vastly different from that of Germany, it has been noted that 'university reform during the Third Republic was an exceedingly complex process'. However,

If there was a single continuing thread in this complex story, it was the struggle to expand the social role of higher studies in France, with German universities serving as a model. Indeed, for much of the nineteenth century, German universities and academics enjoyed incomparably greater status than did their French counterparts.[43]

---

[42] Friedrich Paulsen, 'Wesen und geschichtliche Entwicklung der deutschen Universitäten', in *Die deutschen Universitäten. Fuer die Universitätsausstellung in Chicago 1893*, ed. W. Lexis (Berlin, 1893), 10 (my translation); Paulsen, *Die deutschen Universitäten und das Universitätsstudium* (Berlin, 1902). For Meinecke, see also H. Stuart Hughes, *Consciousness and Society. The Reconstruction of European Social Thought, 1890–1930* (New York, 1958), 229–48.   [43] Weisz, *Emergence*, 369.

The role of German universities as exemplary institutions was extremely important in the American debate as well. One effect of this influence was a growing emphasis on new settings for research and graduate training. Such institutional innovations were grafted onto colleges and universities mainly devoted to the provision of a liberal education or to a professional training in the older professions of law or medicine or – as in the land grant colleges – to providing qualifications in agriculture, mining, and engineering. Sometimes, however, entirely new institutions were created where the research-orientation came to play a guiding role for the institution as a whole. Johns Hopkins, established in 1876, was the first American institution of this type. It was – in the words of Abraham Flexner, a leading American university reformer of the early twentieth century and former student at Johns Hopkins less than ten years after its creation,

the nearest thing to a university and practically nothing else that America has yet possessed ... Instruction proceeded, as in Germany, through lectures to larger groups and seminars in which the professor and a limited number of students pursued intensively advanced studies and research, methods now in common use in all American graduate schools.[44]

When Flexner, in the late 1920s, looked back upon the rise of the research-oriented university in the United States, he saw this diffusion of a German model of research and graduate training as a key element, 'the most meritorious part of the American university'. However, it was an element he perceived to be far from firmly instituted and still 'in imminent danger of being overwhelmed' by 'overcrowding, vagaries especially in the fields of education and sociology, and incomprehensible institutes' within a higher education system which 'catered thoughtlessly and excessively to fleeting, transient, and immediate demands' and gave 'degree courses that belong in technical and vocational schools, not in a university – not even in a sound secondary school'.[45]

It is easy to see, with the benefit of hindsight, that Flexner grossly underestimated the achievements of the American research universities.[46] Some would argue that he was – in the words of Clark Kerr – 'too respectful of the German university ... [and] did not realize how many functions can be combined within a single university ... did not understand

---

[44] Flexner, *Universities*, 73.   [45] *Ibid.*

[46] Possibly the most comprehensive overview of the history of American research universities in the early part of this century is given in Geiger, *To Advance Knowledge*. His two articles, 'The Home of Scientists: A Perspective on University Research', and 'Hierarchy and Diversity in American Research Universities', appear in *The University Research System*, ed. Wittrock and Elzinga, 53–74 and 77–100. They contain discussions of more recent developments in the light of historical experiences as well as classical conceptions of the role of a university.

324   *Björn Wittrock*

that quantity and quality can be combined'.[47] It was exactly the kinds of combinations and permutations of different institutional traditions and models which Flexner deplored that came into being in the United States. Thus far from a Wilhelminian-style imperial research university transposed to 'Stateless' America, only some parts of the German research-oriented university influenced reformers. The result was that graduate training and research, along with liberal education and professional education, all came to characterise American higher education institutions, either in the form of single-campus institutions or multi-campus federations.

Much the same type of reconstitution and restructuring occurred in other countries. Thus, no matter how appealing the German model of a research-oriented university may have been to French reformers, it is quite obvious that their innovations were, at best, only half successful:

The reform movement's most conspicuous failure, of course, was its inability to create universities that broke completely with the existing system of professional faculties. The reasons are clear enough. If everyone had something to gain from a nominal change to institutions called universities, the administration's desire to create only a few large and unified educational centers conflicted with many vested interests. Local elites and academics... were threatened with a reduction in status and privileges... The powerful *grandes écoles*, of course, had even more to lose.[48]

The process of institutional transformation was a highly complex one in Britain as well. The modern university emerged in Britain in the same period in the late nineteenth century as it did elsewhere. This transformation, however, had as its backdrop a complex threefold development. First of all, in the mid nineteenth century, there had been a renewed emphasis on the importance of a liberal education free from narrow considerations of utility and vocational interests. John Henry Newman was the most articulate proponent of this notion of a liberal education as 'gentleman's knowledge', but it was an ideal which exerted a powerful influence on British intellectual life generally. John Stuart Mill's well-known statement in 1867 that 'universities are not intended to teach the knowledge required to fit men for some special mode of gaining their livelihood. Their object is... to make... capable and cultivated human beings', is just one of many expressions of this widespread view of the proper role of a university.[49]

However, it is important to see that this view was in many ways a forceful articulation of an age-old set of opinions about the primary task of the colleges of the old British universities, namely to form the characters

---

[47] Kerr, 'Remembering Flexner', xvii, ff.   [48] Weisz, *Emergence*, 374.
[49] Cited in Rothblatt, *The Revolution of the Dons: Cambridge and Society in Victorian England* (1968; Cambridge, 1981), 248.

and minds of their often very young students rather than to, say, expand the domains of knowledge beyond their present boundaries. It is equally important that many of the proponents of this type of liberal education may have advocated a form of detachment from the values of modern industrial life and civilisation and repudiation of the ideals of professional training. However, the character formation provided came to be intimately linked to the formation of the political and administrative elite not only of Britain but of the British empire. There is actually – as shown by Rothblatt and Reba Soffer – a close tie between elite higher education on the one hand and the growing political and administrative demands of the British polity on the other:

In the last quarter of the nineteenth century, the college teacher transformed Oxford and Cambridge into domestic communities capable of molding their members to a degree never attained before by the earlier universities, by the home or by the church. The universities largely succeeded in creating a homogeneous governing class because they organized liberal education, in all its social, intellectual and moral aspects, within the college... After the eighteen-fifties, the universities set out to be places of intensive training for the eventual governance of the outside world. But they also remained privileged retreats into personal and peer satisfactions which guarded them against the conflicting imperatives characteristic of ordinary life.[50]

Many scholars have highlighted the persistence of these educational ideals and their continuing deep-seated influence on British social and political life. Don Price's well-found phrase, 'Specializing for Breadth', nicely captures the duality of elite liberal education.[51] These university developments were also parallelled by changes in the public schools where from the 1850s onwards a strong emphasis on physical education and sports not only served to effectively discipline unruly adolescents but to form the character of members of the military corps and a civil service which was to serve as an imperial ruling class.

A second feature of the British development occurring in the second half of the nineteenth century was a renewed emphasis even in the old universities of Oxford and Cambridge on the role of universities in preparing students for a professional career. This process – which entailed a deep-seated restructuring of the universities, what Rothblatt has identified as 'the revolution of the dons' – involved the professionalisation of science and scholarship. One consequence of this development at

---

[50] Reba Soffer, 'The Modern University and National Values, 1850–1930', *Historical Research*, 60 (June 1987), 169ff.

[51] Don K. Price, 'A Yank at Oxford: Specializing for Breadth', in *The American Scholar* (Spring 1986), 195–207. See also Cyril Smith, 'Networks of Influence', in *Social Sciences*, ed. Wagner *et al.*

Cambridge was that new schools for medicine and engineering were established.[52] Another one was not only the intellectual but also material manifestations of a new scientific professionalism. Museums, lecture halls, and most importantly perhaps, new laboratories became an integral and important part of university life.[53] This is what Paulsen noted when he spoke about the re-emergence of the university as a real entity in England. However, he failed to see that these developments did not mean that the colleges were being superseded. Rather it meant that the collegiate and the university parts of Oxford and Cambridge were complementary and that liberal education was but one of many types of educational practices. It was a practice, furthermore, which was not so much fitted to professional requirements as constituting a specific form of training for the members of the future national elite, a form based on the duality of detachment and elite integration. A third development refers to the whole new set of institutions of higher education that emerged in Britain in the latter part of the nineteenth century. These institutions became known – but only after the turn of the century – as 'civic universities' to highlight their role as manifestations of the civic pride of the different towns and cities in which they were located. Scholars often contrast these institutions to Oxford and Cambridge and describe them in terms of their commitment to the promotion of more professional, not to say vocational, types of higher education.[54] Sometimes, however, it is rather their distance from utilitarian

---

[52] See Rothblatt, *Dons*, for a detailed study of this process.

[53] A suggestive analysis of the changing physical shape and architecture of English universities in the late nineteenth century is given by Sophie Forgan, 'The Architecture of Science and the Idea of a University', *Studies in History and Philosophy of Science*, 20 (December 1989), 405–34. Interestingly enough, even though British higher education institutions are usually said to be less influenced by German models than American ones, the influence was certainly apparent in laboratories, both in their construction and in the teaching carried out therein:
With regard to general teaching at a university level, British scientists carefully studied the large German laboratories...Germany seems to have been regarded as the fount of all knowledge as far as labs were concerned. Even Kelvin, who loyally promoted the antiquity of Scottish labs, was obliged to pay homage to Liebig.
(Forgan, 'Architecture', 422 and note 37 on the same page).

[54] For a fascinating account of the evolution of a field of knowledge in terms of its actual teaching in British universities in the late nineteenth century, see Keith Tribe, 'Political Economy to Economics via Commerce: The Evolution of British Academic Economics 1860–1920', in *Discourses*, ed. Wagner *et al.*, 273–302. For an historical analysis of the development of economic reasoning in the German context in the late eighteenth century and early nineteenth century, see Tribe, *Governing the Economy: The Reformation of German Economic Discourse, 1750–1840* (Cambridge, 1988). The American development in this field in the nineteenth century is discussed in the various contributions to William J. Barber (ed.), *Breaking the Academic Mould: Economists and American Higher Learning in the Nineteenth Century* (Middletown, CT, 1988). Mention should also be made of Soffer's careful research on the teaching of history in English universities in the late

aims that scholars emphasise in order to stress their connections to traditions of education associated with the prestigious traditional university – connections of which their proud provincial supporters boasted. Sophie Forgan has convincingly argued that in practice these institutions encompassed a range of different educational traditions and ideals, involving liberal education, professional education, and research. Furthermore, as already indicated, the very term 'civic university' is a slight misnomer:

> Most institutions were heavily dependent on patronage and their ability to tap local resources, which was not always easy... Few town councils initially considered such an institution would be an ornament to the town, a view no doubt reinforced by the shabby premises many institutions started off in – Leeds in converted shops; Liverpool in a lunatic asylum; and Durham-Newcastle in the attics and cellars of the Coal Chambers... In short, such costly enterprises, doubtful of success, should not be regarded as ornaments of civic culture in their early years.[55]

Historically, the emergence of a range of new institutions in conjunction with reforms in the old English universities led to a situation where several traditional missions of the English universities, including their emphasis on a liberal education, were retained and even strengthened but nevertheless – in Rothblatt's words – it became 'apparent that character formation and the ideal of a liberal education could only be one of several functions of a university in national education'.[56] This was equally true of Cambridge and Oxford and of the new 'civic' universities. In all types of institutions, old and new, there was also a clear recognition that professional training and professional scientific activities in disciplined form were integral parts of a modern university.

This confluence of different missions was not only a matter of educational ideals and practices. It also had an immediate influence on the physical shape of a university – whether ideally conceived as a scholarly temple, a detached semi-monastical setting, or as secularised institutions that, in accordance with the industrial machine-age that served as the ultimate backdrop for their very support, not to say existence, represented factory-like large-scale teaching machines.

At the turn of the century all ideals met and confronted each other, resulting in universities which both architecturally and institutionally

nineteenth and early twentieth century ('The Modern University'). For a comprehensive study of the evolution of the social sciences in Britain in this period, see also her *Ethics and Society: The Revolution in the Social Sciences 1870–1914* (Berkeley, 1978). A comprehensive study of the sociology of academic careers in Britain, which includes governance and administration in historical context, is Albert H. Halsey and Martin A. Trow, *The British Academics* (London, 1971). [55] Forgan, 'Architecture', 411.
[56] Rothblatt, *Dons*, 250.

encompassed and reconstituted a variety of different educational traditions
and values. This shaping of the modern research-oriented university
cannot be captured in terms of a simple functional response to a secular
process of industrialisation and differentiation. There is no way of
accounting for the vastly different patterns of institutionalisation which
emerged in different national settings. Nor can this process be reduced to
a question of mere national styles or educational ideals and cultures. It can
only be described as a process in which individuals actively strove to
realise, resurrect, or assert educational programmes and visions of higher
education, but always against the background of a whole set of well-
entrenched institutional legacies and social practices. Some of them could
be resuscitated, but others had become hopelessly outmoded.

In this process of constitution and restructuring, Germany – or rather a
perception of the Berlin university with its heavy emphasis on research and
research training – came to serve as an exemplar for university reformers
all over the world. Ironically, and as already pointed out, the original
philosophical underpinning of the university once conceived by the
Humboldt brothers was an institution vastly and irrevocably different
from the Friedrich-Wilhelms-University of late-nineteenth-century Berlin.
German scholars such as Max Weber were fully conscious of this fact and
actually perceived – at precisely the moment when the Berlin university
was most admired and cherished, not least by American scholars and
reformers – that an alternative model of a modern research-oriented
university was already present, namely the American enterprise-like
university. The German university was facing a deep dilemma.

This dilemma might perhaps be expressed as the realisation of the
inevitability of ever-increasing specialisation in both cognitive and
institutional terms. This had concomitant tendencies toward an enterprise-
like organisation, or – to use Weber's expression – a 'state-capitalist
enterprise'. On the other hand there was also a sense that the Humboldtian
university was truly different from purely professional schools or research
laboratories. It had, in the final instance, an ability to be a real community
of teachers and students. Humboldt had once expressed this by emphasising that in contrast to the situation in a specialised or vocational
school, the university teacher's role was not to transmit ready-made pieces
of knowledge but to share with students a quest for knowledge and to join
with them in serving science. The university should also approximate the
vision of a community which would be 'the summit where all that concerns
the moral culture of the nation comes together'. Paulsen regarded 'the
German university' as being exactly that, deriving its ultimate strength
from the fact that it was able to attract 'the leading spirits' (*die fuehrenden
Geister*) and that these intellectually distinguished scholars maintained

direct communication with young students. To Weber, however, the assertion of the desirability of such a relationship was no guarantee of its possibility in an age of growing specialism and bureaucracy. Weber, much like his contemporary Meinecke and much like leading scholars in later generations such as Habermas, was caught on the horns of this dilemma. Finally all he could do was forcefully highlight the problem rather than provide a clear-cut solution.

As already mentioned, the University of Berlin came to occupy an outstanding position in the late nineteenth- and early twentieth centuries. To this very day, the pre-Nazi University of Berlin can still boast of more Nobel prizes than any other institution in the world. However, the universities in Germany were not just intellectually important. They also played a significant part in the process leading to the expansion of the State's administrative capacities. Even in less centralised America, the State grew stronger and more interested in its higher education institutions. In the late nineteenth century, the American Federal State underwent a major transformation from – to use Stephen Skowronek's terms – a State of courts and parties to a State which, no matter how unwillingly and hesitantly, had undergone major reforms and increases in both its public administrative capacities and its armed forces. It too had a growing capacity to intervene, often enough inadvertently and reactively, in the promotion and governance of the economy of the nation.[57]

In the case of Germany, it has been convincingly and repeatedly argued that the pre-eminence of German researchers in the fields of the natural and technical sciences was an important prerequisite for Germany's rise to an internationally leading role in a number of branches of industry.[58] Similarly, it is clear that German legal scholarship, notably the doctrines of

[57] Stephen Skowronek, *Building a New American State: The Expansion of National Administrative Capacities: 1877–1920* (New York, 1982). Also Peter Manicas, *A History and Philosophy of the Social Sciences* (Oxford, 1987), particularly chapters 10–12, as well as his 'The Social Science Disciplines: The American Model', in *Discourses*, ed. Wagner et al., 45–71.

[58] These developments had, as already mentioned, an effect on institution building in other countries as well. It has been observed that the Japanese development towards 'techno-nationalism' in the late nineteenth century was heavily dependent on close interaction between national research institutes, governmental agencies, and emerging private industrial enterprises. In this process the Prussian *Chemisch-Technische Versuchsanstalt* served as one important model – see Miwao Matsumoto's review of Chikatoshi Kamatani's work (in Japanese), 'The Road to Techno-Nationalism: Japanese Modernization and National Research Institutes from the Meiji Era', in *Historia Scientiarum: International Journal of the History of Science Society of Japan*, 38 (November 1989), 75–80; and Miwao Matsumoto, 'The Structure of Technology Transfer in the Japanese Shipbuilding Industry in the First Decade of the 20th Century: The Navy Connection', unpublished paper presented at the International Sociological Association Twelfth World Congress, Madrid, 9–13 July, 1990.

legal positivism, supplied the central bureaucracy of the newly united nation with both its ideological underpinning and the instruments for effectively regulating and administrating the new Reich.[59] German universities were also able to breed that vast group of prominent policy intellectuals who constituted the backbone of the *Bildungsbürgertum*, the German Mandarins, to use Ringer's term. Charles McClelland, among others, has documented the rapid growth of scientific institutions in Wilhelminian Germany. During the period between the Franco-Prussian War and World War I, between 150 and 200 new research institutes were formed as part of direct State action. Many of them were models for reformers in other countries. Furthermore, there was a sharp increase in the number of students enrolled in German universities. This number more than doubled between 1870 and 1900 and nearly doubled once again between the turn of the century and the outbreak of World War I in 1914 when the figures exceeded 60,000.[60]

However, around the turn of the century the corresponding figures for the United States were more than six times larger and increasing at least at the same rate as in Germany. As in Germany (or Britain), America's emergence as a great international power was in some respects connected to the restructuring of its universities. The modern research-oriented universities, both private and public, appeared, and their leadership fell into the hands of what might be termed large-scale educational entrepreneurs. American academic leaders were attracted to the management styles of business firms, and ties between industrial and academic elites were made on a scale previously unknown. Older traditions of liberal and medical and legal education – often with roots in the ancient universities of England and Scotland – survived to mix with research seminars and laboratories of German inspiration. But German influence notwithstanding, the end result both in institutional and cognitive terms was a far cry from what existed in Central Europe. Even the disciplinary organisation of the cognitive universe of professional scholarship, which was in large measure a legacy of the German university, was developed to a degree of specialisation far exceeding Germany itself.

One possibility was not open to German-trained American academics. Obviously they could never hope to acquire the high status of a civil

---

[59] For an excellent overview, see Wagner, *Sozialwissenschaften und Staat*.
[60] See McClelland, *State, Society, and University*. Also his 'Professionalization and Higher Education in Germany', in *The Transformation of Higher Learning 1860–1930*, ed. Konrad H. Jarausch (Chicago, 1983; originally published in Stuttgart in 1983 as volume 13 of *Historisch-Sozialwissenschaftliche Forschungen*). This volume as a whole represents a systematic effort to describe in consistent, and often enough quantitative categories the transformation of higher education in the four countries of England, Germany, Russia, and the United States.

servant in a strongly State-centred society. In Germany the professors were not members of a legal 'free' profession but were (and remain) public-sector *Beamten*, with all the rights and obligations this entailed. The same has been the situation in Sweden, where to this day the professors are customarily appointed by 'the King in Council', or to use the language of the 1974 constitution, the Cabinet. American scholars, unable to emulate the status of their German professors, instead sought their prestige through voluntary professional associations divided along clearly-defined disciplinary lines. For better or for worse, corresponding divisions did not fully materialise in the European context until well after the Second World War.

To recapitulate, the 'idea' of a university was resurrected at the turn of the nineteenth century, despite the competition of other kinds of institutions – professional schools on the one hand and academies and even literary salons on the other. Regarded by rivals as antiquated and obsolete, the university returned as the home of modern research and in so many ways became the axial institution of the modern world. Internally, however, deep-seated tensions in the very conception and operation of the university also existed, as well as a widening gulf between the generally acknowledged models of such institutions as they had developed in Germany. The newly emerging practices of the American institutions were – although largely unrecognised by their practitioners at the time – destined to overtake the German universities as leading international influences already early in the twentieth century.

Expansion and fragmentation: higher education in the age of the great programmes

The essays in this volume clearly bring out the crucial role of the universities in the process of strengthening the industrial and technological capabilities of new nation-states, of providing them with competent administrative and technical personnel, and in serving as the loci for cultural discourses which helped make the world of modernity, of industrialism and urbanism, intelligible and meaningful. These different aspects of the modern university have been captured in such notions as liberal education and *allgemeine Bildung*, of professional education, and of research. Yet at least rhetorically, there was remarkable agreement on the proper role of a university across national boundaries. Somehow, a Cambridge historian of Methodist upbringing such as Herbert Butterfield, a German scholar of a classical national-liberal persuasion such as Meinecke, or for that matter, Weber, or a Swedish Social Democrat like Myrdal all seemed to cherish cultural values concerning the university and its appropriate functioning which were not only compatible but largely identical.[61] The university for them is a place for genuine discourse and non-manipulative interaction. That in fact is its ultimate rationale.[62]

Such international agreement on the purpose of a university lasted long after 1945. Thus on the eve of the harshest political controversy in Sweden for decades to come, that over a 'free' or a 'planned' economy in the late 1940s, Myrdal – then a member of the Cabinet as well as a professor at

---

[61] As already mentioned, *The German Catastrophe* represents an effort by a major representative of the classical tradition of German high culture to come to terms with the disastrous events of his recent past. The dilemmas inherent in translating such interpretations into institutional realities in the immediate post-war period is vividly illustrated by the choices and commitments made by different representatives of the world of classical learning (the German Mandarins). For two different perspectives on the early post-war history of higher learning in Berlin, see Hubert Laitko, 'Befreiung – Besinnung – Neubeginn. 1945–1949', in *Wissenschaft in Berlin*, ed. Laitko *et al.*, 594–691, and James F. Tent, *The Free University of Berlin: A Political History* (Bloomington, 1988), 1–176. In this period Meinecke, at the age of 86 and despite ill health, considered it his obligation to accept the nomination to the post of *Rektor* of the new Free University of Berlin. Another 'mandarin', the classicist Johannes Stroux, served as *Rektor* of the resurrected Berlin University, renamed Humboldt-Universität. Even under harsh Soviet and communist pressure, he tried to preserve some of the basic features of free intellectual life.

The dilemmas were perhaps most clearly illustrated in the person of Eduard Spranger, the renowned pedagogue and philosopher. Spranger had been a student of Wilhelm Dilthey and represented the very core of German philosophical idealism. During the war he had – like Stroux and Werner Heisenberg – been a member of the so-called Wednesday Society, a circle of sixteen distinguished intellectuals, civil servants, and members of the military, several of whom had links to the groups behind the attempt on Hitler's life on 20 July 1944. (The origins of the *Mittwochgesellschaft* of Berlin are discussed in Behrens, *Society, Government and the Enlightenment*, and Dieter Hoffman and Wolfgang Schlicker, 'Wissenschaft unter dem braunen Stiefel', in *Wissenschaft in Berlin*, ed. Laitko *et al.*, 587. See also the relevant passages by Liedman in chapter 2 of this volume.) Spranger was imprisoned and subjected to harsh interrogation by the Gestapo in the aftermath of those events, but he was eventually released. Remaining in Berlin, almost immediately after the fall of the Nazi regime he assumed a key role in the efforts to resurrect the University, which he wanted to be a collegial institution with a heavy emphasis on teaching. As the first but provisional *Rektor* of the about-to-be-opened Berlin University, he worked energetically to solve immense practical, intellectual, and ethical tasks, such as the budget, suitable locations for the university, and assembling a de-Nazified faculty. He made rapid progress but almost immediately found himself in the middle of disagreements by the occupying powers over Cold War policies. He received little or no support from the Western allies. A main question was whether the Berlin University should be under four-nation control or under that of the Soviet-dominated central education authority in the Soviet sector and zone. Spranger was never able to establish real support with the key higher education official in the American zone, Edward Hartshorne, a former student of Meinecke's and later professor of sociology at Harvard. Apparently he was able to satisfy none of the contending parties. The Americans arrested him in July 1945, and the Soviets removed him from office in the following October. A fascinating account appears in Tent, chapter one, and from a very different perspective in Laitko, 'Befreiung'.

[62] Butterfield, *The Universities and Education Today. The Lindsay Memorial Lectures* (London, 1962), 3ff; Paulsen, 'Wesen', and *Die deutschen Universitaten*; Jürgen Habermas, 'The Idea of a University – Learning Processes', in *New German Critique*, 41 (Spring-Summer 1987), 3–22.

what was still the private Stockholm university college – passionately pleaded not only for increased resources to the universities but also for the protection of their autonomy and academic freedom:

Research and higher education are the sources of national culture...The newly aroused interest in some quarters for the practical application of science must not be allowed to conceal the fact that science itself like all the rest of our culture depends on the existence at our universities and colleges of free research activities, conducted with an interest in the search for truth and unaffected by immediate utilitarian interests. We must step forward to protect basic research...We must also guard and support the humanities. They nurture the deeper cultural values that are the soul of national culture. I for one, hope and believe that the socialist · labor movement, which is now taking over the decisive political power in society, will feel its identity with the ideals of humanity and will see to it that our research will not have a short-term utilitarian orientation.[63]

It is difficult to imagine that this passionate plea for university autonomy was written by someone who had little interest in preserving autonomy for other spheres of social activity, and perhaps most notably those concerned with the economy. It is even more difficult to imagine that Myrdal was the major policy intellectual of a political party which two decades *after* it had given up any serious idea of far-reaching plans for the economy nevertheless introduced one of the most comprehensive policies for the restructuring of a higher education system ever undertaken in Europe. This was, furthermore, a restructuring which had as its almost exclusive guiding principle exactly those types of short-term utilitarian ambitions which Myrdal had cautioned against and where the very mention of 'deeper cultural values' would have resulted in sneers of incomprehension and demands for 'bread and butter' policies and short-term labour market relevance.

True enough, the Second World War had convincingly demonstrated the immense direct applicability of research findings. Thereby, as noted by several scholars, signs emerged which heralded if not the end then at least a threat to the long period of academically self-organised knowledge production which had been ushered in by the creation of the École polytechnique in France and the Berlin university in Germany.[64] Initially, however, representatives of academia proved highly successful in accommodating the new research. The United States was the undisputed leading country in this development. Far from being threatened by the new developments, American research universities were greatly strengthened

---

[63] Myrdal, *Universitetsreform*, 28–30 (my translation).
[64] Jerome R. Ravetz, *Scientific Knowledge and its Social Problems* (Oxford, 1971, and Harmondsworth, 1973), 37ff. I am indebted to Peter Weingart for calling this book to my attention in his unpublished paper, 'The End of Academia? The Social Organization of Knowledge', Science Studies Unit, University of Bielefeld, 1988.

by public approval. One major reason for this relatively smooth accommodation was the fact that increasing resources were channelled
through a system of grants which was entirely compatible with the basic
operating mode of the university research system.[65] This system was based
on peer-review, and the newly-founded 'research council', the National
Science Foundation, served as an important supporting and coordinating
body at the federal level. Thus the professional ethos of academic science
was strengthened rather than undermined, and in the post-World-War II
era the American university system emerged as the undisputed model for
university reformers across the world. In Germany the Kaiser-Wilhelm-
Gesellschaft – resurrected after 1945 as the Max-Planck-Gesellschaft –
had played a somewhat analogous if quite different role earlier in the
century as a collection of highly prestigious basic research institutes
connected to but independent from universities.

Thus the growing role of research did not spell the end of academic
science but rather its efflorescence. Science as 'the endless frontier' held the
promise of on-going expansion. Science as a source of wealth and power
helped underpin the prestige and position of the research universities.
Gradually, this was also reflected in a re-definition of public policies for
research and development everywhere in the modern world. The industrial-
nation consortium called the Organisation for Economic Co-operation
and Development (OECD), with origins in the Marshal Plan of the
immediate post-war period, was established in Paris in 1960 and served as
an important forum for discussions on the crucial relation of research to
economic growth and innovation.

In the 1960s and 1970s, higher education itself became a key concern for
policy-makers in all Western countries. In overall enrolment, government
expenditure, the number of institutions, and staff size, the higher education
systems of Western Europe and North America at least doubled and often
tripled or quadrupled within a period of less than a decade and a half.[66] In
short, growth was phenomenal, but it was also historically different.
Policy-makers and scholars alike have tried to grasp the significance of the
transformation. Martin Trow called it a 'sea change' from elite to mass
higher education eventually leading to universal higher education.[67]

[65] Argued by Price, 'Endless Frontier or Bureaucratic Morass?', *Daedalus*, 107 (1978),
75–92.
[66] An excellent overview of this development is given in Clark Kerr, *The Great Transformation in Higher Education 1960–1980* (Albany, 1991).
[67] Trow has analysed these features of modern higher education with unusual sensitivity and
conceptual imagination in a series of articles: 'Reflections on the Transition from Mass to
Universal Higher Education', *Daedalus*, 99 (Winter 1970); 'The Expansion and
Transformation of Higher Education', in *International Review of Education* (February
1972); *Problems in the Transition from Elite to Mass Higher Education* (University of
California, Berkeley, Institute of International Studies Reprint 444, 1974); 'The Public

Essentially what observers saw was an increasing *diversification* within higher education as a whole. 'Higher education' became a comprehensive term embracing all kinds of different establishments, each fulfilling important societal functions in a mutually-dependent universe of institutions. Colleges of further education co-existed with institutes for advanced graduate training and research; vocational schools sat side-by-side with well-endowed institutions still in the business of elite education. In a growing number of institutions, many of what were once rival forms of education were comprehended within the same institution.

This process of increasing diversity, of the emergence of the modern multiversity, to use Clark Kerr's fortuitous neologism, was much more of an American than a European phenomenon. One reason for this was that American higher education had always been characterised by the confluence of different educational practices. The early colonial colleges followed the curricular lead of Oxford and Cambridge, but Scottish influences followed. Lay control (borrowed from the English law of charities) and presidential leadership in particular were distinctly American features, replacing the guild-like governance of Oxbridge, although at one point in its history the University of Edinburgh had 'lay' leadership when it was virtually governed by the town council.

In the late nineteenth century, the land-grant colleges and universities had added a strong practical dimension of training and service to society to more familiar traditions, but so had the new ideals of research and research training. At the same time, another component was added to this system, namely the graduate school and the idea that higher education was the natural home of science and scientists. Inspired by the example of German universities, research and specialism nevertheless took different shape in the American setting. Instead of the German single-professorial chair system, for example, multi-professorial departments were created.

It is impossible to exaggerate the significance of the partly inadvertent and unplanned confluence of different educational ideas and traditions. Ralf Dahrendorf has recently reminded present-day reformers and politicians of 'the fact that with the mountains of literature and lakes of commission reports in recent decades nothing of comparable significance has been produced since'. Yet, as Dahrendorf also stresses,

and Private Lives of Higher Education', *Daedalus*, 104 (1975), 115–27; 'Elite Higher Education: An Endangered Species?', *Minerva*, 14 (1976), 355–376. See also David Riesman, Joseph Gusfield, and Zelda Gamson, *Academic Values and Mass Education: The Early Years of Oakland and Monteith* (Garden City, New Jersey, 1970); and the delightful account of efforts to re-create the small scale and intimacy of a traditional college environment in a modern multiversity at the University of California, Santa Cruz, as described by Riesman and Gerald Grant in a chapter in their volume, *The Perpetual Dream: Reform and Experiment in the American College* (Chicago, 1978).

the effect of this change was by no means immediate. For several decades yet, continental European – and again, especially German – universities (and technical universities) remained places of innovation as well as superior education. But when the great expansion of higher education began, the American hybrid turned out to be uniquely appropriate.[68]

But a different note had already been sounded. To many of the late-nineteenth- and early-twentieth-century American reformers, the inter-mingling of quite diverse educational traditions and ideals was an imperfection, a regrettable deformation which prevented the proper ideals of higher learning from permeating the institutions of the New World. Thus in 1930 it had still been possible for a leading American university reformer such as Flexner to write that 'neither Columbia, nor Harvard, nor Johns Hopkins, nor Chicago, nor Wisconsin is really a university, for none of these possesses unity of purpose or homogeneity of constitution'. In this respect they were, in his view, not up to the high standards of a real university of the neo-Humboldtian model of late nineteenth-century Berlin. They were not 'organisms' but 'administrative aggregations', full of 'trivial courses, trivial chairs, trivial publications, ridiculous research', catering to 'fleeting, transient and immediate demands' and the purported needs of 'make-believe professions'. Not even the oldest university, Harvard, could be a real university of the German type unless it rid itself of its business school. A Boston School of Business could function like a *Handelshochschule* and cater to whatever narrowly professional and utilitarian ends it wished. Never, however, should it be allowed to thwart the pursuit of pure knowledge and truth.

In the United States of the 1940s and 1950s, such an attitude appeared hopelessly backward. The massive utilisation of research in the war effort constituted a forceful practical rejoinder to Flexner. Vannevar Bush, who had played a prominent role during the war as Director of the Office of Scientific Research and Development (OSRD) and afterwards became president of the Massachusetts Institute of Technology (MIT), coined the new suggestive formula, 'Science – the Endless Frontier', the name of an OSRD report. In these years the foundation was being laid for a new type of science policy which would respect the value of the autonomy of science while also recognising its practical potential. A major recommendation of the OSRD report which bore fruit was the creation of the National Science Foundation in 1950. Later came the National Institutes of Health. All of these developments had implications for the social sciences, and their changing foci were highlighted by titles such as the 'behavioral sciences' and the 'policy sciences'.

[68] Ralf Dahrendorf, 'Education for a European Britain' (the Edward Boyle Memorial Lecture, June 5, 1991).

On a theoretical level, the vague echoes of German idealist philosophy resonating through Flexner's rhetoric had never been very compatible with the pervasive pragmatism dominating the American intellectual scene throughout most of the nineteenth and twentieth centuries. In the 1940s, however, the self-understanding of American university representatives was greatly bolstered by the emergence of functionalism as the dominant theoretical framework in social science. It was ideally suited to provide a comprehensive and credible justification for the very diversity and pluralism which characterised American educational practices; these were but the logical responses of higher education to the very diversity and plurality of American society and the educational needs and demands of a society much less troubled by 'class' than those in Europe.

Functionalism gave American university representatives a self-understanding which seemed to make perfect sense of the realities of their institutional situation. Furthermore, the two towering functionalist sociologists of the times, Talcott Parsons and Robert Merton, both wrote extensively about science and higher education, as did some of their foremost students: Martin Trow, Neil Smelser, and James Coleman. Not even the present demise of functionalism in social science generally has been able to shake its prominence within higher education research. Neither 'rational choice theorizing', nor structuralism, nor ethnomethdology, nor structuration theory, nor any other more or less fashionable intellectual trend appears to give nearly as good, if any at all, a clue as to the complexities of higher education institutions seen in their entirety.

If functionalism was a help to American academics in acquiring the self-identity which the German professoriate had found in their civil service standing, so were the professional associations discussed by Peter Manicas. The new disciplinary identity was often described in more or less technocratic language which was a far cry from the broad-ranging humanistic vocabulary of earlier European social science.

However, if the secular trends indicating expansion and diversification presented few fundamental problems to the self-understanding of American academics and policy-makers, the situation in Europe was almost exactly opposite. Far from diversity being the normal operating practices of higher education systems, most European countries had for decades embraced a more or less well-articulated belief in the necessity of holding to high and uniform standards of quality. To Europeans, diversity meant variations in educational standards and differential funding for different educational missions. Both possibilities were regarded as unsatisfactory, whether we speak of Britain and France, Sweden and Germany. Thus the University of London, the first new university in England since the middle ages, had in the course of the nineteenth century come to function as a kind of benchmark for academic examinations not only throughout England but throughout the British Empire. This helped secure a 'gold standard' for examinations in English-type institutions. In a country like Sweden, a major ambition of the new private institutions in Stockholm and Gothenburg in the late nineteenth century was to prove that they could live up to the standards set by the older universities of Uppsala and Lund. The general European inclination to avoid diversity (except marginally) was further strengthened in the course of the twentieth century by the large-scale higher education reforms undertaken in the 1960s and 1970s. Bureaucratic centralisation of policy and direction has been the main beneficiary, and European governments have been able to increase their central overview and coordination of entire higher education systems.[69]

Still, the dilemmas inherent in policies aiming at diversity were much less apparent in the late nineteenth and early twentieth centuries than in the period of mass higher education from the 1960s onwards. In the 1800s practically all higher education in Europe was an elite education both in form and numbers. The fact that in some countries such as Sweden, there had always been a substantial share of 'peasant students' (the *bonde-studenter* mentioned by Liedman) who did not have the means to study at the same intense pace as other students did not do much to change the elite nature of higher education. Until well after the Second World War, only a tiny fraction of an age cohort went on to higher education in European

[69] I discuss some of these problems in 'Excellence of Analysis to Diversity of Advocacy: The Multiple Role of the Leverhulme Study into the Future of Higher Education', in *Higher Education*, 13 (1984), 121–38. In the European context, probably no scholar has raised these issues more persistently than Torsten Husén. See his *Universiteten och forskningen* (Stockholm first published 1975, 2nd edn 1986). For the British context, see Dahrendorf, *Education*, but also Tony Becher (ed.), *British Higher Education* (London, 1987). Additional studies are Tribe, 'The Accumulation of Cultural Capital: The Funding of UK Higher Education in the Twentieth Century', *Higher Education Quarterly*, 44 (Winter 1990), 21–31; and Peter Scott, 'All change or no change at all?', *The Times Higher Education Supplement*, 9 August 1991, 12.

For an interesting German report discussing the problems and potentials of higher education pluralism in a European setting, see *Kommission Forschung Baden-Wuertemberg 2000. Abschlussbericht* (Stuttgart: Ministerium fuer Wissenschaft und Kunst Baden-Wuertemberg, July 1989). This is a discussion of how a larger element of choice and diversity of missions can be introduced into the higher education system of the state of Baden-Wuertemberg with its mixture of older universities (Heidelberg, Tuebingen, and Freiburg) and newer (Ulm and Konstanz). The authors of the report wish to preserve the dynamism of the newer institutions, which they fear will be sacrificed if the traditional prestige norms of the older ones are taken as models.

Ulrich Teichler, 'Hochschulen in Europa. Studiengänge, Studiendauer, Übergang in den Beruf', in *Aus Politik und Zeitgeschichte*, 8 (December, 1989), 25–39, offers a brief but insightful overview of the contemporary scene.

Flexner's 1912 Report for Carnegie contains what is still a sensitive and sensible discussion of diversity and uniformity in university education. His position may be summarised by saying that diversity requires a certain minimum degree of uniformity. He was, of course, thinking particularly of medical education.

countries, especially and particularly if we take the situation of women students into account. It is, for instance, often mentioned that the distinguished mathematician Sonja Kowalevska was the first female professor in Sweden and that typically she was not chaired at one of the universities but held a position at the new private, elite Stockholm university college largely through the intervention of Gösta Mittag-Leffler, then pro-rector. It is also pointed out that she had to take her doctorate at Zürich despite the fact that she had studied under Weierstrass in Berlin. The astounding fact, however, is not that she was unable to take her doctorate in Berlin or was not appointed to a university chair, but that in the 1870s she was even allowed to attend Berlin classes or lectures at all! Women undergraduates were only really admitted almost a quarter of a century later, in 1896.[70]

From the 1960s onwards, higher education student expansion created a real dilemma for European academics and policy-makers. A traditional elitist higher education system could not easily accommodate the growing numbers. Early efforts to trim the system by various means could do little to change this fact, especially since interventionist-minded welfare states were placing more and more demands upon the higher education sector.

Higher education was viewed as a key arena for policy intervention both in principle and because higher education could be used to promote specific social and political objectives. Thus higher education was directly and indirectly used to help stimulate economic growth, not least by being geared to policy-perceived labour market needs. It was also used to support such general governmental social aims as furthering national conceptions of social equality. How were these ambitious objectives to be achieved? Across the member countries of the OCED, the two basic traditional parameters of higher education – *governance arrangements* and *curricula* – were being redesigned. Often enough, a combination of central political planning and incentives combined with a change in the composition of governing bodies within higher education institutions were intended to bring about the desired changes in performance and curricular activities.

Although the general trend of changes was fairly uniform across countries, some nations went further than others in the comprehensiveness

---

[70] This, incidentally, was also the same year when it was officially stipulated that all docents at the Berlin University were explicitly prohibited from taking part in the activities of social democratic organizations – and this in a country with the largest and most well-organised social democratic party in the world. For a detailed account of some of these developments in critical perspective, see Fabian, 'Die lange Geburt', and two other chapters: Wolfgang Grinius, 'Zwischen Reichsgruendung und Jahrhundertwende 1870–1900', and Annette Vogt, 'Berliner Wissenschaft im Abgesang des Wilhelminischen Reiches 1900–1914', all in *Wissenschaft in Berlin*, ed. Laitko *et al.*, 174–303, 306–95.

of the changes. Sweden stands out as having undertaken probably the most thorough-going reform efforts of any European country in this period. In a sequence of sweeping reforms, a highly traditionalist professorial system was amended to allow students and administrators representation on departmental boards. On university-wide bodies, the professors were actually outnumbered by outside political appointments. Subsequently, all of undergraduate education was re-designed into so-called study programmes oriented towards various sectors of the labour market. The traditional teaching disciplines were relegated to the status of 'single courses'.[71]

In their contributions to this volume, Liedman and Aant Elzinga argue that a combination of 'implementation deficits', active resistance, and the weakness inherent in the original, highly technocratic planning schemes, widely symbolised by the acronym 'U 68' referring to the key government commission which supplied the rationale for the new system, have led to a situation where almost all of the utilitarian schemes of the 1960s and 1970s are now being dismantled, albeit incrementally. In the spring of 1991, the Social Democratic government proposed that the old university degrees be restored and universities be given the right to cancel whatever remained of the old system of 'study programmes' should they wish to do so. The major non-socialist opposition parties which replaced the Social Democrats following the autumn 1991 general elections have even suggested that the system of State universities, introduced at the Reformation, be abolished, and that universities should be transformed into private foundations supported by huge endowments transferred to the universities from government wage earners's funds scheduled for dissolution. Probably the most amazing feature of this stunning reversal of policy is that it has been accompanied with little or no harsh political controversy.

Similar though less drastic changes have been occurring in most other European countries. The belief in a pre-programmed and politically-oriented process of production and knowledge-use has been waning for at least a decade and a half. In its stead has come the call for a return to fundamentals, 'back to basics', both in research and teaching. On a

[71] There is a vast literature on these developments in the Swedish context. For a brief introduction to the literature, see the contributions by Wittrock, Olof Ruin, and Elzinga to *University Research System*, ed. Wittrock and Elzinga, and the contributions by Elzinga to this volume, as well as Lennart G. Svensson, *Higher Education and the State in Swedish History* (Stockholm 1987). Also the contributions to Martin A. Trow and Thorsten Nybom (eds.), *Universities and Society, Essays on the Social Role of Research and Higher Education* (London, 1991). A highly perceptive view from the outside (as it were), especially in undergraduate education, is provided by Peter Scott, *Higher Education in Sweden – A Look from the Outside* (Stockholm: UHÄ (National Board of Universities and Colleges, 1991), in a report commissioned by a Swedish government committee on higher education.

rhetorical level this is sometimes mistaken for a return to the general type of quality-guided research policies favoured in the OECD area in the early- and mid-1960s before the period of the Rothschild principle, contractualisation policy, and sectoral science policy.

However, rather than a return to the days of pre-mass higher education institutions, what we seem to be witnessing are dramatically increasing efforts to build up real research strength in broad areas of strategic importance to long-term technological health. The words 'strategic research' and 'targeted basic research' have become fashionable. Recent changes in public policies for research as well as for higher education therefore have little or nothing to do with longings for an idyllic past on the part of a conservative professoriate or with the anti-technocratic critique of radical intellectuals. Rather they are a reflection of the changing position of knowledge in the most advanced production processes. That this is indeed the case is indicated by the string of so-called 'mega-buck-deals' concluded between large companies, not least in the pharmaceutical industry, and selected university environments, and also in the growing bulge of 'science parks' and 'silicon valleys' surrounding the more prominent university centres in Western Europe and North America.[72]

Friedrich Wilhelm III once declared that the creation of a new university at Berlin would mean that the country could regain in intellectual excellence what it had lost in military power. To most current policy-makers, the resuscitated interest in universities and higher education seems basically to be a matter of regaining employment opportunities and stimulating economic growth of a new type to compensate for the decline and obsolescence of older types of production technologies and industries. Thus the university is not a tarnished ornament of dubious and uncertain value, a relic inherited from a foregone age unlikely to be of much immediate use to the world of action and practice, but once again a real asset to the new entrepreneurial city elites.

So, as Harold Perkin observed some years ago, universities have never before had larger resources at their disposal, as many students enrolled, or as much public attention paid to them. But also never before have they 'been in so much danger of losing the *sine qua non* of their existence, the freedom to pursue their primary function of conserving, advancing, and disseminating independent knowledge'.[73] Nobody with experience of today's higher education institutions in Europe and North America, or

---

[72] An overview and analysis of some of these developments is made by the different contributors to *Science as a Commodity: Threats to the Open Community of Scholars*, ed. Michael Gibbons and Wittrock (London, 1985).

[73] Perkin, 'Historical Perspective', 44. Also Ronald Brickman, 'The University Research System: Policies, Performances and Paradoxes', in *University Research System*, ed. Wittrock and Elzinga, 39–52.

even with an average interest in them, can avoid being confronted with a host, not to say an avalanche, of descriptions and prescriptions and reports all highlighting the anonymous and vaguely bureaucratic nature of the modern university, the distance between rhetorical statements invoking the reality of a community of scholars, of teachers and students on the one hand, and the very absence of a living, intellectual sense of cohesion and community on the other.

The three transformations in perspective

The modern research-oriented university emerged in the latter part of the nineteenth century in what has here been termed the second of the three major transformations in the relationship between universities and societal institutions in the period since the French Revolution. This, however, as has been repeatedly argued in the course of this chapter, was only possible because of the deep-seated transformation which occurred first at the turn of the nineteenth century. The transformation of the university, normally associated with the Humboldt brothers and with the creation of the new university at Berlin, was co-terminous with the emergence of a new type of epistemic regime, that of academic science.

This new epistemic regime entailed a break with previous types of academic and intellectual discourse. It also entailed, as already emphasised, new social identities for scientific practitioners, separating amateurs from 'serious' scholars and scientists. The new, more closely regulated intellectual activities had as their institutional backdrop re-designed universities of the nineteenth century.

However, it has been a major argument of this chapter that although the emergence of a new epistemic regime is co-terminous with the institutional events manifested in the resurrection of the idea of a self-governing university along the lines proposed by the Humboldt brothers, institutional renovation itself was grounded in a philosophical conception which in many ways was at odds with the whole process of ever-increasing disciplinary specialisation. In the late nineteenth century, during what has here been termed the second transformation, tensions surfaced, but they tended to be glossed over in rhetoric and everyday life. Instead, a history of heroic continuities conveniently served as the dominant self-understanding of European university representatives.

In the course of the twentieth century, a functionalist explanation of the evolution of the different fields of knowledge and of social developments reinforced the view that modernisation was an inevitable process requiring both specialist intellectual activity and the application of knowledge thus gained to the solution of concrete social problems. But the functionalist explanation – which is simultaneously normative and instrumental – has now been shattered by developments from the 1970s onwards. Consequently we must carefully rethink the role of universities and institutions of higher education in the modern world.

The 'idea' of the university and the three transformations

Harold Perkin's phrase describing the university as 'the axial institution' of the modern world may appear to be a rhetorical flourish for flattering academic professionals. It is, however, important to see that the research-oriented university really does occupy a position at the crossroads of major societal transformations.

Three major dimensions of these transformations can be identified:

First is the economic and technological, the process of establishing new modes of production and utilising resources, including natural resources, in new ways. Inevitably these processes require different forms of social relationships, but they also affect the physical surroundings. Increasingly the notion that nature was something separate from and largely unaffected by human activities, or possibly just a source of wealth, came to be at odds with the living experiences of human beings shaped by industrialism and technology.

Second are social processes which influence meaning and cultural identity in societies where conventional bonds of obligation, obedience, and loyalty can no longer be taken for granted. Throughout the nineteenth century, the concern for 'the social question' of industrial-technological civilisation was paralleled by a concern for what may be called the 'cultural question'. This question arose because of changing identities resulting from the joint effects of new forms of production and spatial organisation and the French wars of upheaval which fundamentally and irreversibly shook the established political and cultural order in Europe.

All these alterations immediately affected the existing institutions of higher education and produced new and imaginative responses, as well as dilemmas. Thus while some branches of scientific activity were becoming increasingly professionalised within the framework of internationally constituted communities of scholars, others were increasingly called upon to help undergird or construct a sense of cultural and national community in the new nation-states of Europe and beyond.[74]

Third is the process of searching for a new political order to address the social and cultural questions. The solution, arrived at gradually, was the

[74] Some of the contributions to *The Internationalization of Science, Sociology of the Sciences: A Yearbook*, 16 (forthcoming 1992), ed. Elisabeth Crawford, Terry Shinn, and Sverker Sörlin, address exactly this dilemma in different fields of science.

notion of a modern nation-state. Higher education institutions greatly benefited from this solution. They were given access to much greater resources than had previously been the case, and for almost a century it largely seemed as if the knowledge explosion and occupational special-isation were but two different aspects of one and the same pervasive process of modernisation.

Consequently it was tempting to see the proper role of the State as one of coordination and synchronisation. The State's role was to assure that sufficient resources were channelled to universities to permit them to continue their work of supplying society with a steady stream of competent personnel, but this could only be effectively achieved if universities were also granted sufficient independence. The dilemmas inherent in this 'contract' or idealised trade-off have simply become more apparent in the age of the great programmes of the interventionist State. So while during the course of the last century the university emerged as the axial institution or mediating ground of society's many strivings, its days of almost un-questioned pre-eminence have now gone. The problematic features of the former, fragile balance are very evident, even if university representatives continue to depict their institution as the 'powerhouse' of society.[75]

The dilemmas so obvious to us were smoothed over by the new, exhilarating centrality of universities in economic and social affairs. Drawn increasingly into activities that were in some sense 'practical' or 'applied', universities responded with a dual justification for the importance of research. True academic work, it was maintained, should or must be 'pure'. Even so, there was always the possibility that from such investigations great social benefits might ensue. Admittedly there were research activities tainted from the outset, but the existence of such 'impure' work did not undermine the university's proper mission. On the contrary, it ended up by reinforcing the university's claim on public resources.

The justification produced (or mirrored) the desired results. Universities became rich, relatively speaking, and the new *écoles* of France, Germany, Switzerland, and Sweden also rose in standing to rival the universities. They were certainly useful and successful. No one was likely to say, as did

---

[75] The fragility of the 'social contract' between State and university is nowhere better illustrated than in the perversions of the Nazi period. In a short period, the Nazi regime irreparably damaged and destroyed some of the greatest universities ever known. This horrific period, however, is not properly speaking part of the three great transformations. Readers may wish to consult two recent works bearing on National Socialism and higher education, science, and technology. The first is Michael Burleigh, *Germany Turns Eastwards: A Study of 'Ostforschung' in the Third Reich* (New York, 1988); and the second is Mark Walker, *German National Socialism and the Quest for Nuclear Power, 1939–1949* (New York, 1989).

a French visitor to the eighteenth-century colleges of Oxford University, that they were 'occupied by rich idlers who sleep and get drunk one part of the day, and the rest they spend in training, clumsily enough, a parcel of uncouth youths to be clergymen'.[76]

Universities had of course long 'served' society. What was genuinely new was the mission of advancing not just transmitting knowledge. University self-identity is so strongly associated with original and applied science that research and research training are now taken to be 'the core sector of the university' and 'the hall-mark of the university: that which differentiates it from other institutions offering post-secondary education and training'.[77]

The euphoria could not last. Even as universities were arriving at a new relationship with State and society in the late nineteenth century, the ambiguities of their situation were surfacing. The ideology of 'detachment' could hardly be sustained when, for example, German higher education was so heavily involved in chemicals, optics, and electrical engineering. The foundation at the turn of the century of the Kaiser-Wilhelm-Gesellschaft (KWG) as a collection of advanced research undertakings not only dramatised the State's expectations of higher education, it also meant that universities would not enjoy a monopoly on research funds. The KWG foreshadowed what would ultimately be referred to as a 'strategic research' policy, with industrial (later hi-tech) corporations playing a major financial support role.[78]

In his speech on the occasion of the centennial of the Friedrich-Wilhelms-University, the Kaiser legitimated the creation of non-university research institutes by making them an integral part of the old Humboldtian conception:

Humboldt's great plan for science demands besides the [Berlin] Academy of Sciences and the [Berlin] University independent research institutes as integral parts of the overall organism of science.

The creation of such institutes in Prussia has not kept pace with the development of the universities and this lack, specifically in our natural science equipment, becomes ever more tangible as a consequence of the gigantic expansion of the sciences. We need institutions that transcend the framework of the universities and

[76] Quoted in Penry Williams, 'From the Reformation to the Era of Reform 1550–1850', in *New College Oxford 1379–1979*, ed. John Buxton and Penry Williams (Oxford, 1979), 59, where Williams' comment also appears: 'No doubt he was unfair, but the attractive scent of luxury in Restoration Oxford is inescapable'.

[77] Talcott Parsons and Gerald Platt, with the collaboration of Neil J. Smelser, *The American University* (Cambridge, 1973), 103ff; and Stuart S. Blume, 'After the Darkest Hour... Integrity and Engagement in the Development of University Research', in *University Research System*, ed. Wittrock and Elzinga, 140.

[78] A detailed analysis of the early history of the society is given in Guenther Wedel, *Die Kaiser-Wilhelm-Gesellschaft 1911–1914* (Berlin, 1975).

colleges and that can serve research unimpeded by educational tasks but in close relation to Academy and University.[79]

These remarks notwithstanding, it was evident that even at the peak of its intellectual power and prestige, the research-oriented university was and had been diverging from the Humboldtian conception in at least two drastic ways. It had accepted specialism and the ordering of the disciplines that came with the intellectual division of labour, and it had shown itself unable to combine advanced research with the model of teaching and personality formation which to the early nineteenth century humanists was seen as the ultimate rationale of an institution of higher learning.[80] In the decades to come, universities in countries other than Germany faced similar problems, whether in connection with weapons development during war-time or because of industrially useful research in the age of the 'mega-buck deals', but in all cases they demonstrated that in several important respects they were in danger of losing their claims to a real universality. The choice appeared to be either to admit that important segments of the cognitive universe were outside their historical purview, or to renounce important aspects of their heritage, notably the belief in the university as an open community of peers, of scholars freely sharing with one another their thoughts and findings. The latter possibility is so dispiriting that some commentators today speak of the university as losing its essence or 'soul'. Peter Scott has explicitly dismissed any Humboldtian self-perceptions that may remain in universities by labelling them 'a shared bureaucratic environment'.[81] It may well be asked whether after two centuries anything at all remains of the idea of the university.

Burton Clark, however, is more optimistic or just factual. Modern universities have in-built tensions, but they also have a certain coherence. In order to capture both, he has introduced the powerful metaphor of the 'master matrix' which consists of two different but connected dimensions. Within the matrix, the scholarly disciplines represent professional identity and commitment; and the institution itself is represented by 'enterprise'.[82]

[79] From the *Berliner Local-Anzeiger* (11 October 1910, Evening edition, S. 1), quoted in Vogt, 'Berliner Wissenschaft', 357 (my translation). As already indicated, it was indeed the case that Humboldt discussed the relationship between the University, the Academy, and their respective role *vis-à-vis* different scientific institutions. On the other hand, Humboldt's brief sketch cannot in any real sense be said to have entailed the necessity of establishing an institution such as the KWG.
[80] Ravetz, *Scientific Knowledge*, discusses some of these developments and the internal tensions in academic science already apparent at an early stage. See as well as Wolfgang Nitsch, Uta Gerhardt, Claus Offe, and Ulrich Preuss, *Hochschule in der Demokratie: Kritische Beiträge zur Erbschaft und Reform der deutschen Universität* (Berlin, 1965), 240–346.   [81] Scott, *Crisis*, 68.
[82] Burton Clark (ed.), *The Higher Education System: Academic Organization in Cross-National Perspectives* (Berkeley, 1983) still stands out as a landmark of higher education

To early nineteenth-century thinkers in Germany and England like Humboldt and Coleridge, to take but two examples, the idea of a university highlighted those features which were not co-incidental and accidental but essential, permanent, and independent of specific circumstances. Clearly, this type of essentialism clashed with empiricism as an epistemology and with utilitarianism as a political philosophy. Beyond this, however, it certainly had political implications – conservative in the case of England, radical in the case of Germany. It is only too obvious today, with the benefit of almost two centuries of hindsight, that reducing all the functions and activities of universities to a single essential idea so remarkably clear and self-evident that it could not be resisted is unimaginable.[83]

However, it should be equally obvious that 'ideas' about universities are not quixotic, for they do in fact exist, and moreover they are functional. Each and every effort to shape or reform a university or an institution of higher learning does by necessity rely on some idea of its form or mission. Clearly, then, an 'idea' is not a free-floating abstraction but a guiding conception, rooted in the experiences, traditions, and life-worlds of individuals who have memories and hopes and attachments. Modern universities are in fact very much part of the age of modernity and the traditions and values which have helped shape the modern world since the French Revolution and the Enlightenment. All reforms and changes since then have indicated the pervasive influence of 'ideas' about what a university ought to be in relation to other educational and social institutions, and the academic communities who make universities and associated institutions their homes have implicitly or explicitly attempted to relate their working lives to some sort of notion of the 'universal' in the university. Their self-image has certainly depended upon their doing so.

None of the three transformations of the university in the 200-year period of modernity since the French Revolution occurred as an automatic response to social differentiation. None of them was a mere reaction to the educational needs inherent in the secular process of modernisation. They occurred because leaders, thinkers, scholars, and scientists continually questioned the basic nature and meaning of higher learning.

This is eminently apparent in the case of the first major transformation. The resurrection of the idea of a university in early nineteenth-century

scholarship, as do Clark's research programmes at Yale and the University of California at Los Angeles.
[83] A fascinating overview of the way in which the notion that an idea of a university can exist and how it developed in the Anglo-Saxon world from the early nineteenth century onwards, with some comparative observations on developments elsewhere, is given in Rothblatt, 'The Idea of the Idea of a University and Its Antithesis', *Conversazione* (La Trobe University, Bundoora: Seminar on Sociology of Culture, 1989).

Germany is all the more remarkable since in drastic ways it entailed a break with what many perceived to be the dominant trends of the times. The habitual invocation of the Humboldtian ideals by university representatives throughout the nineteenth and twentieth centuries make it all too easy to forget that the very survival of the 'university' was a completely open question around 1800. To the new elites of Revolutionary France and to large sections of the traditional elites of Continental European monarchies, the university appeared to be an outdated and impractical relic of the middle ages, badly managed and essentially irrelevant. The rebirth of the university was intimately linked to an uneasy process of social and political reform in Prussia under the impact of an imminent external threat to the ruling circles. It was actually only under extreme circumstances, involving the forced absence of King and Cabinet from the capital, that a coalition of radical philosophers and aristocratic reformers had any possibility of overcoming the resistance of a traditionalist court camarilla.

The idea of a university embraced by the reformers was elaborated differently by thinkers such as Schelling, Fichte, Schleiermacher, Steffens, and von Humboldt. However, underlying their different proposals was a common vision of a university which featured the unity of teaching and research, of general education and research, of the different scientific specialties within a community of knowledge. This vision, the thinkers and idealists believed, would benefit the world at large, for they thought of the university as an ideal moral community supporting the values of enlightenment and personal development.[84] It is also clear that in anchoring their vision to some kind of practical institutional reality, they were able to fulfil their ideal of intellectual and moral unity and universal learning by selecting a subject such as philosophy. It is hardly coincidental that Hegel came to play a pivotal role as chairholder in philosophy at the Berlin university.[85]

However continuous, the moral vision of a university was destined to become incompatible with the realities of modern life and with the epistemic and institutional realities of science itself. The constant rhapsodic evocation of the Humboldtian heritage inevitably underscored the differences which were occurring. In the German and the American contexts, Paulsen and Flexner, the two major proponents of the modern research

[84] See Anrich, *Idee der deutschen Universität*, for the classical texts on the university by these different authors. Habermas, 'The Idea of a University', has nicely captured the basic common features in the reform movement of the early nineteenth century.

[85] Dickey, *Hegel*, gives an interesting, carefully-researched analysis of the philosopher's conception of *Bildung*. See in particular the epilogue, '*Bildung* and Politics: The "First Class", Christian Pride, and "Absolute Spirit"', 278–93.

university in the early twentieth century, were both firmly committed to the classical heritage of the Humboldtian university, but they were also very much aware of institutional realities. Their basic positions may be characterised as optimistic interventionism. To the extent that higher education institutions actually deviated from the historic model of a university, Flexner was inclined to favour corrective reform.

In this respect, the Americans actually departed from the Europeans in the inter-war period. In the American setting, the policy activist impulse, propelled by a basically pragmatic philosophical outlook, did not get blunted but was strengthened after two world wars, especially after the second. Optimism did indeed typify major American university leaders. For all their differences, for example, Flexner and Clark Kerr represent the same energetic reformism. Both were ceaselessly active in trying to combine various legacies, to make certain that American universities were intellectually equal to or as 'effective' as the best German universities (later the Japanese higher education system) and to retain the highest standards of quality even in a period of mass higher education. Both were very much the products of a higher education culture where size, diversity, and plurality had made rankings, assessments, and measurements an integral feature and concern, some would uncharitably say a culturally-conditioned obsession.

In this respect the end of the First World War is a deep dividing line. Before the war Paulsen had written with the self-confidence not only of a representative of the model university of the modern world but also of a triumphant scientific and industrial nation. The post-war representatives of German academia were all writing in the shadow of a disastrous political and military defeat, writing from within a strong and living intellectual tradition, but one which could never again be invoked just as a matter of course. Was there indeed any role for that visionary entity such as the 'idea' of a university? If so, how, if at all, could it be joined to the institutional realities of scientific and educational institutions in the modern world?[86]

In the early and mid twentieth century, such questions seemed hopelessly outdistanced by events. After World War I, Max Weber, Karl Jaspers, and Martin Heidegger – to name but three of the most profound critics and defenders of the German university tradition in this period – all engaged in a penetrating self-critical inquiry into the state of German universities. All concluded that the traditional conception of the constitutive features of a

[86] An interesting perspective on Paulsen's intellectual orientation is provided by the correspondence between him and his Schleswig-Holstein 'compatriot', the great German sociologist Ferdinand Tönnies. It can be found in Ferdinand Tönnies and Friedrich Paulsen, *Briefwechsel 1876–1908* (Kiel, 1961).

university was a myth when confronted by the institutional realities of the twentieth century. Nevertheless, not one of them was thereby willing to dismiss the idea of a university as just an expression of disembodied metaphysics. Why? Because the alternative was no less than admitting that the university existed only to cater to the demands of State and society for usefully-trained personnel. Success as measured by adaptation to a universe of ever-evolving sets of social sub-systems, of technology, technocracy, and experts, was the apparently new idea of a university. To admit to this was to surrender everything worth preserving in the German intellectual tradition since Hegel and Hölderlin. It was to exchange an often disconnected idealism for a mindless functionalism, a capitulation to the dispirited realities of factory-like mass higher education processing. Weber, Jaspers, and Heidegger viewed such accommodation as intolerable. They each sought ways of revitalising the historic conception of a university.

Jaspers, in analysing the idea of a university, was still searching for an ultimate enlightening and comprehensive role for philosophy, not least because in the absence of such reflective guidance the various scientific specialties were inevitably drifting apart. This role, however, could not be the one conceived by early-nineteenth-century philosophical idealism. Rather it had to be a Kantian-inspired open quest for those elements of truthfulness and sincerity informing truly intellectual work within all disciplines. Jaspers had published a book with the title *Die Idee der Universität* in 1923, and a new edition appeared immediately after the Second World War in 1946. A third edition containing contributions by Kurt Rossman was published in 1960 on the eve of what has here been termed the third major transformation of the modern university.[87]

In the preface they made clear that it was no longer enough to express a commitment to the traditional features of the German university.[88] The increasing specialisation of the sciences was an inevitable process, and pure philosophical reflection could not overcome or encompass an ever-expanding cognitive universe. However, Jaspers was sceptical, not to say contemptuous, of the idea of a university that passively accepted fragmentation and superficially glossed it over with something called 'general education' or crash courses in *allgemeine Bildung* (which had social class overtones). One is reminded of the similarly sharp literary

[87] Karl Jaspers and Kurt Rossman, *Die Idee der Universität. Fuer die gegenwärtige Situation entworfen von Karl Jaspers und Kurt Rossmann* (Berlin, 1961).
[88] 'Die Alternative ist: Entweder gelingt die Wiedergeburt der Idee im Entschluss zur Verwirklichung einer neuen Organisationsgestalt oder sie findet ihr Ende im Funktionalismus riesiger Schul- und Ausbildungsanstalten fuer wissenschaftlich-technische Fachkräfte.' *Ibid.*, 'Vorwort'.

critique of the superficial and habitual invocation of classical *Bildung* expressed by the *alter ego* in Hermann Hesse's *Der Steppenwolf* when coming across the inevitable Goethe picture in a traditional German middle-class home.

The plurality of scientific activities had to be accepted, but Jaspers went on to argue that within each and every scholarly pursuit it was possible to reflect about the foundations of these activities and to reach out to other fields, thus preserving some aspects of the unity of a university. Indeed, if this were genuinely the situation, the potential for an open universalism might be greater than ever. Thus, there is preserved in Jaspers' notion of higher education a portion of the continuities reaching back to the generation of Humboldt, but also a sense of transcendence and renewal. The two cornerstones of this renewal might be described as existential choice and a kind of universalistic realtivism.[89]

Self-reflection as a precondition for the restoration of the German idea of a university is part of the original heritage, and in the post-Second World War period sophisticated and self-conscious variations on the theme were provided by Helmut Schelsky and Habermas. Schelsky emphasised the point of critical-reflection from within disciplines leading to a broader grasp of the discipline and its relation to other fields of study. At the new University of Bielefeld his ideas were given an actual lease on life in the form of an institute for interdisciplinary research along the lines of an institute for advanced study. Actually, in a speech at the West German Rectors' conference at Göttingen on 22 June 1966 on the occasion of the bicentennial of Wilhelm von Humboldt's birth, Schelsky stated that the lively intellectual encounters of a truly universalistic community of scholars were, in the contemporary era, more likely to be found in centres for advanced study in America than in traditional universities in Germany.[90]

Habermas was even less optimistic. He did not think that some form of transcendent meta-reflection would preserve an element of unity and enlightenment in modern scholarship. However, Habermas's pessimism,

---

[89] For a discussion of Jasper's place in the intellectual development of Hannah Arendt, see Martin Jay, *Permanent Exiles: Essays on the Intellectual Migration from Germany to America* (New York, 1986), chapter 14.

[90] This speech is reprinted in Helmut Schelsky, *Abschied von der Hochschulpolitik oder Die Universität im Fadenkreuz des Versagens* (Bielefeld, 1969). As the title indicates, this volume is characterised by deep pessimism about the future of the German universities. In many ways, Schelsky shares all the fears of Weber, Jaspers, and other intellectuals that universities would become mindless vocational institutions, except that for him the university as a factor for mass-producing trained manpower was a reality. Hoping to preserve some of the features of the classical heritage in the new era, Schelsky wrote *Einsamkeit und Freiheit. Idee und Gestalt der deutschen Universität und ihrer Reformen* (Reinbeck bei Hamburg, 1963).

many would say realism in this respect, was in a sense more than balanced by his confidence in the communicative process itself, inherent in all discourse and teaching, in its ideal form, unaffected by strategic considerations of power and professional interest. This, he thought, epitomised everything that Humboldt and Schleiermacher valued. Thus despite the utopianism of the belief that all living members in a university should subscribe to some sort of common ideal whether of an epistemic or normative nature, Habermas with all his critical insights into the sociological realities of scientific practices retains confidence in the process of communication which he believes inheres in real intellectual work. His confidence appears to be just as strong as that of his nineteenth-century forebears, who were also fully aware of the drastic deviation of the ideal university they envisaged from the practical realities of German university life.

Two other significant positions in German intellectual life in the inter-war period may be contrasted with the classical tradition. One of them derives from one of the most notorious statements of a major European intellectual in this century, namely Heidegger's address upon assuming the rectorship of the University of Freiburg im Breisgau in May 1933, a position from which he resigned in February 1934. This address, 'The Self-Assertion of the German University', is ill-famed because it is normally interpreted as a betrayal of the most fundamental features of the intellectual heritage of humanistic scholarship and the Enlightenment tradition. Not even the postmodern pluralism of Lyotard is able to discern in it anything but 'an unfortunate episode in the history of legitimation', a statement which though 'theoretically inconsistent...was compelling enough to find disastrous echoes in the realm of politics'.[91]

It is only in the last few years and through the work of some radical philosophers of the younger generation in France and the United States, and with the concomitant publication of Heidegger's actual text in English and French, that some observers have found reason to question Lyotard's assessment.[92] It is not clear that the address really found any echoes at all in the realm of politics or the university at the time of its delivery. More importantly, an effort has been made to place the address within the overall framework of Heidegger's thought. The most important of the recent interpretations of the Heideggerian position are Gérard Granel's book *De l'université* and Christopher Fynsk's provocative article on Heidegger

[91] Jean-Francois Lyotard, *The Postmodern Condition: A Report on Knowledge* (first French edition in 1979; English translation in 1984, reprinted Manchester, 1986), 37.
[92] Martin Heidegger, 'The Self-Assertion of the German University: Address Delivered on the Solemn Assumption of the Rectorate of the University Freiburg', and 'The Rectorate 1933/34: Facts and Thoughts', *Review of Metaphysics*, 38 (March 1985), 467–502.

and Granel, 'But Suppose We Were to Take the Rectoral Address Seriously... Gérard Granel's *De l'université*'.[93]

The rectoral address cannot be severed from Heidegger's method of reasoning. Rather than proposing a simple blueprint for a university, Heidegger urged scholars to 'question' its reliance on a narrow definition of science (derived, he said, from Greece):

Science is the questioning of one's ground in the midst of the ever-concealing totality of what is. The active perseverance knows, as it perseveres, about its impotence before fate. This is the original essence of science... Such questioning shatters the division of the sciences into rigidly separated specialties, carries them back from their endless and aimless dispersal into isolated fields and corners.

In the absence of such a fundamental questioning, science 'remains an accident we fall into or the settled comfort of a safe occupation, serving to further a mere progress of information'.[94]

This line of argument had been pursued by Heidegger in his inaugural address as chair-holder in 1929 when he stated that the 'fragmented multiplicity of disciplines is held together only by the technical organisation of universities and faculties, and retains some importance only because of the practical aims pursued by the different specialties. But the roots of the sciences in their essential ground have withered.'[95]

There is no reason to assume that Heidegger's basic philosophical stance did not resonate in his Rectoral Address. Granel and Fynsk are right in that we can indeed take the address seriously as a fundamentally critical assessment of the idea of the university in the twentieth century. However, it is difficult not to side with Lyotard. The address contains a disastrous conflation between Heidegger's desire, however sincere, to reject all rhetorically pleasing complacency with existing university life and an effort to legitimate his position by invoking a vaguely but radically nationalistic short-term political rhetoric. Thus the unfortunate triad of *Arbeitsdienst* (labour service), *Wehrdienst* (military service), and *Wissensdienst* (knowledge service) figures prominently in the address, as do references to the fate and community of the German people.[96] The absence of any anti-semitic pronouncements and of any references to either the Nazi party or its leader

---

[93] Gérard Granel, *De l'université* (Paris, 1982). Christopher Fynsk, 'But Suppose We Were to Take the Rectoral Address Seriously... Gérard Granel's *De l'université*', *Graduate School Journal of Philosophy* (June 1991). Also Philippe Lacoue-Labarthe, *Heidegger, Art and Politics: The Fiction of the Political* (Oxford, 1990).

[94] Heidegger, 'The Self-Assertion of the German University', 473ff.

[95] Heidegger is quoting from his Freiburg inaugural address. *Ibid.*, 482.

[96] The common English translations do not capture the true meaning of this triad, which implies State service. There is also an implicit reference to the three fixed estates of Plato's *Republic* – workers, warriors, and philosophers.

does not change the fact that it is no exaggeration to characterise Heidegger's political language as fascistic.

With the benefit of hindsight – and many would surely add foresight – it is hard to imagine two less compatible university and science policy stances than those taken by Heidegger and by the Nazi party: a fundamental hermeneutic questioning crossed with the most ruthless and short-term oriented technocratic utilitarianism. The party of storm-troopers, as Heidegger almost immediately came to experience, was not overly interested in an inquiry into the Greek roots of science. Such an inquiry – or really 'questioning' as he termed it, 'the highest form of knowing' – would in his view have far-reaching implications. For Heidegger regarded Greek science as the beginning of the history which led to a denatured technological civilisation, and for a moment he thought that the 'questioning' he advocated would lead to genuine spiritual renewal, a rebirth but in German not Greek form. He allowed himself to believe that the Nazi movement meant spiritual regeneration. But abandoning 'questioning' as the means to self and national renewal, he substituted 'philosophy', that is to say, advocacy, and threw away any value that lay in his original approach. So much for questioning as 'the highest form of knowing'. The actual result was a personal and national tragedy.

Nevertheless, in his reflections on office, Heidegger depicts his own stance as involving a clear resistance to this, hence his refusal to bow to Nazi demands for the dismissal of two famous Jewish professors, his appointment of deans, none of whom belonged to the NSDAP, and his account of an endless sequence of day-to-day controversy with various minor Nazi officials in the ministry and student union. However, it also seems undeniable that Heidegger personally was, indeed, a Nazi and that in his capacity as Rector he openly declared his willingness to participate in the process of trimming the university to the demands of the Nazi State. The fact that he had to resign from this position within a year cannot change this reality. Thus it seems futile to depict Heidegger as an unknowing and basically apolitical philosopher who was unfortunate enough to be caught up in the midst of a maelstrom of political events, being exploited by the ruthless representatives of the new regime for a brief moment before being discarded.

There was a fundamentally anti-individualistic streak in Heidegger's thought which had a profound affinity with Nazi ideology. However, it would be equally misleading to reduce his critique of the modern university to this ideological position. Heidegger's actual standpoint as Rector is clearly related to a more comprehensive view of the role of knowledge in the modern world and to a deeply pessimistic vision of the situation of humanity in an age of technologically oriented forms of knowledge. This general *problematique*, however, was one that in different formulations occupied intellectuals in many different quarters. How otherwise can it be explained that philosophers as different as Hannah Arendt and Herbert Marcuse were his students?[97]

The very first article of the first issue of the journal of the marxian Frankfurt School, the *Zeitschrift fuer Sozialforschung*, was devoted to this theme of the sociology of knowledge. It was a relatively brief piece entitled 'Notes on Science and Crisis' written by the Director of the Frankfurt Institute for Social Research, Max Horkheimer. His original intention was to publish a major article on science and society which for reasons of illness, was replaced by a shorter version.[98]

The theme of the technocratic deformation of modern science came to be a pervasive theme throughout the activities of the Frankfurt School both in Germany and in exile. Horkheimers' and Adorno's *Dialektik der Aufklärung* (1944) was certainly one of the most important works in the tradition of Critical Theory, being a fundamental critique of a perceived perversion of the whole Enlightenment tradition. The *problematique* is not altogether dissimilar from Heidegger's and is equally critical. It is hardly coincidental that both Marcuse and the young Habermas were influenced by various strands in Heidegger's philosophy and his analysis of the ways in which technological civilisation penetrated into and deformed the life-worlds of human beings.

Similar themes were also, in roughly the same period, broached in literary terms by authors worlds apart in their political views, such as the extreme right-wing author Ernst Jünger – both in his *Der Arbeiter. Herrschaft und Gestalt* (*The Worker: Domination and Gestalt*) which played an important role in Heidegger's intellectual development, and *Auf den Marmorklippen* (*On the Marble Cliffs*) – or the later Nobel laureate and pacifist Hermann Hesse in his major war-time epic, *Das Glasperlenspiel* (*The Glass Bead Game*).[99]

Heidegger's analysis is, compared to, say, Paulsen's or Weber's,

[97] An interesting overview of Heidegger's intellectual stance, his relation to classical traditions in Germany, not least to Hölderlin, but also to political events and to National Socialism as well as to other intellectuals, not least to his contemporary Ernst Jünger, is given in Michael E. Zimmerman, *Heidegger's Confrontation with Modernity: Technology, Politics, Art* (Bloomington, 1990). Heidegger's influence on Arendt and Marcuse is also discussed in Jay.

[98] Max Horkheimer, 'Bemerkungen ueber Wissenschaft und Krise', *Zeitschrift fuer Sozialforschung* (Jahrgang 1, 1932, Doppelheft 1/2), 1–7 (reprinted Munich, 1980).

[99] Ernst Jünger, *Der Arbeiter, Herrschaft und Gestalt* (Hamburg, 1932), and *Auf den Marmorklippen* (Zurich, 1939); Hermann Hesse, *Das Glasperlenspiel. Versuch einer Lebensbeschreibung des Magister Ludi Joseph Knecht samt Knechts hinterlassenen Schriften* (Zurich, 1943). See also Theodor W. Adorno and Max Horkheimer, *Dialektik der Aufklärung* (New York, 1944, English translation 1972).

persistently and fundamentally critical, even of the whole Enlightenment. In some fundamental ways, it signals a break with traditional German Mandarin culture. In another way, Heidegger is working from within a major German intellectual tradition that was highly prominent also among the idealistic philosophers around 1800, namely in his insistence on the necessity to return to the Greek origins of Western civilisation.

This theme – what one observer has termed 'the German infatuation with Classical Greece', an infatuation dating back to Winckelmann and the mid eighteenth century – also recurred in literary works of the early nineteenth century, most prominently perhaps in the poetry of Friedrich Hölderlin, in his youth a close friend of Hegel's and like him deeply affected by the revolutionary upheavals in France.[100] Hölderlin's poetry, both the most romantic and the most classicistic of the times, had of course been the subject of the most varied interpretations. Clearly much of Hölderlin's early poetry is carried by a 'vision of re-establishing the Golden Age of Greece'.[101] The vision of classical Greece did not mean a vague interest in distant history. It meant a search for the answers to the most existential questions affecting contemporary Germany. In Heidegger's philosophy, a return to the questions of the pre-Socratic-philosophers had similar existential meaning. They were regarded by him as necessary for breaking decisively with modern mass society and technologically-driven civilisation and therefore crucial for the renewal of Germany. Heidegger also devoted himself to interpretations of Hölderlin – as did, for example, one of the greatest poets of the German language of the war years and the post-war period, the Rumanian Jewish poet Paul Celan, during the war in the Red Army and for most of the post-war period living in exile in France.

In his statements on the university, Heidegger urged a search for the origins of science, not just for convenience and certainly not as just an exercise in humanistic scholarship. There is a sense in which this attitude is quite compatible with extreme nationalism and anti-individualism, namely in the conviction that somehow Greece and Germany represent two fundamental beginnings, and in the belief that the political transformation of Germany, its national revolution as it were, involved such an historical moment of choice and transcendence. The cost was a ruthless subjection of individual preferences and wishes to the demands of the historical and political moments. So there is indeed a connection between Heidegger's university conception and his philosophy, as well as his political vision, and the connection is far from accidental.

Still, these correlations do not eliminate the poignancy of the questions

---

[100] Ronald Taylor, *The Intellectual Tradition of Modern Germany* (London, 1973), I, 134.
[101] *Ibid.*, 136.

Heidegger was trying to force upon the scholarly communities of a modern university. Nor is it possible to brush his remarks aside either as only an expression of fascist politics or philosophical interest. On the contrary, they are at least as relevant as many of the more conventional formulations of an idea of a university precisely because they are grounded in an insight into the intellectual and institutional realities of modern university life. Heidegger refuses to relapse either into a half-cynical rehearsal of conventional formulas or into a mere functionalism unredeemed by reference to the life-worlds of human beings within and without academia.

However, it is equally reasonable to state that the Heideggerian position for all its audacity and critical stance provides little or no guidance for an extended institutional analysis of the university and its embeddedness in modern society. For that we turn to one of Weber's most famous lectures, namely *Science as a Vocation* (*Wissenschaft als Beruf*, 1919). This lecture is often discussed in relation to the objectivity of scientific work or in connection with science and society. But first and foremost it is an effort by a leading social scientist and historian to make a long-term assessment of the position and prospects of German and American universities at the end of the second great transformation of the modern university. Most other observers at the time either tended to eulogise or, as in the case of Flexner, to reflect critically on the accomplishments of the universities of their native country. Weber was certainly an archetypical representative of the German mandarins and their culture of intellectual aristocracy. However, as noted by Keith Tribe, 'in Weber's comments on the respective features of the German and the American university system, his disparaging comments are reserved for the German, not the American system'.[102] Instead of recalling the notable past achievements of the German university system, Weber tried to identify those features most conducive to the rise to pre-eminence of the leading American universities. These he saw, quite in correspondence with his general social theory, as an irreversible process of increasing specialism and rationalisation.

Germany's loss of scientific leadership to the United States, Weber continued, was just as inevitable as the process by which the handicraft based putting-out system of early manufacturing was replaced by a modern factory system. German university life, centered around the full professors, the *Ordinarien*, was largely reminiscent of the pre-capitalist

---

[102] Tribe, 'Strategy and Structure in the Modern University', *Higher Education Quarterly* (forthcoming). Tribe's article is a brief but highly perceptive and interesting analysis of the situation of the university in modern society. He takes Weber's analysis as a point of departure and argues for the fruitfulness of linking him to contemporary advances in institutional analysis and in the history and sociology of science. This suggestion is very much in keeping with the kind of analysis adopted in this chapter.

handicraft master, except that the journeymen and apprentices were *Assistenten* and disciples who had little influence and remuneration but also few distractions from the pursuit of learning. Even the successful amongst them, who were able to go beyond the doctorate to the *Habilitation* and were given the formal right to lecture on themes of their own choosing as *Privatdozenten* (if students cared to listen), were, as Weber emphasised, still in a highly subordinate position. Thus a *Privatdozent* would rarely, if ever, insist upon his – and it certainly was a 'his' – formal lecturing rights if this entailed a perceived transgression of a professor's accepted right to give a 'great' lecture course.

The American higher education system was analagous to 'state capitalist' (the quotation marks are those of Weber himself) enterprises. The basic division was a department whose chairman or head hired and fired his employees. Younger scholars were paid to work and teach. The worker-scholars were separated from the means of production; the system was subjected to rational production processes, and a premium was put on efficiency. Needless to say, Weber was the first to admit that this drastically painted picture required any number of qualifications. He did, however, insist that the general trend towards increasing specialisation and bureaucratisation was real indeed and had already affected the German universities as well.

As an old handicraft master, Weber could only deplore the changing intellectual atmosphere portended by these developments; but they possessed technical and organisational advantages which could not be dismissed by an appeal to an outdated university ideology. Furthermore, it was apparent that many of the features of German universities which were taken to be constitutive – and which, one might add, so many Germany university representatives before and after Weber were to recall rhetorically – had largely become fictitious. Weber painted a harsh picture of a system that required young people to gamble on an academic career and seriously rigged the game against radicals and Jews. Instead of indulging in nostalgic reminiscences of student life in small romantic German university towns, Weber highlighted its ridiculous pettiness.

However, when all is said and done, he still appealed to the necessity for an inner 'calling' in the hopeful future scholar. He still argued that scientific work for all its compartmentalisation can only yield lasting results if it is carried forward by passion. Indeed, a human activity devoid of passion is, in Weber's words, virtually inhuman.

The force of Weber's position is that he did not shy away from the dilemma of bridging the 'life-worlds' (to use the terminology of Habermas and the hermeneutic scholars) of human beings and the structures and systems of society. Almost all other scholars tried to solve this dilemma rhetorically by invoking the solution of a Humboldt or a John Henry Newman, or, more recently, a Flexner or Robert Hutchins.[103] Or else through functionalism to eliminate the dilemma entirely by creating sub-systems and abstract institutions without people and by afterwards populating this universe with some empirical features which give a sense of social reality. But social reality really means living human beings with memories and hopes, talking and walking in particular places at particular times. They are not the accidental instantiations of abstract rule systems or the temporary locations of preference orderings. Weber forces us to confront this simple but methodologically uncomfortable fact.

Weber placed science in the whole process of modernisation and demystification, *Entzauberung*. Thus viewed, the advancement of science helps human beings to see the world more clearly. However, for precisely the reason that scientific activities themselves are subjected to the very same processes of increasing bureaucratisation and fragmentation that characterise modernity at large, the scientific disciplines themselves are becoming less, not more, able to yield any kind of comprehensive understanding of the present age. They cannot, it is true says Weber, claim the over-arching knowledge and guidance characteristic of traditional religion. But if rational knowledge cannot give guidance to the modern world, what can? For Weber charismatic leadership pointed to a possible way out of the iron cage of bureaucracy. But within a decade and a half of his death, it was clear that a version of it was leading towards, to use Meinecke's term, the German 'catastrophe'. The dilemma Weber posed in its starkest form is still with us. Modern social studies of science have rather highlighted than diminished its importance by trying to demonstrate than even the residue of unambiguous rationality which Weber let reside in the practices of different scientific specialties might have been an overestimate.

Weber's analysis of the constitutive features of the changing university systems of Germany and the United States is directly attributable to his more general theory of bureaucratisation. It also owes much to the general methodological position he adopted in an heroic effort to straddle the ever diverging positions taken by the main antagonists in the so-called *Methodenstreit*. They had divided into the advocates of the descriptive approach of the old historical school on the one hand, and the proponents of modern marginalist economics on the other.

---

[103] Robert M. Hutchins, *The Higher Learning in America* (New Haven, CT, 1936).

Conclusion

Higher education research cannot shrink back from an effort to understand the processes which historically have formed the current set of disciplines and specialties, have reshaped intellectual and institutional life, have ordered anew the cognitive universe of teaching, and have affected scholarly notions of collegiality. Any rhetorical exercise invoking the idea of a university must one way or the other come to terms with the real diversity of professional and institutional allegiances. In fact, no one with experience of today's higher education institutions in Europe and North America can avoid being confronted with a host, not to say an avalanche, of descriptions and prescriptions and reports all highlighting the anonymous, impersonal, and vaguely bureaucratic nature of the modern university, and no one can miss seeing how separate rhetoric is from reality.

Still the notion of a university as universal and unified persists and has been argued for in three basic ways.

First: a university consists of all relevant domains of discourse which altogether reflect the sum total of human knowledge, a true universe of intellectual activities.

Second: a university is a place governed by non-particularistic concerns, be they the norms of a disinterested pursuit of truth of an open community of scholars or some equally encompassing set of normative commitments.

Third: a university is a set of institutional arrangements which guarantee that the recognised representatives of the different domains of discourse comprise an institutionally self-governing community; it is a community epistemically and normatively committed to universalism, yet clearly situated in space and time.

It is the case that both micro-oriented institutional research and modern sociologies of knowledge have tended to highlight the difficulty in sustaining any notion of universality. More macro-oriented research on the real diversity of cultural commitments and identities has certainly added weight to the original assessments.

Interestingly enough, the archetypical functionalist analysis of the largest and in many ways most successful university system in the world, namely that of the United States, in *The American University* by Talcott Parsons and Gerald Platt, with the collaboration of Neil Smelser, is characterised by a keen awareness of the difficulties.[104] For these

---

[104] Parsons and Platt, *The American University*.

authors, the university is central to the educational, industrial, and democratic revolutions which have shaped the modern world. It is 'the culminating focus of the educational revolution'. However, its 'core cognitive interests' are in danger of being radically subverted by other interests. It is an institution living under threat.

Thus even in this late stage of functionalist theorising, a somewhat complacent belief in a systematically and functionally safeguarded evolution of systemic differentiation and adaptation has been replaced by anxiety, a concern over whether the axial institution of modernity can survive an overload of increasingly large and contradictory external demands.

My own argument, and one thesis of this chapter, is that functionalist theorising itself is conceptually inadequate for capturing the meaning of the current challenges to the integrity and the history of the modern university. By its very nature as a system of analysis, functionalism is only able to render those challenges as a 'problem' of systemic adaptation (or it may invoke the very different rhetoric of philosophical idealism). But to truly understand the current dilemmas of higher education, it is necessary to have an analytical theory which can comprehend the interplay between cognitive claims and the realities of institutional authority.

Today it is easy to see that two of the three key institutions of modernity, namely, the nation-state and the university, can no longer take their continued existence for granted – certainly not in the form in which they have appeared for over a century. Moreover, the third key institution, the modern large-scale corporation, has, many would argue, also seen its nature altered in fundamental ways. Thus, although there is no reason to expect the demand for higher education and scientific knowledge to decline – quite the opposite – such may well occur in a fashion that makes any discussion of the 'idea' of a university appear to be hopelessly antiquated, as indeed many leading politicians and academics felt it was some two hundred years ago.

How in fact can an 'idea' emphasising the universality of the university survive amidst urgent needs for professional training in an ever-more differentiated society where academic life itself follows the economic laws of the division of labour and academics seem distant or uncoupled from the wider social reality outside universities? And who but unrepentant Popperians and old-fashioned Marxists would even consider 'social reality' to be a useful notion? Who, indeed, needs the universality of the university today besides Weber and Heidegger? They presented the dilemmas and asked the difficult fundamental questions, questions that are increasingly uncomfortable in light of what we now know about disciplinary developments, cognitive growth, and institutional complexity.

Are the Enlightenment and emancipation ideals of the von Humboldt brothers really just another set of Eurocentric words which should have been buried once and for all along with the boring white males who spent their lives debating them? But whatever epithets may come to mind in describing Wilhelm and Alexander, 'boring' is surely not one of them. And Hegel, an exceedingly persistent thinker already in his revolutionary youth, is certainly demanding but never boring. The world spirit he tried to trace still haunts us and refuses to come to rest no matter what Francis Fukuyama tells it to do.

Cultural diversity is real and the particularistic use of scientific knowledge is not a new invention. The idealised scientific community of Francis Bacon's House of Solomon engaged in industrial and scientific espionage under the guise of 'merchants of light'. Yet even in an age dominated by applied science and technology, or an age in which linguists, philosophers, and literary critics proclaim the impossibility of communication, science, knowledge, and learning – to include the discourses of the humanities and the social sciences – crash through all sorts of allegedly closed and impenetrable cultural gates.

The particular does not necessarily have the last word. The problem of the universality of the university will not go away. It remains with us because it is a 'real' problem and a 'real' concern. But to deal with it, we shall have to think and act as if we were freely communicating colleagues in the university that the Humboldt brothers and other reformers envisioned but never saw fully realised.

Index